CHRISTIAN SPIRITUALITY
IN THE CATHOLIC
TRADITION

ABOUT THE AUTHOR

Director of the Institute of Spirituality at the Pontifical University of St. Thomas Aquinas in Rome.
Consultor to the Sacred Congregation for the Clergy and Catechetics and also to the Sacred Congregation for Evangelization.
Former editor of *The Priest*, published by *Our Sunday Visitor*, and of the *Cross and Crown Series of Spirituality*, published by B. Herder Book Company of St. Louis, Mo.
Has preached retreats to priests and religious and given lectures internationally – Nigeria, Philippines, Taiwan, Singapore and throughout the USA and Canada.
Honorary Professor at University of Santo Tomás in Manila.

AUTHOR OF

Spiritual Theology, published by Our Sunday Visitor Incorporated, Huntington, Ind., and Sheed & Ward Limited, London, in 1980.
History of Spirituality: A Compendium, published by Daughters of St. Paul in Manila in 1981.

CO-AUTHOR OF

The Meaning of Christian Perfection
Sex, Love and Life of the Spirit
Devotion to the Heart of Jesus (1982)
Theology of Christian Perfection

CHRISTIAN SPIRITUALITY
IN THE
CATHOLIC TRADITION

Jordan Aumann, O.P.

IGNATIUS PRESS   SAN FRANCISCO

Original edition published in 1985 by
Sheed & Ward Limited, London
All rights reserved
New edition printed by permission

Nihil obstat: Anton Cowan, Censor
Imprimatur: John Crowley, Vicar General
Westminster, January 17, 1985

Cover design by Roxanne Mei Lum

Reprinted in 2001 by Ignatius Press, San Francisco
ISBN 0-89870-068-x
Library of Congress control number 2001092118
Printed in the United States of America ∞

CONTENTS

PREFACE

The present work has been written as a companion volume to a previous book entitled *Spiritual Theology* and currently published by Sheed & Ward of London. In the first work we offered a comprehensive and systematic study of the theology of Christian perfection. There we established the theological principles that constitute the doctrinal basis of the ascetical and mystical life and then proceeded to the application of those principles to Christian living.

In the present volume we move from theory and principles to life and witness. The history of spirituality serves not only to acquaint one with the origins and development of Christian spirituality but, equally important, it projects into our contemporary scene the lives and teachings of men and women who have reached a high degree of sanctity throughout the ages. It likewise demonstrates the marvelous variety among the saints and the fact that the perfection of charity can be attained by any Christian in any state of life.

In an age that is unsympathetic to systematic theology but attracted to the experiential approach, perhaps the historical survey will be of great help in discerning what is of perennial value in Christian spirituality. And since there were heterodox tendencies and movements almost from the beginning, one can likewise learn from history the mistakes and errors of the past and thus perhaps avoid repeating them in the present.

In a one-volume history of spirituality our goal is necessarily a modest one, namely, to provide a survey of the evolution and adaptation of Christian spirituality through the centuries, with particular emphasis on the spiritual teaching of outstanding individuals. Moreover, as the title of this volume indicates, we are concerned exclusively with the history of Catholic spirituality. Those who are interested in a more detailed and scholarly treatment will find it in the classical *Christian Spirituality* by P. Pourrat (four volumes), the more recent *History of Christian Spirituality* by L. Bouyer, J. Leclercq, F. Vandenbroucke and L. Cognet (three volumes), or the as yet unfinished *Dictionnaire de Spiritualité*, pub-

lished by Beauchesne in Paris. Finally, we have provided detailed
bibliographical references in the footnotes for those who may wish
to study an author, movement or historical period in greater depth.

Jordan Aumann, O. P.

CHAPTER I

SACRED SCRIPTURE AND THE SPIRITUAL LIFE

"Sacred theology relies on the written Word of God, taken together with sacred Tradition, as on a permanent foundation.... Therefore, the 'study of the sacred page' should be the very soul of theology.... In the sacred books the Father who is in heaven comes lovingly to meet his children, and talks with them. And such is the force and power of the Word of God that it can serve the Church as her support and vigor, and the children of the Church as strength for their faith, food for the soul, and a pure and lasting fount of spiritual life."[1]

The Fathers of Vatican Council II have officially recommended a return to Sacred Scripture and Tradition. Yet, it is not without its difficulties, both for Scripture scholars and for theologians, as is pointed out by Yves Congar, a highly respected leader of the movement back to the biblical sources.

> There is bound to be at times an alarming confusion among theologians in possession of a centuries-old heritage. The unfortunate consequence is not that they are upset; it is the resulting divorce that might be established between the research of biblical scholars and the conclusions of theologians. An unhealthy situation of "double truth" might ensue, which must be avoided at all costs. One group must pay close attention to the work of the other in a common fidelity to the tradition of the Church....
>
> But the problems created for classical theology by exegetes returning to biblical sources must be recognized and faced. For centuries past, especially since the great Scholastics who proposed such a seemingly definitive and perfect elaboration of sacred doctrine, theology has been formulated satisfactorily in ontological terms. Its work was to contemplate and define by means of revelation the *en-soi* of God and of Christ, that is, *what* they are in themselves. And now biblical scholars agree more and more in affirming that revelation comes to us essentially in the framework of history and that it is essentially "economic" or "functional": there is no revelation of the mystery of God and Christ except in the testimony handed on about what they did and are doing *for us*, that is, except in relation to our salvation.[2]

The primary witness of Scripture, therefore, is that God has acted in the life of man, so that the Bible is not so much a code of laws or a book of questions and answers as it is "a history of what God has done in the lives of men, for humanity as a whole, in order to fulfill in them the design of grace."[3] One does not go to the Bible to get ideas about God and to talk about God (although it does reveal God to us as he is in himself, e.g., Ex. 3:14), but to understand what God is to us and to respond to his presence. "Man wants to experience God's presence somehow, through signs that manifest it unambiguously; and he wants to live in communion with God on a quasi-experiential level."[4] The Fathers of Vatican II expressed the same sentiments:

> It pleased God, in his goodness and wisdom, to reveal himself and to make known the mystery of his will (cf. Eph. 1:9). His will was that men should have access to the Father, through Christ, the Word made flesh, in the Holy Spirit, and thus become sharers in the divine nature (cf. Eph. 2:18; 2 Pet. 1:4). By this revelation, then, the invisible God (cf. Col. 1:15; 1 Tim. 1:17), from the fullness of his love, addresses men as his friends (cf. Ex. 33:11; Jn. 15:14–15), and moves among them (cf. Bar. 3:38), in order to invite and receive them into his own company.[5]

Since God makes himself known to us by what he does for us, by the extent to which he intervenes in our human history, we must always speak of the mysteries of God, says Congar, "in such a way as to unite a profound perception of what they are in themselves with a vital expression of what they are *for us*."[6] The new relationship which results from God's personal intervention in human history causes something unique among the various religions of humanity; it is a relationship in which God approaches man, and man, by a free act of faith, offers himself to whatever God wants to effect in and through him. As Hans Urs von Balthasar puts it:

> The question of the relationship between God and man ... is settled in the Bible from God's point of view.... God chooses, promises, demands, rejects and fulfills.... Man must no longer listen to his nostalgia for the divine in himself but in God's word. Action is led beyond all purely human self-realization and becomes obedience to God and law, and this obedience contains a very concrete will of God which demands fulfillment in fellowship, among people, in the world. Lastly, resignation, guided by God's word, becomes a faith ready to accept all and a patience ready to endure all, even the dark suffering of Israel as the Servant of God.[7]

The Bible, therefore, is the word of God that reveals to man his high destiny and also answers man's innate desire to rise from a fallen condition and to experience the divine. It is the rule and standard of all authentic supernatural life and it demands everything; it will not be reduced to our measure because its aim is to fashion us in the image of God. It cannot be replaced by any *ersatz* spirituality or religious experience which some may seek in spiritism, drugs, group therapy, psychedelic experience or pentecostalism. Even the charisms enumerated by St. Paul (cf. Rom. 12:6–8; 1 Cor. 12:8–10) are reducible to the original apostolic mission as stated in the New Testament. Everything must be understood and evaluated in the light of Scripture, and the closer any spirituality is to the Bible, the more authentic it is. This does not mean that the application of biblical teaching to the spiritual life does not admit of any variety whatever, but it does mean that Sacred Scripture ever remains the unifying factor and the ultimate standard. It transcends all diversity.

Our task, then, is to determine the basic principles of the Christian life as revealed in the Bible; that is to say, the truths that are valid for every Christian of every age and state of life. And since we are concerned with the fundamental framework of Christian spirituality, the New Testament will have priority, although, as Grelot has stated, unless we understand the Old Testament we cannot understand the New.[8] Further, in order to avoid the risk of fitting the Bible to preconceived notions or of using it as a vehicle for private interpretation, we shall accept Charlier's principle that the Bible is "the word of life *because* it is the word of truth, and for no other reason."[9] In that way we can accept the teachings of Scripture on God's terms and not try to force it into our own intellectual context.

THE OLD TESTAMENT

"The first chapter of Genesis is the first chapter of faith,"[10] as opposed to the pagan religions that were born out of fear of an unknown deity. The first law of the Decalogue is stated thus: "I am the Lord thy God; thou shalt not have strange gods before me." This is to designate that the God of the Bible is completely different and set apart from the deities of paganism. Man of antiquity had an awareness of the sacred which he expressed in a cultic religion that was shrouded in various mythologies. His religion was a projection of his instinctive needs, such as health, life, fertility, protection against the unknown. Eventually paganism developed a contemplative type of religion, as a response to man's higher needs, but in the beginning, the fertility cults were perhaps the primitive forms of religious worship.

> The basic notion behind every fertility cult was this: they recognized that there is a god or gods.... Secondly, they knew that man was completely dependent on the gods in some way. Their question was, *how*.... They recognized that man must participate in the creative powers .... of these gods, and therefore he must do everything in his power to express the intensity of the desire that is his to participate. And so the fertility cults, which were sexual cults, were basically a form of worship and they were concerned with expressing the intensity of the desire of men to participate in the power of the gods.[11]

Genesis records that the first step in man's relation with God was his creation in the image of God and his situation in a state of innocence which was later lost because of man's sin. What the sin was, remains a mystery; we do not know whether it was a particular action or simply the end-product of an accumulation of evil. We do know that man became acutely aware of sin and therefore found access to the one, true God much more difficult. "For man, God is both present and absent, both near and far away. He is present and near as the Creator, since man is dependent on God for his very existence. He is absent and far away insofar as man looks for him from within the framework of his own sinful condition."[12] Eventually, however, and almost unexpectedly, God intervened once more in human history to resume his dialogue with man.

> Yahweh said to Abram, "Leave your country, your family and your father's house, for the land I will show you. I will make you a great nation; I will bless you and make your name so famous that it will be used as a blessing.... Here now is my covenant with you: you shall become the father of a multitude of nations.... I will establish my covenant between myself and you, and your descendants after you, generation after generation, a covenant in perpetuity, to be your God and the God of your descendants after you" (Gen. 12:1-2; 17:1-8).

Genesis 4-11 records that a few men, such as Abel and Noah, were found worthy in the sight of God, but he chose Abraham for an alliance of friendship and it was through Abraham that God raised up a people who will be *his* people and he will be *their* God. He established his presence in their midst, not only in the Temple, but ultimately in their hearts (Jer. 31:31-34). In keeping with his promise, God showed the same goodness to the descendants of

Abraham, reaching a climax in the golden age under David and Solomon.

Time and again, God revealed himself through his actions, which were often accompanied by signs. Perhaps the sign *par excellence* was the exodus from Egypt, accompanied by so many miraculous events that the people could not doubt that they were under the special care and protection of their God. As a result, "the people venerated Yahweh; they put their faith in Yahweh and in Moses, his servant" (Ex. 14:31). Moreover, the fact that Israel was provided with water and food in the desert could be interpreted to demonstrate that God himself became intimately involved in man's earthly existence. It also serves to demonstrate that God is at once transcendent and immanent. Congar says in this regard:

> The living God of rich biblical monotheism is posited as being the source and measure of all goodness, of all truth, of all authentic existence. The God of biblical monotheism is something other and more than the great clock-maker or great architect of the theists who posit him only as the Creator of the world; after this initial act the world and man have no longer any rapport with anything but themselves and their own nature. The living God is affirmed by the Bible as sovereign source and measure, to which man and all things must unceasingly be referred and must conform so that one does not just exist but exists *truly*, realizing the meaning, the fullness of one's existence.[13]

God's initiative, however, demands a response from Israel, both by obedience to the law given on Sinai and by religious worship. Thus, "the obligation of the people to observe the terms of the covenant is solemnly ratified by the holocaust, the sacrifices and the sprinkling of blood (Ex. 24:3–8). On the other hand, the leaders of the community . . . are brought into God's presence and commune with him in a sacred meal (Ex. 24:1–2; 9–11)."[14] Lest the cultic actions be merely empty gestures, it was necessary that they proceed from and bear witness to a living faith and obedience to God's word. Numerous prophets insisted on this point with great zeal (Am. 5:21–27; Is. 1:10–16; Jer. 6:20), indicating that although Israel had the Ark and the Temple, God's truest presence is not in any material place but in the hearts of men. There was always a temptation to yield to empty ritualism.

Thus, the prophet Isaiah (765–740 BC), whose mission it was to proclaim the fall of Israel and the punishment of the nation's infidelity, described Israel as "a sinful nation, a people weighed down with guilt, a breed of wrong-doers, perverted sons. They have abandoned Yahweh, despised the Holy One of Israel, they have turned away from him" (Is. 1:4). A century later, Jeremiah (b. 646 BC), who witnessed the fall of the kingdom and the exile of many of the Israelites, accused Israel of infidelity and predicted dire punishment in the name of Yahweh (Jer. 1–25). Not only have they wandered away from the presence of God, but God himself seems to disown them: "Even if Moses and Samuel were standing in my presence I could not warm to this people. Drive them out of my sight; away with them!" (Jer. 15:1).

It appears that the divine plan had reached an impasse, but such was not the case; God was disposed to receive Israel back into his presence if the people would repent and give perfect obedience:

> I will not make an end of you, only discipline you in moderation, so as not to let you go entirely unpunished.... And you shall be my people and I will be your God.... I have loved you with an everlasting love, so I am constant in my affection for you (Jer. 30:10–11, 22; 31:3).

With Ezekiel, whose ministry spanned a time marked by the fall of Jerusalem and the destruction of the Temple, the sacred is clearly distinguished from the profane, and great insistence is placed on observance of the Law. The prophet announces that out of pure benevolence God will make a new covenant with his people: "I shall make a covenant of peace with them, an eternal covenant with them.... I shall settle my sanctuary among them forever. I shall make my home above them; I will be their God, they shall be my people" (Ez. 37:26–27).

But God also demands repentance and conversion, not only collectively but individually, and Ezekiel insists that this requires the proper interior dispositions: "House of Israel, in future I mean to judge each of you by what he does – it is the Lord Yahweh who speaks. Repent, renounce all your sins, avoid all occasions of sin. Shake off all the sins you have committed against me, and make yourselves a new heart and a new spirit" (Ez. 18:31; cf. also 11:19; 36:26). The emphasis here is clearly on the necessity for each person to make a commitment and assume personal responsibility.

Toward the end of the exile (between 548 and 538 BC), the people finally responded to the prophets by confessing their infidelity and acknowledging the one true God. Thus, Second-Isaiah (the Book of Consolation)[15] depicts the perfect disciple of Yahweh as one who confesses the true faith, atones for his sin and is exalted by God:

You whom I brought from the confines of the earth
and called from the ends of the world;
you to whom I said, "You are my servant,
I have chosen you, not rejected you,"
do not be afraid, for I am with you;
stop being anxious and watchful, for I am your God.
I give you strength, I bring you help,
I uphold you with my victorious right hand (Is. 41:9–10).

Remember these things, Jacob,
and that you are my servant, Israel.
I have formed you, you are my servant;
Israel, I will not forget you.
I have dispelled your faults like a cloud,
your sins like a mist.
Come back to me, for I have redeemed you (Is. 44:21–22).

Does a woman forget her baby at the breast,
or fail to cherish the son of her womb?
Yet even if these forget,
I will never forget you (Is. 49:15).

Your redeemer will be the Holy One of Israel,
he is called the God of the whole earth.
Yes, like a forsaken wife, distressed in spirit,
Yahweh calls you back.
Does a man cast off the wife of his youth?
says your God.
I did forsake you for a brief moment,
but with great love will I take you back.
In excess of anger, for a moment
I hid my face from you.
But with everlasting love I have taken pity on you,
says Yahweh, your redeemer (Is. 54:4–8).

We have reached a high point in God's revelation of himself, no
longer simply as God of power and majesty, as Yahweh Sabaoth,
the God of armies, but as Father of love and mercy. The marriage
symbol used by the prophet, portraying God as a husband, is an
echo of the stirring passages of the Book of Hosea, who perhaps
lived to see the fall of Samaria in 721 BC. The same wedding imagery is found in Jeremiah (2–3), Ezekiel (16) and the Song of Songs.
Hosea, however, saw God's love for man as a future triumph over
Israel's infidelities; the author of Second-Isaiah sees it as actually

victorious. Then, if we accept the allegorical interpretation of the Song of Songs, as understood by the Jewish tradition and the writers of the early Christian Church, we are justified in applying it to the love between God and Israel, and between God and the individual soul.

The message that comes to us from this rapid survey of the patriarchs and the prophets is that God loves us and asks our response to his love through faith and obedience. The Old Testament does not simply record this in a series of statements; God himself makes it known by his intervention in human history, and especially in his relations with Abraham and Moses and his revelation through Hosea and the author of Second-Isaiah.[16] As to man's response to God's love, the Old Testament provides him with maxims according to which he can guide his life. The "wisdom" books (Job, Proverbs, Ecclesiastes, Ecclesiasticus, Wisdom) base their moral teaching on the principle that good will be rewarded and evil will be punished; they then offer directives for the acquisition of virtue and the avoidance of sin.

It is not, however, simply a matter of acquiring virtues by one's own strength, for frequently the virtuous are those who suffer most from injustice and uncharity; consequently, the Old Testament morality is one of personal effort based on a deep trust in God (cf. Job, Proverbs, Ecclesiastes). Finally, in the Book of Psalms the Old Testament provides more moral instruction plus prayers of adoration, petition, thanksgiving and contrition.[17]

The promises and the entire movement of the Old Testament are orientated to the perfect communication of God to man; the newness of the eternal covenant consists precisely in the Word made flesh, through whom the kingdom of God will be definitively established. Christ, says Congar, is "the last revelation.... When God became man, something that was already true in the previous stages of salvation history reached its highest degree: man resembles God and, therefore, in a totally transcendent way, God resembles man."[18]

Whatever the value of the Old Testament in itself as a source of the spiritual life, and however inspiring it is as a witness to the religious experience of the patriarchs and the prophets, for us it is seen primarily as a preparation for Christ and his kingdom. Such, in fact, is the teaching of Vatican Council II:

"The economy of the Old Testament was deliberately so orientated that it should prepare for and declare in prophecy the coming of Christ,

Redeemer of all men, and of the messianic kingdom.... For in the context of the human situation before the era of salvation established by Christ, the books of the Old Testament provide an understanding of God and man and make clear to all men how a just and merciful God deals with mankind.... Christians should accept with veneration these writings which give expression to a lively sense of God, which are a storehouse of sublime teaching on God and of sound wisdom on human life, as well as a wonderful treasury of prayers; in them, too, the mystery of our salvation is present in a hidden way."[19]

THE NEW TESTAMENT

The continuity between the Old and the New Testaments is evidenced in the fact that Christ frequently supported his teaching by references to the Old Testament and insisted that he had not come to abolish the Law and the prophets "but to complete them" (Mt. 5:17). Christ is the realization and the fulfillment of all that had been promised and signified by the word and action of God in the history of salvation from Adam to the last of the prophets. Christ is, therefore, the embodiment of authentic spirituality and, quite logically, from our point of view the spiritual life must be a participation in the "mystery of Christ." Consequently, Christ is for all times – yesterday, today and forever – and any attempt to construct a spirituality that is "more contemporary" or "more up-to-date" is purely an illusion.

This does not mean, however, that we should consider the spiritual life as Christ-centered to such an extent that we would fail to give proper emphasis to God the Father, God the Holy Spirit, and the Trinity of Persons dwelling in the soul through grace. What Congar has stated in regard to theology in general may be applied also to the theology of the spiritual life: "Of course we reach a knowledge of the intimate mystery of God only *through* Jesus Christ (*inventionis, acquisitionis*) and from God (*revelationis*), but it is only by means of the mystery of God that we can believe fully in the mystery of the Incarnation and, therefore, can understand Jesus Christ."[20]

Nevertheless, having made this precision, we can repeat that the spiritual life is centered in Christ and is, in fact, a participation in the mystery of Christ. To know what this life is, it is necessary to understand as much as possible about Christ; and to achieve this, it is necessary to turn to the New Testament, which records much of what Christ said and did for our instruction.[21] At this point several observations should be made. First of all, we do not read the New

Testament as we would read the biography of a great historical figure whom we wish to remember and perhaps imitate. This could all too easily result in a religion of hero-worship, a liturgy of memorial services and a spirituality of nostalgia for the past. Our objective is rather to live the mystery of Christ here and now, which requires that we somehow identify with Christ as he is here and now – in glory at the right hand of the Father.

Secondly, Christ did not leave us a detailed code of morality, a fully explicated body of dogmas, a directory of liturgical rubrics and ceremonies, or even a completed pattern for the structure of his Church. Rather, he seems deliberately to have allowed for evolution in dogma, prudential decisions in morality, adaptation in liturgy, and the gradual development of the Church, not to mention the charismatic operations of the Holy Spirit. Therefore the Christian life is not the present trying to recapture the past, but the present striving to become the future; it is a Christianity *in via*, on the march.

Thirdly, what we should seek in the New Testament is a spirituality that is valid for all persons everywhere and in every age, whether it be the twentieth century, the Middle Ages or the primitive Church. But Christ lived within a particular historical context; the New Testament represents a variety of viewpoints, such as that of St. Matthew or St. Luke as compared with that of St. John or St. Paul; in primitive Christianity there was a Jewish-Palestinian and a Jewish-Hellenistic trend. Consequently, it is not always easy to abstract the essential and perennial elements of Gospel spirituality from the New Testament writings or from the life of Christians in apostolic times. Further, Gospel spirituality must be lived by particular persons at a particular time and in a particular place. In other words, the Gospel must be constantly inserted into the historical situation; that is why there is a history of spirituality and schools of spirituality.

If Christian spirituality signifies a participation in the mystery of Christ, our first task is to contemplate that mystery with the help of the New Testament and then to discover how we share in it. Stated succinctly, the mystery of Christ is the mystery of the Incarnation, the Word made flesh and dwelling among us (Jn. 1:14), the God made man. The Old Testament had progressively revealed God as Father, as one who approaches man, but his presence was never so intimate as when he sent his only begotten Son into the world that we might live through him (1 Jn. 4:9). The mystery of the Incarnation reveals that God is not only the transcendent and majestic God, but he is God "for us," a God of generous love (cf. Eph. 2:5; 1 Jn. 4:9). In Jesus Christ, who possesses "the fulness of divinity" (Col. 2:9), God unites himself to our humanity and to our world so intimately and so definitively that there can be no "opposition or disjunction between the glory of God, which is the ultimate end of everything, and the happiness of man or the completion of the world."[22] Jesus Christ is thus the central mystery of the entire universe and through him, God is not only present to us but dwells in us, as Christ himself had promised (Jn. 14:23).

The Incarnation of the Word of God marks a new stage in the development of God's plan for the world and for mankind. The Mosaic cult yields to the sacrifice of Christ, and fallen man is healed and elevated to the state of friendship with God. It is the manifestation of a new life through Jesus Christ that will be transmitted uninterruptedly through his Church.

The very mystery of the Word made flesh indicates to us how we are able to participate in the mystery of Christ. The Word condescended to "humanize" himself, so to speak, by assuming human nature, but in so doing, he elevated that nature to the supernatural order by "divinizing" it through its union with the divine Person. The Father "sent into the world his only Son so that we could have life through him" (1 Jn. 4:9) and Jesus said to himself: "For the Father, who is the source of life, has made the Son the source of life" (Jn. 5:26). Consequently, to participate in the mystery of Christ means to share in the selfsame life which animated the God-man, the life which the incarnate Word shares with the Father and the Holy Spirit; and through this life, man is regenerated and elevated to the supernatural order.

A correct understanding of the supernatural order is a necessary prerequisite for a correct understanding of the spiritual life and the mystery of Christ. The natural and the supernatural are intermingled in such a way that the natural is not destroyed but perfected and elevated, but they are always distinct and separable. So also in Jesus Christ the God-man, the human and the divine are marvelously blended in the hypostatic union but the human nature is distinct from the divine Person and nature. Arintero summarizes the doctrine as follows:

This is precisely what constitutes the supernatural order, the manifestation of eternal life: entrance into fellowship or familiar and friendly relationship with God by sharing in the communication of his life and his intimate secrets. The supernatural order is not, then, anything that our reason can trace out by analogy with the natural order. Nor is it a superior order which has been "naturalized" so as to fit our mode of being. . . .

The true supernatural order, that unique order which actually exists in union with the natural order, is much more than this. It not only exceeds natural exigencies, but it transcends all suppositions and rational aspirations. . . .

God so loved the world that he gave his only-begotten Son, so that all those who believe in him may have eternal life. This life is the intimate life of the sacrosanct Trinity in the ineffable communications of the three Persons because all three, and each of them in his own way, contribute to the work of our deification. . . . It is the Father who adopts us; the Son who makes us his brothers and co-heirs; the Holy Ghost who consecrates and sanctifies us and makes us living temples of God, coming to dwell in us together with the Father and the Son.[23]

The New Testament frequently speaks of the new life which is given to us through Jesus Christ (cf. John 1:12; 3:14; Col. 2:13; Eph. 4:23; Tit. 3:14; Rom. 5:19; 1 Cor. 1:21; 2 Pet. 1:4). In substance, the divine teaching reveals to us that through Christ we become children of the Father by the power of the Holy Spirit:

Everyone moved by the Spirit is a son of God. The spirit you received is not the spirit of slaves bringing fear into your lives again; it is the spirit of sons, and it makes us cry out, "Abba, Father." The Spirit himself and our spirit bear united witness that we are children of God. And if we are children we are heirs as well: heirs of God and co-heirs with Christ, sharing his suffering so as to share his glory (Rom. 8:14–17).

Dom Columba Marmion states that "we shall understand nothing – I do not say merely of perfection, but even of simple Christianity – if we do not grasp that its most essential basis is constituted by the state of child of God, participation – through sanctifying grace – in the eternal filiation of the incarnate Word. . . . All Christian life, all holiness, is being by grace what Jesus is by nature: the Son of God."[24]

Christ himself spoke most frequently of "the kingdom" and of entrance into the kingdom.[25] But even before Christ began his public ministry, John the Baptist had preached the kingdom of God and had stated explicitly that repentance and forgiveness of sins was a necessary prerequisite for entrance into the kingdom (Lk. 3:1–18; Mt. 3:1–12). When, at the very beginning of his own preaching,

Christ announced the kingdom of God, he made the same demands as John the Baptist: "From that moment Jesus began his preaching with the message, 'Repent, for the kingdom of heaven is close at hand' " (Mt. 4:17).

The kingdom of God (or kingdom of heaven) was a constant theme in Christ's preaching and it was developed especially in the Sermon on the Mount (Mt. 5–7), the sermon on the plain (Lk. 6:17–49) and the parables.[26] In regard to the parables, it should be noted that some of them are eschatological: they point to a kingdom of the future (e.g., the prudent and foolish virgins [Mt. 25:1–13]); others are descriptive of a kingdom already present (e.g., the sower, the mustard seed and the yeast [Mt. 13:18–23, 31–32, 33]).

"At no time," says Bonsirven, "did Jesus give a definition of this 'kingdom of God'. ... [The various conceptions of it] can be classified into two diametrically opposed types: according to one of them, Christ had in mind a spiritual kingdom, already existing at the time and progressive – an *evolution*; according to others, he was looking forward to it as something which had to come into existence suddenly as the result of an eschatological *revolution* which would shake the whole world."[27]

In the context of the spiritual life, the kingdom of God is interior, it is within us (Lk. 17:21), it is capable of growth and evolution, and from the individual it reaches out to all humanity, to the entire world. The kingdom is life in Christ, with whom the Father and the Holy Spirit are present (Jn. 14:23). It is a kingdom that is present but always evolving, and therefore we must always pray: "thy kingdom come."

On several occasions Christ identified himself with the kingdom: "If it is through the finger of God that I cast out devils, then know that the kingdom of God has overtaken you" (Lk. 11:20); "I confer a kingdom on you, just as my Father conferred one on me: you will eat and drink at my table in my kingdom" (Lk. 22:29–30). Origen coined the expression *autobasileia* to indicate that Jesus is himself the kingdom of God and that membership in the kingdom is determined by the relationship of the individual to Christ.[28] Thus, we are brought back to the basic teaching that in, with and through Jesus Christ we become children of God. God the Father, acting in Christ, establishes his kingdom in the hearts of men and in the world.

Since God is our Father, the kingdom of God likewise refers to God's rule or authority over all.[29] It is his rule or reign that must be established. This entails, on the part of the individual, a total commitment to God which admits of no compromise. Its ultimate objective was stated by Christ in the Sermon on the Mount: "You must therefore be perfect just as your heavenly Father is perfect" (Mt. 5:48). The question that arises is how one makes this commitment to God, which is the same thing as to ask what are the conditions for entering the kingdom of God or how one begins to participate in the mystery of Christ and becomes a child of the Father.

The first thing that must be acknowledged is that it is a question of the kingdom of God; therefore it is God who stipulates what is required for membership in the kingdom. The conditions are sufficiently clear and sufficiently demanding. Before anything else, the individual must repent for sin, and this presupposes an acknowledgement of one's guilt before God (Mt. 4:17; Mk. 1:15; Lk. 3:3). Secondly, liberation from sin should lead to a regeneration, a new life in God through Christ and the Holy Spirit (Rom. 6:5). This, in turn, requires two more conditions: reception of the word of God through faith, and baptism by water and the Holy Spirit. "You have been washed clean, and sanctified, and justified through the name of the Lord Jesus Christ and through the Spirit of our God" (1 Cor. 6:11). Thus, through repentance, faith and baptism one enters the kingdom of God and subjects oneself to the rule of God.

But entrance into the kingdom is not a static achievement; it involves a new life as sons of God, and this new life also makes its demands by way of a Christian morality.

> This inherent situation of the Christian is thus described by Jesus: The disciple is a child of the heavenly Father, he is a member of the kingdom of God, he has fellowship with brothers and sisters, he lives in the world of matter and of men who can fail to appreciate him and persecute him. Next, there is the host of concrete, changing situations, innumerable and unforeseeable, in which it is the duty of the Christian to work out his fundamental situation by creatively giving to each concrete situation a Christian meaning, by responding to it as a child of God and a sharer in the kingdom.[30]

As we have already stated, Christ did not give a detailed code of moral laws to his followers, although he did demand a total commitment and the practice of virtue. His Sermon on the Mount contains the fundamental principles for the Christian life-style; it is in reality "a preliminary draft of Christian situation ethics."[31] Two characteristics in particular reveal that the moral teaching of Christ is a fulfillment and a perfection of the Mosaic law of the Old

Testament. First of all, he placed much greater emphasis on the interior than the exterior, as when he condemned the purely external observances and legalistic practices of the Pharisees (Mt. 6:1–18) and called for interior mortification (Mt. 6:16) and the practice of private prayer (Mt. 6:5–7). It is not, however, a question of choosing the interior to the exclusion of the exterior, for Christ was equally insistent that his followers must prove their faith and commitment by obedience to his commandments and by the performance of good works (Mt. 19:16–22; Lk. 6:43–49).

Secondly, the Sermon on the Mount not only fulfills and perfects the laws of the Old Testament; it is an ethic that points to an ideal of ever greater perfection. Christ did not concentrate on the minimum requirements of the law and of justice as the Mosaic Law had done; rather, he repudiated the old legalism with its restrictive moralizing and opened new horizons in the relationships of men with God and their fellow men.

> You have heard that it was said, "an eye for an eye and a tooth for a tooth." But I say to you, do not resist one who is evil. But if anyone strikes you on the right cheek, turn to him the other also.... You have heard that it was said, "You shall love your neighbor and hate your enemy." But I say to you, love your enemies and pray for those who persecute you (Mt. 5:38–44).

But if the morality taught by Christ is not restricted to a minimum, neither does it point to a maximum. No limits are set; there is no terminus. As a result, the follower of Christ is made constantly aware of his own sinfulness and weakness, but without pessimism or despair; and he is also urged to strive for excellence. "You must therefore be perfect just as your heavenly Father is perfect" (Mt. 5:48). This last command, as well as the entire structure and tone of the eight beatitudes, indicates that Christ is positing an ideal that is not fully attainable in this life and is certainly not within the grasp of man by his own natural efforts. It is an ideal that is not of this world, but one that must be the goal of all man's striving while he is in this world.

Moreover, the command to be perfect is not to be understood as a precept that obliges here and now, as does the command to love one's neighbor here and now. Rather, it should be seen as a principle of dynamic evolution, a law of constant progress in one's relationship with God. Christ urges all his followers to respond with all their capacity to the call to the perfection of charity. "For I have given you an example, that you also should do as I have done to you. ... I am the way, and the truth, and the life; no one comes to the Father, but by me. ... If a man loves me, he will keep my word, and my Father will love him, and we will come to him and make our home with him" (Jn. 13:15; 14:6, 18). Thus, as Congar states: "The morality of the New Testament is always 'an imperative coming from an indicative': do this because Christ did it. It is the imitation of Jesus, but an imitation that is not moralistic, narrowly individualistic and pessimistic.'"[32]

What Christ taught in the Sermon on the Mount was summarized in his farewell address at the Last Supper. Previously, when questioned concerning the commandment, Christ had quoted from the Old Testament: "You shall love the Lord your God with all your heart, and with all your soul, and with all your mind (cf. Dt. 6:5). This is the great and first commandment. And a second is like it, you shall love your neighbor as yourself (cf. Lev. 19:18)" (Mt. 22:37–39).

At the Last Supper, however, Christ gives love an entirely new dimension, not only by relating love of neighbor to the love of God, but by placing love of neighbor in a central position in the Christian life:

> A new commandment I give to you, that you love one another; even as I have loved you, that you also love one another. By this all men will know that you are my disciples, if you have love for one another. ... As the Father has loved me, so have I loved you; abide in my love. If you keep my commandments, you will abide in my love, just as I have kept my Father's commandments and abide in his love. ... This is my commandment, that you love one another as I have loved you (Jn. 13:34–35; 15:9–12).

St. John, the theologian of charity par excellence, states explicitly that charity is not a love that is acquired and perfected by purely human effort; it is a gift infused in us by God. It makes us one with God, through Christ, and must then extend to all whom God loves – all men in general and our neighbor in particular:

> Beloved, let us love one another; for love is of God, and he who loves is born of God and knows God. ... In this is love, not that we loved God but that he loved us and sent his Son to be the expiation of our sins. Beloved, if God so loved us, we also ought to love one another. No man has ever seen God; if we love one another, God abides in us and his love is perfected in us. ...

Whoever confesses that Jesus is the Son of God, God abides in him, and he in God. So we know and believe the love God has for us. God is love, and he who abides in love abides in God, and God abides in him.... We love, because he first loved us. If anyone says, "I love God," and hates his brother, he is a liar; for he who does not love his brother whom he has seen, cannot love God whom he has not seen. And this commandment we have from him, that he who loves God should love his brother also (1 Jn. 4:7–21).

It has been stated that the love of neighbor occupies a central position in Christian spirituality; the logical question that follows immediately is: Who is my neighbor? Christ himself answered this question with the parable of the Good Samaritan (Lk. 10:25–37). In the parable the priest and the levite had several bonds of relationship with the victim, and therefore a greater obligation to come to his assistance, but it was the stranger, the Samaritan, who proved to be a true neighbor. Therefore, in the vocabulary of Christian charity the love of neighbor calls for personal involvement in the particular situation or need of another person, and precisely because we have a care or concern for him. Therefore, love of neighbor is not fulfilled by a vague, general love for people in general; it is activated in the concrete circumstances surrounding individual persons. It is because of this interpersonal aspect of fraternal charity that Christ could say: "A new commandment I give to you" (Jn. 13:34).

What then did Jesus really do with the concept of "neighbor"? He made of it a notion that is of itself unlimited and unconditioned, defined only by the concrete situation in which one finds himself. My neighbor is the person with whom I find myself in a circumstance of proximity, that is, anyone with whom I by my love establish a relation of nearness, which in turn engenders a response. It is not determined beforehand who is my neighbor; anyone can become this. It is he, toward whom *in concreto* I have a relation of neighborliness, not the one whom I may casually meet, but him with whom I hold communication. My neighbor is the one, anyone at all, whoever he may be, whom I wish to encounter in the total concrete situation of my being-in-the-world and not because of something which has been added to my human status.[33]

It is evident, then, that there can be no authentic Christian spirituality and no authentic Christian charity which consists exclusively in love of God or love of man; the arms of love must embrace both objects of that love. Neither can there be a purely secularized or humanized love that is charity; true charity is always a gift from

God through Jesus Christ, which must return to God, either directly or indirectly (through neighbor). If, as St. John says, it is an illusion to think we can love God without loving our neighbor (1 Jn. 4:20), it is likewise erroneous to say that we can love our neighbor in Christian charity without loving God. As St. Augustine states in his commentary on the First Letter of St. John: "When therefore you love the members of Christ, you love Christ; when you love Christ, you love the Son of God; when you love the Son of God, you also love the Father. Love therefore cannot be separated into parts. Choose what you love; all the rest will follow."[34]

With this we close our brief description of the spirituality of the Gospels, which is Christian spirituality *par excellence*. Nothing more can ever be added substantially to the theology of Christian perfection, and if one were to attempt to reduce the spirituality of the New Testament to a formula, it would read as follows: *Conversion to God through faith and baptism in the Holy Spirit, and love of God and neighbor in the fellowship of Jesus Christ.*

Gospel spirituality adapts itself to every age, but each historical situation and each culture responds to the imperatives of the Gospel in accordance with the needs and capabilities proper to itself. The spirituality of the Gospel is therefore a dynamic evolution which cannot be restricted to any particular age or fixed permanently in any historical context. But taking the New Testament as the authentic foundation of the Christian life, we can now examine the living witness and Catholic tradition of that life throughout the centuries.

CHAPTER 2

SPIRITUALITY OF THE EARLY CHURCH

In his sermons and parables Christ frequently stated that the kingdom of God would be rejected by the Jews and accepted by the Gentiles, although the Jews remained the Chosen People. Jerusalem was in fact the cradle of the Church; the majority of the first converts were Jews and the early Church followed the Jewish observances until the Council of Jerusalem, about the year 51. The rule of conduct promulgated by the Council dispensed the Christians from the Jewish observances but, following the suggestion of St. James, obliged them to abstain from things sacrificed to idols, from blood, from things strangled and from fornication (Acts 15:28 ff.). In spite of the protests and tactics of the Judaizers, the Gentile Christians ultimately prevailed and the conflict gradually subsided.[1]

In the *Didache* or *Teaching of the Twelve Apostles*, written sometime between 70 and 100, we find a great deal of information about the Christian life in the early Church. It mentions, for example, the organization of the hierarchy that emerged at this period: apostles, prophets, doctors, bishops, priests and deacons.[2] The moral teaching of the *Didache* is explicit and severe, as a protection, no doubt, against the immorality and superstition of the pagan world in which the early Christians lived. It is probable that, except for the Gospel of St. John, his Letters and the Book of Revelation, the entire New Testament was composed before the writing of the *Didache*. Consequently the *Didache* is an important link between the Acts of the Apostles and the Apostolic Fathers, and it is to their writings that we turn for a more detailed description of the spirituality of the early Church.

THE APOSTOLIC FATHERS

As the writings of the apostles were an authentic record of the teachings of Christ, so also the works of the earliest Christian writers, called the "Apostolic Fathers," were a transmission of the teaching of the apostles. They were, for the most part, men who had either known the apostles themselves or had known persons closely associated with them. Yet, the written documents of this period are few in number and, as Bouyer points out, "the importance of an oral tradition . . . makes the few original texts bequeathed to us from this period of quite secondary importance."[3]

The patrologist Cotelier seems to have been the first to classify some of the early writers as "Apostolic Fathers" (in 1672). He listed them as follows:

– Barnabas, considered by ancient writers such as St. Clement and Origen to be the apostle by the same name and a companion of St. Paul, but modern criticism rejects this theory and refers to a pseudo-Barnabas who was an intellectual and possibly a Gnostic. He was the author of a work consisting of 21 chapters and known as the *Letter of Barnabas*. It gives an allegorical interpretation of the Old Testament and not only insists that Christ is the culmination of the law and the prophets, but affirms that the covenant belongs exclusively to the followers of Christ. The Jews have been definitively rejected. Nevertheless, the *Letter* is permeated with a sense of joy at the reception of the good news of the Gospel, and the author lists hope, justice and love as the fundamental Christian virtues.

– St. Clement of Rome, the third successor of St. Peter as Bishop of Rome, who addressed a *Letter to the Church of Corinth* in the year 95 or 96, during or immediately after the persecution by Domitian. The occasion of the *Letter* was the division caused in the Church of Corinth by certain proud, ambitious and envious members. Recalling the former glory of the Church of Corinth, St. Clement pleads for a return to peace and unity in the name of Christ, who shed his blood for our salvation.

– Hermas, author of *The Shepherd*, a work that enjoyed such prestige that St. Irenaeus, Tertullian and Origen considered it to be part of Sacred Scripture. Although he was once considered to be the Hermas referred to in St. Paul's *Letter to the Romans* (16:14), it is now believed that he was a brother of Pope St. Pius I, whose pontificate extended from 140 to 155.

The Shepherd consists of a description of five visions received by Hermas, and in the fifth vision the Shepherd appears and dictates to Hermas twelve precepts and ten parables. The work is valuable because it offers a rather complete description of the daily life of fervent Christians in the early Church.

– St. Ignatius of Antioch, bishop and martyr, who added the pseudonym "Theophorus" to his given name. He was a disciple of St. Peter, who named him as his successor to the See of Antioch. During his voyage to Rome, under arrest, St. Ignatius wrote seven letters that are marvelous testimonies of his steadfast faith and his ardent desire for martyrdom. In his letters he develops three themes that were characteristic of early Christian spirituality: Christ, the Church and martyrdom.

– St. Polycarp, who had heard the preaching of St. John the Apostle and was named by St. John to be the Bishop of Smyrna. He was also a dear friend of St. Ignatius of Antioch. In a letter written by St. Irenaeus to the Roman priest Florinus we find conclusive evidence that St. Polycarp is one of our most important links with apostolic times. St. Polycarp received the martyr's crown in 156. Two documents are extant concerning him: his *Letter to the Philippians* and the account of his martyrdom, recorded in the *Martyrium*.

In 1765 the Oratorian Gallandi added to the list of Apostolic Fathers the names of Papias, Bishop of Hierapolis (said to have been among those who heard the preaching of St. John the Evangelist) and the unknown author of the *Letter to Diognetus*. Papias is the author of a work that explains the teaching of Christ and is valuable as a link with the preaching of the apostles, but only fragments of his work remain. The author of the *Letter to Diognetus*, however, would more properly be classified among the Greek apologists than among the Apostolic Fathers.

Finally, the *Didache* (mentioned previously) was discovered in 1873 by the Greek Archbishop Bryennios in the library of the Hospital of the Holy Sepulchre in Constantinople. The codex also contained two letters of St. Clement of Rome and the *Letter of Barnabas*. The author is unknown, as is the date of composition of the *Didache*. The presumption is that it was composed by a person of authority in the Church in either Syria or Palestine, but while some historians place the date of composition between the years 50 and 70, others place it anywhere from 70 to 100.

The doctrine contained in the *Didache* is eminently liturgical and sacramental and in that sense served well as a catechesis for the reception of baptism. There is also a distinction made between the precepts and the counsels and a reference to Christian perfection, although there is no attempt to classify Christians into vocations or states of life. The Church is seen as a community of saints and one enters the community through baptism, but within that community everything converges on the Eucharist. And since the term "Christian" appears in the *Didache*, some historians have conjectured that the work was composed at Antioch, where the followers of Christ were first called Christians.[4]

It should be evident from the foregoing brief description that the Apostolic Fathers are not a homogeneous group. They differ in many respects – as regards their authority, places of origin, subjects treated – and to such an extent that the only thing they have in common is that all of them are witnesses to the spirituality of the primitive Church. Consequently, the various writings from the apostolic era do not have the same value for the history of spirituality; in fact, authors usually name the following as the most important documents: St. Clement of Rome's *Letter to the Church of Corinth*, the *Didache* and the letters of St. Ignatius of Antioch.

None of the writings offer a systematic and structured theology of the Christian life; that had to await the rise of the schools of theology under the guidance of St. Clement of Alexandria, Origen and St. Gregory of Nyssa. Nevertheless, the experience of Christian living and the theology of the spiritual life were already developed and at least partially described in St. John the Evangelist, St. Paul, and their disciples, St. Ignatius of Antioch, St. Polycarp, Papias and the author of the *Didache*.

The Church was not yet "institutionalized" in this first century of its existence, nor was it "one and catholic" in the sense that we understand those terms today. There was, however, a hierarchical structure, with recognition of the primacy of St. Peter and his successors, and there was a liturgical tradition focusing on the Eucharist. The local churches, such as the Church of Corinth or of Philippi, enjoyed great autonomy, and within these churches there was as yet no organized grouping of Christians into various states of life such as religious life or presbyterate. That would soon evolve, but for the present the distinctions were as often as not on the basis of charismatic gifts or ministries, as St. Paul described them in 1 Cor. 12–14. We can, however, describe the spiritual life of the early Church in general terms by listing its predominant themes or characteristics.

CHRISTIAN LIFE

First of all, early Christian spirituality was *Christocentric*, both because the words and deeds of Christ were still fresh in the minds of Christians (thanks to those who had been witnesses to the Lord) and because Christians lived in anticipation of the return of the risen Christ. "We should have but a very incomplete idea of the spirituality of this period," says Pourrat, "if we did not note the altogether preponderating position which the person of Christ holds in it.... Jesus is constantly set before the faithful as a pattern for the Christian and as the ideal of sanctity.... Jesus was to the first Christians no abstract ideal. The very definite feeling of his presence in the Church and in the hearts of the faithful was everywhere displayed."[5] The presence of Christ was experienced especially in the liturgical context of Eucharist, prayer and biblical homily.

Of the writings that remain from this period, the Christological emphasis is especially noteworthy in the letter of St. Clement of Rome to the Church of Corinth, the letters of St. Ignatius of Antioch and the letter of pseudo-Barnabas. So intense was St. Clement's love for Christ that some have suggested that he may have been the author of the *Letter to the Hebrews*, but this theory is without foundation. Nevertheless, his Christocentric teaching is amply evident in his Letter to the Corinthians, and especially in the sublime passage contained in Chapter 36, where St. Clement refers to Christ, the High Priest, as our road to salvation and our protector and support in our weakness. He repeatedly uses the expressions "in Christ" and "through Christ", which still appear in the prayers of the Church's liturgy. Christ is the Mediator between God and the Church, and the entire economy of salvation is effected in three stages: Christ is sent by the Father; the apostles are sent by Christ; and from the apostles we receive the good news of salvation.

The unknown author of the *Letter of Barnabas* was one of the earliest defenders of the divinity of Christ and he shares this honor with St. Ignatius of Antioch. Two great heresies were flourishing in the churches of the East: the one was a denial of the divinity of Christ, and it gained great acceptance in the churches of Magnesia and Philadelphia; the other was a denial of the humanity of Christ and was rampant in the churches of Tralles, Smyrna and Ephesus. St. Ignatius responded to both of these heterodox doctrines, as the following citations demonstrate:

> There is one God, who manifested himself through Jesus Christ, his Son. . . . Be diligent therefore to be confirmed in the ordinances of the Lord and the apostles . . . in the Son and the Father and the Spirit. . . . God manifested himself through Jesus Christ, his Son, who is his Word proceeding from silence.[6]

> [Christ] is in truth of the family of David according to the flesh . . . truly born of a virgin . . . truly nailed to a tree in the flesh for our sakes. . . . I know and believe that he was in the flesh even after the resurrection.[7]

Finally, St. Ignatius recognizes the unity between Christ and his Church and urges his readers to imitate Christ in order to be united with him as individual Christians:

> My charter is Jesus Christ . . . his cross and his death and resurrection, and faith through him; wherein I hope to be justified.[8]

Even as where Jesus may be, there is the universal Church.[9]

Jesus Christ is our only teacher, of whom even the prophets were disciples in the Spirit and to whom they looked forward as their teacher.[10]

Even the things you do in the flesh are spiritual, for you do all things in union with Jesus Christ.[11]

Do as Jesus Christ did, for he also did as the Father did.[12]

Secondly, early Christian spirituality was *eschatological*, for the primary concern of the first Christians was vigilant preparation for the *parousia* or second coming of Christ. This expectation was fortified by a literal interpretation of Revelation 20:1–10, which in turn gave rise to the doctrine called Millenarianism.[13] On numerous occasions Christ had announced his second coming and he had likewise insisted that his followers are not of this world, that they have not here an abiding city. Consequently, the early Christians experienced the tension of living in an intermediate state; they were a Church in vigil, and since they felt that the second coming was imminent, they lived as if the Church was already in the last days.

The eschatological element is especially evident in the *Didache*, the letters of St. Ignatius of Antioch, Papias, and to some extent in the letter of pseudo-Barnabas. For example, we read in the *Didache*:

Watch for your life. Let not your lamps be quenched, nor your loins be loosed, but be ready, for we know not the hour in which our Lord will come.

Gather yourselves together frequently, seeking the things that are fitting for your souls; for the whole time of your faith shall not profit you unless you be made perfect in the last time. For in the last days the false prophets and corrupters shall be multiplied, and the sheep shall turn into wolves, and love shall turn into hate.

Because of the increase of iniquity men shall hate and persecute and betray each other; and then shall the deceiver of the world appear as the Son of God, and shall do signs and wonders, and the earth shall be given over to his hands, and he shall do unlawful things that have never happened since the world began.

Then shall come the judgment of men into the fiery trial, and many shall offend and perish. But those who remain steadfast in their faith shall be saved from the power of the curse.

And then shall the signs of the truth appear: first the sign of the unrolling of heaven, then the sign of the sound of the trumpet, and the third shall be the resurrection of the dead.

Yet not of all the dead; but as it was said: "The Lord shall come, and all his saints with him."

Then shall the world see the Lord coming above the clouds of heaven.[14]

Thirdly, primitive Christian spirituality was *ascetical*, but the word "ascetical" should be understood in its original meaning of the practice and growth of the virtues rather than acts of austerity and self-denial. Later, asceticism would develop into a way of life practiced by a particular class of people within the Church, but in these early days asceticism was a logical consequence of the Christocentric and eschatological aspects of Christian spirituality.

Following the teaching of St. Paul, St. Ignatius of Antioch had urged the imitation of Christ as a duty for all Christians. Martyrdom, of course, was considered the supreme example of the imitation of Christ, and of this, St. Ignatius gives the clearest and most inspiring testimony; but for the generality of Christians as yet untouched by persecution, the imitation of Christ was achieved by the practice of virtue. Thus, the early Christians were renowned for the virtues of fraternal charity, humility, patience, obedience, chastity and the practice of prayer, as we learn from the moral teaching of the *Didache*. To cultivate and safeguard these virtues, they soon found it necessary to resort to practices of austerity and some degree of separation from the world. Eventually the forms of asceticism most widely respected were the practice of celibacy, freely accepted by both sexes, and the continence of widows. Yet St. Clement and St. Ignatius never allowed the early Christians to forget that the greatest of all the virtues is charity. Thus, in lyrical terms reminiscent of St. Paul's hymn to charity, St. Clement writes:

Who can explain the bond of divine charity? Who is capable of describing its sublime beauty? The height to which charity raises us is ineffable. Charity unites us with God; charity covers a multitude of sins; it suffers all and bears with all. There is nothing base in charity, nothing of pride. It does not foment schism; it is not seditious; it does everything in concord. Charity achieves the perfection of all the elect of God, but without charity nothing is pleasing to God. The Lord has gathered us all to himself in charity and by the charity he had for us, Jesus Christ our Lord, in obedience to the will of God, gave his blood for us, his flesh for our flesh, his soul for our souls. Now you see, dearly beloved, what a great and admirable thing is charity and that there are no words to describe its exalted perfection.[15]

We have seen that St. Ignatius of Antioch urged the imitation of Christ as a duty of all Christians; we have likewise seen that St. Clement of Rome praised charity as the bond of perfection. For St. Ignatius the greatest act of charity and the most perfect imitation of Christ was found in martyrdom. For that reason he wrote in his letter to the Romans: "Permit me to be an imitator of the Passion of my God." In the same letter to the Romans we find a passage that was extracted by Eusebius and through the efforts of St. Jerome has been handed down through the centuries as a stirring testimony to martyrdom as the perfection of charity and the sure means of union with Christ:

> Pray for me, that God will give me both inward and outward strength, so that I may not only be called a Christian but found to be one. . . . I write to the churches and signify to them all that I am willing to die for God. . . . Suffer me to be food to the wild beasts, by whom I shall attain to God. For I am the wheat of God; and I shall be ground by the teeth of the wild beasts that I may become the pure bread of Christ. . . . Let fire and the cross, let the band of wild beasts, let the breaking of bones and the tearing of members, let the shattering in pieces of the entire body and all the wicked torments of the devil come upon me; only let me enjoy Jesus Christ.[16]

The relationship between asceticism and eschatology is likewise evident in the early Church. Living as they did under the impression that the second coming was imminent, though uncertain as to the exact hour, the first Christians realized that it profited them little to accumulate worldly possessions or to be preoccupied with the affairs of this life. They were expecting the Lord's return, and even when it became evident that the waiting period would be longer than first anticipated, they never lost sight of the *parousia*.

In the literature of the period, ascetical and moral instruction can be found in the *Didache*, the letter of St. Clement and the *Shepherd* of Hermas. Finally, in the *Letter to Diognetus*, the life of Christians is described as follows:

> They dwell in their own fatherlands, but as if sojourners in them; they share all things as citizens, and suffer all things as strangers. Every foreign country is their fatherland, and every fatherland is a foreign

country. They marry as all men, they bear children, but they do not expose their offspring. They offer free hospitality, but guard their purity. Their lot is cast "in the flesh," but they do not live "after the flesh." They pass their time upon the earth, but they have their citizenship in heaven. They obey the appointed laws, and they surpass the laws in their own lives. They love all men and are persecuted by all men. They are unknown and they are condemned. They are put to death and they gain life.[17]

Fourthly, primitive Christian spirituality was *liturgical*. Bouyer notes that "it is to Clement, apparently, that we owe the meaning which Christianity was to attach precisely to this word, 'liturgy.' Using it in the traditional Greek sense of the public service rendered by an individual to the community, Clement applies it for the first time to Christian worship."[18] The focal point of the liturgical life was the Eucharist and "nothing is more revealing both of the newness of Christianity and also of its permanent root in the ground of Jewish spirituality than an examination of the eucharistic formulas left to us by the primitive Church as compared with those of Judaism."[19] The *Didache* contains a series of eucharistic prayers which are in reality Jewish blessings with Christian insertions.

> We give thee thanks, our Father, for the holy vine of David, thy servant, which thou hast made known to us by Jesus Christ thy Servant. Glory be to thee forever.

> We give thee thanks, our Father, for the life and knowledge which thou hast made known to us by Jesus Christ thy Servant. Glory be to thee forever.

> As this broken bread was scattered upon the mountains, and being gathered together became one, so let thy Church be gathered together from the ends of the earth into thy kingdom; for thine is the glory and the power, through Jesus Christ, forever.[20]

According to the Acts of the Apostles, three important rites dominated the liturgy of the apostolic times: baptism, the imposition of hands and the breaking of bread. By baptism the candidate was admitted as a full-fledged member of the Christian community; the imposition of hands on baptized Christians conferred the Holy Spirit, and this was sometimes accompanied by special graces or charisms; but the most solemn ceremony of Christianity was the breaking of bread, done in memory of the Last Supper as Christ had commanded. It was in this ceremony more than any other that the Christian experienced the presence of Christ. Here Christ, in his paschal mystery, was present; here the *parousia* or second coming was anticipated.

As in the Passover celebrated by Christ at the Last Supper, there were two distinct parts to the Eucharistic liturgy. First was the common meal, celebrated in the evening and accompanied by prayer formulas that were essentially Jewish. At the close of the meal the celebration of the Eucharist or the breaking of bread took place. The reception of the Eucharist was preceded by a prayer over the bread and wine and followed by a prayer of thanksgiving. As Evdokimov describes it: "At the time of the liturgy, the people are convoked first to hear and then to consume the Word."[21] We should also note that the apostles and their disciples met three times each day for prayer, preferably at nine o'clock in the morning, at midday and at three in the afternoon. Wednesdays and Fridays – and later Saturdays – were observed as days of penance.[22]

Finally, early Christian spirituality was *communal* or social. From the beginning, as we know from the Acts of the Apostles, the common life was an essential element of the Church. Theologically, it provided a setting in which the Christians could practice fraternal charity; liturgically, it was required by the very nature of the Eucharistic liturgy and common prayer. Community life, in turn, required the sharing of common possessions, if only to prevent the separatist individualism that is occasioned by personal dominion. Of all the elements of the apostolic life, the common life was most fundamental, and of all the practices of the common life, the sharing of goods seems to have received the greatest emphasis. This, at least, is the testimony of the Acts of the Apostles:

> These remained faithful to the teaching of the apostles, to the brotherhood, to the breaking of bread and to the prayers. . . . The faithful all lived together and owned everything in common; they sold their goods and possessions and shared out the proceeds among themselves according to what each one needed. They went as a body to the Temple every day but met in their houses for the breaking of bread; they shared their food gladly and generously; they praised God and were looked up to by everyone. Day by day the Lord added to their community those destined to be saved (Acts 2:42–47).

> The whole group of believers was united, heart and soul; no one claimed for his own use anything that he had, as everything they owned was held in common. The apostles continued to testify to the resurrection of the

Lord Jesus with great power, and they were all given great respect. None of their members was ever in want, as all those who owned land or houses would sell them, and bring the money from them, to present it to the apostles; it was then distributed to any members who might be in need (Acts 4:32–35).

As the membership of the Church grew, however, the communal life could no longer be observed as it was in the days of the apostles. Changes were inevitable in a developing and expanding Church. As more and more Gentiles were converted, it became necessary to dispense them from the observance of certain Judaic customs that still prevailed in the Church. As the Church grew in numbers, becoming more universal and less parochial, it was not possible to preserve the close personal relationships in community that had previously characterized the local churches. Finally, with the end of the persecutions and the freedom granted to Christians to practice their religion openly and without fear, there was no longer any external pressure causing the Christians to cling together for mutual protection and security.

Unfortunately, the growth and expansion of the Church during the first few centuries did not proceed without conflict. Even before the persecutions ended, the Church was beset by internal crises caused by heresy, schism and controversy. The first crisis was that of the Judaizing spirit caused by excessive nationalism; the second was the Hellenistic influence that gave rise to the various forms of Gnosticism; the third was the exaggerated autonomy of the local churches that led to controversies about baptism, penance, Easter and hierarchical authority. The most perduring of these crises was the one caused by Gnosticism, which in one form or another has plagued the Church throughout the centuries.

CHRISTIAN GNOSTICISM

Because of the excesses to which it led, Gnosticism is generally condemned outright as an attempt to Hellenize Christianity by adapting the Gospel to Greek philosophy. This was not so from the beginning, however, for the first phase of Gnosticism was simply an effort to express in philosophical terms the moral and doctrinal content of Sacred Scripture. It is only later, toward the end of the second century, that some Gnostics promulgated the doctrine of the dual principle of creation and the erroneous conclusions that follow from such a doctrine. Thus, according to Bouyer, Gnosticism "was not originally a heterodox idea, either in Christianity or in Judaism.

The Alexandrian Christians did not need to introduce it into orthodox Christianity, for the simple reason that it had always had an important place in it. Even with these Christians, even with Clement – the Christian theologian doubtless most infatuated with Greek philosophy – gnosis was never defined by the combination of Christianity and philosophy. As Clement says: '. . . Gnosis is the knowledge of the Name and the understanding of the Gospel'."[23] As a matter of fact, Dupont concludes that the meaning of gnosis as used by St. Paul owes nothing to Greek philosophy and that even in later Hellenism (e.g., in Philo's works) gnosis refers to knowledge of God only as a result of the Greek Bible.[24]

In St. Paul, therefore, gnosis signified the knowledge of God, knowledge of the mysteries or secrets of God, and the understanding of the mystery of Christ (Eph. 3:14–19). In St. John, gnosis is united with love and takes on mystical qualities. Reflections of the Pauline and Johannine doctrine are found in the *Didache*, in the *Shepherd* of Hermas and in the letters of St. Ignatius of Antioch, but it is in St. Clement of Rome and the pseudo-Barnabas that the doctrine of gnosis is clearly set forth. Then, when heretical Gnosticism began to flourish, St. Justin and St. Irenaeus defended Christian gnosis against "pseudo-gnosis."[25] It has been said of St. Irenaeus that he destroyed Gnosticism and introduced orthodox Christian theology.

St. Justin's first defense of Christian doctrine was published around the year 150; his second defense appeared in 155; his *Dialogue with Trypho* around the year 160. According to St. Justin, Christianity is the one, true and universal religion because the truth is fully manifested in Jesus Christ. Nevertheless, the ancient religions and even the Greek philosophers possess the seed of truth, and to the extent that they do, they are partakers of Christ, the Word. Therefore, the teachings of the Greek philosophers are not entirely contrary to Christian truth and need not be rejected *in toto*. But St. Justin insists that natural reason alone is not sufficient for attaining salvation or the complete truth; one also needs interior grace and external revelation. Accordingly, although St. Justin and the other Christian apologists tried to express the Christian truths in philosophical language, they were not philosophers primarily, but Christian theologians, defending and explaining the truths of revelation by reason. Revelation of the truth and acceptance of that truth through faith were always the starting point of their philosophizing.

As a witness to the faith and teaching of the Church, St. Justin speaks with great authority, and this is especially true of his description of the Eucharistic liturgy. He was one of the first apologists to divulge the "secret" of the liturgy which, up to that time, was carefully concealed from the pagans.

On the day called Sunday, all who live in cities or in the country gather together in one place, and the memoirs of the apostles or the writings of the prophets are read, as long as time permits. Then, when the reader has ceased, the president verbally instructs, and exhorts to the imitation of these good things. Then we all rise together and pray. . . .

Having ended the prayers, we salute one another with a kiss of peace. There is then brought to the president of the brethren bread and a cup of wine mixed with water. And he taking them, gives praise and glory to the Father of the universe, through the name of the Son and the Holy Spirit, and offers thanks at considerable length for our being accounted worthy to receive these things at his hands. And when he has concluded the prayers and thanksgivings, all the people present express their assent by saying Amen. . . .

And when the president has confected the Eucharist, and all the people have expressed their assent, those who are called by us deacons give to each of those present to partake of the bread and wine mixed with water, over which the thanksgiving was pronounced, and for those who are absent they carry away a portion.

And this food is called among us the Eucharist, of which no one is allowed to partake but the person who believes that the things which we teach are true, and who has been washed with the washing that is for the remission of sins and unto regeneration, and who is living as Christ has enjoined. For not as common bread and common drink do we receive these, but in like manner as Jesus Christ our Savior, having been made flesh by the Word of God, had both flesh and blood for our salvation, so likewise we have been taught that the food which is blessed by the prayer of his Word, and from which our blood and flesh by transmutation are nourished, is the flesh and blood of that Jesus who was made flesh.

For the apostles, in the memoirs composed by them, which are called Gospels, have thus delivered unto us what was enjoined upon them: that Jesus took bread and, when he had given thanks, said: "This do ye in remembrance of me; this is my Body"; and that, after the same manner, having taken the cup and given thanks, he said: "This is my Blood." And he gave it to them alone. . . . Sunday is the day on which we all hold our common assembly, because it is the first day on which God made the world, and Jesus Christ our Savior on the same day rose from the dead.[26]

The second outstanding defender of Christian doctrine against the

heterodox Gnostics was St. Irenaeus, Bishop of Lyons, who probably suffered martyrdom in 202. In his monumental work, *Against
Heresies*, St. Irenaeus refuted the errors of Marcion, who taught a
heretical dualism and denied the humanity of Christ. After demonstrating that Marcion's Gnosticism must necessarily lead either to
dualism or pantheism, St. Irenaeus presents a synthesis of orthodox
Christian theology. Like St. Justin, he rested his case on the deposit
of faith as found in Scripture and handed down by apostolic tradition: "The only true and lifegiving faith, the Church has received
from the apostles and imparted to the faithful. For the Lord of all
gave to his apostles the power of the Gospel, through whom also we
have known the truth, that is, the doctrine of the Son of God; to
whom also the Lord declared: 'He who hears you, hears me. . . .
The Church is the Church of God. . . . Where the Church is, there is
the Spirit of God.'"[27]

While Tertullian was defending the synthesis composed by St.
Irenaeus – sometimes almost too zealously – Clement of Alexandria
and his disciple Origen were expounding a truly Christian Gnosticism at the School of Alexandria. For Clement the Christian life is
composed of stages through which the individual passes to the state
of perfection; the various stages are called "mansions of the soul."
The mansions are classified as holy fear, faith and hope, and finally
charity. Actually, not all souls reach the final stage and therefore
Christians are divided into those of "ordinary faith" and those who
are true gnostics (perfect faith).[28] The gnostic or perfect Christian is
characterized by contemplation, obedience to the precepts, and the
instruction of good men. Contemplation, of course, is for St. Clement the summit of gnosis, which consists in knowing God, seeing
God and possessing God. Therefore, gnosis is closely related to
prayer (which, says St. Clement, tends to become interior, silent
and constant) and to charity, in which gnosis becomes firmly established.[29] "God is love," says St. Clement, "and he is knowable to
those who love him."[30] The final state of Christian gnosis is
apatheia, which is the result of complete control of the passions and
desires as well the detachment from created things. It is the peace
and unity that flow from charity.[31]

Origen, severely ascetical in his personal life and hailed as the first
scientific exegete in the Church and the first to produce a systematic
manual of dogmatic theology, was placed in charge of the School of
Alexandria in 203 at the age of eighteen. In his treatise on prayer,
which had a profound influence on later monastic spirituality, he
teaches a mysticism that reaches the Trinity through Christ. Though

he speaks of gnosis, as did St. Clement, the treatment is not the same, as Bouyer points out:

> The greatest difference between the two gnoses is that Clement's so easily turns back on itself, in order to understand itself, to describe itself, and perhaps to savor itself. Origen's, on the contrary, hardly describes itself at all . . ., wholly taken up as it is with its one unique object: the mystery of Christ, contemplated in the Scriptures. It was in this way, probably, that Origen exercised the deepest and most enduring influence on all later Christian spirituality.[32]

Perfection, says Origen, consists in becoming as much like God as possible, and in order to do this, the soul must progressively detach itself from this world and gain mastery over its desires and passions. To achieve this, the soul must acquire a knowledge of self by means of examination of conscience and it must also imitate the life of Christ. However, Origen agrees with St. Clement in stating that only the perfect attain to gnosis; the multitudes do not.

Once the soul has passed from the state of a beginner to an advanced state, its spiritual combat is no longer with itself but against the devil. But when the soul approaches the state of the perfect, it enjoys various types of visions and the wisdom or gnosis that constitutes the mysticism of the Logos. At this point, participation in the mystery of Christ terminates in the Trinity and in the mystical marriage. In this state, says Origen, the soul "is divinized in what it contemplates"[33] and "it is raised to friendship with God and to communion with him by participating in the divinity."[34]

By the third century there were communities of Christians in France (Lyons, Vienne, Marseilles, Arles, Toulouse, Paris and Bordeaux), in Spain (León, Mérida and Zaragoza), and in Germany (Cologne, Trier, Metz, Mainz and Strassburg). Carthage was the center of Christianity for North Africa and in Egypt the focal point was at Alexandria. Beyond Europe and the countries of northern Africa, Christianity had spread to Asia Minor, Armenia, Syria, Mesopotamia, Persia, Arabia, and perhaps to India.

This does not mean that the expansion of Christianity was peaceful and unimpeded; on the contrary, it encountered serious obstacles because of occasional doctrinal disputes from within and because of periodic persecutions by Roman authority. With the conversion of Constantine, Christianity was accepted as a legitimate religion and during the reign of Theodosius I (379–395) it became the official religion of the empire. Meanwhile, under

Pope Damasus, who governed the Church from 366 to 384, the monastic movement spread quickly to Egypt, Syria and Asia Minor. At the same time, the *Life of Antony the Hermit* by St. Athanasius was a major factor in the rise of monasticism in Italy and France.

CHAPTER 3

MONASTICISM IN THE EAST

Monasticism began toward the end of the third century as the result of the efforts of ascetical Christians to live a more perfect life. Although it would eventually constitute a distinct state of life in the Church, at the beginning it was a manner of life available to any Christian who wanted to give an authentic witness to the teaching of Christ. The monastic movement began so quietly that historians are unable to describe its origin with exactitude and it was not until the 1930's that there was any serious investigation into the matter.[1] However, there seems to be some connection between the end of the persecution of the Church and the flourishing of asceticism that was a prelude to the monastic movement. Thus, according to Fénelon: "The persecution made less solitaries than did the peace and triumph of the Church. The Christians, simple and opposed to any softness, were more fearful of a peace that might be gratifying to the senses than they had been of the cruelty of the tyrants."[2]

CHRISTIAN VIRGINS AND ASCETICS

In the earliest days of the Church the supreme witness to Christ was martyrdom, although even in those times there were ascetics and also men and women who vowed to live a celibate life. When the persecutions ended, the ascetics and the celibates were placed in a difficult situation; in a world that was tolerant of Christians it was almost inevitable that relaxation should set in and that some Christians should become worldly.[3] As long as they were considered enemies of the State, it was relatively easy to avoid contact with pagan society and to practice their religion within the confines of the small Christian communities; and if they were arrested, they could hope for the coveted crown of martyrdom. But once Christians obtained their freedom and Christianity became the official religion, "it is no longer the pagan world that fights and eliminates the martyr; it is the hermit that takes up the attack and eliminates the world from his being."[4]

From the beginning of the second century there are references to ascetics who lived a life of continence and it seems that the state of virginity was approved by the Church and held in reverence by the faithful. Both St. Clement of Rome and St. Ignatius of Antioch speak of Christian men and women who had embraced a celibate life, and for both of these authors the primary purpose of the celibate life is to imitate Christ in that respect.[5] There are numerous texts from the third century that describe the role of virgins and other celibates in the life of the Church; the treatises by Tertullian and St. Cyprian are especially noteworthy.[6] Finally, in the fourth century the authors who praised virginity were even more numerous: St. Athanasius, St. Basil, St. Gregory Nazianzen, St. Gregory of Nyssa, St. John Chrysostom, St. Ambrose, St. Augustine and Cassian.[7]

At the start, the ascetics, virgins and other celibates remained in their own homes, living with their families and sharing in the common life of the local church. Sometimes they organized themselves into groups, similar to confraternities or chapters of a Third Order. Eventually a rule of life was composed and promulgated by various authors such as St. Ambrose, St. Jerome and St. Caesarius of Arles. Moreover, in order to be approved by ecclesiastical authority, men and women desirous of consecrating themselves to God in celibacy could make a vow to this effect into the hands of the bishop. Thus as early as 306 the Council of Elvira in Spain imposed sanctions on virgins who had been unfaithful to their consecration to God and their vow of virginity. At the same time the Council of Ancyra (314) declared that consecrated virgins who marry were guilty of bigamy, since they were espoused to Christ. In 364 the civil law, under Valens, declared that anyone who married a consecrated virgin was subject to the death penalty.

According to the canonical legislation, virgins were required to wear a black tunic and a black veil, which was to be blessed and bestowed on them by the bishop at the time of their consecration. They could live in their own homes but they were not to leave the house without real necessity. The prescribed prayers were to be recited, alone or in a group, at the traditional hours of nine o'clock in the morning, at twelve noon, and at three o'clock in the afternoon. In addition to this, they were to rise during the night to chant psalms. At Jerusalem both men and women celibates usually joined the clergy for prayer at the prescribed hours. In the fourth century at Rome Marcella and Asela welcomed the virgins and widows into their home for prayer and spiritual reading.

The regulation on fasting was severe and it lasted throughout the entire year, exceptions being made for reasons of health. One meal a day was permitted, and only after three o'clock in the afternoon. It consisted of bread and vegetables and was preceded and followed by appropriate prayers. As regards works of mercy, the virgins were encouraged to share their simple fare with the poor, to visit the sick and to perform any works of mercy befitting their state of life.

Both in the East and in the West the practice of cohabitation was introduced for a time. Clerics or celibate men shared the homes of the virgins to protect them and to provide for their spiritual needs. Inevitably this situation led to abuses that were sharply criticized by bishops and preachers, such as St. John Chrysostom, St. Jerome, and the pseudo-Clement (author of the treatise *Ad Virgines*, composed in the middle of the third century). Ultimately ecclesiastical legislation was drawn up for the protection of the virtue of consecrated virgins and to guarantee that they would be faithful to their commitment. These regulations contributed in no small measure to the development of truly monastic communities of consecrated virgins and the recognition by the Church of the religious life as a distinct state of life.

It should be noted, however, that the vocation to married life among the early Christians was not only the normal calling but that Christian matrimony and family life were a forceful witness to the teachings of Christ. St. Paul not only offered advice to husbands and wives and their children (cf. I Cor. 7:1–40; 2 Cor. 6:14–18; Eph. 5:21–33; 6:1–4; Col. 3:18–24), but he used the union of husband and wife as a symbol of Christ's union with the Church (cf. Eph. 5:25–30). In fact, the ceremony of the consecration of virgins was itself based on the marriage rite. The veiling of the virgin, taken from the Roman wedding custom, was a symbol of her marriage with Christ, and in the Middle Ages it was customary to give the consecrated virgin a ring and a crown, which were also marriage symbols. The celibate life and separation from the world did not connote a disdain for marriage or a Manichaean condemnation of created things.

EREMITICAL AND CENOBITICAL LIFE

A variety of opinions persists throughout the centuries concerning the sources of Christian monasticism. The following non-Christian types of monastic life have been proposed at one time or another as the inspiration and model of Christian monasticism: the recluses of Serapis in Egypt; the ascetical life of the Buddhists; the Essenians who dwelt as monks near the Red Sea about 150 BC;

the Jewish ascetics, called Therapeutae, who lived near Alexandria; the gnostics of Neoplatonism; the asceticism of the religion of Mithra. Vicaire, who is an authority on this question, draws the following conclusion:

> Note that, regardless of the error on which Eusebius and Cassian rest a good part of their theories, ... it is indeed exact that monasticism was inspired from its beginning – not exclusively, but truly – by a desire to imitate the apostles and the first Christians.
>
> Certainly there are elements in monasticism which are not specifically Christian but common to every effort for interior perfection. This general basis of human spirituality explains the existence of real analogies between the monastic institution and institutions far from it both in time and in space.... Nevertheless the most fundamental Christian factor which historians have discovered in the origins of monasticism is a powerful "nostalgia for the early Church." The principal expression of this was the wish to take up the "apostolic life," that is to say, the Christian mentality communicated by the apostles to the early Church and lived by them. This is not surprising if it is remembered that the early monks were convinced of the universality of the formula of the Christian life described in the Acts.[8]

Dom Germain Morin substantiates the foregoing statement when he says that what was new at the beginning of the fourth century was not the monastic type of life but the adaptation to the world by many Christians when the persecutions ended. Actually, the monks and hermits did nothing but try to preserve intact the ideal of the Christian life as lived from the beginning.[9] St. John Chrysostom (+ 407) asserted that monasteries were necessary because the world was not Christian; let it be converted, and the need for the monastic separation will disappear.[10]

Indeed, St. John Chrysostom presents an interesting paradox in the last half of the fourth century. An ascetic by temperament and by practice and always a lover of the contemplative life, he nevertheless dedicated all his energies to the active life as a preacher and a director of souls. In his younger days he had spent four years in the cenobitic life and two years as a hermit, but he seems to have practiced such harsh austerities that his health was endangered and he had to return to Antioch. There he devoted himself to the ministry, first as a deacon, then as a priest, and finally as bishop of Constantinople.

Among his earliest writings are three treatises in defense of the monastic life which contribute nothing to the theology of Christian monasticism; Bouyer refers to them as an "asceticism without mysticism."[11] His treatise on the priesthood, however, written while he was still a deacon, indicates St. John's awareness of a spirituality that is truly sacerdotal and not monastic. He later extended his efforts to the promotion of the spirituality of the laity. He insisted that their basic spiritual exercises should consist in reading and meditating on Scripture and the worthy reception of the sacraments, especially the Eucharist. Perfection, said St. John Chrysostom, is the vocation not only of monks but also of Christians in the world.[12]

Monasticism in the East was of two types: the eremitical life of hermits or anchorites and the cenobitic life of monks. The model of the eremitical life was Antony of Egypt, who retired to the solitary life at the age of twenty and died in 356 at the age of 105. The *Life of St. Antony*, written by St. Athanasius in 357, is the most important source of information on the eremitical life. Another helpful document is the *Apophthegmata Patrum* or sayings of illustrious hermits. Finally, as representative of a later and more structured monastic life, we should mention the *Historia monachorum in Aegypto*, which describes the life of the monks at the end of the fourth century, and the *Historia Lausiaca*, written by Palladius (+ 431) to describe the monastic life in Egypt, Palestine, Syria and Asia Minor.[13]

As recorded by St. Athanasius, St. Antony taught that meditation on the last things strengthens the soul against one's passions and against the devil. If Christians would live each day as if they were to die that day, they would never sin. In the struggle against the devil's wiles, the unfailing weapons are faith, prayer, fasting and the Sign of the Cross. Since the hermit carries with him into solitude his own imperfections and evil tendencies, and since the devil seems to attack the hermit with special ferocity, the life of a solitary is essentially a warfare and a struggle. An individual may flee from the world, but in the desert he will be brought face to face with his own sinfulness and the devil, who goes about seeking whom he can devour (I Pet. 5:8).

Another important lesson taught by St. Antony is that the hermit seeks both interior and exterior solitude in order to give himself completely to God. Consequently, he cannot allow any created thing to occupy his heart, because only he who has practiced total detachment can experience the full force of charity. But lest the hermit fall a victim to pride and self-love, he must, as a disciple of Christ, practice love of neighbor; and he can do this by immolating himself for the salvation of souls, by his prayers for others, and by supporting them in the faith through his spiritual counseling. Indeed, according to St. Antony, the solitary must be willing to leave his desert when the good of the Church or the good of souls require it.

A number of disciples were attracted to St. Antony by his austere manner of life and they frequently sought his advice. Gradually, the eremitical life spread to other places. St. Ammon (+ 350), who had lived as a celibate with his wife, retired with her to the Nitrian Valley and founded a monastic colony. There was no common rule, and each solitary occupied himself as he saw fit, although they all gathered together on Saturdays and Sundays for liturgy and a homily in the church. According to Palladius, there were at one time approximately five thousand hermits in the Valley of Nitria.

To the south, in the desert of Scete, Macarius of Egypt (+ 390) and his disciples led an even more solitary life. Meanwhile, Macarius of Alexandria (+ 394) settled with his followers in the desert of Cellia. Evagrius Ponticus also joined that colony and remained there until his death in 399. The austerities practiced by these solitaries were incredibly severe and some of them would today be branded as masochistic. Palladius, the author of *Historia Lausiaca*, also describes many of the prodigies and marvels performed by the ancient hermits but even in doing so, he stated that he feared that nobody would believe some of them; for example, that Macarius of Alexandria spent an entire season of Lent on his feet, day and night, and during that time subsisted on nothing but cabbage leaves.

The anchorites of Egypt seem to have had a great influence on those of Syria, but there the solitaries became eccentric to the extreme. Rejecting any kind of discipline, they preferred to lead a nomadic existence in wild and desert places; they refused to do any manual labor because they were committed to a life of perpetual prayer. In Palestine, on the other hand, the ascetics observed greater stability, attaching themselves to the holy places in order to be protected and to carry on divine worship. By the fourth century numerous pilgrims joined their ranks and among their visitors were St. Jerome, St. Paula and John Cassian.

At the same time that the eremitical life was flourishing in Egypt, another form of monastic life – the cenobitic – was introduced by St. Pachomius, who was born at Esna, near Thebes. In 318, after having served in the army and then having lived for some time under the guidance of the monk Palamon, Pachomius settled on the eastern bank of the Nile, north of Thebes. The gradual development of the cenobitic life took place as other ascetics joined Pachomius. He regarded this style of life as superior to that of a simple solitary:

> The life of a cenobite is more perfect than that of an anchorite, by reason of the virtues which daily association with the brethren obliges one to practice. Moreover, the brethren are inspired by seeing the labors and virtues of others. Those who are imperfect enable us to practice mortification, and those who are perfect show us the path we should follow.

When the number of monks reached 100, Pachomius constructed a second monastery, some distance from Thebes, and within a few years there were nine such monasteries. Each monastery was like a little town, consisting of several buildings, each housing about forty monks, and the entire complex surrounded by a wall. St. Pachomius also founded a monastery of nuns, at the request of his sister, and he located it near the men's monastery, but separated by a swift-flowing river which no monk was allowed to cross, except the priest who celebrated the liturgy for the nuns.

The rule composed by St. Pachomius consisted of 192 regulations that reveal the prudence and moderation of the legislator. Each monastery was governed by an abbot or archimandrite, to whom the monks were to give complete obedience. Various monks were named as officials in lesser categories, such as infirmarian, hebdomadarian, bursar, etc. Meals and prayers were community exercises and each monk contributed any earnings to the common fund. Unfortunately, some of the monks saw only the material advantages to the common life but refused to obey Pachomius in other matters. His patience served only to encourage them in their egotism and disobedience. Finally Pachomius took a stand; the monks must either obey according to the rule or leave the monastery.

> Now, when you are called to the synaxis, you will all come, and you will not act toward me as you have done. . . . Likewise, when you are called to meals, you will come together, and not behave as you have been doing. . . . If you are still inclined to disobey the instructions I have given you, you may go wherever you please. "The earth is the Lord's, with all that is in it" (Ps. 23:1). And if you want to go somewhere else, do as you will; so far as I am concerned, I will not keep you here any longer, unless you conform to the instructions I have given you.[14]

For Pachomius, obedience was the very foundation of the cenobitic life – obedience to the rule and to the superior. At the same time, he was willing to make adaptations so that all the monks could feel that they were living up to their commitment to the monastic life. Thus, Pachomius stated: "Don't you know that certain brethren, especially the younger ones, have need of relaxation and rest?" On another occasion he commanded: "Provide an abundance at table, so that each one may deny himself and grow in virtue in the measure of his fervor." In other words, each monk was permitted to eat as much as his health or work required, and the manual labor assigned to the individual was in proportion to his strength.

The monastic observances prescribed by the rule of St. Pachomius were adopted by the *lauras* of Palestine, founded by St. Hilarion and perfected by St. Theodosius. In fact, many of the customs later observed by the monastic and mendicant orders of the West had their origins in the Pachomian monasteries. Thus, St. Pachomius insisted on a period of postulancy and novitiate before a candidate could be definitively admitted to the monastic life. There was a vestition ceremony at the beginning of the novitiate, at which time the postulant was clothed in the habit of a monk, consisting of a linen tunic, a cowl and a cloak made of goatskin. Admission to the novitiate was contingent on the favorable vote of the professed monks; and after a successful novitiate, dedicated largely to manual labor, formation in obedience, and the memorizing of lengthy portions of Scripture, the young monk made his vow to live according to the rule.

In the Pachomian monasteries the superior gave spiritual conferences to the community several times a week; the monks assisted at the liturgy and received the Eucharist on Saturdays and Sundays – in a nearby church if none of the monks were priests. Manual tasks were assigned each morning by the superior of the monastery, and silence was strictly observed, especially at meals. Fasting was prescribed on Wednesdays and Fridays throughout the year, and on those days only one meal was eaten, but in Lent every day was a fast day. The monks abstained totally from meat and wine and never took food outside of meal-time. They wore their cowls while they ate; they slept fully clothed, not in a bed, but on a reclining chair, and the doors of their cells were always open.

By the time St. Pachomius died in 346 a large number of monastic communities were flourishing in Egypt. However, it was in Asia Minor, under the leadership of St. Basil (+ 379), that monasticism took a new turn; from a popular, ascetical form of life available to all, "it was to become a school of learned spirituality, wholly permeated with the heritage of Alexandria and, above all, of Origen."[15] As a result of his contributions to the theology and structure of the cenobitic life, St. Basil is commonly hailed as the father of monasticism in the East, at least of monasticism as a well-defined way of life or particular vocation.

Born in 330, Basil studied at Caesarea, Constantinople and Athens. At Caesarea he met Gregory Nazianzen and the two became fast friends. Both of them came into contact with the pagan Gnosticism of the Greeks and the Arian heresy; later, Gregory Nazianzen and Gregory of Nyssa (the brother of Basil) defended the transcendence of God and the divinity of Christ against the Arians. They also incorporated orthodox, Christian Gnosticism into monastic spirituality.

While still young, Basil felt called to the ascetical life. He travelled to Egypt, Syria and Mesopotamia, where he followed the monastic style of life for a time. Then, returning to his homeland, he distributed all his possessions to the poor and lived as a solitary until he was named bishop in 370. Although he gained great renown as an anchorite, St. Basil never considered the monastic life as exceptional or as a special vocation; he even avoided using the term "monk" and referred to hermits and monks simply as Christians. For St. Basil and for some of the other Fathers the monastic life was the logical consequence of the commitment made by the Christian at baptism. The fact that the monastic life was held up to the ordinary faithful as the ideal demonstrates that in these early centuries there was only one spirituality for all Christians: the authentic *vita apostolica*, and it constituted the perfection of the Christian life.[16]

Yet this very insistence on the monastic life – and indeed the contemplative life – as the perfection of the Christian life gave rise to further questions. Are there, after all, two classes of Christians – the perfect and the ordinary? If monasticism is the ideal, are married Christians excluded from the possibility of attaining Christian perfection? Or are there two kinds of perfection, one ordinary and the other extraordinary? These questions have been posed again and again throughout the history of Christian spirituality.

St. Basil, however, did not look favorably on the strictly eremitical life nor on total separation from human society. When asked whether a monk formed in the cenobitic life could retire to the desert, he replied: "This is nothing but a mark of self-will and remains foreign to those who honor God."[17] In his defense of the common life of cenobites, Basil bases his argument on the precept of charity:

Who does not know, indeed, that man is a gentle and sociable being, and not solitary or savage? Nothing is as proper to our nature as to enter one another's society, to have need of one another, and to love the man who is of our race. After having given us these seeds which he has cast into our hearts, the Lord came to claim their fruits and he said: "I give you a new commandment: to love one another" (Jn. 13:34).... What did he say to them? "All will know that you are my disciples by the love that you have for one another" (Jn. 13:35). Everywhere he unites these precepts to such an extent that he refers to himself the good deeds of which our neighbor is the object.... "Everything that you did to the least of my brethren, you did to me" (Mt. 15:35–40). And so, by means of the first precept, it is possible to observe the second, and by the second to go back to the first.... "My commandment is that you love one another as I have loved you" (Jn. 15:12).[18]

St. Basil was not in favor of large communities; he preferred that they be small so that the common life could foster the recollection of the monks and the superior could relate to the monks, and the monks to each other, on a more personal level. The daily schedule called for community prayer, the study of sacred doctrine (and especially of the works of Origen), manual labor, mitigated asceticism and an apostolate that was compatible with the monastic life. The rule composed by St. Basil became the standard legislation for monasticism in the East, and it had a great influence on the monks of the West as well.

THE CAPPADOCIAN FATHERS
Unlike his close friend Basil, St. Gregory Nazianzen (+ 389 or 390) was strongly attracted to the eremitical life and in particular to the gnostic meditation of Origen. Together with St. Gregory of Nyssa, he introduced what has been called "learned monasticism." These three men were not only monks but bishops as well, yet their personalities differed greatly. St. Basil was a practical man, totally dedicated to the service of the Church in a position of responsibility and authority; St. Gregory Nazianzen was basically a poetic and contemplative type, drawn to solitude, asceticism and study, although outstanding as a preacher when he engaged in the pastoral ministry; St. Gregory of Nyssa was an intellectual and, according to Bouyer, "one of the most powerful and most original thinkers ever known in the history of the Church."[19]
During his monastic period St. Basil collaborated with St. Gregory Nazianzen on an anthology of the works of Origen, but after he became a priest and later a bishop, his literary productions were in

the fields of moral theology and spirituality. His *Moralia* (PG 31,700–869) is a collection of eighty rules and instructions based on texts of Scripture, and although they were addressed to Christians in general, they also served as a doctrinal basis for the monastic life. The *Regulae fusius tractatae* (PG 31, 889–1052) and the *Regulae brevius tractatae* (PG 31, 1080–1305) were written in the form of questions and answers, based on Basil's conversations with monastic communities he had visited.[20]

St. Basil has been called a Roman among the Greeks because on the one hand he was eminently practical and moralistic and on the other hand he did not disdain to make use of philosophical ideas and expressions in the formulation of his ethical teaching. Like Plato and Plotinus, he could see that the human person was a strange blending of the spiritual and the physical; consequently the renunciation of sensate pleasures constitutes the very core of the ascetical life. Another element of asceticism is the obligation to comply with all the moral precepts and commandments, and even to observe the evangelical counsels. This does not mean that St. Basil was proposing the monastic life as suitable for all Christians, but simply insisting that all should strive to live the Gospel teaching as perfectly as possible. He did not condemn marriage, but neither did he extol it. As we have stated previously, St. Basil considered the monastic community to be the best possible imitation of the primitive Church in Jerusalem; that is why he was so energetic in promoting the monastic life and why he considered cenobitic monasticism superior to the eremitical life.

St. Gregory Nazianzen, close friend of St. Basil, led a life of continual fluctuation between the contemplative life and the sacerdotal ministry. Having spent some time as a monk, he would have remained so if he had been able to resist the insistence of the Christian faithful that he be ordained a priest. Later, ordained a bishop by Basil, he eventually accepted the administration of the Church at Constantinople. After two years, during which time he became renowned as an orator, he resigned from Constantinople and returned to his former diocese of Nazianzus but remained there for only two years. The five or six years prior to his death in 389 or 390 were spent in study, contemplation and monastic practices.

The writings of St. Gregory Nazianzen consist of the following: numerous sermons (PG, Vol. 35 and 36), approximately 400 poems (PG, Vol. 37 and 38), his letters (PG, Vol. 37) and an autobiography. Gregory reveals himself in his works as eminently mystical and contemplative; indeed, he taught that the perfection of the Christian life culminates in contemplation. The goal of Christian spirituality is as perfect an imitation of Christ as is possible, and to attain this, one must eliminate everything that could be an obstacle to union with Christ. Hence, says Gregory:

> I must be buried with Christ, rise with him, inherit heaven with him, become son of God, become God.... This is what is the great mystery for us; this is what God incarnate is for us.... He has come to make us perfectly one in Christ, in the Christ who has come perfectly into us, to put within us all that he is. There is no longer man nor woman, barbarian nor Scythian, slave nor free man (Col. 3:11), characteristic of the flesh; there is now only the divine image that we all bear within us, according to which we have been created, which must be formed in us and impressed on us.[21]
>
> Then we shall be deiform, because we shall possess in ourselves God whole and entire and God alone. Such is the perfection to which we are tending.[22]

As if to justify his constant yearning for the eremitical life, St. Gregory Nazianzen delivered a beautiful tribute to that style of life shortly after his ordination to the priesthood:

> To me, nothing seems preferable to the state of the man who, closing his senses to exterior impressions, escaping from the flesh and the world, re-entering into himself, retaining no further contact with any human beings except when necessity absolutely requires it, conversing with himself and with God, lives beyond visible things and carries within himself the divine images, always pure, untouched by any admixture with the passing forms of this earth; having become truly and becoming each day more truly the spotless mirror of the divinity and of divine things, receiving their light in his light, their resplendent brightness in his more feeble brightness, in his hope gathering already the fruits of the future life, living in association with the angels, still on this earth and yet outside of it, carried even to the higher regions by the Spirit. If there is one of you who is possessed by this love, he knows what I am trying to say and will pardon my weakness.[23]

St. Gregory of Nyssa was educated by his brother, St. Basil, and afterwards ordained a lector, but he soon abandoned that function, opened a school of rhetoric and married. After the death of his wife he was persuaded by Gregory Nazianzen to enter the monastery founded by Basil in Pontus. In 371 Gregory was ordained bishop of Nyssa, but five years later he was accused of financial negligence and deposed by a synod in 376. However, when the Arian Emperor Valens died in 378, Gregory returned to Nyssa, and when his brother Basil died in 379, he dedicated himself to ecclesiastical affairs and became a great leader of the Church in Cappadocia until his death in 394.

Most of Gregory's writings were composed in the period extending from 382 to 394. His dogmatic works were directed to the refutation of the Arian heresy and the Christological heresy of Apollinaris, and an explanation of Catholic belief in the Trinity. He also composed a summary of Catholic doctrine, *Oratio catechetica magna* (PG 45, 9–106), and wrote several works of scriptural exegesis, one of them a continuation of Basil's commentary on Genesis and the other a treatise on man. The rest of his exegetical works treat of Christian perfection and mystical union: *De vita Moysis* (PG 44, 297–430); *In psalmorum inscriptiones* (PG 44, 431–608); *In ecclesiasten homiliae* (PG 44, 616–753); *In Canticum Canticorum* (PG 44, 756–1120); *De oratione dominica* (PG 44, 1120–1193); *De beatitudinibus* (PG 44, 1193–1302). Finally, among his strictly ascetical writings we find *De virginitate* (PG 46, 317–416), composed before he became a bishop; *De vita Macrinae* (PG 46, 959–1000), the life of his own sister and a marvelous example of early hagiography; *De instituto christiano* (PG 46, 287–306), a definitive synthesis of his teaching on Christian spirituality; *De perfectione* (PG 46, 251–286) and *De castigatione* (PG 46, 307–316). It is only in recent times that St. Gregory of Nyssa has been properly appreciated, and this is due in large part to the scholarly work of Hans Urs von Balthasar, Jean Daniélou, Werner Jaeger and Walther Völker.[24]

The first thing the reader notices in the writings of Gregory of Nyssa is his generous use of concepts and terminology borrowed from Greek philosophy; so much so, that he has been accused of pure Platonism.[25] As a philosopher, Gregory did follow the system of Plato; as a theologian he was influenced by Origen, but without falling into the errors of the latter.[26] Quasten has shown that Gregory did not hesitate to criticize pagan philosophy and to compare it with the barren daughter of the Egyptian king (Ex. 2:1–10): "Childless indeed is pagan philosophy; always in pains of childbirth, it never engenders living offspring. What fruit has philosophy brought forth worthy of such labor?" Nevertheless, "there is, indeed, something in pagan learning which is worthy of being united to us for the purpose of engendering virtue. It must not be rejected."[27]

St. Gregory states the following rule for the use of philosophy in relation to revealed truths: "We are not allowed to affirm what we please. We make Holy Scripture the rule and the measure of every tenet. We approve of that alone which may be made to harmonize with the intention of those writings."[28] Bouyer describes Gregory's method as follows:

> The basis of Gregory's thought, in fact, remains Christian and biblical, at the school of Origen, whom he understood perhaps better than anyone else, but used with the sovereign freedom which is always his.... In general, his thought goes through three successive stages. At the starting point comes the biblical, Christian intuition, grasped in a text or a theme that he draws from tradition, Philo or Origen often being his guides. Then comes the compact and very personal expression of this intuition in the philosophic language that is his own, and here we must be on guard against too quickly interpreting its terms as we might if we found them in Plato, in later Stoicism, or even in Plotinus. And, finally, this thought is unfolded by a return to the Bible in which the connections, not only with a single isolated text, but with the whole current of tradition, are indicated and justified.
>
> One last feature characteristic of his time has been brought out very happily by Fr. Daniélou: we must never forget that the context of his most personal meditations always remains liturgical. It is within baptismal and eucharistic perspectives that his thoughts develop and that his spirituality is to be understood.[29]

St. Gregory of Nyssa never denied for a moment the duality of matter and spirit, as described by Plato, but he prefers the Pauline and theological duality of the will of the sinner and the will of God. The integration of the two extremes can be effected only through the sacraments of baptism and the Eucharist, by which the redemptive mystery of the risen Christ is applied to man. The perfection of the Christian, therefore, consists in participation in the mystery of Christ. What man must do to achieve this participation, apart from the sacraments of baptism and the Eucharist, is explained by Gregory in his *De instituto christiano*.[30]

What Gregory proposes to teach in this work, written specifically for monks, is that Christian perfection is the goal of life and that it is possible of attainment because of the knowledge of the truth that God has provided for those who wish it. What St. Gregory understands by knowledge or gnosis is the knowledge of the distinction between good and evil (Heb. 5:14) or the difference between true good and apparent good. Ultimately, it is the knowledge of God himself as revealed in the word of God and expressed in the tradition of the Church. But true contemplation of the Scripture is given only to those who act under the impulse and guidance of the Holy Spirit. And how does the monk prepare himself to receive the Holy Spirit? St. Gregory answers:

> He who desires, therefore, to lead his body and his soul to God in accordance with the law of religion and to consecrate to him a pure worship ... must make the faith which the saints have taught in the Scriptures the guide of his life and he must give himself up to the pursuit of virtue by obeying this faith perfectly. He must free himself completely from the chains of earthly life and put away once and for all any slavery to what is base and vain. By this and his life, he must become wholly God's possession, knowing well that he who has faith and purity of life has the power of Christ as well, and where there is the power of Christ there is also deliverance from the evil and the death that ravage our life.[31]

For St. Gregory, therefore, baptism is the pledge of the work of the Spirit in man and the Eucharist is its sustenance, but the Christian does not arrive at the full stature of Christ until he exerts increasing efforts in the ascetical life. "For the body grows without us," says Gregory, "but the measure and beauty of the soul in the renewal of its conception, which is given it by the grace of the Spirit through the zeal of him who receives it, depends on our disposition: to the degree that you develop your struggles for piety, to the same degree also the grandeur of your soul develops through these struggles and these efforts."[32] Eventually the soul can reach the heights of gnosis, which is "a mutual compenetration, God coming into the soul and the soul being transported in God." This is the high point of *agape*.[33]

In Homily XI on the *Song of Songs*, St. Gregory describes the three stages in which God revealed himself to Moses: first in the light of the burning bush, then in the cloud of the exodus, and finally in total darkness. Similarly, the soul first finds God in the visible things of creation; but as the soul advances, the intellect serves as a cloud to cover everything sensate so that the soul may be prepared to contemplate that which is hidden; and when the soul has abandoned all earthly things, so far as is possible to human nature, it enters the sanctuary of the knowledge of God, completely enveloped in the divine darkness. It is this experience of God in darkness that St. Gregory calls true theology (*theognosis*).

St. Gregory has been described by Harvanek as a dogmatic theologian, a philosopher and an ascetico-mystical writer.[34] His writings serve as a link with the great theologians of Alexandria, with Maximus and with the Byzantine school. According to

Bouyer, the teaching of St. Gregory had three well-defined effects on Christian spirituality: it was popularized by Macarius of Egypt (+390) among the monks; it was further developed by Evagrius Ponticus (+399); and it prepared the way for the writings of the pseudo-Dionysius (+530).[35]

EVAGRIUS, PSEUDO-DIONYSIUS AND MAXIMUS

According to Bouyer, "Evagrius is one of the most important names in the history of spirituality, one of those that not only marked a decisive turning-point, but called forth a real spiritual mutation."[36] Greatly influenced by the teachings of Origen, Evagrius Ponticus (+399) developed a theology of the spiritual life which affected many subsequent writers, and especially Cassian. However, Evagrius does not escape criticism on the grounds that he was too much of a philosopher. He was condemned, together with Origen, by the Council of Constantinople (553) and by three subsequent councils. In modern times Hans Urs von Balthasar has stated: "There is no doubt that the mysticism of Evagrius, carried to the strict conclusions of its premises, comes closer, by its essence, to Buddhism than to Christianity."[37]

Evagrius attempted to synthesize the doctrine of the spiritual life in treatises that would be of particular benefit to monks. The *Practicos* (PG 40, 1221–1252) contains the ascetical teaching of Evagrius; the *Gnosticos*,[38] a continuation of the previous work, is a compilation of practical counsels and precautions; his masterpiece, *Kephalaia gnostica*, was published under the editorship of A. Guillaumont at Paris in 1958.[39] Of the other works attributed to Evagrius we mention only a treatise on the cenobitic life and another directed to nuns,[40] discussions of evil thoughts and the eight spirits of malice,[41] and a work on prayer.[42]

The positive contributions made by Evagrius can be summarized as follows: he defined the stages of growth in the spiritual life;[43] he tried to show the interconnection of the virtues, beginning with faith and terminating with charity; he expounded a theology of prayer that reaches its perfection in "mystical theology" or gnosis of the Trinity; he enumerated and commented on the eight capital sins; and he attempted to refine the stoical doctrine of *apatheia* by relating it to charity.

With pseudo-Dionysius it is "surprising to see *apatheia*, the importance of which from Clement to Evagrius was always being explained and affirmed, here disappearing, or almost so; while *gnosis*, if it has not disappeared, is at least considerably less emphasized."[44] Yet, the pseudo-Areopagite is truly in the mainstream of the Cappadocian school, although he also represents an advance in the theology of the spiritual life, particularly in his treatment of the three stages, his distinction between theology as a science and theology as mysticism, and his explanation of mystical contemplation. It would be difficult to overemphasize his importance in spiritual theology, especially as an influence on the medieval theologians. His impact was much greater in the West than in the East.

It is generally admitted that the works of the pseudo-Dionysius were composed toward the end of the fifth century or early in the sixth century. There is also common agreement on the authentic works that constitute the *corpus dionysiacum: De divinis nominibus, Theologia mystica, De caelesti hierarchia*, and *De ecclesiastica hierarchia*. As the title indicates, the first work is an explanation of the various names attributed to God, both in Sacred Scripture and by the philosophers. *Theologia mystica* treats of the divine darkness and the necessity of total detachment in order to be united with God and then, after explaining the difference between positive theology and negative theology, shows why the transcendental is not contained in any sensate form or intellectual concept. The last two works are treatises on the hierarchy of angels and on the sacraments respectively.[45]

It has been said that pseudo-Dionysius was the originator of the division of the "three ways" or "three stages" of the spiritual life. However, except for a passage in *De caelesti hierarchia*, where the catechumens, the ordinary faithful and the monks represent three stages of progress toward perfection, pseudo-Dionysius does not apply the concept of ways or stages to the individual Christian. Rather, he is speaking of the ways in which men or angels participate in the divine perfections; therefore it is in this context that one should understand the expressions "purification, illumination and perfection." Thus, in *De caelesti hierarchia*, various choirs of angels perform the functions of purification, illumination and perfection; in *De ecclesiastica hierarchia*, on the other hand, these same functions are performed by the liturgy, the clergy and the faithful. Liturgically, baptism is the sacrament of purification; the Eucharist is the sacrament of illumination; chrismation (confirmation) is the sacrament that perfects the graces of baptism. Applying the same terms to the clergy, the ministers or deacons perform the function of purifying, the priests illumine, and the bishops perfect the work by the ministry of the word and the liturgy.

At the beginning of *De ecclesiastica hierarchia* pseudo-Dionysius remarks that the goal of all purification, illumination and perfection is "constant love of God and divine things ..., the vision and knowledge of sacred truth, a divine participation in the simple perfection of him who is sovereignly simple, and the enjoyment of that contemplation which nourishes the soul and deifies all who attain it."[46]

In *De divinis nominibus* he speaks of a knowledge of God that is attained, not by study but by an impression of the divine; it is a kind of empathy and intuition resulting from a supernatural illumination from God and, on man's part, a love that becomes ecstatic.[47] But it is in the short treatise, *De mystica theologia*, that pseudo-Dionysius develops his doctrine on the two types of theology and the nature of mystical contemplation. At the very beginning he describes "mystical theology" and the means to attain it:

> O Trinity superessential, superdivine, supergood, ... lead us to that supreme height of mystical words that transcends understanding and manifestation, there where the simple, absolute, unchangeable mysteries of theology are unveiled in the superluminous cloud of silence that initiates into hidden things, super-resplendent in the deepest depths of darkness in a manner beyond any manifestation, which, wholly intangible and invisible, fills to overflowing with superbeautiful splendors our blinded spirits.
>
> Such is my prayer, and you, my friend Timothy, applying yourself with all your strength to mystical contemplations, abandon the senses and the intellectual energies and everything that is sensible or intelligible; everything that is not and that is, and raise yourself in unknowing toward union, so far as this is permitted, toward what surpasses all essence and gnosis; indeed, it is purely by a free and absolute ecstasy out of yourself that you will be carried toward the superessential ray of the divine darkness.[48]

Stated briefly, pseudo-Dionysius' doctrine on the knowledge of God (theology) starts from the assertion that no sensible or imaginative image can lead man to a knowledge of God; rather, these images are obstacles. God can be known in only two ways: by the intellect or by mystical contemplation. The former is a rational knowledge called demonstrative or apodictic theology; the latter is a mystical theology that is supernatural and intuitive. Moreover, demonstrative or reasoned theology is of two kinds: affirmative and negative. Theology by way of affirmation consists in attributing to God all possible being and all perfections; God is all and God is everything. Theology by negation is the attempt to express the fact that whatever be our concepts of God, they are more expressive of what God is not than what he is; they fall far too short of the God who is unknowable, transcendent and mysterious. Consequently, our knowledge of God by negation is often more accurate than our affirmative theology, and this is so because the negation of our images of God purifies our concept of God. Thus, all the goodness of created things is likewise found in God (affirmative theology), but the goodness of God is infinite and therefore it is not the same as the goodness in created things (negative theology).

In order to understand pseudo-Dionysius' doctrine on mystical theology, it is necessary to accept his use of the word "mystical" in a Christian sense. In spite of the fact that some scholars have seen purely Platonic doctrine in the mysticism of the pseudo-Dionysius, Bouyer maintains that the expression *"mystikos"* did not have a religious meaning for the Greek philosophers.

> The only uses of the word that we find in the Hellenistic world in connection with religious things concern the ritual of the "mysteries." But in this case they mean quite simply that the ritual is and must remain hidden. . . .
>
> What was hidden in the Hellenistic mysteries was the rites and nothing but the rites. These did not include any "mystical" doctrine, for the very good reason that they did not include any doctrine at all. . . .
>
> However, the symbolic usage that literary men soon came to make of the images and formulas of the mysteries made ready for an intellectual and spiritual utilization of the term. . . . This vocabulary came to be used in the domain of philosophy: . . . to signify any knowledge difficult to penetrate, such as the most academic and arid subtleties of Stoic physics or psychology.
>
> It is in connection with this very loose and very commonplace usage that . . . the first Christian use of the word *mystikos* came to be introduced. It was used to describe what Clement and Origen considered the most difficult theological problem in Christianity: Scriptural exegesis as they understood it, that is, the discovery of the allegorical sense of the Scriptures. . . .
>
> Other doctrinal uses of the word "mystical" are encountered in the ancient Fathers to designate the teaching of the objects of faith in contrast to visible realities. . . . It was in a kindred sense that Clement had previously described the divine name as the "mystical tetragram," and

also that Eusebius, St. Cyril of Alexandria and many others later on would call the Christian Trinity the "mystical Triad" or its teaching a science "in a superior way, ineffable and mystical."

From here we go on to a third sense in which mystical becomes merely a synonym for "spiritual" in contrast to "carnal"....

All these texts in which "mystical" is used in the Fathers, in a biblical context, show us, then, that the word, in its Christian usage, is primarily connected with the divine reality which Christ communicates to us, which the Gospel reveals to us, which gives its whole meaning to the whole of Scripture. Hence we see how the word "mystical" came to be applied to any knowledge of the divine realities to which we have access through Christ, and then, by derivation, to these realities themselves. And, finally, the word is applied, in the same line of thought, to the spiritual reality of the "worship in spirit and in truth" as opposed to the emptiness of an external religion not vivified by the Lord's coming....

The use of the term "mystical," then, came to pass from the Christian interpretation of the Scriptures to the content of the Christian sacraments. Here it designates at once the spiritual reality of the latter and the fact that his reality remains hidden....

We might say, therefore, that, for the Fathers, the sacraments and, above all, the Eucharist, are "mystical" in that they envelop the reality of the "mystery" which the Gospel proclaims and unveils to the eyes of faith in the whole Bible.

The first uses of the term which began to orient it toward designating a particular spiritual experience are visibly rooted in these two primordial senses.[49]

For pseudo-Dionysius mystical theology applies both to the intuitive knowledge of the revealed truths of Scripture and the experience of divine realities, either in those revealed truths or in the Eucharistic liturgy. In *De divinis nominibus* he makes a distinction between the theology that results from one's own effort in thinking about divine truths and that which is the result of "some more divine inspiration, not only learning the things of God but experiencing them, and through this sympathy with them, if we may say this, having been consummated in initiation into mystical union and faith in them, which cannot be taught."[50]

The experience of divine realities, which is infused contemplation, involves three things: suspension of all sensible and intelligible images, entrance into darkness and obscurity, and the vision of God and intimate union with him.[51] The apparent contradiction between vision and darkness is explained as follows by pseudo-Dionysius:

> The divine cloud is that inaccessible light in which it is said that God dwells. Being invisible by the excess of its splendor, and inaccessible by the hyperbole of the superessential expansion of its light, whoever has been judged worthy to see God attains to this by the very fact of not seeing or knowing, having arrived truly in him who is above all vision and gnosis, in knowing that he is above everything that is sensible or intelligible.[52]

With pseudo-Dionysius, Evagrius and Macarius Christian spirituality as expressed in monasticism reached its highest point of development in the East. Their spiritual teaching and practice are far removed from the asceticism of the anchorites and they contributed greatly to a shift of emphasis in monastic life from work and asceticism to the mystical elements of knowledge and prayer. Although this "interiorized" monasticism[53] was completely orthodox, it also gave grounds for the heretical movement of Messalianism, which was an exaggerated doctrine on the role of prayer and mysticism in the monastic life. It led ultimately to a mysticism that was physical, sensual and passive, resulting in an antimystical reaction that was corrected by Diadochus.[54]

After Messalianism, another crisis arose in monasticism and it occasioned the emergence of St. Maximus (+662), whom Bouyer calls "the last great theologian of Greek patristics."[55]

From the time that he entered the monastic life in 613, St. Maximus spent most of his time in the defense of orthodox doctrine against the heretics, frequently moving from one monastery to another because of persecution. Ultimately he was arrested in Rome, together with Pope Martin I, and sent into exile. In 662 he was again in Constantinople, where the heretics condemned him to be scourged and to have his tongue and his right hand cut off. He died in that same year as a result of his sufferings.

Aside from his dogmatic and polemical writings, St. Maximus composed the following works in ascetico-mystical theology: *Liber asceticus*, a dialogue between an abbot and a young monk concerning the obligations of monastic life; *Capita de caritate*, containing the doctrine on charity and the spiritual applications of the doctrine; *Capita theologica et oeconomica* and *Alia capita*, which are a continuation of the treatise on charity; and *Mistagogia* and his commentaries on the works of pseudo-Dionysius, based on the *De ecclesiastica hierarchia* of pseudo-Dionysius, for whom Maximus had the greatest reverence.

What is distinctive about the spiritual doctrine of St. Maximus is that he centers everything on Christ. Having defended orthodox Christology against the heretics, he was thoroughly imbued with love for the Savior. He saw Christ not only as the meritorious cause of our salvation but also the exemplary cause, for which reason the great law of the Christian life is the imitation of Christ. By imitating Christ, the soul can achieve victory over the enemies of the spiritual life, the greatest of which is self-love. This involves a detachment from created things and one's own selfish desires so that egoistic love can be replaced by the love of God and of neighbor.[56] Thereby the soul attains the state of *apatheia* or peace of soul which is also the fruit of prayer and grace.

St. Maximus classifies Christians into three groups: the beginners, who are led by fear; the advanced souls, who have the well-founded hope of a reward and are therefore somewhat mercenary; and the perfect, who are true children of God and motivated by filial love. The perfect enjoy a contemplative prayer that is activated by the gift of wisdom, which Maximus calls "the eyes of faith." It is also through wisdom that the soul receives a knowledge of God that is called theology. It is a fruit of prayer. But the greatest of all the spiritual gifts enjoyed by the perfect is divine charity. It is charity that deifies the soul, enables it to experience its adoptive filiation, and unites it to God in the bond of mystical marriage. And all this comes through Christ. In St. Maximus, therefore, the model and cause of Christian perfection is Jesus Christ, and the soul of Christian perfection is charity. With St. Maximus, says Bouyer, Christian spirituality "regains something of the first upsurge of the vigor of the Gospel."[57]

CHAPTER 4

MONASTICISM IN THE WEST

There is little documentary evidence of monasticism in the West before the middle of the fourth century, at which time it was already flourishing in the East.[1] However, since there was constant communication between Rome and the centers of monasticism in Egypt, Palestine and Alexandria, it is probable that Christians in Rome knew about the monastic movement. What is certain is that St. Athanasius visited Trier during the time of his first exile between 336 and 338, and he was in Rome in 340. His *Life of Antony*, which had such a great role in the popularization of the monastic life, was quickly translated into Latin for Christians in the West.

On the other hand, it is possible that monastic life in the West could have developed without any direct influence from the East. The ascetics, virgins and widows were already observing some of the practices proper to a monastic life style. Eusebius even speaks of an ascetic living in solitude as early as the middle of the third century.[2] But one of the distinguishing elements of monastic life was absent in the first few centuries of the Church in the West, namely, separation from the world. The early ascetics preferred life in community to a solitary life separated from the world. Consequently, although we cannot say with certainty that monastic life in the West was strictly an importation from the East, during the fourth and fifth centuries eastern monasticism was a dominant influence on the development of monastic communities in the West.

ORIGINS OF WESTERN MONASTICISM

Writing in the 380's, St. Jerome states that the name "monk" was held in contempt, probably because of certain male and female ascetics who were excessively charismatic and lacking in discipline.[3] At the same time he spoke favorably of the monastic life of certain noble Roman ladies for whom he served as spiritual director. In spite of some opposition to the ascetical movement, St. Jerome fostered this type of life during his three years in Rome.

Another promoter of the ascetical life was St. Ambrose (+ 397) whose own sister Marcellina began to live the ascetical life in Rome in 353 and later moved to Milan.[4] As bishop of Milan, he was the patron of a community of men near Milan, and it was here that St. Augustine first encountered anything resembling the monastic life.

It has been said that Eusebius, Bishop of Vercelli from 344 to his death in 371, founded the first monastic community in the Latin Church. However, since he was exiled to the East in 355 for refusing to sign the condemnation of St. Athanasius at the synod at Milan, it is likely that he established the community after his return from the East in 363.

St. Paulinus of Nola was also a founder of monastic life. Born in Bordeaux around 353, he married Therasia, a Spanish lady and devout Christian. When their only child died in infancy, they decided to dedicate their lives to asceticism, continence and prayer. They left Barcelona and settled at Naples in 395, where they organized a *fraternitas monastica* composed of relatives and friends, all from the upper class. Paulinus had been ordained a priest – possibly before leaving Barcelona – and after Therasia died in 408, he became bishop of Nola. He was in contact with most of the ecclesiastical figures of his day, for example, St. Jerome, St. Ambrose, St. Martin of Tours, St. Augustine and St. Honoratus.[5]

St. Martin of Tours completed his military service in 356 and in 360 he went to Poitiers with St. Hilary, where he formed a semi-eremitical community. In 371 he became bishop of Tours, the first monk-bishop in the West, and he promoted monasticism until his death in 397. Having been formed in the monastic life by St. Hilary, who was a great admirer of St. Athanasius and eastern monasticism, St. Martin founded numerous monasteries, among them the famous ones at Ligugé and Marmoutier. So great was the veneration paid to St. Martin as a founder and patron of monastic life that St. Benedict dedicated a chapel to him at Monte Cassino.[6]

Shortly after the death of St. Martin, a monastery was founded by St. Honoratus between 400 and 410 on the island of Lerins, near Cannes. The monks were for the most part educated men from the upper class and as a result numerous bishops were chosen from their ranks. The monastery at Lerins became a focal point of religious culture for several centuries, producing such eminent figures as St. Caesarius (+ 542), author of monastic rules for men and for women, and Vincent of Lerins, author of the *Commonitorium*, a treatise on Catholic doctrine.

Meanwhile, St. Jerome, who had become so unpopular in Rome

that he left for Palestine after the death of Pope Damasus in 384, founded and directed monasteries for men and for women until his death in 420. The monasteries followed the Rule of St. Pachomius, and in 404 St. Jerome translated the Rule of St. Pachomius, his *Monita*, and his letters into Latin. Previously, Rufinus, onetime friend of St. Jerome, had translated the Rule of St. Basil and the *Historia Monachorum in Aegypto* into Latin. In this way both St. Jerome and Rufinus exerted a great influence on monasticism in the West.

JOHN CASSIAN

In John Cassian (+435) we have the greatest exponent of the monastic life and the most influential figure prior to St. Benedict. Most likely he was born in the Balkans in 360 and took the name of John as a remembrance of his teacher and patron, St. John Chrysostom.

With his friend Germanus, Cassian entered a monastery in Bethlehem in his youth, and after a short time he went with Germanus to visit the monks in Egypt. He visited the famous monasteries of Cells, Nitria and Scete, and in the last-named place most probably met Evagrius, who died in 399. The two friends returned to Bethlehem and later made a second visit to Egypt. In 400 they were in Constantinople, where Cassian was ordained a deacon by St. John Chrysostom. When Chrysostom was sent into exile in 405, Cassian and Germanus travelled to Rome to plead his cause with the Pope. The next fact that we know for certain is that Cassian was in Provence by 415 and had been ordained a priest.

Here Cassian entered upon a very productive work. Since the days of St. Martin of Tours many monasteries had been founded in the area of Provence, but there was no specific rule of life universally accepted and therefore no uniformity of monastic observances. With his background of experience in eastern monasticism and his acquaintance with the various types of monastic life, Cassian was considered an authority on the subject. Not only did he respond to questions and give advice, but he founded a monastery for men near Marseilles – very likely the Abbey of St. Victor – and one for women.[7]

His spiritual teachings are contained in his *Institutions* and *Conferences*. In the former treatise, Cassian speaks of the monk's garb, prayer and psalmody, ascetical practices, and the eight capital sins that had been enumerated by Evagrius.[8] In the *Conferences* he discusses the nature of monastic life, prudence, the three renunciations, sources of temptation, prayer, Christian perfection, charisms, chastity and spiritual knowledge.

According to Cassian, the purpose of the monastic life is the interior perfection of the individual monk, and this perfection is not found in the monastic manner of life as such, but in the virtues of the monk himself. The essence of perfection is charity, and the perfection of charity is reached by the way of asceticism. Yet Cassian repeats time and again that the monk is not to seek ascetical practices as a goal in themselves; rather, he is to aspire to the positive spiritual values that are made possible by negation. The asceticism of the monk should pass through three successive phases until the monk attains the perfection of contemplative love:

> The tradition of our Fathers and the authority of Scripture teach us that there are three kinds of renunciation which each of us must endeavor to carry out with all his strength. The first is to reject all the pleasures and all the riches of this world. The second is to renounce ourselves, our vices, our wicked habits, and all the unruly affections of the spirit and of the flesh. And the third is to withdraw our heart from all things present and visible and apply it only to the eternal and invisible. . . . We shall then arrive at this third renunciation when our spirit, no longer weighed down by the contagion of this animal and earthly body, but purified from the affections of the earth, is raised to heaven by continual meditation on divine things, and is so taken up with the contemplation of the eternal truth that it forgets that it is still enclosed in fragile flesh and, ravished in God, it finds itself so absorbed in his presence that it no longer has ears to hear or eyes to see and it cannot even be impressed by the greatest and most perceptible objects.[9]

Thus, the fruit of asceticism is for Cassian the gift of contemplative prayer. Indeed, the practice of prayer is so essential to Christian spirituality, says Cassian, that just as there can be no prayer without the virtues, so there can be no true virtues without prayer. In the *Conferences* he distinguishes four kinds of prayer: the prayer that asks pardon for sins, which is proper to beginners in the spiritual life; the prayer that makes good resolutions to God, which is characteristic of those who are progressing in the spiritual life; prayer for the salvation of souls, which is practiced by those who have grown in charity and love of neighbor; the prayer of thanksgiving for graces received, which is proper to those who contemplate God in what Cassian calls the "prayer of fire."[10] And as if to stress that contemplative prayer is not to be identified with a pagan gnosis, Cassian insists that it has its source in the reading of Sacred

Scripture and it leads the monk back to Scripture. The one and only perfect good is "the contemplation of God, which must be placed above all merit, above all the virtues of the just, even above all that we read in St. Paul of what is good and useful."[11]

The monastic movement was not without its detractors, however, who found a powerful leader in the ex-monk Jovinian. In his efforts to stem the tide of asceticism, he preached and practiced a Christian life that was so sensate and worldly that St. Jerome branded him "the Christian Epicurus."[12] Jovinian's attack on monasticism led to his denial of the virginity of the Mother of Christ and a rejection of the practice of celibacy among the Latin clergy.[13]

At the other extreme we find the heresy of Messalianism, against which St. Augustine wrote the treatise, *De opere monachorum*. The basic error of Messalianism was the contention that since monks had left all things for a life of solitude and prayer, all forms of manual labor must be rejected in favor of recollection, silence and prayer.[14] In spite of the attacks on the monastic life, it continued to flourish, although in the West it would undergo radical adaptation, especially at the hands of St. Augustine.

ST. AUGUSTINE

St. Augustine (354–430) has been hailed as the father of theology in the West and the greatest doctor of the Church. His theological accomplishments were so great and so varied that he is at once the depositary of the theological tradition of the East and the source of a new theology for the West. In many areas, such as the theology of creation, the problem of evil, ecclesiology, the virtue of faith, and eschatology, his teaching has been accepted as practically definitive. He attained an insight into the doctrine of the Trinity that no Greek Father had ever equalled, and his theology of grace still dominates our theological investigations.

St. Augustine developed a theology of the spiritual life that was rooted in charity, perfected in wisdom and intimately united to Christ and the Church. In order to understand his teaching, it is helpful to review briefly the doctrine on original sin and grace that emerged from his struggle with the Pelagians.

The fundamental principle that lies at the heart of Pelagianism is the autonomy of human liberty. Man was created free, and although his freedom is a gift from God, it is so essential to man that he could not exist without it. Having given man this freedom, God cannot intervene without destroying it, and therefore man is his own master; his freedom "emancipates" him from God. Man's free choice is the sole determinant of his actions and whether he chooses good or evil, the act proceeds entirely from his own free choice.

Moreover, since man was in no way affected by original sin or its effects, according to the Pelagians, man is fundamentally good and his free will suffices to keep him sinless. For the Pelagians grace was not considered a principle of divine life within the soul nor a power that affects man's faculties interiorly; it is something exterior to man. The teaching and example of Christ assist our power to do good, but the actual willing and doing are exclusively in our own hands. And since man can achieve holiness by his own efforts, it is of obligation that he do so. Every good act is of obligation; there are no counsels, nor is there any real need for prayer of petition. There is no distinction between mortal sin and venial sin, for all sins are equally serious. All that remains is duty and obligation: what a man *can* do, he *must* do.

St. Augustine's response to the Pelagians can be summarized as follows: Out of divine goodness, God created the world and man; the latter was created for an intimate union of personal fellowship with a personal God. To this end, God created our first parents in the state of innocence and endowed them with preternatural gifts of bodily immortality, immunity from sickness and death, infused knowledge and perfect integrity. Their state in relation to sin was *posse non peccare*, and after attaining glory, their state would be *non posse peccare*. In spite of all his gifts, man committed the original sin, not because God's prohibition conflicted with man's desires, but because man as a creature was subject to change and therefore able to turn away from his true good. The root of the sin was pride; man wanted to be his own master. As a result of his fall, Adam was placed in the state of *non posse non peccare*. His love of God was changed to love of self; his intellect was clouded with ignorance and his will was inclined to evil; he lost the subordination of his lower powers to reason; he was doomed to die; sexual concupiscence became the strongest inclination of his flesh. And since Adam sinned as the father and head of all humanity, all men were in Adam when he sinned, and all men have inherited his sin as well as its effects.

Since original sin, the human race is a mass of corruption. Man still retains a restless longing for God and for the good, but his freedom to accomplish the good is lost; therefore, without God's help, man can only sin. Justification and salvation are exclusively the work of God. The first requisite for justification is faith in

Christ, but faith is impossible without the "prevenient" grace of God. It is not a question of man's accepting or rejecting God's gift of grace and faith, for if that were so, everything would ultimately depend on man and not on God. That a man accepts the grace of God is due to the grace of God.

St. Augustine defended the reality of sanctifying grace against the Pelagians by stating that justification implies a positive element besides remission of sins, some new reality inhering in the soul. He speaks of this reality as a divine adoption, a divinization of the soul which thereby becomes an image of God, a participation in the justice and holiness of God himself. Thus, commenting on Romans 5:5: "The love of God has been poured into our hearts by the Holy Spirit which has been given us," St. Augustine says: "Indeed, the love of God is said to be diffused in our hearts; not the love whereby he himself loves us, but the love whereby he makes us lovers of him; just as the justice of God whereby we are made just through his gift. . . . This is the justice of God which he not only teaches through the precept of law but he also gives through the gift of the Spirit."

It is, however, on the question of actual grace that the teaching of St. Augustine seems ambivalent; at least, it has been interpreted in contrary senses. Certain expressions seem, for example, to deny man's freedom under grace: "God works in us, to will and to do"; "God's will and grace always obtain their effect in us"; "Whichever delights us most, that we must necessarily choose." And yet, the entire treatise De gratia et libero arbitrio was written by St. Augustine as a defense of man's freedom. According to Portalié, three fundamental principles are at the basis of St. Augustine's theology of actual grace: 1) God, through his grace, is absolute master of all the determinations of the human will; 2) man is as free with grace as he is without it; 3) the compatibility of these two principles rests on the mode of divine government.[15]

In view of his teaching on grace, wherein St. Augustine valiantly defended the gratuitousness of grace and the freedom and responsibility of man's cooperation with grace, his teaching on the spiritual life likewise places great emphasis on these two elements. First of all, St. Augustine requires docility to the Holy Spirit, through humility, faith and the practice of prayer; secondly, he demands a response to grace through the imperation of charity, which bears fruit in good works. From the subjective point of view, charity is the summation of the entire moral life and it is likewise the essence of Christian perfection: perfect charity is perfect justice.[16] Indeed, Scripture commands nothing else but charity. And this charity is for

Augustine nothing other than the love of God for himself and the love of self and neighbor because of God.[17]

However, the perfection of charity is attained only after the soul is strengthened and purified by the practice of the virtues; and even then it is always a relative perfection, since there is no terminus to charity. "We shall have perfect charity," says Augustine, "when we see God as he is. For there will be nothing more that can be added to our love when we have attained vision."[18] Here on earth, however, "it is the property of perfection to recognize that it is imperfect," yet "the more you love, the more you will be raised up."[19] When the soul's love reaches its perfection, the soul enjoys intimate union with God, since love by its very nature tends to become one with the beloved. At this point the soul enjoys that true wisdom which for Augustine constitutes mystical contemplation.

In the treatise, *De quantitate animae*, St. Augustine lists seven stages through which the soul normally passes as it advances to contemplation. The first three stages refer to the vegetative, sensitive and rational levels of human life. But the Christian does not begin to make true progress toward perfection until the fourth stage, which is that of virtue, accompanied by purification. The fifth stage is called tranquillity, to denote the peace that follows from control of the passions. The sixth stage is called the entrance into the divine light (*ingressio in lucem*), in which the soul seeks to penetrate the divinity; there, if it succeeds, it passes on to the seventh and final stage which is that of habitual union and indwelling (*mansio*).[20] That this last stage is truly mystical contemplation and not the philosophical contemplation of a neo-Platonist is evident from St. Augustine's commentary on Psalm 41:

> But is the God for whom [the soul] seeks, something like its own spirit? Certainly, we can see God only by means of the spirit; and yet God is not what our own spirit is. For the spirit of the prophet seeks something that is God, so that, having found him, he will no longer be exposed to the scorn of those who say to him: "Where is your God?". . . .
> Seeking my God in visible and corporal things, and not finding him; seeking his substance in myself, as if he were something similar to what I am, and not finding him; I perceive that my God is something superior to my soul. Then, to succeed in attaining to him, "I meditated on these things and I poured out my soul above myself." How indeed can my soul attain what it must seek above itself if my soul does not pour itself out above itself? If it remains within itself, it will see nothing but itself, and in itself it will not see its God. . . . "I have poured out my soul above myself" and there remains nothing more to lay hold of other than my

God. Indeed, it is there, it is above my soul, that the house of God is.[21]

In the doctrine on the contemplative and the active life, St. Augustine surpasses all the theologians who preceded him, and together with St. Gregory the Great and St. Thomas Aquinas, he must be recognized as an authority on the subject. In *De civitate Dei*, Augustine discusses the active and contemplative aspects of wisdom: the active part pertains to the cultivation of virtue and the contemplative part refers to the consideration of truth. In *Contra Faustum* he symbolizes the active life by Leah and the contemplative life by Rachel, but in such a way that the active life is taken for man's mortal life on earth, in which he lives by faith, and the contemplative life is reserved for eternity, where man will enjoy the eternal contemplation of God. This same notion is found in St. Augustine's commentary on the Gospel of St. John: "The active life is signified by the apostle Peter, the contemplative by John. The first is wholly carried out here until the end of this world, and there finds an end; the last is deferred, to be completed after the end of this world, but in the world to come it has no end."[22] However, St. Augustine also treated of the contemplative and active phases of life here on earth and he maintains that no man can be exclusively active or exclusively contemplative, but that these two types of operation alternate in the lives of individuals.

> There are two powers set before the human soul, the one active and the other contemplative. Through the former one makes progress, through the latter he attains his goal. By active power he labors to purify his heart for the vision of God; by contemplative power he is at rest, beholding God. Therefore, the one consists in observing those precepts by which we must toil in this temporal life, while the other fills us with truths concerning that everlasting life to come.
>
> Consequently, the active power is engaged in struggle, but the contemplative power enjoys repose.... A second consequence is that in this mortal life the active power consists in the pursuit of a good manner of living, but the contemplative power consists especially in faith and, for a very few, in some partial vision of the unchangeable truth, seen through a mirror in an obscure manner (I Cor. 13:12).[23]

When comparing the active with the contemplative life, as he does when he speaks of Martha and Mary, St. Augustine does not hesitate to give the superiority to the contemplative life. "Martha chose a good part, but Mary the better.... She has chosen to contemplate, to live by the word."[24] He repeats the same doctrine in *Sermon 179*;

> Martha's part is holy and great, but Mary has chosen the better part, for while her sister was solicitous and working and attending to many things, Mary was quiet and sat still and listened. Mary's part will not be taken from her, but Martha's will, because the ministering to the saints will pass away; to whom will food be given, where no one is hungry? Mary's part will not pass away because she found her delight in justice and in truth, and this will be her delight in eternity.

From the active and contemplative exercises of life, St. Augustine turns his attention to the various ways of living. He states that there are three modes of life: the life of contemplation or study of the truth, the life dedicated to human affairs, and the life which is a combination of the two. In attempting to decide which of the three forms it is best to choose, St. Augustine insists that the choice should be determined by the degree to which any one of the three will facilitate the attainment of a man's ultimate end.

> As to these three modes of life – the contemplative, the active or the composite – although a man may choose any one of them without detriment to his eternal interests, as long as his faith is preserved, yet he must never overlook the obligations of truth and duty. No man has a right to lead such a life of contemplation as to forget the service he owes to his neighbor; nor has any man a right to be so immersed in the active life that he neglects the contemplation of God.[25]

St. Augustine's teaching on the three modes of Christian living was carried into practice, for it was he, says Pourrat, who "began the cenobitic life for men in Africa."[26] Indeed, Bouyer advises that "the work of Augustine directly related to spirituality should not be considered apart from what might be called his work with regard to institutions, particularly in the domain of the monastic life."[27]

Unlike John Cassian, St. Augustine did not promote an eastern type of monasticism; rather, he introduced a new form of cenobitic life. He had first come into contact with the monastic life at Milan and in 386 he retired with a few companions to a quasi-monastic retreat. When he returned to Tagaste, North Africa, in 388, he continued his cenobitic life; then, after his ordination to the priesthood in 391, he founded his first monastery. The members of the community were called "servants of God" and they held all possessions in common.

When St. Augustine became a bishop in 386, he converted his

household into a monastery, insisting on the common life and the renunciation of all personal possessions. He likewise made this a condition for ordination to the priesthood in his diocese. One of the motivating factors for Augustine's insistence on the common life, personal poverty and celibacy was not only the obvious advantage of the mutual support that the clergy could offer each other, but also the proper environment for a life of study and reflection. However, as Bouyer observes, "this common life little by little abandoned its contemplative purpose to become directed toward an ideal of pastoral service."[28] In this way, a foundation was laid for the later emergence of the canons regular and the mendicant friars.

Three separate treatises on monastic life have been attributed to St. Augustine: *Obiurgatio*, *Praeceptum* and *Ordo monasterii*. The task of determining the origin and authenticity of these documents has been one of the most challenging investigations in patristic research. Although there is still some disagreement, it is generally believed that the *Praeceptum* or *Regula ad servos Dei*, known as the Rule of St. Augustine, is an authentic work, composed most likely in 397 for St. Augustine's community at Hippo. The *Obiurgatio*, addressed to a community of virgins at Hippo, is also probably authentic. Later a feminine version of the *Regula ad servos Dei* was added as an appendix, and this is Letter 211. The *Ordo monasterii* is now attributed to Alypius rather than to St. Augustine and the Rule of St. Augustine as it now stands consists of the opening sentence of the *Ordo monasterii* and the rest is the complete text of the *Praeceptum*.[29]

St. Augustine's concept of monastic life was firmly rooted in the description of the *"vita apostolica"* found in Acts 4:32–35. In accordance with the western mentality, he had the highest regard for the common life, admonishing the members of the community to be of one heart and one mind in God, because the purpose of their coming together was to exercise fraternal charity. St. Augustine goes so far as to give his own original interpretation to the Greek word *monachos*, which means one, alone or solitary:

Since the Psalm says: "Behold how good and how pleasant it is that brothers should dwell together in unity," why then should we not call monks by this name? For monos is "one," but not one in just any way; for an individual in a crowd is "one" and although he can be called "one" when he is with others, he cannot be *monos*, that is, "alone," for *monos* means "one alone." Hence those who live together so as to form one person, so that they really possess, as Scripture says, "one mind and one heart," ... can properly be called *monos*, that is, "one alone."[30]

The monastic practices in the Augustinian community were the traditional ones: community and personal prayer, silence, humility, austerities, obedience, celibacy, poverty, but the emphasis was always on fraternal charity. As one author puts it: "If the basic observances were the same as in the East or in Europe, there was nevertheless a difference of tone in the monasticism of Augustine. His concern with the value of community led to an emphasis upon the relationships of brothers to one another, whereas the Egyptian tradition was more concerned with the relationship of each individual to God via the spiritual father."[31]

The influence of St. Augustine on monasticism was extensive, especially in France, Italy and Spain. Even the Rule of St. Benedict contains traces of Augustinian doctrine.

Later the Rule of St. Benedict was likewise influenced by Augustine; though here the actual quantity of literary borrowing is rather discreet, the qualitative influence of Augustine's thought, derived not only from his rule but from numerous other works as well, is extremely significant. While the [Rule of St. Benedict] remains primarily in the tradition of Egypt as mediated by Cassian and the [Regula Magistri], the second most important influence upon it is that of Augustine, whose humaneness and concern for fraternal relationships have contributed to the [Rule of St. Benedict] some of its best known and most admired qualities. It has rightly been said that "with the Rule of Augustine western monasticism entered upon the road which led to Benedict.[32]

ST. BENEDICT

Early in the fifth century – in 410 to be exact – the civilized world was shocked at the news of the fall of Rome at the hands of Alaric. Soon all of Italy was ravaged by the Goths, while the Vandals pillaged North Africa and in 455 invaded the city of Rome. During the reign of Theodoric, from 493 to 526, there was an era of relative peace, but in 535 the eastern emperor Justinian waged war throughout Italy in an attempt to regain the West. The Goths were defeated in 553 but in 568 the Lombards waged a destructive war before settling in the north of Italy.

At the same time, the Church was torn apart by heresies. The Christological controversies were centered in the East but because of the close political and ecclesiastical ties between the East and the West, the Holy See had to exert great effort to preserve orthodoxy. In the West the most serious challenges came from Pelagianism and the controversies about grace, the semi-Pelagian teaching that posed a problem for monastic asceticism, and the effects of the Arian heresy.

Such was the civil and ecclesiastical turmoil during the lifetime of St. Benedict of Nursia (480–547), called the father and legislator of western monasticism. Born of an illustrious family and educated in Rome, he retired to a life of solitude at Subiaco, about forty miles from the city of Rome. Three years later he reluctantly accepted the invitation of some monks to act as their spiritual director but when they refused to follow the monastic observances, Benedict returned to Subiaco. There he attracted followers and within a short time he had organized twelve monasteries of twelve monks each, somewhat similar to the *lauras* of St. Pachomius in the East. As yet there was no basic rule for the government of these small monasteries, although each one was subject to a superior and all were under the direction of Benedict.

According to one account, a neighboring priest named Florentius exerted every effort to discredit Benedict and to poison the minds of the young monks. Whether that was the reason for his departure or not, Benedict went with Maurus, Placidus and several companions to Monte Cassino, eighty miles south of Rome, and there, in 529, began the construction of a monastery. Later, he sent monks to establish another monastery at Terracina. St. Benedict spent the rest of his life at Monte Cassino and died in 547, a little more than a month after the death of his sister, St. Scholastica, abbess of a monastery of nuns near Monte Cassino.[33]

Unlike Caesarius, Cassiodorus and other monastic figures of the period, St. Benedict is not mentioned by any of his contemporaries nor in any literature that can be dated earlier than the end of the sixth century. He does not even identify himself in the Rule, and hence it cannot be used as a source of information about him until his authorship can be otherwise established. Nor has he left any other writings. For our knowledge of him, we are entirely dependent upon a single source, the *Dialogues* of Pope Gregory the Great.[34]

The Rule of St. Benedict is the most influential document in all of western monasticism, for although there were numerous other monastic rules in this period, it was the Rule of St. Benedict that the Council of Aix-la-Chapelle, in 817, proposed as the basic rule for monastic life. It is not, as some have asserted, an entirely original innovation, but it draws on a number of previous sources such as St. Pachomius, St. Basil, Cassian, St. Augustine and the *Regula Magis-*

tri.[35] St. Benedict had a gift for synthesizing the essential elements of these diverse sources, with the result that his Rule is at once a faithful continuation of the monastic traditions and practices and at the same time a personal contribution to the necessary adaptation of monasticism to contemporary needs.

The Rule of St. Benedict can be divided, as was the *Regula Magistri*, into two main sections: the Prologue and the first seven chapters consist of spiritual doctrine; the remainder (chapters 8–73) provides regulations for the life and discipline of the monastery. Most of the first section is taken almost literally from the *Regula Magistri*, and it begins with the well-known phrase, "Listen carefully, my son, to the master's instructions, and attend to them with the ear of your heart." Then follows the challenge: "This message of mine is for you, then, if you are ready to give up your own will, once and for all, and armed with the strong and noble weapons of obedience to do battle for the true King, Christ the Lord."[36] The central concept in the Prologue is that the monastery is a "school for the Lord's service," and St. Benedict concludes the Prologue with the words:

> Do not be daunted immediately by fear and run away from the road that leads to salvation. It is bound to be narrow at the outset. But as we progress in this way of life and in faith, we shall run on the path of God's commandments, our hearts overflowing with the inexpressible delight of love. Never swerving from his instructions, then, but faithfully observing his teaching in the monastery until death, we shall through patience share in the sufferings of Christ that we may deserve also to share in his kingdom. Amen.

In the first chapter of the Rule St. Benedict lists four types of monks: the *cenobites*, who live in community under a rule or an abbot; the *hermits* or anchorites, who have lived in the monastery for a long time and are now sufficiently strong to live a life of solitude in the desert; the *sarabaites*, self-willed monks who followed their own inclinations instead of living according to a monastic rule; and the *gyrovagues*, who are constantly on the move, drifting from one monastery to another and never settling down in one place. After stating his preference for the cenobitic monastic life, St. Benedict discusses the qualities and duties of the abbot, the regulations concerning the community council, and then offers a series of maxims for the spiritual life. The first section concludes with an explanation of three fundamental virtues required of a monk: obedience, the practice of silence, and humility.

The first step of humility, then, is that a man keeps the fear of God always before his eyes and never forgets it.... The second step of humility is that a man loves not his own will nor takes pleasure in the satisfaction of his desires.... The third step of humility is that a man submits to his superior in all obedience for the love of God. ... The fourth step of humility is that in this obedience under difficult, unfavorable, or even unjust conditions, his heart quietly embraces suffering and endures it without weakening or seeking escape. ... The fifth step of humility is that a man does not conceal from his abbot any sinful thoughts entering his heart, or any wrongs committed in secret, but rather confesses them humbly. ... The sixth step of humility is that a monk is content with the lowest and most menial treatment, and regards himself as a poor and worthless workman in whatever task he is given. ... The seventh step of humility is that a man not only admits with his tongue but is also convinced in his heart that he is inferior to all and of less value. ... The eighth step of humility is that a monk does only what is endorsed by the common rule of the monastery and the example set by his superiors. ... The ninth step of humility is that a monk controls his tongue and remains silent, not speaking unless asked a question. ... The tenth step of humility is that he is not given to ready laughter. ... The eleventh step of humility is that a monk speaks gently and without laughter, seriously and with becoming modesty, briefly and reasonably, but without raising his voice. ... The twelfth step of humility is that a monk always manifests humility in his bearing no less than in his heart....[37]

In the second section of the Rule the lengthiest treatment is devoted to liturgical prayer, chapters 8–20. In this section also the original contribution of St. Benedict to monastic life is much more evident, especially in his discussion of fraternal relationships among the monks, his sense of community, his insistence on prudence as a necessary virtue for the abbot, and his concern that the monk fulfill his monastic duties for spiritual motives. In order to attain his goal as a contemplative, the monk must devote himself to three daily activities: liturgical prayer, *lectio* and some type of labor.

Besides the traditional night office (after midnight), the monks assembled seven times during the day for common prayer consisting of psalms and readings from Scripture. In addition, approximately four hours each day were devoted to *lectio*, which included prayerful reading of Scripture or commentaries by the Fathers and monastic authors, private mental prayer, and the memorizing of biblical passages. The labor prescribed by the Rule was for the support of the monks and also to provide help for the needy. There is no mention in the Rule of work as related to the apostolate, nor is there any academic or scholarly motivation given for the reading of Scripture and the Fathers. Since most of the monks were laymen – as was St. Benedict – there was no priestly ministry and St. Benedict laid down detailed regulations concerning the admission of priests to the monastic life (chapter 60) and the ordination of monks to the priesthood (chapter 62).

As if to emphasize that the monastic life is a "school for the Lord's service," as stated in the Prologue, St. Benedict concludes the Rule with the following words:

> The reason we have written this rule is that, by observing it in monas- teries, we can show that we have some degree of virtue and the begin- nings of monastic life. But for anyone hastening on to the perfection of monastic life, there are the teachings of the holy Fathers, the observance of which will lead him to the very heights of perfection. What page, what passage of the inspired books of the Old and New Testaments is not the truest of guides for human life? What book of the holy catholic Fathers does not resoundingly summon us along the true way to reach the Creator? Then, besides the *Conferences* of the Fathers, their *Institutes* and their *Lives*, there is also the rule of our holy father Basil. For observant and obedient monks, all these are nothing less than tools for the cultivation of virtues; but as for us, they make us blush for shame at being so slothful, so unobservant, so negligent. Are you hastening toward your heavenly home? Then, with Christ's help, keep this little rule that we have written for beginners. After that, you can set out for the loftier summits of the teaching and virtues we mentioned above, and under God's protection you will reach them. Amen.[38]

IRISH MONASTICISM

The magnificent history and apostolic zeal of the monks of Ireland can be summarized in the life and works of St. Patrick and St. Columbanus.[39] St. Patrick (+ 493), of course, is the patron of Ireland and the founder of Irish monasticism. Born in 389 – some say in Scotland; others, in France – he was taken prisoner by pirates and at the age of sixteen found himself in servitude as a shepherd in Ireland. Six years later he escaped and found his way to France, where he received an education in monastic schools, either at Mar- moutiers, founded by St. Martin of Tours, or at Lerins, founded by St. Honoratus. After being ordained a bishop, he was sent to Ireland by Pope Celestine and worked zealously for the conversion of the Celts. He founded numerous monasteries, the most famous being that at Armagh.

The Church in Ireland developed along the lines of the clan and the way of life in the local churches was almost monastic. Both monks and nuns accompanied St. Patrick on his missionary journeys and throughout the centuries the Irish monks were famous for their evangelization of foreign lands. The Celtic monks also cultivated a love of learning, so that Ireland became known as the isle of saints and scholars.

During the sixth century monastic foundations were made in Ireland in rapid succession: St. Enda established a monastery in the Aran Islands near Galway; St. Finnian founded Clonard; St. Brendan, the abbey of Clonfert; St. Columcille, the monastery at Derry. Later, St. Columcille crossed over to Scotland and founded Iona, from which St. Aidan went to Northumbria to make the foundation of Lindisfarne. Finally, St. Comgall founded the famous monastery of Bangor in Ulster, which sent out the greatest of the Irish missionary-monks, St. Columbanus.

Born around the year 540, St. Columbanus led a group of Irish monks to France, where he founded several monasteries which became centers of learning and evangelization. Since the Irish abbots were not subject to bishops, in due time Columbanus came into conflict with the French espiscopate and both for that reason and for criticizing the royal family, he was expelled from France. He made his way across the Alps to Switzerland and to Italy, and at Bobbio he founded a monastery. He died there in 615.[40]

St. Columbanus composed the *Regula monachorum* but it was such a severe rule that the Columban monks soon began to transfer to other monasteries in Europe or adapt their monastic observances to a more moderate norm. Gradually the monasteries founded by St. Columbanus in France, Switzerland and Italy adopted the more moderate Rule of St. Benedict. They did so not only because the *Regula monachorum* was too rigorous and demanding, but also because St. Benedict's legislation enabled them to adjust more easily to the Roman liturgical practice and thus abandon the Celtic liturgy.

Meanwhile, in England, St. Illtud founded a monastery on the island of Caldey and an abbey in Wales at the beginning of the sixth century. His foremost disciples were St. Gildas, who later emigrated to Brittany, and St. David, patron of Wales. Then, in 596, Pope Gregory the Great sent forty monks from his former monastery on the Coelian Hill in Rome, with the superior Augustine at their head, to evangelize England. The monks settled at Canterbury with the king's permission but almost immediately a conflict arose between the Roman and the Celtic liturgical practices. This tension subsided, however, in 664 when the English Church allied itself with the Roman faction.

St. Gregory (+604) is the first monk to become a pope and throughout his pontificate he never lost his nostalgia for the monastic life. Thanks to his influence, Benedictine monasticism became, as Cayré puts it, "the conquering army of the Roman Church."[41] When the need arose, Gregory did not hesitate to ordain monks to the priesthood and even to assign them to apostolic work. As regards the spiritual life, his teaching on the active and contemplative life, on the grades of spiritual progress, and on contemplation is especially significant. More than the other Fathers of the Church, he devoted much of his writing to pastoral concerns, and especially directives for the pastoral ministry, the requirements of candidates for the priesthood, and the apostolate of preaching.

Born around 540 of a noble family, he became prefect of Rome in 570. Five years later he converted his home on the Coelian Hill into a monastery and was the founder of six other monasteries in Sicily. It has frequently been stated that Gregory was a Benedictine monk but the truth of the matter is that we do not know what the monastic observance was at St. Andrew's on the Coelian Hill. According to Peifer, "it is an anachronism to speak of Gregory and his monks as 'Benedictine' in the later sense of that term, for in the sixth century a rule did not serve as a detailed code regulating the life except in the monastery for which it was written. Monasteries frequently made use of several rules, taking from each what they found suitable."[42]

In 579 Gregory was sent to Constantinople as papal nuncio, where he continued to live the monastic life, and in 586 he returned to his monastery in Rome. Named a deacon to Pope Pelagius II, Gregory was elected Pope in 590 and reigned for fourteen years.[43] As pope he worked unceasingly for the conversion of the pagans; he combated the vices of his contemporaries; he defended the temporal possessions of the Holy See and the primacy of the Bishop of Rome. Although a contemplative by temperament, Pope Gregory dedicated all his efforts to live up to his preferred title, "Servant of the servants of God." In spite of his demanding pastoral work, Gregory left an extensive literary production: 850 Letters, a moral treatise entitled *Expositio in Job* or *Moralia*, his famous *Regula Pastoralis* on the priesthood, some homilies on the Gospel and on Ezechiel, and most important, the *Dialogues*. Known as *Dialogorum Libri*, the last-named work was written in the form of a conversation with his deacon, Peter, and it presents the spiritual and moral teaching of Pope Gregory in the form of stories about the saints of Italy. It is in this work, for example, that we have the best and practically only source of information about St. Benedict.

Although he belongs to the patristic age, St. Gregory exerted an influence on the entire medieval period. He wrote for all – laity, monks and clergy – and the primary sources of his doctrine are Scripture, St. Augustine and Cassian. If one attempts to discover what dominated the vital synthesis of his doctrine, he will find that it is the basic problem of the states of life. Like his predecessors, St. Gregory gives the superiority to the contemplative life. He is, in fact, as Leclercq calls him, "the doctor of contemplation."[44]

Before considering St. Gregory's teaching on the active and contemplative life, it is useful to recall his teaching on the stages of progress in the spiritual life. In the first stage the Christian strives to combat vices and gain control of the passions. The second stage is a period of growth in virtue, and especially the moral virtues, although the theological virtues are also necessary, since without them nothing is pleasing to God. Finally, all the virtues are brought to their perfection by the actuation of the gifts of the Holy Spirit.[45] St. Gregory is, in fact, with St. Thomas Aquinas and John of St. Thomas, an outstanding authority on the theology of the gifts of the Holy Spirit.[46]

As did his doctrine on the gifts of the Holy Spirit, Gregory's teaching on the types of life influenced theology throughout the middle ages. For him, the active life pertains to the operations of the moral virtues which, in turn, dispose the soul for contemplation. The contemplative life is the area of the theological virtues, leading to the perfection of the virtues through the actuation of the gifts of the Holy Spirit. Thus, the operations of the active life are listed as follows: "to give bread to the hungry, to teach the ignorant the word of wisdom, to correct the erring, to recall to the path of humility our neighbor when he becomes proud, to care for the sick, to give to all what they need, and to provide those in our charge with the necessities of life."[47] In the contemplative life, on the other hand, one preserves with all his strength the love of God and neighbor but he "rests from all external activity and clings only to the will of the Creator, so that the mind takes no pleasure in doing anything but, having spurned all cares, may be aglow to see the face of its Creator."[48]

Of the two lives, the active life is necessary for salvation, says St. Gregory, since no man can be saved without good works, but the theological virtues are necessary for merit. Therefore, Gregory's distinction between the active life as the life of the moral virtues and the contemplative life as the life of the theological virtues should be understood in the sense that in the latter the theological virtues are more clearly manifested. And of the two lives, says St. Gregory, "the contemplative life is greater in merit than the active. ... Although the active life is good, the contemplative is better."[49]

Since the Christian life should be patterned after Christ, the contemplative life is possible for men of every state and condition. Christ himself, says St. Gregory, gave the example of both the contemplative and active life in his own person; "he gave his faithful ones an example not to neglect the care of their neighbors through love of contemplation, nor again to abandon contemplative pursuits by being too immoderately engaged in the care of their neighbors."[50] And since St. Gregory realized the difficulty involved in keeping the two types of activity in proper balance, he warns preachers not to neglect service to others because of their devotion to contemplation and not to neglect contemplation because of involvement with the apostolate.[51]

St. Gregory never lost sight of the fact that the precept of charity is twofold, and therefore the contemplative activity which fosters intimacy with God should never be completely separated from the apostolate which provides service to one's neighbor. Indeed, the active life serves as a preparation for the contemplative life and likewise is a consequence of the contemplative life. The Christian should therefore be "able to pass to the contemplative life and yet not abandon the active life. ... And he who arrives at contemplation does not abandon the activity of good works whereby he is able to be of use to others."[52] And although relatively few persons may actually attain to contemplation, it is of its nature available to all:

It is not the case that the grade of contemplation is given to the highest and not given to the lowest; but often the highest and often the most lowly, and very often those who have left the world, and sometimes also those who are married, receive it. If therefore there is no state of life among the faithful from which the grace of contemplation can be excluded, anyone who keeps his heart in custody may also be illuminated by the light of contemplation, so that no one can glory in this grace as if it were extraordinary. It is not the high and eminent members of the holy Church only who have the grace of contemplation, but very often those members receive this gift who, although by desire they already mount to the heights, are actually occupying lowly positions.[53]

St. Gregory sees God and man as the two contrasting terms that are united by man's salvation through Christ and in the Holy Spirit. Aided by God's grace and his own ascetical practices, man can traverse the path to God which terminates in contemplative prayer. Along this "way of salvation" Christ is the Mediator, Model, Redeemer and Intercessor, and St. Gregory advises all Christians to meditate on the mysteries of Christ, both in his humanity and in his divinity, in his sufferings as well as in his glories.[54] But the work of man's salvation is perfected by the Holy Spirit, whom Christ sent after he had ascended to his Father. The Holy Spirit is the gift *par excellence* and he works in man by his sevenfold gifts. And when the Holy Spirit works in the soul through his gifts, whereby man is led successively from fear to wisdom, the soul is able to enjoy union with God through contemplation.[55]

From the time of St. Gregory's pontificate until the middle of the eighth century, Christianity enjoyed a tremendous expansion throughout all of Europe. As could be expected, there was a long period of adjustment, adaptation and confusion as Christianity absorbed the cultural and temperamental differences of the Saxons, the Franks, the Visigoths, the Lombards and others. But there was also discernible a basic unity which enabled the various races, in spite of accidental differences, to embrace the one, catholic faith.

Leclercq mentions certain factors that contributed to the unity of Christian life during this period.[56] First of all, the Roman Church and monasticism preserved a unified Christian heritage that could be presented to races of people who had no strong traditional culture that had to be rejected and replaced by Christianity. Secondly, the literary sources that nourished this vast evangelization were less abundant and less varied than in other periods. There were treatises of a practical nature, with counsels on asceticism, the practice of prayer, and Christian virtues, but most of them bore the imprint of the teaching of St. Gregory the Great. Even the two outstanding authors of the period – St. Isidore of Seville and Bede the Venerable – were greatly indebted to St. Gregory the Great.

In spite of the ambiguity of words which were used to designate the various classes of Christians – priests, monks, nuns, laity – the distinctions laid down by St. Gregory the Great and St. Isidore of Seville were still observed. Each state of life retained its own identity and there was a gradual development of a spirituality proper to each. Thus, there were two classes of the laity: the ordinary faithful and the more fervent or devout Christians. The first class, whose form of Christian living was classified by Bede as *vita popularis*, received a basic instruction on the duties of Christians prior to their baptism; they were given a preparation for marriage, with emphasis on the indissolubility and the purpose of marriage and the duty of fidelity; they received the rest of their religious formation from the ordinary preaching of the clergy. But their knowledge of the faith was rudimentary at best and many of them were greatly attracted to magic, superstition and the occult or preternatural.

The "fervent" Christians, however, constituted an elite and they normally grouped themselves around the churches or monasteries in order to live a penitential life, either for their own past sins or as a voluntary way of life. Both men and women embraced this type of life, which consisted in attendance at the Divine Office in a church or monastery, the practice of private prayer, and a life of austerity. They dressed simply and often the unmarried took the vow of celibacy while the married observed continence. They thus constituted a class of Christians that was clearly differentiated from the "ordinary faithful" and resembled very much the "third orders" and the secular institutes that would come into existence much later. Since many of these "penitents" were uneducated, they were given their own "little office," made up of a litany of Christ or the Blessed Virgin or a specified number of *Our Father*'s and *Hail Mary*'s. The prayers of lay brothers in later centuries and the Rosary itself seem to have their origin in the prayers of the penitents.

Thanks to St. Gregory the Great, the spiritual life of the clergy was guided and protected during this period of confusion and adjustment. What gradually emerged was a grouping of the diocesan clergy around their bishop, both for pastoral work and for the celebration of the Divine Office. Priests were assigned to a designated church for the administration of the sacraments, the liturgy, and preaching; community life was encouraged for the safeguarding of celibacy and for common prayer and liturgy; great stress was placed on the necessity for personal holiness in the life of the priest. A letter written by Bede the Venerable to Egbert of York in 734 contains directives which are typical of the spiritual program for the clergy of the period.[57] Bede also advised priests to instruct the faithful in the recitation of the *Creed* and the *Pater Noster* of the Mass in the vernacular and to encourage the faithful to frequent Communion.

However, the predominant influence in the spirituality of this epoch was still monasticism, especially Benedictine monasticism. This was true not only because the monks gave Christians the example of a life of asceticism and virtue, but because a large number of the bishops were selected from among the monks. Once again, two forms of monasticism emerged – the cloistered monk and the wandering evangelizer – and Dom Leclercq points to Bede the Venerable and St. Boniface as outstanding examples of the two types.[58]

In the areas of ascetical practices and prayer, we should note the following developments during this epoch. The severe asceticism of the ancient monks and hermits, preserved to a great extent among the Irish monks, gradually gave way to the asceticism of service to neighbor and manual labor. The corporal works of mercy were offered by the bishops as suitable manifestations of Christian love and asceticism. Yet, the individuals who devoted themselves to these services were still motivated to a great extent by the spirit of penance and a fear of the last judgment.

The prayer life of this period was still communal and liturgical. For all classes of Christians the spiritual life was nourished by the Mass, the Divine Office, homilies, the reading of Scripture, and the teachings and sermons of the Fathers of the Church. The Psalter was the basis even of private prayer and meditation, and the more difficult psalms were synthesized in a few verses and interspersed with prayers or "collects." Many of the hymns that are still preserved in the Divine Office were composed in this period, as were numerous litanies.

"In spite of what it lacked," says Dom Leclercq, "the period was a truly formative and fruitful one for the Christian West, and left a definite mark on later centuries."[59]

CHAPTER 5

BENEDICTINE SPIRITUALITY

In the seventh and eighth centuries the Church was still carried along by the momentum received from the fruitful pontificate of St. Gregory the Great. The Council of Orange (529) had given the Holy See great prestige and had confirmed the doctrinal authority of St. Augustine. Prior to this, the writings of Boëthius (+ 524) had also helped to propagate Augustinian doctrine. However, the predominant influence and unifying force was monasticism, and especially Benedictine monasticism.[1]

At Toledo in Spain the entire Visigoth nation had embraced Christianity, and St. Isidore of Seville (+636) emerged as an influential theologian and a promoter of monasticism.[2] In Italy the Lombards, tainted with Arianism, were gradually assimilated into orthodox Christianity. Meanwhile, the Anglosaxons, who had arrived in England as pagans, were now sending forth missionary monks to the continent. Willibrord evangelized the Low Countries and St. Boniface, assisted by monks, nuns and clerics from England, labored from 718 until his martyrdom in 754 to establish the Church in Germany and to reform the Church in the Frankish empire. The successors of St. Boniface also preached the Gospel in Hungary and in Scandinavia. Back in England, Bede the Venerable (+735) dedicated himself to a life study and literary productions based on the teaching of St. Augustine, St. Gregory the Great and Cassiodorus.[3]

When Charlemagne (*Carolus Magnus*) came to the throne in 768 he achieved by peaceful means what the Visigoths, the Vandals and the Lombards had failed to do by warfare and pillaging: a unified Europe. It was not, to be sure, a reincarnation of the ancient Roman Empire, but Charlemagne did succeed in bringing the Roman and Germanic peoples together under one emperor and the universal authority of the Holy See. During his long reign (768–814) the liturgy was stabilized, the biblical text was unified, the *Gelasian Sacramentary* was revised, Gregorian chant was promoted and new hymns and prayers were introduced. The monasteries played a significant role in all of this renewal and reform; in fact, Charlemagne had desired to see all monasteries under one rule but the first move in that direction was made only after his death.[4]

BENEDICT OF ANIANE

The first representative writer on the theology of the monastic life, according to Leclercq,[5] was Ambrose Autpert, who died in 784 as abbot of a monastery in southern Italy.[6] His doctrine was fully in accord with that of St. Augustine and St. Gregory the Great, since he saw the monastic life as a distinctive form of ascetical combat in which the monk seeks personal sanctification by separation from the world and loving meditation on the mysteries of Christ. Although Benedictine spirituality did not subscribe to the speculative contemplation and gnosis of the Alexandrian Fathers, it did esteem that affective or loving contemplation which is superior to pure intelligence.

However, the man selected by Charlemagne to work for the desired unification and renewal of monastic life was Alban Flacco, whose pen-name was Alcuin (+804). Educated in the tradition of Bede the Venerable and imbued with the spirit of the Rule of St. Benedict, he developed a series of liturgical devotions for each day of the week. Perhaps he contributed as much as anyone to the numerous additions to the prayer life of the monks, thus extending the hours of community prayer and interfering with the manual labor and *lectio* of the monks.[7]

Charlemagne also called to his service the Spanish intellectual, Teodulfo (+821), and the Italian, St. Paulinus (+802). And although Paulinus praised Charlemagne extravagantly, he nevertheless had the courage to defend the rights of the Church whenever the emperor tended to overreach his authority. Cilleruelo observes that in Spain the ecclesiastics controlled the kings, but in the Carolingian period the emperor controlled the ecclesiastics.[8]

When St. Benedict of Aniane appeared on the scene as a reformer, he endeavoured to restore the observance of the Rule of St. Benedict, but at the same time he imposed lengthy ritual prayers in addition to the Divine Office and he extended the *lectio divina* to the study of the writings of Origen, St. Jerome, St. Augustine and St. Gregory the Great. Benedict did not attempt to restore a primitive observance; he tried rather to adapt Benedictine monasticism to a new age and new needs, accepting the customs and usages that had been introduced.

Born in 750, Benedict became a monk in 774 and later founded his own monastery at Aniane, near the Pyrenees. At the outset he was greatly inclined to the monasticism of St. Pachomius, considering the Rule of St. Benedict too lax. Eventually, however, he changed his mind and adopted the Rule of St. Benedict as the only practical solution. Benedict of Aniane was convinced that the only way to prevent monasteries from falling into laxity was to discover a basis for constant renewal and to provide some kind of central organization.

When Louis the Pius became emperor in 814, Benedict became a kind of visitor for all monasteries and he sent monks from his own monastery to reform other monasteries. In this way he formed a federation of monasteries with himself as the "abbot primate." He also composed two monastic documents: the *Codex Regularum*, a collection of existing Latin rules, and the *Concordia Regularum*, a kind of commentary on the Rule of St. Benedict with parallel passages from other monastic rules.[9]

The Synod of Aix-la-Chapelle in 816 and 817 promulgated legislation touching the lives of clerics (*De institutione clericorum*) and a capitulary for the reform of monastic life.[10] Unfortunately, for the most part the laws were ignored and when Benedict of Aniane died in 821, the empire was torn apart by strife among the sons of Louis the Pious and by invasions by the Northmen and the Saracens. Monastic reform was thus delayed, but when it did begin to materialize, it was on the foundations laid by St. Benedict of Aniane.[11]

He is one of the most important figures in Benedictine history; what he envisaged, or something very like it, became the pattern of Benedictine life for most of the middle ages. . . . This does not mean that a Benedictine monastery according to the conception of Benedict of Aniane was exactly like Montecassino of the sixth century. The introduction of the Rule of St. Benedict did not displace the numerous layers of tradition that had already accumulated in Gaul. The Gallic monasteries still bore the imprint of the old Martinian monasticism, of the tradition of Lerins, of the Celtic and Anglo-Saxon contributions, and especially of the vastly changed social and economic situation of the feudal period.

A great Carolingian abbey was a vast establishment that might have several hundred monks and a number of boys to be instructed in the monastery school. It might be surrounded by a town whose life was dominated by the monastery. The abbey was supported by large tracts of land worked by serfs and had to fulfill obligations toward its feudal overlord. The life of the monks was highly ritualized: many additional psalms and prayers were added to the Benedictine *opus Dei*; churches, altars and private Masses were multiplied; there were daily processions for the veneration of altars and relics. ... The life of the monks was indeed a continual seeking of God through prayer, asceticism and liturgical service. But the monastery was conceived of as an organ of the Christian state; the abbot became an important political functionary, the abbey was a powerful economic force, and the state assured control by reserving the right to appoint the abbot in most cases. This factor was to have disastrous consequences.[12]

HILDEMAR

In an effort to achieve greater uniformity of monastic life and observance, "customaries" or "statutes" began to appear in the eighth and ninth centuries. These were necessary because the Rule of St. Benedict was not a detailed code of law; particular matters were left to the abbot of the monastery. Benedict of Aniane had already set the pattern for congregations of monasteries under one head and eventually the Benedictines would be recognized as a religious order.[13]

At the same time, a more intensive study of the Rule of St. Benedict led to the composition of numerous commentaries. Four of them appeared in the first half of the ninth century, although some scholars prefer to reduce them to two distinct and independent commentaries. The first was attributed to Paul the Deacon, around 800; the second was composed by Smaragdus around 820; the third was written by Hildemar between 840 and 845; and the fourth was written shortly thereafter by the abbot Basil.[14]

Hildemar concedes that the perfect life can be lived either as a hermit or as a member of a community, but he emphasizes the value of the spiritual community which is based on one baptism, one faith, one hope, one spirit and one Church. In fact, the common life is much better for the majority of monks; the solitary life of a hermit is possible for only a few.

According to Hildemar, Benedictine spirituality should be characterized by a profound sense of the supernatural, an intense love of Jesus Christ, total renunciation, an awareness of the presence of God, and the virtues of holy fear, obedience and patience. In order to have a rightly formed conscience and grow in humility, the monk should likewise be faithful in confessing his actions and thoughts, either to the abbot or to a spiritual brother. The life of the monk should be divided between the contemplative and the active life, but by this Hildemar means that the monk applies himself to the practice of prayer and to manual labor.

The commentator offers some specific regulations concerning the practice of prayer, which is the primary function of the Benedictine monk. Since preoccupation with the things of this world tends to destroy the simplicity of one's recollection in God, the monk should give himself to the psalmody with great attention and fervor. Chanting the words of prayer which come from God himself, the monk is able to enjoy God's presence in a special manner.

In speaking of private mental prayer, Hildemar asserts that it is difficult for most people and therefore it should be brief. The reason given for the difficulty of prolonged mental prayer is that the human mind cannot normally fix its attention on silent prayer for a long period without being invaded by distracting thoughts. When this occurs, says Hildemar, the monk should leave silent prayer and occupy himself with reading, the psalmody or manual labor. The monk who continues his silent prayer while troubled by bad thoughts would act against the Rule; the same is true of one who abandons silent prayer for a light reason when he has received the grace to continue his prayer without being interrupted by distracting thoughts. And if, through God's grace, a monk receives contemplative prayer while he is occupied with *lectio divina* or manual labor, he should leave his reading or work and go to the oratory. This will occur rarely, says Hildemar, and there is always the danger of illusion. The psalmody is the normal prayer for a monk and it should be followed by a brief period of silent prayer; but some – and they are always few in number – will also practice silent mental prayer for long periods.[15]

CLUNIAC REFORM

As the Benedictine monks gradually moderated their practices of asceticism and gave less importance to the place of manual labor in the monastic life, they concentrated more and more on the liturgy and *lectio divina* as the essential elements of monastic life. As a result, the influence of Benedictine spirituality on the Church at the dawn of the Middle Ages was predominantly in the areas of Scripture and the liturgy. It was in this period that Teodulfo and Alcuin made a revision of the Latin Bible and Rabanus Maurus wrote his scriptural commentary. The purpose was eminently spiritual, namely, to provide Christians with the truths of revelation as a basis for their pious reading and meditation.

In the area of the liturgy the Benedictine monks contributed to the success of the liturgical reform inaugurated by Charlemagne. The literary output was tremendous, especially by way of new hymns, and the monks also restored the chant to its primitive purity. New feasts were introduced into the Church calendar; original hymns and invocations, the expressions of private devotions, were interwoven in the public liturgical prayers. The diocesan clergy were obliged to the daily community Mass and choral Office in their churches, although the Council of Aix-la-Chapelle (817) refused to impose on the clergy the obligation to private recitation of the Divine Office.[16] The liturgical themes were centered on Christ – especially under the titles of Redeemer, King of kings, Lord and Holy Cross – and on his Blessed Mother. The use of the Saturday votive Mass in honor of Mary was already in vogue and during this period there was a noticeable increase of prayers and hymns in honor of Mary. Two doctrinal questions that attracted the attention of theologians of the time were the virginity of Mary and her assumption.[17]

The Eucharist also received a great deal of attention, as did the Mass. This is to be expected, of course, in a spirituality that was centered on the liturgy. The Eucharist was seen as a memorial of the passion and death of Christ and the means by which Christ communicates to men the fruits of his paschal victory. Great insistence was placed on the dispositions required for the worthy reception of Communion.

Such were the characteristics of Christian spirituality under Benedictine influence at the end of the Carolingian era, just prior to the dissolution of the Roman Empire. The history books recount the scandalous and damaging effects of the destruction of central authority in civil government and the seizure of Church power by the laity: schisms and scandals in the papacy, confiscation of churches and monasteries by the laity, simony and sins against celibacy among the clergy, investiture of laymen as abbots of monasteries. During the eleventh and twelfth centuries the Church would oscillate between decadence and reform, but eventually, under the leadership of Pope Gregory VII (1073–1085), Christian renewal would prevail.

There were, however, centers of reform in the tenth century and the first and most influential was Cluny, founded in 910. This monastery had a glorious history and its impact was felt not only in spirituality but in literature as well. What had been initiated by Benedict of Aniane was carried forward by Cluny, namely, the establishment of a federation of monasteries under the control and guidance of Cluny. The formation of such a federation of monasteries was considered necessary in order to achieve "exemption" from control by laymen or bishops. In some instances abbeys were placed under the protection of the Holy See, as was Cluny itself.

What developed at Cluny was "a monastic empire of almost incredible proportions and yet for more than two centuries, under a series of abbots whose sanctity was equal to their discretion and administrative ability, it maintained a disciplined and fruitful monastic life that constituted the most powerful reforming influence in the Church."[18] It was not, however, a question of strict reform in the sense of literal observance of the Rule of St. Benedict. The changed times and social conditions called for an adaptation, and this was achieved by composing a customary based on the text of Benedict of Aniane.

> Characteristic of this form of Benedictine monasticism was a certain centralization and uniformity of observance, an enormous development of ritual, a refined monastic culture based upon intensive study of the Bible and the Fathers, a genuinely contemplative orientation, a far-reaching charitable activity, serious though limited work, especially that of the scriptorium, and a discreet practice of the eremitical life alongside and subject to the *coenobium*.[19]

Numerous other Benedictine monasteries rallied to the reform and although they differed in some details of observance, all of them followed the Rule of St. Benedict as interpreted by Cluny. The reform spread to other parts of France and to Belgium and England in the tenth century, and to Italy, Germany and Spain in the eleventh century. The effects of the renewal of monastic life extended far beyond the cloister and contributed greatly to the reform of the diocesan clergy and the ordinary faithful. The monasteries were ultimately freed from domination by the laity and civil power and also protected against undue intervention on the part of bishops.

Unfortunately, the very structure of the Benedictine congregations, the necessary traveling and visitations by abbots, and the increasing apostolic activities of the monks took their toll on the contemplative aspect of Benedictine life. Moreover, as more and more monks confined their work hours to the scriptorium, manual labor was more and more neglected. Finally it led to the introduction of *conversi, familiares* or oblates to whom the monks entrusted the manual labor and the maintenance of the monastery. Eventually this led to a division of the monastery into "choir monks" and "lay brothers."[20]

In the eleventh century and well into the twelfth, while these monasteries were still prosperous and fervent, a reaction was nevertheless developing. They had become the Establishment; they had not changed with the times, whereas society was beginning to undergo profound transformations. For this reason there developed a fervent and widespread desire for a life that would be more simple, less institutionalized, more solitary, less involved in the political and economic fabric of society – in short, a return to monastic origins. It is not surprising, then, that it often led to a reintroduction of the eremitical life. This movement, which sprang up spontaneously all over Europe, brought about a revolution in the monastic world and produced a whole variety of new "orders" and observances alongside the established houses.[21]

Monasticism remained Benedictine at basis but it moved in two different directions. Thus, St. Romuald founded the Camaldolese in 1010, fostering a strictly eremitical life under the Rule of St. Benedict; St. Robert of Molesmes, on the other hand, founded the Cistercians in 1098 in an effort to promote a cenobitic life of greater separation from the world, poverty and strict observance of the Rule of St. Benedict. During this period two men worked most assidously for reform, both in the Church and in monastic life: John of Fécamp and St. Peter Damian.

JOHN OF FÉCAMP

Thanks to the work of Dom Wilmart,[22] the name and the works of John of Fécamp have been rescued from oblivion, although John himself perhaps would have preferred to be forgotten. He always referred to himself in deprecatory terms, calling himself "poor John" (misellus Johannes), and for many years his writings were wrongly attributed to such great authors as St. Ambrose, Cassian, Alcuin, St. Anselm and St. Bernard. For example, John of Fécamp was the author of the prayer, Summe sacerdos, that is given under the name of St. Ambrose in the prayers before Mass. Until the wide popularity of The Imitation of Christ, beginning in the fifteenth century, the devotional works of John of Fécamp were the most widely read in Christendom.

Born near Ravenna, he lived as a hermit until he went to the monastery of St. Benignus at Dijon and then, in 1017, to the monastery at Fécamp. After travels that took him to England and back to Italy, he died in 1076.

The spirituality of John de Fécamp is eminently Christocentric and he loved to dwell on those aspects of the life of Christ that show his love for mankind. In his longing to enjoy the sweetness of union with God, he realized that there are no methods that can provide this sweetness. Nevertheless, he provided contemplative souls with a kind of *lectio divina* that could dispose them for an experience of the divine.

Indeed, Sitwell maintains that John of Fécamp's writings illustrate perfectly the type of spirituality that developed from the *lectio divina*.[23] Wilmart praises him as the most remarkable spiritual author of the Middle Ages before St. Bernard.[24] His descriptions of prayer are a refinement and advancement of the silent mental prayer to which Hildemar referred in his commentary on the Rule of St. Benedict. After chanting the Divine Office or reading the word of God in Scripture, the monk may be moved by divine inspiration to enjoy an affective, silent prayer which will sometimes blossom into genuine infused contemplation. John describes this type of prayer in his *Confessio theologica*:

> There are many kinds of contemplation in which the soul devoted to thee, O Christ, takes its delight, but in none of these do I so rejoice as in that which, ignoring all things, directs a simple glance of the untroubled spirit to thee alone, O God. What peace and joy does the soul find in thee then. While my soul yearns for the divine vision and proclaims thy glory as best it can, the burden of the flesh weighs less heavily upon it, distracting thoughts subside, the weight and misery of our mortal condition no longer deaden the faculties as usual; all is quiet and peaceful. The heart is inflamed with love, the spirit is filled with joy, the memory is powerful, the mind is clear, and the whole soul, burning with a desire for the vision of thy beauty, is ravished by a love of things invisible.[25]

The foregoing passage illustrates clearly the importance of prayer in the Benedictine spirituality of the early Middle Ages. However, John of Fécamp, like St. Benedict himself, while recognizing the validity of a purely contemplative life, believed it was better to live in a monastic community and thus combine the active with the contemplative life (*orare est laborare*).

ST. PETER DAMIAN

Born in 988 and educated at Ravenna, St. Peter Damian entered the eremitical monastery founded by St. Romuald at Fonte Avellana, where he became superior in 1044. Created a cardinal, he dedicated the rest of his life to the much-needed reform of the Church. His activities extended into three distinct areas: reform of the diocesan clergy, renewal of monastic life, and adjustment of

Church-State relations. Although he was interested primarily in reform and the spiritual life, St. Peter Damian also composed a treatise, *De fide catholica*, on the interpretation of Scripture, and a work entitled *De divina omnipotentia*, in which he discussed the relationship between theology and philosophy and coined the expression *"philosophia ancilla theologiae."*

The regulations of St. Peter Damian in view of reform were often severe to the point of harshness, and yet when he wrote about Jesus or Mary, the reformer could be as tender and loving as a child. In this respect he resembled John of Fécamp and St. Romuald and was at the same time typically medieval. Like St. Augustine, he insisted that ascetical practices (which were extremely harsh for the hermits of the Middle Ages) are not an end in themselves, but a means to attain to the perfection of charity and divine wisdom.

Nevertheless in his teaching on the reform of monastic life he advocated the use of the discipline and other severe bodily mortifications. In some cases his advice was met with resistance and resentment on the part of monks and clerics alike. In addition to fidelity to the Divine Office and the night vigils, he sought to impose on the monks an almost continual fast and a strict observance of poverty. His concept of monastic life was that of separation from the world and concentration on the things of God; a life of penance and prayer.

As regards the reform of the diocesan clergy, St. Peter Damian was tireless in his efforts to combat the sexual immorality and the ignorance of secular priests and to correct the abuses of simony. He drew his arguments from Scripture, the Fathers and the canonical legislation of the Church. To help the clergy overcome their ignorance, avarice and incontinence, he advocated the study of Scripture and the practice of meditation on the word of God. Later, the Church would propose the community life for the diocesan clergy.[26]

CAMALDOLESE HERMITS

Since Benedictine monasticism developed indirectly out of the colonies of hermits in Egypt, some traces of the eremitical life still remained within the framework of the cenobitic character. The first rule for hermits in the Western Church appeared in the tenth century under the authorship of Grimlac, a solitary from the environs of Lorraine.[27] Unlike the Benedictine practice of prayer, the prayer of the hermit, according to Grimlac, should not be common, vocal prayer, but continual mental prayer. In Italy, however, St. Romuald founded the Camaldolese Order in 1010. It follows the Rule of St. Benedict as adapted to the eremitical life. The Constitutions for the Camaldolese were composed by Blessed Rudolph, between 1080 and 1085, and they list the following as the occupations of the Camaldolese hermit: prayer, reading, bodily flagellation and prostrations, accompanied by recitation of specified prayers. Great discretion was urged in the use of penitential practices, which were to be gauged by one's bodily strength, personal need or an inspiration of grace. The life of the hermit was totally contemplative; chant was reduced to an absolute minimum; solitude was jealously safeguarded as a means of death to self and exile from the world.[28]

During this period two predominant characteristics of contemplative religious life emerged clearly and definitively: separation from the world and asceticism. Partly because of the reaction against the abuses and excesses of the times, Christians in and outside the monastic life felt the need to do penance and to flee from the world. Given the violent passions of men of that period, conversion was often accompanied by austerities and penances carried to the extreme. It was not unusual for monks to leave their monasteries and become hermits; nor was it unusual for bishops to renounce their dioceses in order to become monks. Uneducated peasants and members of the nobility could also be found among those who sought admission to the monastic life; sometimes husbands and wives would separate by mutual agreement and each would leave the world for the cloister or a hermitage. Those who did not embrace the monastic life, but still felt the need for asceticism, could flee from the world temporarily by a self-imposed exile or pilgrimage or they could remain at home and make use of the discipline in self-flagellation.

The Rule of Grimlac provides a detailed description of the life of a hermit. The candidate was examined for four or five days as to his past life and his ability to live the eremitical life. Religious profession was indissoluble and the hermit also made a vow of stability. He was then led to his hermitage, carrying the clothes he would henceforth wear, and the abbot or the bishop would close and seal the door. There were two openings in the hermitage: a small window to the outside, and another small opening through which the hermit could assist at Mass in the church and receive Communion. Priest-hermits could have an oratory, consecrated by the bishop for the celebration of private Mass. Each hermit also had a small enclosed garden for taking fresh air or for planting vegetables.

Since hermits are also obliged to love of neighbor, they were to be sufficiently versed in sacred doctrine so that they could instruct candidates or disciples and give spiritual direction to persons who asked for it. In many respects the life described in the Rule of Grimlac is similar to the life of the Carthusians.

THE CARTHUSIANS

The Carthusian Order, established by St. Bruno of Cologne (+1101) in the valley of La Chartreuse, near Grenoble, in 1084, provided for its members an eremitical life within the framework of the primitive Benedictine *coenobium*. They do not follow the Rule of St. Benedict but their own *Consuetudines*. Their mode of life resembles that of the anchorites in the deserts of the East. Carthusians are totally cut off from the world; their sole occupation is to cultivate and maintain a direct and immediate contact with God. Even within the charterhouse the community aspects of religious life are minimal, and seem to be allowed with a certain reluctance. Pope Innocent XI said of the Carthusians, in 1688, "*Cartusia numquam reformata, quia numquam deformata.*"

Typical of all Carthusians, who are extremely reticent about their own spirituality, St. Bruno left only two letters, and these were written toward the end of his life. One of them, addressed to the lay brothers of the Order, states that the "key and seal of all spiritual discipline" is obedience, safeguarded by humility and patience and accompanied by chaste love of the Lord and true charity.[29] It remained for Guigo I, the fifth successor of St. Bruno, to formulate the Carthusian *Book of Customs* between 1121 and 1128.[30] Leclercq does not hesitate to classify Guigo as "one of the most remarkable spiritual authors of his century."[31]

In his prologue to the *Book of Customs* Guigo I refers to St. Jerome and the Rule of St. Benedict but he does not follow them slavishly. Throughout the entire treatise the emphasis is on simplicity, moderation and peace. The hermits are to observe an austere simplicity in the ceremonies of the liturgy and Divine Office; poverty is to be observed with great diligence; as hermits, the Carthusians are to observe strict silence and keep to the solitude of their cells.

There are two classes of Carthusians – monks and lay-brothers – but all are hermits, and their residence is to be called "hermitage" or "charterhouse" rather than monastery. The use of the discipline and other penitential instruments is allowed, but always with permission of the prior. Moderation is observed, in accordance with the example and teaching of St. Bruno, so that an atmosphere of joy may pervade the silent but occupied solitude of the hermits. Guigo states in one of his letters that the Carthusian life is given to the study of Scripture and spiritual writings.

Everything that the Carthusian needs for his health, work and prayer is provided for him so that he need never depart from his cell for anything at all. Everything in the life is ordained to solitude and prayer, and perhaps the only reason for prescribing the minimal community prayer and liturgy – and in modern times the weekly walk – was for the sake of the moderation and balance that are so characteristic of St. Bruno. The Carthusians never intended to be recluses, but hermits who live in a communal setting.

Although in a strict sense there has never been a "school" of Cathusian spirituality, it is characterized by the following traits: wise discretion, joy and simplicity, constant care not to lose sight of the lowly struggles of the purgative way, even in the heights of the contemplative life, and a tender love for Jesus and Mary.

This is evident in the writings of Guigo "the Angelic," also known as Guigo II because he was the second Guigo to be prior at the Grand Chartreuse (1174–1180). His letter on the contemplative life, known also as *Scala Claustralium* and *Scala Paradisi*, was more widely read and more highly praised than any other work of its kind.

Guigo II describes four stages in the development of the spiritual life of the contemplative: reading, meditation, prayer and contemplation. "Reading," says Guigo, "is the careful study of the Scripture, concentrating all one's powers on it. Meditation is the busy application of the mind to seek the help of one's own reason for knowledge of hidden truth. Prayer is the heart's devoted turning to God to do away with what is evil and obtain what is good. In contemplation the mind is in some way lifted up to God and held above itself, so that it tastes the joys of everlasting sweetness." He then proceeds to explain each of these "rungs" on the ladder of perfection. Then, in summary, he again returns to a brief description of the four stages:

> Reading comes first, and is as it were the foundation; it provides the subject matter which we must use for meditation. Meditation considers more carefully what is to be sought after; it digs, as it were, for treasure which it finds and reveals, but since it is not in meditation's power to seize upon the treasure, it directs us to prayer. Prayer lifts itself up to God with all its strength, and begs for the treasure which it longs for,

which is the sweetness of contemplation. Contemplation, when it comes, rewards the labors of the other three; it inebriates the thirsting soul with the dew of heavenly sweetness. Reading is an exercise of the outward senses, meditation is concerned with the inward understanding, prayer is concerned with desire, contemplation outstrips every faculty. The first degree is proper to beginners, the second to proficients, the third to devotees, the fourth to the blessed.[32]

Guigo then offers some conclusions that are stated in the terse manner characteristic of Carthusians: "Reading without meditation is sterile; meditation without reading is liable to error; prayer without meditation is lukewarm; meditation without prayer is unfruitful; prayer, when it is fervent, wins contemplation, but to obtain contemplation without prayer would be rare, even miraculous."[33]

CISTERCIAN SPIRITUALITY

The third outgrowth of monasticism in the Middle Ages, and the most popular, was the Cistercian Order, founded by St. Robert of Molesmes at Citeaux in 1098. After making the foundation, the Pope commanded Robert to return to Molesmes but the other members remained at Citeaux, living in great austerity under St. Alberic and St. Stephen Harding. St. Bernard arrived at Citeaux with thirty companions in 1112, and so great was the expansion of the Cistercian Order that when St. Bernard died in 1153, there were 343 monasteries of strict observance covering Europe and reaching into the Balkans and the Holy Land.

Following the regulations laid down by Stephen Harding in his *Carta caritatis* in 1114, the Cistercians moved away from the centralization of the Cluniac system and introduced government by a general chapter, which became a model for religious orders in the future.[34] The Cistercians succeeded in adapting monastic life to the needs of the times by adjusting the perennial values of monastic life to changing conditions. As a result, while many of the other newly-founded orders flourished for a time and then disappeared, the Cistercians have prospered to the present day.

The Cistercians did not differ essentially from the Benedictines in general as regards their concept of monastic life; what they sought to do was to restore the primitive observance in all its simplicity and austerity. Consequently, they greatly reduced the liturgical accretions, restricted the activities in the scriptorium, and returned to manual labor. This, says Sitwell, constituted the fundamental difference between the "black" monks of Cluny and the "white" monks of Citeaux.[35] It was, therefore, a difference that sprang from two distinct customaries or constitutions based on the same Rule of St. Benedict.

However, there was yet another difference between Cluny and Citeaux: the desire of the Cistercians to seek a more eremitical life, not in the manner of the Camaldolese and Carthusians, but as a community totally separated from the world and observing the Rule of St. Benedict as literally as possible. Nevertheless, the Cistercians, while endeavouring to restore primitive Benedictine monasticism, also made adaptations to suit their purpose. Consequently, they tended to subordinate everything else to the ascetical and contemplative elements of monastic life, while the Cluniac interpretation gave the primacy to the liturgy and *lectio divina*.

For the Cistercians, separation from the world was as complete as for the monks of the East, and for that reason they sought more remote places for their monasteries and observed strict cloister. Their asceticism consisted in manual labor and an austere mode of life, thus embracing the cross of Christ without mitigation. In order to safeguard their contemplative recollection, they withdrew from all forms of apostolate and priestly ministry, observed perpetual silence, and avoided the accumulation of wealth. And to those who would ask how the Cistercians fulfilled the precept of love of neighbor, they could reply with the teaching of St. Bernard, who stated that the practice of fraternal charity was amply evident in the community life of the monks themselves.

Whether or not one can go so far as to speak of a "school" of Cistercian spirituality as distinct from Benedictine spirituality,[36] there are certain characteristics that distinguish the monks of Citeaux. First of all, in accordance with the monastic axiom of *solo Deo*, there was an eschatological quality to Cistercian life. Their gaze was fixed on eternal realities and on the goal of life in glory. They considered themselves very much as pilgrims on the road to heaven, and to keep themselves ever prepared for the coming of Christ, they divested themselves as much as possible of all earthly interests and attachments.

Paradoxically, however, the Cistercians always preserved a deep appreciation for created things and a delicate sensitivity to human needs. They cultivated the fields, became experts in animal husbandry, and even became renowned for the production of such domestic items as bread, cheese, and other edibles. In liturgical art they did away with the ornate style characteristic of so many abbey churches and returned to the pure lines of nature that provide the simplicity of beauty. In the area of human relations, following the example of St. Bernard, William of St. Thierry and especially St. Aelred, they gave an example of authentic spiritual friendship in the monastic *milieu*.[37]

Another characteristic of Cistercians was their prudent adaptation of monastic observances. Holding fast to the beneficial traditional practices, the Cistercians did not hesitate to abandon or change those elements that no longer served the purpose for which they were instituted, but always with a view to preserving the pure monastic sources. This did not lead to rugged individualism, however, for the basic statutes of Cistercian life were rigorously observed by all the monasteries, while allowing individual abbeys to make necessary adjustments as regards implementation.

Two other qualities of Cistercian life are poverty and manual labor. For the Cistercians, poverty went beyond the interior detachment and the extirpation of a possessive spirit, as required of all monks; the Cistercians practiced poverty as a means of personal privation and asceticism as a community witness. They did not go to the extremes that the mendicant friars would propose in the thirteenth century, but they did add a new meaning to the concept of monastic poverty. As regards manual labor, they saw it as a logical consequence of their concept of poverty. St. Benedict had stated in his Rule that the monks should not be distressed if local conditions or their poverty make it necessary for them to do their own harvesting, for when they live by the labor of their hands, they are truly monks (chap. 48). The Cistercians, desiring to be "truly monks," made manual labor a required element of their life. One could say that for the Cistercians, manual labor was as essential to monastic life as liturgical prayer and the *lectio divina*. However, with the emergence of the lay brothers or *conversi*, a certain imbalance was created in this threefold division of Cistercian monastic activities.

Lastly, and perhaps as a result of the foregoing characteristics, Cistercian life was marked by utter simplicity. Whether one considers their liturgy, which was drastically abridged and simplified, or their architecture or their whole style of living, the impression received is always that of a simplicity marked by discretion. Doing away with all pomp and ceremony and avoiding any trace of triumphalism or ostentation, the Cistercian monks desired nothing more than to live the Rule of St. Benedict with all fidelity and to devote themselves entirely to a life of prayer and manual labor.[38]

ST. BERNARD

In order to have a better understanding of Cistercian spirituality and to appreciate the impact of the monks of Citeaux, it is necessary to discuss the teachings of their three most influential writers: St. Bernard, William of St. Thierry and St. Aelred of Rievaulx. Mabillon refers to St. Bernard as the "last of the Fathers,"[39] and Sitwell says that he "towers over the whole of the first half of the twelfth century."[40]

Born in Burgundy, near Switzerland, around 1090, Bernard entered the abbey at Citeaux in 1112 with four of his brothers, an uncle and twenty-five friends. After three years of spiritual formation, Stephen Harding sent Bernard to make a new foundation at Clairvaux, if only to ease the crowded conditions at Citeaux. So great was the influence of Bernard in attracting vocations to the Cistercian life that he has been called "the second founder of the Cistercians."[41]

As to his activities, it is almost impossible to recount the various works and movements with which he was involved. He composed an *Apologia* in defense of the Cistercian reform; he worked for the reform of the diocesan clergy and the laity; he helped to end the schism in the Church by defending the rights of Pope Innocent II against the pretender, Anaclete II; he argued against the errors of Abelard, who was condemned later by the Church; he obliged Gilbert de la Porée, bishop of Poitiers, to retract his errors at the Council of Reims; he preached against the Manichaeans in southern France; he went on missions as a peacemaker between warring factions and preached the Second Crusade; he sent to Pope Eugene III, his former disciple at Clairvaux, the treatise *De consideratione* for reforming the Church. Unfortunately, Pope Eugene III died in July, 1153, and St. Bernard died in August of that same year. The biography of St. Bernard was written during his lifetime; William of St. Thierry and Arnold of Bonneval wrote what is called the *Vita prima*, and it was completed by Geoffrey of Auxerre. St. Bernard was canonized in 1174 and proclaimed Doctor of the Church in 1830.[42]

In spite of his varied and demanding activities, St. Bernard was also a prolific writer. His voluminous correspondence comprises more than 500 letters and there are 332 sermons, including the well-known series on the *Song of Songs*. His first spiritual work was written about 1124 and was a treatise entitled *The Degrees of Humility and Pride*. The following year he wrote his *Apologia* or defense of the Cistercian reform, and between 1126 and 1141 he wrote *The*

Love of God, Grace and Free Will, The Customs and Obligations of Bishops, Conversion (for the reform of diocesan priests), *Precepts and Dispensation*, and various tracts on such topics as baptism, the Cistercian *Antiphonary*, and the errors of Abelard. Toward the end of his life he composed the *De consideratione* and a *Life of St. Malachy*, an Irish bishop who died suddenly during a visit to Clairvaux.[43]

In accordance with the tradition and practice of Benedictine spirituality, St. Bernard drew the inspiration for his spiritual doctrine from Scripture, directly by meditation on the Bible and indirectly by reading the biblical commentaries of Origen, St. Jerome, St. Augustine and St. Gregory the Great. For St. Bernard, "the Bible contains no other mystery than that of Christ, for it is he who gives the Scriptures their unity and their meaning. It is Christ who is the principle of that unity for he is everywhere present, pre-figured in the Old Testament and revealed in the New."[44] As a result, the spiritual doctrine of St. Bernard is eminently Christocentric. The Christian is perfect to the extent that he is assimilated to the mystery of Christ. This, in turn, can be effected only by participation in the doctrinal, sacramental and liturgical life of the Church, because Scripture – which reveals the mystery of Christ – can be understood truly only in and by the Church.

Again, as would be expected in the spiritual teaching of a Cistercian, the central theme of St. Bernard's spirituality is expressed in the words of St. John: "God is love; he loved us first, his love for us was revealed when he sent into the world his only Son so that we could have life through him."[45] Asking, then, how God is to be loved, St. Bernard replies: "The reason for loving God is God himself; the measure of loving God is to love him without measure."[46] In this respect, St. Bernard rivals St. Augustine for the title, "Doctor of charity." He is likewise a forerunner of the style of spiritual writing found in St. Francis de Sales.

Neither in his life nor in his doctrine, however, was St. Bernard a sentimentalist; rather, his ascetical teaching is realistic and demanding. Its starting point is humility, which is basically the fruit of self-knowledge that reveals to man his sinful condition.[47] St. Bernard then develops a psychology of asceticism in which he demonstrates that man's free will is the key to conversion and progress in spiritual perfection. Whether speaking of the degrees of humility through which the soul must pass in its conquest of sin or the grades of love that culminate ultimately in a mystical union with God, priority of emphasis is always given to man's will, though never divorced from intellect and memory.[48] Although he admits that there is no terminus to the love of God in this world nor can man attain absolute perfection *in via*, St. Bernard nevertheless stresses the obligation of the Christian to strive constantly for ever greater perfection: "No one can be perfect who does not desire to be more perfect, and he shows himself to be more perfect in the measure that he aspires to yet greater perfection.[49] One who refuses to be better is certainly less good; as soon as you refuse to become better, you cease to be good."[50]

The love of God, therefore, should grow constantly in the Christian desirous of perfection and in so doing, it passes through four basic stages which St. Bernard identifies as carnal, mercenary, filial and mystical. Carnal love is a natural, instinctive love which a man has for himself and when it becomes supernaturalized by grace it normally concentrates on the sacred humanity of Christ and the mysteries of his life on earth. Mercenary love is a servile love whereby a man loves God because of the benefits received from God and it springs from man's awareness of his need for God. Filial love is a disinterested love of God as our Father and it enables us to taste the sweetness of the Lord. The fourth and highest stage of love is a pure love of God, totally devoid of self-interest but St. Bernard says that this fourth type of love is one in which the individual no longer loves himself except for God's sake, and his only prayer is: Thy will be done on earth as it is in heaven.[51]

The means of growth in perfection proposed by St. Bernard are the following: God's grace, the humanity of Christ, and Mary co-redemptrix and mediatrix; meditation, especially on the mysteries of Christ; prayer (here St. Bernard follows the teaching of Cassian); examination of conscience; custody of thoughts and affections; and spiritual direction. It is worth noting that the spiritual teachings of St. Bernard exerted a strong influence on the Victorines, the Franciscans, Thomas à Kempis, the Rhineland mystics, St. Ignatius Loyola and St. Francis de Sales.

The mystical theology of St. Bernard is found in his treatise on the love of God and in his commentary on the *Song of Songs*, delivered as sermons to his monks. He identifies Christ as the bridegroom, and the Church or the individual soul as the bride. In the beginning the love for Christ is sensible or carnal; it focuses on the humanity of Christ and the events of his life on earth. And although love for Christ in his humanity is a great gift of the Holy Spirit, it is, says St. Bernard, "none the less carnal as compared with that other love which is not so much related to the Word made flesh as to the Word as wisdom, the Word as justice, the Word as truth, and the Word as holiness."[52] When St. Bernard speaks of mystical union, he is speaking of a spiritual love that passes beyond the humanity of Christ in order to concentrate on his divinity. He says: "Be careful to think of nothing corporal or sensible in this union of the Word with the soul. Let us call to mind here what the Apostle says: 'He who is joined to the Lord is one spirit with him' (I Cor. 6:17). The rapture of the pure soul in God or the loving descent of God into the soul is expressed as best we can by comparing spiritual things with spiritual."[53]

When the soul is completely purified and is well exercised in spiritual love, it may, if called by God, enter a mystical union and become the bride of the Word; it contracts a spiritual marriage with the Word and is completely identified with the divine will in the transforming union.[54] St. Bernard makes use of the same imagery as the *Song of Songs* to describe the phenomena that accompany mystical union: embrace, kiss, ecstasy, marriage. Although he was aware of the danger of such language and constantly insisted that these images describe experiences that are totally spiritual and produced by grace, the history of spirituality is dotted with cases of persons who interpreted these expressions in a sensual manner.

Like St. Gregory the Great, St. Bernard saw the apostolate as the fruit of love and an overflow from the interior life of prayer. In the same sermons in which he discussed mystical union, he frequently referred to the pastoral ministry, and especially that of preaching.[55] Those who have received the gift of divine love are able to understand its language, says St. Bernard, and they respond to it "by works of love and piety."[56] And since grace and divine love come to the soul during the time of its communings with God, those who have the care of souls should be especially devoted to meditation on divine truths; then they should pass from the quiet of contemplation to the labor of preaching.[57] Consequently, the apostle should be at once a contemplative and a man of action. Indeed, St. Bernard insists that the apostle must first be concerned with the sanctification of his own soul before dedicating himself to the sanctification of others. St. Bernard also offers some practical observations on pastoral service:

Know that you must be mothers to those that are submitted to you and not masters. If, from time to time, severity must be employed, let it be fatherly and not tyrannical. Show yourselves mothers in encouragement and fathers in correction.[58]

Zeal without knowledge is insufferable. When love is very ardent, discretion, which regulates charity, is especially necessary. Zeal unenlightened by knowledge always loses its force, and sometimes becomes harmful. ... Discretion, indeed, regulates all the virtues, and thus makes them moderate, beautiful and stable. ... It is not so much a virtue itself as the chastener and guide of the other virtues. ... Take it away, and virtue is changed to vice.[59]

According to Yeomans, "Bernard is led through Christ to the Trinity. His devotion to the Savior fructifies into consciousness of the presence of the three divine Persons in his soul and in the whole of creation."[60] It is true that the mystery of the Trinity is at the core of the spirituality of St. Bernard, as it must be for all Christian spirituality, but St. Bernard has been characterized in the tradition as a theologian of Jesus and Mary. It is, rather, in his contemporary and fellow-Cistercian, William of St. Thierry (1085–1148), that we find a spiritual theology which is, as Leclercq calls it, a *"mystique trinitaire."*[61]

WILLIAM OF ST. THIERRY

For some reason, which is not very well understood, before the end of the twelfth century itself, the treatises of William began to be attributed to St. Bernard and other writers, and from the end of the Middle Ages until some thirty years ago, apart from a few references by the mystics, little or no attention was paid to them. Modern scholarship, however, has vindicated the claim of William of St. Thierry to be considered as a theological and spiritual writer of the first importance.[62]

William of St. Thierry (1085–1148) ruled for fifteen years as abbot of the Benedictine monastery near Rheims. In 1135 he transferred to the Cistercian abbey at Signy, where he remained until his death, except for a visit to the Carthusians at Mont-Dieu. This visit occasioned his famous *"Golden Epistle"* or *Epistola ad Fratres de Monte Dei.*

In the course of his lifetime he wrote numerous treatises on a variety of subjects: the love of God, the nature of man, the Eucharist, faith, a life of St. Bernard, and commentaries on the Epistle to the Romans and the *Song of Songs.* His masterpiece, however, is the treatise *Aenigma fidei,* written as a defence of the doctrine of the Trinity against Abelard. This work, together with the *Golden Epistle* and *De natura et dignitate amoris,* contain the sum of his spiritual theology.[63]

Although the writings of William on the spiritual life are practical rather than theoretical, Déchanet has discovered that he was greatly influenced by the writings of Origen, St. Gregory of Nyssa and John Scotus Erigena as well as those of St. Augustine.[64] Sitwell points out in this regard that "the fact that he had gone back to the Greek Fathers is of great significance. It represented a development of interest in the theoretical aspect of contemplation. . . . In calling attention to this purely contemplative ideal, in his appeal to the early pre-Benedictine monachism, and in the use he made of its theological background, William of St. Thierry was looking ahead to a movement which was to come after his death."[65]

Like St. Bernard, William sees man's life on earth as a return or an ascent to God, and in his *Golden Epistle* he divides this ascent into the classical three stages: beginners, advanced and perfect. The beginner, in whom the "animal" man predominates, is stimulated to a great extent by his senses and sensate appetites; for that reason he needs the guidance of laws and external authority, to which he responds by obedience, and he needs the ascetical practices of mortification, examination of conscience, spiritual reading and prayer of petition.[66] In the advanced stage the "rational man" takes the ascendancy, and in the third and final stage the perfect man is truly spiritual. Since the *Golden Epistle* devotes three quarters of its contents to a consideration of beginners, we turn to the treatise *Aenigma fidei* to complete the total view of the spiritual doctrine of William of St. Thierry.[67]

In this work William refers to the three stages of man's ascent to God as the periods or stages of: faith, reasoning of faith, and experience. The beginner or "animal" man, as described above, lives by faith, and since he is particularly under the rule of the senses, he is led to the Trinity by that which is perceptible to the senses. Here William stresses the importance of the humanity of Christ and the use of signs and symbols. "This stage," says Brooke, "is closely connected with the Incarnation and the whole temporal economy as a pedagogic preparation leading man by degrees through what is perceptible to the senses toward the eternal, immutable life of the Trinity. The Incarnation is seen as a *Sacramentum*, not as we use the term for the sacraments strictly so called, but in the patristic sense of the word, implying the whole range of signs whereby what is eternal, spiritual and invisible should be manifested through the medium of what is temporal, material and visible."[68]

The second stage, called by William *ratio fidei*, is one in which the soul begins to seek reasons for its faith either by theologizing or meditating on Scripture. In treating of this period of the soul's ascent to God, William never lets the reader forget that the goal of that ascent is the Trinity, although he does not concentrate, as do the Scholastics, on the metaphysics of the mystery. In the stage of "*ratio fidei*," reason is always obedient to faith. William's "contribution lies rather in the fine dialectic with which he leads us at every turn toward the ultimate mystery of the Trinity. After approaching the Trinity from almost every viewpoint, the emphasis of the Latin Fathers on the unity of nature alternating with that of the Greek Fathers on the distinction of Persons, *ratio fidei* confronts us at each conclusion with the impenetrable mystery. We are told that the human mind never understands the Trinity so well as when it is understood to be incomprehensible.[69] The initial mystery of the God who is both three and one is never lessened, yet William's speculations always explain more exactly just where the mystery lies in every aspect of the problem."[70]

Coming to the third and final stage, William describes the state of the spiritual and perfect Christian, who passes beyond intellectual reasoning to mystical experience of the Trinity. At this point, says William, the Father and the Son reveal themselves through the Holy Spirit so that the Christian is not only united with God but he shares and experiences the very life of the Trinity. It is an anticipation of the beatific vision, a loving knowledge or a "love which is understanding" (*amor-intellectus*). "This does not mean that there is no longer a mystery, that the antithesis is now reconciled by reason, so as to see how three and one are compatible. It means that the mind has passed out of the realm of conceptual knowledge, where the question whether reason can in any way explain the mystery no longer arises."[71]

William's concept of the mystical experience of the Trinity involves a transition from man as image of God to man as likeness (*similitudo*) of God. Man in his very nature, even as the "animal" man of the beginner, has an imprint of the Trinity and it can never be destroyed. This innate image gives him the capacity to receive the higher types of image which come to him through the virtues and through the indwelling of the Trinity.[72] But if a man is to enjoy the mystical experience of the perfect Christian he must somehow become transformed into the divine likeness (*similitudo*) and not remain simply an image. And just as the eye cannot see unless it is somehow transformed into that which is seen, so we cannot know God mystically unless we are somehow transformed into his likeness. When does this occur? "We become like him when the image of the Trinity in the soul has been perfected and brought back to a perfect likeness, the *similitudo*, the most perfect union between the soul and God compatible with the distinction between creature and Creator."[73] This is effected by the Holy Spirit, who is the uncreated union of the Father and the Son. Consequently, William concludes: "Through the Holy Spirit the man of God becomes – in some ineffable, incredible way – not God exactly, but what God is by nature, man becomes by grace."[74] Indeed, the Holy Spirit is himself the love by which we love God (*ipse enim est amor noster*).[75]

ST. AELRED OF RIEVAULX

Plagued all his life by bad health, Aelred entered the Cistercian monastery at Rievaulx at the age of 24 and died in 1167, after being abbot for twenty years. During much of this time he administered the abbey from the infirmary and gained great renown as a spiritual director. Aelred was completely monastic in his spiritual teaching and writings, attempting to show the monks how to achieve union with God by abandoning self and sin and, through fraternal love in community, restoring the image of God that had been lost through sin.

His best works consist of sermons and treatises, and of these the best are *Mirror of Charity, Jesus as a Twelve-year-old Boy*, and *Spiritual Friendship*.[76] Aelred appreciated the eremitical life and in fact he wrote a treatise for his sister on the formation of a recluse, but he was much more in favor of the cenobitic life.

According to Aelred, man's whole being longs for God because God has instilled this desire in the human heart. More than that, man seeks to become like unto God, even when he wanders in the "land of unlikeness" because of his sins. It is only through Christ that man can realize his inmost desire, and hence he should love Christ as his dearest friend. Indeed, "God himself is friendship," and "he who dwells in friendship, dwells in God and God in him." This is where human friendship, if it is a spiritual friendship, can be a means of friendship with God. Anyone who enjoys such a spiritual human friendship is by that very fact a friend of God. Friendship with God, therefore, constitutes perfection because "to love God is to join our will to God so completely that whatever the divine will prescribes, the human will consents to."[77]

For Aelred the monastery is not only, as St. Benedict stated, "a school for the Lord's service" (Prologue, 45); it is a "school of love." Under the abbot, who stands in the place of Christ, the monks are brought to friendship with God through their fraternal love in community. Yet this does not mean that the monastic life is a source of continual joy. The abandonment of human will to the divine will involves suffering, and daily life in community often presents trials and crosses. Some monks may even ask themselves, as did Bernard, why they have come to the monastery or what is the value of their hidden life. To this, Aelred would respond by showing the importance of the imitation of Christ and of his apostles who suffered persecution and death.

> It is everyone's affair by charity, and the abbot's by his counsels, to prevent anyone from straying from the path, or any delay on the journey. This peaceful confidence in the monastic life is not peculiar to St. Aelred, but he sets it forth with a charm, a good humor, and at times a humorousness, that are entirely his own. St. Bernard, his master, is a doctor of the Church, whereas St. Aelred is only a doctor of the monastic life; and yet his teaching has a universal value, because monasticism is part of the Church, and he himself lays stress on unity of spirit. Still, he is thinking first of all of monks. The theologian is always the pleasant Father Abbot.[78]

NUNS AND LAY BROTHERS

Throughout the history of the Church women as well as men have embraced the monastic life, both eremitical and cenobitic. Until recently, however, the role played by women in the development of monastic life has been neglected.[79] From the very beginning of monasticism in the East, however, there were female solitaries in the desert, and one legend states that St. Mary Magdalen ended her days as a recluse. We know for certain that St. Pachomius founded a monastery for women; St. Basil wrote legislation for them; and women associates of St. Jerome and Rufinus were ardent promoters of the monastic life. In the West, we need only mention St. Scholastica and the monastery for women near Monte Cassino, the consecrated women of the Irish monastic system, and the female collaborators of missionaries like St. Boniface in Germany.

The laws and customs in the West severely restricted the opportunities for women in monastic life and even among the women themselves there were distinctions based on social class, education or economic level. Thus, some monasteries were for all practical purposes reserved for the women of the aristocracy, either because some royal or noble person had endowed the monastery or because the poorer classes could not afford the dowry. In some cases the young woman of the upper class who entered the monastery as a "choir" nun would bring along one of her maids as a "lay" sister to serve her mistress. As time went on, there were monasteries restricted to aristocrats, others for the middle and lower class, and even some for converts to Catholicism.

While men religious were designated by the term monk (*monachus*) the feminine form, *monacha*, was never commonly used for women religious. The term was used by St. Augustine, St. Gregory the Great and St. Gregory of Tours, and it has survived in Italian as *monaca*, but the more common Latin word was *monialis*, from *sanctimonalis*, designating a person consecrated to God. The term "nun" seems to be of Egyptian origin and is the most common word used in English to refer to a woman religious. However, strictly speaking, the term applies only to a cloistered religious in solemn vows, while the word "sister" (*soror*) applies to a woman religious of the active life. It is interesting to note that the Italian word "*nonna*" means grandmother.[80]

Early in the twelfth century Robert d'Arbrissel organized monasteries of nuns according to the Rule of St. Benedict. He also established communities of men composed of priests and laymen or lay brothers. They lived in adjoining houses and were to take care of the spiritual and material needs of the nuns. The arrangement involved certain risks and was severely criticized in some quarters, but the Holy See took the monastery of Fontévrault under its protection. In England, meanwhile, St. Gilbert made a similar foundation under the Rule of St. Benedict as observed by the Cistercians. Leclercq even refers to a monastic "feminist movement" in this period.[81]

The standard text for the spiritual formation of religious women in the twelfth century was the *Speculum virginum*, composed by an anonymous author, perhaps from the Rhineland, where the monastic life for women flourished to a high degree. It gives examples of the holy women of ancient times, whether wives, widows or virgins, but holds the state of virginity to be the most perfect. Nevertheless, the personal holiness of a wife or widow may possibly surpass that of a nun in given instances. The treatise also insists that the monastic vocation must be the result of the free choice of the individual, although in practice this principle was not always observed.[82]

The two most outstanding nuns of this period are St. Hildegarde and St. Elizabeth of Schönau. Both were German, both were in the Benedictine tradition, and both were highly esteemed mystics. Hildegarde, born in 1098, became a Benedictine nun at the age of eighteen and became abbess in 1136. She was always ill, and she declared that since the age of three she had had visions; and at the age of forty she was commanded by an interior voice to record her visions. When she consulted St. Bernard about the matter in 1141, he wisely told her to practice the virtues and not pay too much attention to visions and revelations. Hildegarde died in 1179 and her revelations were approved by three popes and by the Council of Trèves.

Her writings are a strange mixture of spiritual revelations, the scientific knowledge of her day, and prophetic intuitions. She left a collection of 300 letters and a principal work entitled *Scivias Domini* (*Scire Vias Domini*). Always a humble woman in spite of the many calls upon her for advice and her many travels throughout Germany, Hildegarde taught a prudent asceticism that enabled her monastery to prosper under her guidance. She provided a surprisingly exact account of her mystical experiences and taught that mystical contemplation is available to all who conquer their vices and allow themselves to be set afire by the Holy Spirit. A good predisposition for contemplative prayer is spiritual reading and then meditating on what has been read; but much better than this is the Divine Office.[83]

St. Elizabeth of Schönau, born around 1129, was also a visionary, but unlike Hildegarde, all of her visions were ecstatic and accompanied by extraordinary phenomena and intense suffering. At the command of her confessor, she wrote down her experiences and also composed letters and prayers and a book called *The Ways of God*. Her writings were widely read because she gave spiritual counsel to persons from all states of life. Some critics have theorized that *The Ways of God* is based to a large extent on the *Scivias* by St. Hildegarde, who was a close friend and correspondent. Two other works attributed to Elizabeth are three volumes of visions (although some scholars accept only the first book as Elizabeth's original work), and a treatise on the martyrdom of St. Ursula and companions, which has generally been considered unreliable and the source of many unfounded legends.[84] Neither Hildegarde nor Elizabeth have been officially canonized.

As regards the emergence of lay brothers or *conversi* in the monastic life, we should note that as early as the fourth century Pope Siricius had written to the Bishop of Tarragona: "We desire that monks whom seriousness of conduct, holiness of life, and practice of faith commend, be admitted to the duties of the clergy."[85] In 1311 Pope Clement V stated: "For the increase of divine worship, We prescribe that monks, at the notification of their abbots, must prepare themselves for all sacred orders, once legitimate excuses have been removed."[86] Finally, Pope Clement VIII decreed: "Whoever is received into an order of regulars.... must possess such knowledge of letters or give unquestioned hope of acquiring such knowledge that he may receive minor orders, and in due time the major orders as well, according to the decrees of the Sacred Council of Trent."[87]

The foregoing statements reflect a gradual transition in monastic life which led not only to the ordination of monks to the priesthood and, consequently, the ecclesiastical classification of monastic institutes as clerical religious, but it also led to a new class of monks called lay brothers. A variety of causes led to this development: by the end of the ninth century the Benedictine monks had devoted themselves almost exclusively to *lectio divina* and liturgical worship, to the detriment of manual labor; the intellectual competence and holiness of the monks made them eminently worthy of priestly ordination, while the diocesan clergy of the ninth to the twelfth centuries were often ignorant and immoral; by the eleventh century the monasteries were sorely in need of hands to administer the external goods, do the work of the fields and perform the domestic duties within the cloister. Numerous monasteries had made use of lay help as laborers and servants, but too often this had led to all kinds of difficulties. The solution was found in the institution of a special class of monks who were distinct from the choir monks.

From various documents issued by monasteries of Benedictine life and from statements made by several popes between the twelfth and sixteenth centuries, we can describe the lay brothers or *conversi* as true religious who form an integral part of the monastic community and are dedicated to the manual labor and external services of the monastery so that the choir monks can dedicate themselves to their particular duties. As their form of life became more clearly defined, the lay brothers pronounced only simple vows, wore a distinctive habit, prayed their own Office, assisted at specified monastic exercises such as conventual Mass, compline, chapter of faults and solemn functions, made an annual retreat, received a weekly spiritual conference from their own master or director, and formed a kind of community within the general community of the monastery. Later, when new forms of religious life were approved by the Church provision was usually made for the admission of lay brothers as a distinct but integral part of the religious institute.[88]

To summarize: Benedictine spirituality in the twelfth century still preserved the essential notes that were common to all monastic spirituality, with certain differences in regard to observances. It was, above all, a spirituality firmly rooted in biblical sources and nourished by *lectio divina* and liturgical prayer. The life of the Benedictine monk was a life of prayer and penance, a life withdrawn from the world by a desire to be united with God. As Leclercq describes it, it was a "prophetic life" because it consisted in waiting for the coming of the Lord, in prayer and penance; it was an "apostolic life" because it was a life of community in love, after the example of the disciples in the Cenacle and the first Christians; it was a "life of martyrdom" because it involved separation from the world and a constant warfare against the obstacles to charity; it was an "angelic life" because it sought total detachment through prayer, asceticism and chastity; it was an "evangelical life" because it sought to imitate Christ by walking the way of the Gospel.[89]

Yet, there were also new trends evident in the Benedictine spirituality of the twelfth century, thanks to the Cistercian movement. First of all, there was a vigorous insistence on the place of manual labor in monastic life, and this, as we have seen, was not so much an innovation as a return to the original teaching of St. Benedict. Secondly, there was an equally strong emphasis on the contemplative purpose of monastic life, with the result that the Cistercians explicitly regulated their *lectio divina*, prayer and ascetical practices with a view to contemplation and union with God. It is in this second area that the Cistercians made their greatest contribution to spirituality, especially in the persons of St. Bernard and William of St. Thierry, who bring us a step closer to a systematic theology of Christian perfection and a psychology of the mystical state.

CHAPTER 6

SPIRITUALITY OF THE MIDDLE AGES

The twelfth century was a period of political and ecclesiastical turmoil, intellectual stimulation and challenging adjustment to the changing times. The merchants and artisans of the towns and cities were confronting the ancient feudal system and demanding greater freedom and autonomy as individuals and as members of the guilds. The romance languages were slowly but surely replacing Latin, with the result that people in a given locality were becoming more isolated culturally and somewhat alienated from the Latin liturgy. The masters in cathedral schools and in monasteries, previously immersed in patristic sources and tradition, were reaching out to new methods of scholarship and thus preparing the way for the rise of the universities. Finally, the laity, individually or in groups, began to take a more prominent place in the life of the Church, even in areas that were formerly considered the exclusive domain of monks and the clergy.

MEDIEVAL PIETY

The prologue to the Rule of Grandmont, founded by St. Stephen of Muret (+ 1124), stated that there is only one rule of faith and salvation, namely, the Gospel. All other rules, such as that of St. Benedict or St. Augustine, are simply applications of the Gospel teaching.[1] The reading and knowledge of the New Testament was not, however, the exclusive prerogative of monks; there was an intense interest in Scripture on the part of the laity of the twelfth century. In fact, a group of the laity at Metz translated into the vernacular the four gospels, the letters of St. Paul and the Psalms. Then, in private meetings they discussed and interpreted the various passages, but they excluded from their gatherings all priests and any laymen who disagreed with their exegesis of Scripture. As a result, in 1199 Pope Innocent III issued a letter in which he praised their devotion to Scripture but condemned their secret, exclusive meetings and their anti-clerical attitude. Later, the synods of

Toulouse (1229) and Tarragona (1234) forbade the laity to possess or read translations of the Bible in the vernacular.[2]

Interest in the reading and discussion of the Gospel and the preaching of the Crusades for the liberation of the holy places naturally contributed a great deal to another dominant characteristic of medieval piety: devotion to the sacred humanity of Christ. Some historians have asserted that this devotion was introduced by St. Bernard and popularized by St. Francis of Assisi, but the truth of the matter is that this devotion has existed in the Church from earliest times.[3] It did develop in the twelfth century, however, and because of the worldwide interest in the Crusades and the Holy Land, the devotion of the faithful began to focus more and more on various scenes or "mysteries" of the life of Christ or on the instruments of the passion and death of Christ.

The attention of the faithful was especially fixed on the intensity of Christ's sufferings and, indeed, was preoccupied with that aspect. In succeeding centuries mystics such as St. Brigid described in minute detail the sufferings of Christ. In art, which reflects or animates the devotion of the faithful, the crucifixes were made more realistic and accentuated the agony of Christ. For example, instead of portraying the two feet nailed separately to the cross, one foot was placed over the other and one nail transpierced both feet. As a result, the artist or sculptor could portray more intense suffering of Christ crucified.[4]

A treatise on sacramental confession in the second half of the twelfth century contains a passage in which the author, Peter de Blois, contrasts true devotion with pure emotion:

> There is no merit in any feeling of devotion unless it proceeds from the love of Christ. Many of the characters in tragedies and other poems and songs are wise and illustrious and powerful, and excite our love. . . . The actors put before us the trials they endured, the injustices they suffered, . . . and the audience is moved to tears. You are touched by these fables. When you hear our Lord spoken of devoutly and are so moved, is that truly the love of God? You have compassion for God; and also for Artus! In either case, your tears are in vain if you do not love God, and if your tears of devotion and penitence do not flow from the sources of our Savior; that is, from faith, hope and love.[5]

The name of Jesus was likewise the object of great veneration in this century, propagated no doubt to a great extent by St. Bernard, as was devotion to the sacred humanity of Christ. During this same period an English Cistercian composed the tender hymn: *Dulcis Jesu memoria.*[6] At the same time particular feasts in honor of the "mysteries" of Christ were multiplied; churches and chapels were increasingly dedicated to some aspect of the life of Christ; and artists produced numerous illustrations of the "mysteries" of Christ in painting, sculpture, and theatrical productions.

Flowing likewise from the devotion to Christ and the belief that the Gospel was the sole rule for Christian living was the imitation of Christ, and particularly in regard to poverty. Numerous preachers and writers insisted that by the very fact of his baptism, even if he never becomes a monk or cleric, the Christian is obliged to renounce the world and its pomps.[7] So well was the message understood that in the eyes of the laity the worst and most obvious sin of clergy and religious was avarice, often accompanied by lust.[8] At the same time, numerous laymen tried to live literally the injunction of Christ to give up all worldly possessions and follow him, and they lamented the fact that many bishops, priests and monks were sycophants of the wealthy and interested only in accumulating vast sums of money. Unfortunately, some of the very persons who attempted to live an evangelical poverty, in the face of the greed and luxury of ecclesiastics, often went to excess in their fervor and ended up in heresy.

> Wherever the normal pattern of communities in the Church persisted – dioceses, parishes, monasteries, chapters, confraternities – it seems undeniable that orthodoxy was not seriously threatened. On the other hand, wherever the faithful were seeking to escape from it, they were in danger of losing their spiritual balance and ultimately their orthodoxy. People often tended towards a "private interpretation" of the Gospel. This explains why Western Christianity, when confronted by poverty or, possibly, by the Gospel and its ideal of absolute nakedness, presents a complex picture. On the one hand there were the solid religious organizations; they remained perfectly orthodox, and those of the faithful who did not belong to them were very ready to accuse them of betraying the Gospel. On the other hand, there was a swarm of small groups who wished, for various reasons, to practice the Gospel in all its purity but who easily foundered in heresy. Their spirit was not altogether sound, and they were much in the limelight, as can be seen from references to them in contemporary documents.[9]

Also closely linked to the imitation of Christ was an increasing devotion to the Blessed Sacrament. Until the eighth century Christians firmly believed that the Mass was a continuation of the Last Supper and that Christ was truly present on the altar. But then, theologians such as Paschasius Radbertus, Erigena, Ratramnus of Corbie, and Florus of Lyons began to discuss the Eucharist in order to increase the fervor of the faithful. Eventually the theologizing on the Eucharist led to controversy, in the midst of which Berenguer of Tours denied the real presence of Christ in the Blessed Sacrament. The expression "transsubstantiation" seems to have been introduced into the theology of the Eucharist at this time, perhaps by Bishop Hildebert of Tours (+ 1133). After a prolonged polemic, the Fourth Lateran Council officially settled the controversy and also made particular regulations concerning the Mass and Communion.

During this period a number of changes were introduced regarding the Eucharist. One of the most notable was the elevation of the Host after the consecration of the Mass.[10] It was only later that the chalice was also elevated, but still covered with the pall. Very quickly, however, the authentic veneration of the real presence of Christ was mixed with practices that were almost superstitious. The canon of the Mass was still a period of silence, recollection and mystery, in order to foster the greatest possible reverence.

The reception of Communion was infrequent in spite of the great devotion of the people. As a result, the Fourth Lateran Council commanded that Catholics must receive Communion at least once a year, during the Easter season.[11] One of the reasons why the people received Communion so seldom was their extreme respect for the Eucharist; they felt obliged to go to confession before Communion even when there was no need to do so. Thus, confessions "of devotion" became more and more common.

The reservation of the Eucharist in the tabernacle became standard practice, and in 1246 the first diocesan feast in honor of Corpus Christi was celebrated. Later it was extended and ultimately made a universal feast by Pope Urban IV. The Pope had hesitated about the promulgation until the clergy and faithful of Orvieto brought to him in solemn procession a corporal that was stained red with the Precious Blood that had flowed from a consecrated Host; this was July 19, 1264.

Together with devotion to Christ and veneration of the Blessed Sacrament, the faithful of this period had a filial love for Mary, and a veneration for the saints and the angels. Marian devotion was promulgated particularly in the monasteries (the Cistercians were called the Brothers of holy Mary). In feudal times the title of our Lady, Notre Dame, Madonna, was natural. Known prayers and hymns in the twelfth century were *Salve Regina*; *Ave, Maris Stella*;

Alma Redemptoris and, of course, the *Ave Maria*. However at this time the *Ave Maria* consisted only in the archangel's salutation; the name "Jesus" was added in the fifteenth century. There was also the practice of reciting fifty or even 150 *Ave Maria*'s, but the rosary as we know it did not come into popular use until later. The *Angelus* was recited only at the ringing of the bell in the evening.

As regards the saints, the various guilds placed themselves under saintly protectors and a saint's name was bestowed on a child at baptism. Following upon this devotion was the preservation of saints' relics and the construction of special shrines for their burial. James of Voragine composed the famous book, *The Golden Legend*, lives of the saints, as did James de Vitry, Caesarius, and Thomas of Cantimpré. It should be noted, however, that in the beginning the veneration of the saints was a popular action. Many of the ancient saints have never been officially recognized as such by the Holy See. In order to correct abuses, Pope Alexander II reserved this prerogative of canonization to the Holy See, as had been urged by Pope Gregory IX in 1234. The Fourth Lateran Council insisted that all relics must be authenticated by the Holy See.[12]

MILITARY ORDERS

St. Bernard not only preached the Second Crusade in the name of Pope Eugene III in 1145, but he was also closely related to the emergence of a new religious institute in the Church, that of the soldier-monk. In feudal Christianity there had always been a military concept of the members of the kingdom of God, the Church, whose ruler was Christ the King. But now St. Bernard greets with enthusiasm "a new kind of militia" that has come forth in the Holy Land and has as its object to expel the Muslims from the holy places.[13]

The first of the military orders, the Knights Templar, was founded in the precincts of the Temple at Jerusalem around 1118 and was to some extent affiliated with the Canons of the Holy Sepulcher. Its mission was to defend the Christians in the city of Jerusalem, even by force of arms. The Knights Templar observed poverty, chastity and obedience and therefore they were recognized as religious. Their rule was based on that of canons regular, the Rule of St. Benedict and the Cistercian observances. Consequently, they assisted at the Divine Office, they were obliged to fast and abstinence, and they were to dress simply, in conformity with their military life.

At the same time the Knights of Malta were also founded in

Jerusalem and, like the Templars, they were attached in some way to the canons regular, although their mission was to care for the hospital of St. John the Baptist. They followed the Rule of St. Augustine and members were drawn from clerics and laymen. They observed the evangelical counsels of poverty, chastity and obedience and lived in community.

In a short time these two groups spread throughout Europe and were especially effective in helping to reconquer Spain from the Moors. In Spain another group was formed, known as the Knights of Santiago de Compostela, although they were not religious and therefore did not have to observe the three evangelical counsels. Their whole purpose was to defend the Church and expel the Moors from the Iberian Peninsula. Other organizations affiliated to Cistercian monasteries in Spain were the Orders of Calatrava, Alcántara and Avis.

The problem arises of how to reconcile Christians – indeed men vowed to the evangelical counsels – with dedication to war and the necessary killing of the enemy. Yet even St. Bernard insisted that when they are fighting for the Lord, they are to fear neither the danger of being killed nor the sin of killing an enemy. Yet the crusaders were never considered martyrs, for they were, as St. Peter the Hermit told them, "monks as regards their virtues, but soldiers in their actions."[14]

ST. NORBERT AND PRÉMONTRÉ

Although the canons regular did not exert any notable influence on the life of the Church until the twelfth century, the origins of canonical life can be traced back to St. Augustine. Thus, in a letter addressed to a community of canons in Bavaria, Pope Urban II wrote:

> We give thanks to God that you have resolved to renew among yourselves the admirable life of the holy fathers of the Church. . . . This is the way of life that was instituted by Pope Urban the Martyr, which Augustine organized by his rules, which Jerome molded by his letters, which Gregory commissioned Augustine, the bishop of the English to institute.[15]

Although, as Vicaire points out, the origin of canons "is a cloudy part of history,"[16] there is no doubt that Pope Urban II considered the life of the canons to be as authentically rooted in primitive Christianity, as was the monastic life. Bishop Eusebius of Vercelli (+307) and St. Augustine (+430) introduced the common life among their clergy; in 535 the Council of Clermont defined canons as priests or deacons assigned to a church; Bishop Chrodegang of Metz drew up a rule for his clergy (c. 755) which was based on the Rule of St. Benedict; and the Synod of Aix-la-Chapelle (816–817) promulgated the new *Regula Canonicorum* requiring common life and obedience to a superior but allowing possession of goods. Nevertheless, the canons regular as we know them today did not come into existence until the second half of the eleventh century. At that time the Rule of St. Augustine became the basis for the life of the canons regular and they themselves were recognized as religious but distinct from monks. The diocesan-priest canons continued to exist but they abandoned community life and retained the function of chanting the Divine Office in the cathedral.

In 1059 the Synod of Rome imposed the common life on all clerics who were ordained for a specific church or cathedral, and during the eleventh century many cathedral chapters and collegiate chapters adopted the Rule of St. Augustine. The canons who did so became *canonici regulares* instead of *canonici saeculares* (diocesan-priest canons) because they also pronounced the religous vows of poverty, chastity and obedience. While some chapters remained autonomous, others in due time federated into congregations.[17]

From the beginning the *vita canonica* offered diocesan priests, who are ordained for the ministry, the opportunity to live a community life in poverty. The first question that comes to mind is why diocesan priests should be encouraged to embrace this form of life. In the mind of St. Augustine the reason was for the attainment of the perfection of charity, since he states early in his Rule: "You should wish to live in your house in unanimity, having only one heart and one soul in God, since it is for this that you have come together." Between the ninth and eleventh centuries the *vita canonica* was proposed and then imposed on diocesan priests as a means of reform, to protect them against avarice and lust.[18] The Synod of Rome (1059) proposed the *vita canonica*, a common life in poverty, as a means to return to the apostolic life of the primitive Christians.[19] Thus, St. Peter Damian stated: "It is indeed clear and evident that the rule of the canons is modeled on the norms of the life of the apostles, and that any canonical community which keeps its discipline with exactitude imitates the tender infancy of the Church still at the breast."[20]

It is readily understandable how the emphasis on the "monastic" aspects of the canonical life led to the emergence of the canons regular, a new form of religious life in which the ministry of souls (not generally the work of monks) became one of the purposes of religious life in non-contemplative religious institutes. The principal distinction between the canons regular and the monks is that the former dedicate themselves to the apostolate.[21] Anselm of Havelberg (+ 1158), in his *Apologetic Epistle*, showed that the active life and the contemplative life – later referred to as the "mixed life" – can be perfectly blended in the life of the canons. Vicaire points out several effects of this development which were of special importance in the theology of Christian spirituality:

> The apostolic ideal is thus clearly recalled to the ministry. Once again the new orientation results from the needs of the times. The Gregorian movement, which was an effort to reform the Church by the reform of the clergy, was at the same time the inception of a reformation designed to encompass the whole of Christian society. . . . Putting an end to the equation between perfection and the flight from the world, it sought, on the contrary, to situate this Christian perfection, especially for the clergy, in a return to the world for the purpose of conquering it in order to Christianize it. . . . The Gregorian movement very explicitly sought to call all Christians to the life of sanctity while holding their proper places. . . .
>
> This courageous and original movement affected Christianity . . . by making clear that holiness did not belong only to a small elite which consecrated itself to the life of perfection by fleeing from the world, but that it belongs to all those, whatever their work may be, who bear the name of Christian and live well the role in society that belongs to them. This evolution . . . reacted on the ideal of the *vita apostolica*, which was no longer ordered only to developing virtue in the clergy and to freeing them from temporal ambitions by poverty, but at the same time to preparing them for their ministry in Christianity, as formerly it had prepared the apostles for their ministry of evangelization.[22]

It would not be accurate, however, to conclude that after the emergence of the canons regular as religious institutes, dedication to the ministry and the care of souls superseded in every case the monastic elements of the *vita canonica*. Rather, as Raimbaud of Liége stated,[23] there were two types of canons regular: those who were in contact with the people, and those who were more separated from the world. For our purposes it will suffice to show the effects of this divergence in the two most famous canonical orders: the Premonstratensians and the Victorines.[24]

St. Norbert was originally a *canonicus saecularis* of the diocese of Cologne and in 1115 he retired into solitude to lead a life of prayer and austerity. Shortly thereafter he became a hermit-preacher and travelled from place to place, denouncing the laxity of morals among the clergy and laity. At the request of the bishop of Laon, Norbert gathered a group of priests and laity at Prémontré, where they dedicated themselves to a life of prayer, austerity and manual labor. Preaching was not abandoned, but it was not the primary purpose of the foundation. Named archbishop of Magdeburg in 1126, Norbert assigned to his followers the task of reforming the diocese and doing missionary work in northern Germany. Norbert died in 1134 but even before his death the Premonstratensian communities in France and England tended toward a more contemplative type of life, although they never abandoned the ideal of St. Norbert, which was to combine the life of the cloister with the clerical ministry.[25]

By 1134 the apostolate was for all practical purposes dropped from the statutes of the Premonstratensians and they proposed as a goal the attainment of priestly holiness by monastic asceticism.[26] Perhaps the most outstanding figure of the monastic and contemplative elements in Premonstratensian life was Adam of Dryburgh, who transferred to the Carthusians in 1189.[27]

Attempting as he did to establish a religious order that would combine the monastic observances with the priestly ministry, St. Norbert was a forerunner of the mendicant orders of the thirteenth century. This is especially true as regards the Norbertine orientation to the apostolate and the strict observance of poverty, bordering on indigence. Nevertheless, as regards the religious exercises and the mode of life within the abbeys, the Norbertines preserved a more monastic milieu than did the mendicants: insistence of solitude within the framework of community life, daily recitation of the Office of the Blessed Virgin (in addition to the Divine Office), alternation of liturgical prayer with *lectio divina* and private mental prayer, and dedication to manual or intellectual labor. The Rule of St. Augustine was followed as literally as possible, but the *Statutes of Prémontré*, which greatly resemble those of the Cistercians, gave the Premonstratensians rather more of a Benedictine monasticism than Augustinian *vita canonica*.[28] But eventually the Premonstratensians tipped the balance in favor of the apostolate and priestly ministry.

With regard to [the life of the cloister], there was no great difference between the life of the Premonstratensians and that of the monks; there was the same emphasis on charity in the common life, the same austerities, the same love of that heavenly life of which the life of the cloister is an anticipation, the conception of prayer in which the celebration of the liturgy alternated with the *lectio divina*, meditation and pure prayer; the same guarded attitude towards too intellectual a knowledge, to which is to be preferred an understanding brought about by love, a "tasting," an "experience," and finally the same devotion to the Mother of God, and the same bringing of the new sensibility to bear on the contemplation of the mysteries of our salvation. The originality of the order lies therefore more in the balance between the spirituality of the cloister and the *cura animarun*; in its early days the latter was not as prominent everywhere, but it was always an essential part of the ideal of Prémontré, and gradually became more explicit. In their pastoral trend, as in giving the first place to poverty, the Premonstratensians were a foreshadowing of the mendicant orders of the thirteenth century. They showed that the crisis in monasticism had borne fruit in that it encouraged the appearance in the Church of more and differing states of life; it was not only that there were various ways of fulfilling the ideal of the Gospel; now the differences were recognized and justified on doctrinal grounds, a twofold progress.[29]

CANONS OF ST. VICTOR

With the Canons of St. Victor the trend was in a different direction from that of the Premonstratensians. Although they remained in the monastic tradition and followed the Rule of St. Augustine, the Victorines concentrated their efforts to a large extent on intellectual pursuits, thus contributing to the development of Scholasticism. All of this had its beginning with William of Champeaux (+ 1122), professor at the school of Notre Dame in Paris, who in 1108 retired to a hermitage near Paris with some disciples after a controversy with his student Abelard. In 1113 the group adopted the Rule of St. Augustine and soon the monastery of St. Victor became an outstanding theological center and enjoyed tremendous growth as a congregation of canons regular. William was named bishop of Châlons-sur-Marne and as such he consecrated St. Bernard abbot in 1121.

Following the practico-speculative method of St. Augustine, the School of St. Victor gained great renown, especially through its two greatest luminaries: Hugh of St. Victor and Richard of St. Victor. There were other authors also and they deserve at least a brief mention. Adam of St. Victor (+ 1192) is the poet of the School and author of liturgical *Sequences*; Achard (+ 1171) wrote treatises on the Trinity and Christology; Walter (+ 1180) composed sermons on Jesus and Mary; Godfrey (+ 1194) left a humanistic work called, *Fons philosophiae*, written in poetic form; and Thomas of St. Victor, known as Thomas Gallus (+ 1246), later the founder and abbot of the monastery of St. Andrew at Vercelli, wrote scriptural commentaries and, most important, a commentary and synthesis of the works of the pseudo-Dionysius. Thomas had a strong influence on the early Franciscans: Alexander of Hales, St. Bonaventure, Adam of Marisco, and was a personal friend of St. Anthony of Padua.[30] He is credited with promoting the trend toward "Dionysian" spirituality as opposed to speculative spiritual theology.

Hugh of St. Victor (1097–1141) has been called *"alter Augustinus"* and Villoslada does not hesitate to call him the most outstanding theologian of the entire twelfth century.[31] He is acclaimed by Bihlmeyer as "the most brilliant theologian of the twelfth century"[32] and Grabmann says that Hugh composed the first complete synthesis of dogmatic theology in the period of high Scholasticism.[33] His deep and lengthy study of the works of St. Augustine enabled him to present an Augustinian synthesis that had never before been accomplished.

Hugh's major work is *On the Sacraments of the Christian Faith*, which was an introduction to the understanding of Scripture. It could more properly be entitled "On the Mysteries of the Christian Faith" because Hugh used the word "sacrament" to designate all the holy things treated in Scripture. In the dialogue *On the Sacraments of the Natural Law and the Written Law* he attempted to provide a summary of the Christian faith. His teaching on the spiritual life is found in his treatises on meditation, on the method of prayer, in praise of charity, on the formation of novices, in his commentary on the *Celestial Hierarchy* of the pseudo-Dionysius and his homilies on *Ecclesiastes*.[34] Another work, *De contemplatione et ejus speciebus* is attributed to Hugh but not with certitude.

According to Hugh, although original sin has left disastrous effects, even in his sinful state man still retains a "memory" of God. This serves as a point of departure so that man can return to God, and the path of this return is knowledge and virtue. The spiritual life, therefore, is at once specularive and practical, and its perfection bestows that wisdom which is the unifying principle of the spiritual life.

The three stages of the spiritual life on the speculative level are symbolic knowledge, rational knowledge and mystical knowledge. As Augustine had said, the whole world is a book, but it does not suffice to admire the letters; one must be able to read. Or, following Plato, the world is a mirror in which are reflected the divine ideas, and this constitutes the *symbolic knowledge* that one finds, for example, in Scripture. As to the *rational knowledge*, one ascends to the invisible by means of the visible, and this calls for reflection or meditation. Departing from an awareness of his dissimilarity to God, man can attain to the divine likeness. But this reflection must not be pure speculation; it must be an understanding, an *intus legere*, that stimulates effective love and leads at last to contemplation, which is *mystical knowledge*. Thus, faithful to the method of the Fathers and to the monastic tradition, Hugh sees theology as a practico-speculative science that uses both reason and faith to lead one to mysticism.

In a terminology reminiscent of Guigo I, Hugh describes five steps in prayer that lead to the loving contemplation or *scientia amorosa*, which is the perfection of prayer: reading, meditation, prayer, growth in love and finally contemplation. Then, using an example that we find later in the works of St. John of the Cross, Hugh compares the practice of meditation to the difficulty involved in igniting green wood.

> In meditation there is a kind of struggle between ignorance and knowledge. The light of truth is still obscured by the smoke of error, like fire which catches green wood with difficulty, but when fanned by a strong wind, flares up and begins to blaze in the midst of volumes of black smoke. Little by little the burning increases, the moisture of the wood is absorbed, the smoke disappears, and the flame, with a sudden burst, spreads, crackling and conquering, to the whole log. . . .
>
> Our carnal heart is like green wood; it is still soaked with the moisture of concupiscence. If it receive some spark of the fear of God or of divine love, the smoke of evil desires and rebellious passions first of all rises. Then the soul becomes strengthened, the flame of love becomes more ardent and more bright, and soon the smoke of passion disappears, and the mind, thus purified, is lifted up to the contemplation of truth. Finally, when by constant contemplation the heart has become penetrated by truth, . . . and when it has become transformed into the fire of divine love, it feels neither distress nor agitation any more. It has found tranquillity and peace.
>
> Thus, in the beginning, when, in the midst of dangerous temptations, the soul seeks enlightenment in meditation, there is smoke and flame. Afterwards, when it is purified and begins to contemplate the truth, there is flame without smoke. Then, when it has fully found the truth and charity is perfected within it, it has no longer anything to seek; it rests sweetly in the tranquillity and in the fire of divine love. It is the fire without either smoke or flame.[35]

Hugh distinguishes contemplation from reading, reflection and meditation by saying that it is a penetration of the intellect that comprehends all things in one clear vision. It is the joy of possessing in one glance a great number of truths, as a result of which the soul enjoys great peace and tranquillity. Even natural truths and philosophy itself can provide a type of contemplation but it is much inferior to that *sapientia superior* which constitutes divine theology. Indeed, Hugh seems to hold for the possibility of an immediate vision of God in this life at the height of contemplation, if the work *De contemplatione et ejus speciebus* can rightly be attributed to him.[36]

Richard of St. Victor (+ 1173), born in Scotland, was a disciple of Hugh but he surpasses his teacher as an original thinker. Cayré calls Richard the greatest theoretical teacher of mysticism in the Middle Ages.[37] Nevertheless, Richard owes a great deal to Hugh as well as to Bede the Venerable, Isidore of Seville, St. Gregory the Great and, logically, St. Augustine. His most famous theological work is *De Trinitate*, in which, unlike St. Augustine, he classifies the procession of the second Person from the Father as a procession of love rather than an intellectual generation.[38] In mystical theology, his field of specialization, Richard composed three treatises of special importance: *Benjamin minor* (*Liber de praeparatione animi ad contemplationem*), *Benjamin major* (*De gratia contemplationis*), and *De Quatuor gradibus violentiae amoris*.[39]

The *Benjamin major* is divided into five parts. The first three sections treat of reflection (*cogitatio*) on sensate objects; meditation on realities that are within us; and contemplation, which gives one an experience of divine realities. In the last two parts he discusses the various objects of contemplation and the modes of contemplation.

For Richard the goal of Christian perfection is contemplation, which presupposes a period of preparation through ascetical practices and the cultivation of virtue, starting with self-knowledge and prudence. Like Hugh, he admits of a contemplation which is purely natural and acquired, for he defines contemplation as "the free, more penetrating gaze of a mind, suspended with wonder concerning manifestations of wisdom";[40] and again as "a penetrating and free gaze of a soul extended everywhere in perceiving things."[41] He then proceeds to analyze and classify contemplation by reason of its objects and by reason of its origin or cause.

Three kinds of objects are proposed for contemplation: corporeal objects, spiritual creatures and the divine reality of God himself. In the first and lowest stage of contemplation one considers the material things of the external world which are perceptible through the senses; in the second stage a person perceives the order and interrelationship of material things in the universe; in the third stage one passes beyond the purely sensible to an awareness of the immaterial; and in the fourth stage he contemplates his own soul and also the angelic spirits. Mystical contemplation begins in the fifth stage, when "we come to know, through divine revelation, truths which no human reason can fully understand and no reasoning can enable us to discover with certainty. Such are the teachings of divine Scripture on the nature of God and the simplicity of his essence."[42] But in the sixth stage the truth contemplated not only surpasses reason, but seems to be repugnant to reason, such as the mystery of the Trinity.[43] For this last degree of contemplation, says Richard, the human mind must become in a manner angelic and the heart must be completely purified.

As regards the origin of the various degrees of contemplation, Richard taught that contemplation is purely human if it consists simply in the use of one's natural faculties; it is a mixture of human and divine if it is a consideration of spiritual matters under the impetus of God's grace; it is completely divine if it is the exclusive effect of a grace that is so powerful that it produces a kind of ecstasy or suspension in which the soul operates under the higher power of grace. For Richard the fifth and sixth degrees of contemplation are totally divine; they are the result of a special grace, and therefore not all souls attain to them.[44] Yet all souls should cultivate a desire for a special grace of divine contemplation and all Christians should prepare themselves as best they can to receive this gift from God.[45]

SCHOLASTICISM

The intense intellectual activity of the Victorines was symptomatic of the new trends and the changes taking place in the twelfth century. As the religious life had adapted itself to contemporary needs with the emergence of the canons regular, so also influential centers of learning, of which the Abbey of St. Victor was but one example, were springing up outside the monastic setting. And a great deal more was involved than the founding of schools and universities; there was a definite break with the traditional categories and methods and the introduction of new sources of research provided by the translations of Greek, Arabian and Jewish authors.

Theology henceforward claimed to be a science, and according to the Aristotelian ideal took on a speculative and even deductive character. Like all sciences, it was disinterested; it was no longer concerned with nourishing the spiritual life, as the monastic theologians would have it do. The Scriptures were read, studied and taught with the view of the mind rather than the heart acquiring knowledge, and theological activity assumed a more purely intellectual character, less contemplative, less dependent on the atmosphere created by the liturgy. The study of the Bible had markedly a twofold aim: theological interpretation and literal exegesis; the thirteenth century was to reap the fruit of these efforts.[46]

The focal point of theological ferment was Paris, although there were famous schools at Laon, Chartres, Rheims, Canterbury and Toledo. But Paris was the most influential because of illustrious professors such as Peter Abelard, Gilbert de la Porrée, Alan of Lille, and Peter Lombard.[47] Men of this calibre attracted students from every nation. Later on, other universities would rival the schools of Paris, for example, Padua, Naples, Palermo and Bologna in Italy; Oxford and Cambridge in England; Salamanca and Alcalá in Spain; Coimbra in Portugal.

As early as the ninth century John Scotus Erigena (+ 870) had tried to introduce Platonic philosophy into the traditional study of sacred doctrine, but he was condemned for his efforts. Theology continued to be a study of Scripture interpreted according to the Fathers of the Church. In the eleventh century, however, two factors contributed greatly to the rise of Scholasticism: the concordances of Patristic texts on theological questions and the bitter dispute concerning the respective roles of faith and reason, revelation and speculation, theology and philosophy.[48] It was immediately evident from the compilation of Patristic teaching that many of the texts were incompatible with one another, if not contradictory. It was also evident that human reason must have some role to play in the understanding and development of the truths of faith. Congar summarizes the problem as follows:

> The eleventh century ... is plagued by a fight between dialecticians and antidialecticians. ... The radical question is: Can Christian doctrines be understood in terms of reason's categories? If not, what status should be given to human reason, which is God's creation and man's honor? ... If, on the other hand, the answer is "yes," does this not make Christian realities merely a matter of general laws which the human reason can attain, and, in that case, where is the mystery, where is the supreme, unique, and sovereign character of Christian realities?
>
> This, then, is the stake at issue between the dialecticians and the antidialecticians. Some among these latter take an extreme position. They strongly assert with St. Peter Damian that reason has no teaching authority in Christianity. ... They consider any encroachment of dialec-

tics on the sacred text to be a sacrilege. They affirm very forcefully the transcendence, the character of unique truth of the Christian faith, which has been given us not for the purpose of fashioning it into a science but as a mode of living in penance and avoidance of the world. This is the ascetico-monastic solution which we will soon find again in St. Bernard and later in Pascal. It is an attitude inalienably Christian.

But another attitude is still possible. In fact there is one which later the Church will strongly favor, namely, that all the data are in a hierarchical order. This is what gripped a man like Lanfranc, Bérenger's adversary and the founder of that Abbey du Bec where St. Anselm's important ideas will soon flourish.[49]

St. Anselm (1033–1109) is considered the "Father of Scholasticism." Taking Plato and St. Augustine as his guides, he sought to provide a rational basis for that which is believed. Yet, he never fell into the extreme of Rationalism, since for him faith is always the touchstone of theology. His two basic principles greatly helped to pacify the contenders in the dispute concerning the role of human reason *vis-à-vis* revealed truths: *Fides quaerens intellectum* and *Neque enim quaero intelligere ut credam, sed credo ut intelligam*.[50] As a matter of fact, St. Anselm insisted that without faith, a person cannot possibly understand the revealed truths (*Qui non crediderit, non intelliget*).[51] The following statements, one by St. Anselm and the second by Almer, a disciple, reveal Anselm's understanding of the relationship between faith and reason:

> No Christian should openly discuss why the Catholic Church fully believes and orally confesses a certain doctrine to be true. However, while simply believing and heartily living according to it, he may patiently seek its rational basis. If he understands it, let him give thanks to God. If not, it is stupid to protest. Let him bow his head in submission.[52]
>
> Although we believe whatever the Scriptures direct us to believe (about Christ) ..., it is, nevertheless, sweeter for us if in some manner we come to grasp by reason that the very object of our faith must be so and cannot be other than our faith teaches us. God is the supreme *ratio* and in him resides the certain source of all rational argumentation.[53]

St. Anselm succeeded in combating the excesses of certain dialecticians and at the same time he helped to calm the fears of the inflexible traditionalists. It was Peter Lombard (+ 1160), however, who succeeded in introducing the new methods of theological investigation: the use of Aristotle's philosophy and the response to theological questions by a survey of the opinions (*sententiae*) of theologians and the Fathers of the Church. Peter Lombard's most famous work was entitled *The Four Books of the Sentences* and he became known as the "Master of the Sentences." For several centuries the *Sentences* of Peter Lombard were the basic text for the study of theology.[54]

Inevitably this new Scholastic system substituted questions and answers for a study of the biblical and patristic sources of theology; deductive reasoning gradually replaced *lectio divina*, except in the traditional monasteries. There is no doubt that many theologians saw themselves simply as carrying into effect the statement of St. Augustine: *"Desideravi intellectu videre quod credidi."* It is also true that many of the "new theologians" would maintain, at least theoretically, that speculative theology terminates and is perfected in contemplation. The fact is, however, that asceticism and mysticism were more and more isolated as dogmatic and moral theology became more and more rational. To make matters worse, St. Bernard, William of St. Thierry, Hugh of St. Victor and Robert Grosseteste had to protest strongly against Abelard's excessive dialectic and proclaim the supremacy of faith over all rational knowledge of the truths of revelation. Vandenbroucke sums up the situation in this way:

> The scholastic method of theological research which was born in this century was, in fact, a new one. The Master of the Sentences became the chief authority, or at least the necessary starting point. Hence came the formidable threat, a danger all too real, that the actual reading of the Bible and the Fathers would be forgotten or relegated to a lower level: a foreshadowing of the divorce between theology (now definitely a science) and mysticism, or at least the spiritual life. The province of the latter would then be purely religious sentiment which, at this time, had still a penetrating insight and "taste" of the object of faith; but it was to become a value in itself even to the point of rejecting the intellectual foundations on which it had formerly rested. Soon it would consist in an "unknowing" with a Dionysian flavor, and this would be laid down in principle as a necessary condition for the spiritual ascent.[55]

ST. DOMINIC AND THE FRIARS PREACHERS

Religious life continued to evolve in the thirteenth century as it had in the twelfth, and the evolution necessarily involved the retention of some traditional elements as well as the introduction of original creations. In fact, the variety of new forms of religious life reached such a point that the Lateran Council in 1215 and the

Council of Lyons in 1274 prohibited the creation of new religious institutes henceforth.

Nevertheless, two new orders came into existence in the thirteenth century: the Franciscans and the Dominicans. As mendicant orders they both emphasized a strict observance of poverty; as apostolic orders, they were dedicated to the ministry of preaching. Yet there was a noticeable continuity between the newly founded mendicant orders and the older forms of monasticism and the life of the canons regular. At the risk of oversimplifying, we may say that the Franciscans adapted Benedictine monasticism to new needs while the Dominicans adapted the monastic observances of the Premonstratensians to the assiduous study of sacred truth, which characterized the Canons of St. Victor.

The mendicant orders, however, were not simply a development of monasticism; much more than that, they were a response to vital needs in the Church: the need to return to the Christian life of the Gospel (*vita apostolica*); the need to reform religious life, especially in the area of poverty; the need to extirpate the heresies of the time; the need to raise the level of the diocesan clergy; the need to preach the Gospel and administer the sacraments to the faithful. This was especially true of the Dominicans, who were consciously and explicitly designed to meet the needs of the times and to foster the "new" theology, Scholasticism. The Franciscans, as we shall see, were more in the tradition of the old monasticism and sought to return to a life of simplicity and poverty.

St Dominic Guzmán, born at Caleruega, Spain, in 1170 or 1171, was subprior of the Augustinian canons of the cathedral chapter at Osma. As a result of his travels with his bishop, Diego de Acevedo, he came face to face with the Albigensian heresy that was ravaging the Church in southern France. When they learned of the failure of the legates to make any progress in the conversion of the French heretics, Bishop Diego made a drastic recommendation. They should dismiss their retinue and, travelling on foot as mendicants, become itinerant preachers, as the apostles were.

In the autumn of 1206 Dominic founded the first cloister of Dominican nuns at Prouille; towards the end of 1207 Bishop Diego died at Osma, where he had returned to recruit more preachers. The work of preaching did not end with the death of Bishop Diego, but during the Albigensian Crusade under Simon Montfort, from 1209 to 1213, Dominic continued the work almost alone, with the approval of Pope Innocent III and the Council of Avignon (1209). By 1214 a group of associates had joined Dominic and in June, 1215,

Bishop Fulk of Toulouse issued a document in which he declared: "We, Fulk, ... institute Brother Dominic and his associates as preachers in our diocese. ... They propose to travel on foot and to preach the word of the Gospel in evangelical poverty as religious."[56] The next step was to obtain the approval of the Holy See, and this was of special necessity in an age in which preaching was the prerogative of bishops. The opportunity presented itself when Dominic accompanied Bishop Fulk to Rome for the Lateran Council, which was convoked for November, 1215. According to Jordan of Saxony, Dominic desired confirmation on two points: the papal approval of an order dedicated to preaching and papal recognition of the revenues that had been granted to the community at Toulouse.[57]

Although Pope Innocent III was favorably inclined to the petition, he advised Dominic to return to Toulouse and consult with his companions regarding the adoption of a Rule.[58] Quite logically, the Rule chosen was that of St. Augustine, as Hinnebusch points out:

> The adoption was dictated by the specific purpose St. Dominic sought to achieve – the salvation of souls through preaching – an eminently clerical function. The Rule of St. Augustine was best suited for this purpose. During the preceding century it had become *par excellence* the Rule of canons, clerical religious. In its emphasis on personal poverty and fraternal charity, in its reference to the common life lived by the Christians of the apostolic age, in its author, it was an apostolic Rule. Its prescriptions were general enough to allow great flexibility; it would not stand in the way of particular constitutions designed to achieve the special end of the Order.[59]

In addition to the Rule of St. Augustine, the early Dominicans used the customs of the Premonstratensians as a source for their monastic observances, for which reason they were often called canons as well as mendicant friars. What was peculiar to the Dominican Order was added by the first Chapter of 1216 and the General Chapter of 1220: the salvation of souls through preaching as the primary end of the Order; the assiduous study of sacred truth to replace the monastic *lectio divina* and manual labor; great insistence on silence as an aid to study; brisk and succinct recitation of the choral Office lest the study of sacred truth be impeded; the use of dispensations for reasons of study and the apostolate as well as illness; election of superiors by the community or province; annual General Chapter of the entire Order; profession of obedience to the Master General; and strict personal and community poverty.

On December 22, 1216, the Order of Friars Preachers was confirmed by the papal bull, *Religiosam vitam*, signed by Pope Honorius III and eighteen cardinals. On January 21, 1217, the pope issued a second bull, *Gratiarum omnium*, in which he addressed Dominic and his companions as Friars Preachers and entrusted them with the mission of preaching. He called them "Christ's unconquered athletes, armed with the shield of faith and the helmet of salvation" and took them under his protection as his "special sons".[60]

From that time until his death in 1221, St. Dominic received numerous bulls from the Holy See, of which more than thirty have survived. The same theme is found in all of them: the Order of Preachers is approved and recommended by the Church for the ministry of preaching. St. Dominic himself left very little in writing, although we may presume that he carried on an extensive correspondence. The writings attributed to him are the *Book of Customs*, based on the *Institutiones* of the Premonstratensians; the *Constitutions* for the cloistered Dominican nuns of San Sisto in Rome; and a personal letter to the Dominican nuns at Madrid.

The Dominican friars were fully aware of the mission entrusted to them by Pope Honorius III. In the prologue of the primitive *Constitutions* we read that "the prelate shall have power to dispense the brethren in his priory when it shall seem expedient to him, especially in those things that are seen to impede study, preaching, or the good of souls, since it is known that our Order was especially founded from the beginning for preaching and the salvation of souls."[61]

"This text," says Hinnebusch, "is the keystone of the apostolic Order of Friars Preachers. The ultimate end of the Order, it states, is the salvation of souls; the specific end, preaching; the indispensable means, study. The power of dispensation will facilitate the attainment of these high purposes. All this is new, almost radical."[62] On the other hand, it may be interpreted as a return to the authentic "*vita apostolica*," and that is the way St. Thomas Aquinas would see it: "The apostolic life consists in this, that having abandoned everything, they should go throughout the world announcing and preaching the Gospel, as is made clear in Matthew 10:7–10."[63]

Preachers of the Gospel need to be fortified by sound doctrine, and for that reason the first General Chapter of the Order specified that in every priory there should be a professor. Quite logically, the assiduous study of sacred truth, which replaced the manual labor and *lectio divina* of monasticism, would in time produce outstanding theologians and would also extend the concept of Dominican preaching to include teaching and writing.

Dominican life was also contemplative, not in the monastic tradition, but in the canonical manner of the Victorines; that is to say, its contemplative aspect was manifested especially in the assiduous study of sacred truth and in the liturgical worship of God. However, even the contemplative occupation of study was directly ordered to the salvation of souls through preaching and teaching, and the liturgy, in turn, was streamlined with a view to the study that prepared the friars for their apostolate. Thus, the primitive Constitutions stated:

> Our study ought to tend principally, ardently, and with the highest endeavor to the end that we might be useful to the souls of our neighbors.[64]

> All the hours are to be said in church briefly and succinctly lest the brethren lose devotion and their study be in any way impeded.[65]

Because of the central role which the study of sacred truth plays in the Dominican life, the spirituality of the Friars Preachers is at once a doctrinal spirituality and an apostolic spirituality.[66] By the same token, the greatest contribution which the Dominicans have made to the Church through the centuries has been in the area of sacred doctrine, whether from the pulpit of the preacher, the platform of the teacher or the books of the writer. The assiduous study of sacred truth, so strictly enjoined on the friars by St. Dominic, provides the contemplative attitude from which the Friar Preacher gives to others the fruits of his contemplation. In this restricted sense we may say with Walgrave that the Dominican is a "contemplative apostle."[67]

ST. THOMAS AQUINAS

It is in this area also of the study of sacred truth that the Dominican Order flows into the stream of the history of spirituality, with its most brilliant son, St. Thomas Aquinas, as navigator. Born at Rocca Secca, Italy, in 1225, Thomas entered the Dominican Order in 1244 and until his death in 1274 he dedicated all his talents and efforts to incorporate the new Scholastic methodology into the traditional theological sources.[68] In an age in which a dangerous dualism was rampant between faith and reason, theology and philosophy, Thomas piloted sacred doctrine to safety between the threatening dangers of apostasy from the faith and rejection of human reason. As Sertillanges says:

> So far had things gone that the relation between faith and reason was by now an insoluble question. St. Anselm and others had found it a stumbling block. . . . At the moment when St. Thomas' intellectual life began, the question was not absolutely decided. Albert the Great had undertaken "to render the works of Aristotle intelligible to the Latins". . . . Despite his truly great personal fame, he was not the man to direct his age and lead the Church to safety.
> Abelard, a few decades before, had prepared the way. He was a dialectician of repute, fully aware of the need of providing the faith with rational weapons, by the introduction of philosophy. He became the pioneer of the new reform, but did it more harm than good in the long run. . . . The real leader was yet to come. . . . St. Thomas was providentially raised to fill this role, and he succeeded in spite of all opposition.[69]

What was actually involved in the clash between traditional Augustinian theology and Aristotelian scientific philosophy has been succinctly described by Congar:

> It cannot be denied that Albert the Great and Thomas Aquinas appeared as innovators in the thirteenth century. What set them apart was the fact that they had a philosophy, that is, a rational system of the world, which in its order was consistent and self-sufficient. . . .
> What then did Albert and Thomas Aquinas do? What was the point of the dispute which arose between them and the Augustinians?[70] When Bonaventure, Kilwardby, Peckham, and others opposed Albert the Great and St. Thomas what did they want and why did they act? . . . On the one hand, these opponents were far from rejecting philosophy. They were philosophers as enthusiastically as those they fought. On the other hand, it is clear that neither Thomas nor Albert refused to subordinate philosophy to theology. The formula *ancilla theologiae* (handmaid of theology) was common to the two schools. And still there were two schools. Why?
> Following Augustine, the Augustinians considered all things in their relation to the last goal. A purely speculative knowledge of things had no interest for the Christian. . . . Truly to know things was to refer them to God by charity. So, in the Augustinian perspective, things will be considered not in their pure essence, but in their reference to the last goal, . . . in the use man made of them in his return to God. . . . Again, if "to know things is to determine the intention of their first agent, who is God," then things were to be considered in their relation to the will of God, who made them as he wanted and used them how he willed. . . .
> In the Augustinian school, true knowledge of spiritual things is also

love and union. Moreover, the truth of the true knowledge does not come from experience and sensible cognition, ... but from a direct reception of light coming from the spiritual world, that is, from God. ... Now, this is very important for the notion of theology, for the distinction between philosophy and theology and for the use of "natural" knowledge in a sacred science. ...

Finally, if we consider the utilization of sciences and philosophy in theology, we see that in the Augustinian school ... these have validity or meaning only in their relation to God. ...

For Albert the Great and St. Thomas the sciences represent a genuine knowledge of the world and of the nature of things. ... Therefore, the sciences in their order have a veritable autonomy of object and method, just as in their order they convey their own truth. ...

Now we understand better why Albert and St. Thomas followed the thought of Aristotle. They were looking not only for a master of reasoning but a master in the knowledge of the nature of things, of the world and of man himself. Certainly St. Thomas was not ignorant any more than St. Bonaventure that all things must be referred to God. But alongside that reference to God in the order of use or exercise, he recognized an unconditioned bounty to the speculative intellect in the nature of specification of things, which was a work of God's wisdom. ...

Does it not seem probable that such confidence in reason may endanger the unique, original, and transcendent character of Christian realities? ... Against the naturalism of the Aristotelians this will always be the fear and the objection of the Augustinians, especially of St. Bernard, St. Bonaventure, Pascal, and even Luther. ...

In our opinion St. Thomas really surmounted the danger we have just pointed out. He held that it was not Aristotle but the datum of faith which had the commanding position. Moreover, long before Luther he noted that with regard to the sacred doctrine an undue amount of attention can be given to philosophy. First, and obviously, if the philosophy is false. Secondly, if faith and its revelations are subjected to a philosophical measurement, whereas it is philosophy which should submit itself to the measurements of faith. ...

The theological thought of St. Thomas ... was based essentially on the Bible and tradition. We can never stress too much the fact that in those days theological teaching was profoundly biblical. The ordinary lecture of the master was a commentary on Sacred Scripture. This is why the scriptural commentaries on St. Thomas represent his ordinary teaching as a master.[71]

Since the theology of the spiritual life had not yet emerged as a branch of theology, to be studied as a separate entity, so to speak, we do not find in the works of Aquinas, any more than in the works of

Augustine, a separate treatise on spirituality.[72] For the early Scholastics theology was an eminently unified science which treated of God and of all things in relation to God. Thus, for Aquinas all of moral theology is seen as man's return to God and all human acts receive their moral qualifications ultimately and objectively by reason of their relation to the ultimate end, God. In dogmatic theology all questions are investigated in a spirit of faith which listens to the God who speaks through revelation. In the theology of the spiritual life, Aquinas bases everything and judges everything by that love which is charity, which is perfected as wisdom, and is incarnated in Christ through the Holy Spirit.

Christian perfection for St. Thomas Aquinas is a supernatural perfection and since man is by nature far removed from the supernatural order of the divine, the essential principle of his spiritual life is God's gift of grace, which elevates man to the supernatural order. Grace, however, respects man's nature in the sense that it perfects it at the same time that it works through it. The faculties of these works or operations are the virtues, which again admit of a division into purely natural and acquired virtues, and supernatural, infused virtues. The greatest of the virtues is charity, for it is charity that unites the soul to God. All the other virtues, both theological and moral, are related to charity as means of attaining union with God, but charity is the queen of all the virtues. And when charity so permeates the soul of the Christian that he is docile to God's will, the gifts of the Holy Spirit operate in the soul and constitute the mystical activity of the spiritual life. For St. Thomas the perfection of the Christian life consists in the habitual donal activity of the Holy Spirit, which becomes possible when the individual loves God with his whole heart and all his strength.[73]

Not all Christians will manifest the perfection of charity and donal activity in the same way, and for that reason St. Thomas takes up the questions of the active and contemplative life, understood as the type of activity that predominates in the life of a Christian.[74] Although he follows the traditional biblical and monastic teaching that the contemplative life is objectively superior to the active life, St. Thomas readily admits that there are concrete situations in which the superiority is reversed. In fact, like St. Gregory the Great, whom he quotes extensively, Aquinas shows that the active life may have an ascetical value as a preparation for contemplation, but it may have a mystical value of its own as when the apostolate flows from the perfection of charity and a deep interior life.[75] We do not find in Thomistic theology any restrictive concept of Christian

perfection in terms of contemplation or the contemplative state of
life.

St. Bernard, St. Gregory the Great, Pseudo-Dionysius and
Richard of St. Victor are primary sources for St. Thomas in his
treatment of contemplation.[76] At the outset he investigates the
psychology of the contemplative act and concludes that it is essentially an intellectual operation which originates by a movement of
the will and terminates in delight, which intensifies love.[77] Contemplation for Aquinas is "a simple gaze upon a truth," although
other activities may dispose for contemplation, e.g., reading, listening, meditation, cogitation and so on.[78]

The truth contemplated is divine truth, whether seen directly in
itself or indirectly in its effects. With St. Augustine, Aquinas maintains that the direct vision of the divine essence is possible only if the
soul leaves the body through death or in rapture, where there is a
total suspension of the operations of the external and internal
senses.[79] As regards the types of contemplation, Aquinas seems to
admit the existence of natural or acquired contemplation, for he
states that the six types of contemplation enumerated by Richard of
St. Victor are to be understood as follows:

> The first step is the consideration of things of sense; the second is the
> transition from sensible to intelligible things; the third is the evaluation
> of the things of sense through those of mind; the fourth is the consider-
> ation in their own right of intelligible things which have been reached
> through the sensible; the fifth is the contemplation of intelligible realities
> which cannot be reached through the things of sense but can be under-
> stood by reason; the sixth is the consideration of intelligible things
> which the intellect can neither discover nor exhaust; this is the sublime
> contemplation of divine truth wherein contemplation is finally per-
> fected.[80]

To summarize the teaching of St. Thomas, we may say that the
Christian life is the life of grace, with charity as its principal act.
Charity effects a union between God and the soul, and Aquinas does
not hestiate to call it by the name of friendship.[81] Like any other vital
operation, charity admits of degrees of perfection; in the first degree
of beginners the Christian is intent on the avoidance of sin and the
preservation of God's grace; in the second degree he strives to grow
in the virtues which should flow from charity; in the third degree he
attains the perfection of charity, at which stage he loves God with all
his capacity.[82]

In accordance with his teaching on the superiority of the intellect over the will[83] and his identification of man's ultimate beatitude as essentially (though not exclusively) an activity of the speculative intellect,[84] St. Thomas concludes that in the relative perfection of which man is capable in this life his happiness will consist "primarily and principally in contemplation, but secondarily in the activity of the practical intellect so far as it controls human actions and emotions."[85]

This constant emphasis on the primacy of the intellect sets St. Thomas apart from the voluntarists such as St. Augustine and St. Bonaventure and is reflected in his teaching on the nature of beatitude, the distinction between grace and charity, the origin and nature of law, the relation between obedience and authority, and the contemplative and active life. Nevertheless, the teaching of St. Thomas on the theology of Christian perfection has generally prevailed in Catholic theology since the fifteenth century.[86] Prior to that, between the death of St. Thomas and the emergence of spiritual theology as a well-defined branch of theology, a new current of affective spirituality, more Franciscan in tone, made its appearance. It started interestingly enough, with a group of German Dominicans, not because they were Dominican but because they were German. But of that we shall treat later.

ST. FRANCIS AND THE FRIARS MINOR

Thomas of Celano, the first biographer of St. Francis of Assisi, records that St. Dominic once remarked to St. Francis: "I wish, Brother Francis, that your Order and mine were one, and that we had, in the Church, but one manner of life."[87] There was good reason for such a statement, for the two mendicant Orders were very much alike in their origins, especially as regards the observance of evangelical poverty and the apostolate of preaching. A good reason for this similarity can be found in the fact that as contemporaries, Dominic and Francis were both endeavoring to correct abuses in the Church and restore the Christian life to Gospel standards through their preaching and their poverty. The Gospel was being ignored almost everywhere, due in great part to the wealth of priests and monks and the temporal power of ecclesiastical prelates. Attempts to correct this abuse and the sins that followed from it usually met with failure, not only because many priests and monks resisted conversion, but because some of the reformers resorted to force (as did Simon Montfort and Arnold of Brescia) and others became extremists and disobedient to the Church (e.g., the *Illuminati* and the Albigensians).

With St. Francis of Assisi we see the beginnings of a popular, apostolic movement that proclaims fidelity to the faith, obedience to ecclesiastical authority, and the conversion of people at all levels of society. Sometimes it is difficult to draw the line between orthodoxy and heterodoxy, between the mendicant friar and the revolutionary, but the religious fervor and the joyful poverty of Francis ultimately prevailed. The writings he left are few in number – two Rules, a last testament, a few letters, exhortations and prayers – but the *Poverello* is the source of an evangelical spirituality that has gushed forth like a fountain of living water to refresh and nourish the Church.

Born at Assisi in 1181 or 1182, Francis Bernadone was converted in 1206 or 1207 from a life of wealth and laxity to a life of poverty and penance. By 1209 or 1210 he had attracted eleven disciples and he gave them a rule of life which was approved orally by Pope Innocent III. The Rule of St. Francis stressed poverty, humility and complete submission to the authority of the Church.

Even before he had gathered any disciples, Francis endeavored to live as literally as possible the Gospel teaching on poverty as expressed in Matthew 10:9–10. Later, as his community grew, controversies arose in regard to the degree of poverty that was possible in a religious order dedicated to the apostolate. When the argument of basic necessities was used to justify a relaxation of strict poverty, Francis replied: "It is impossible to satisfy simple necessity without letting oneself lapse into comfort."[88] On another occasion he warned: "The world will turn away from the Friars Minor in the measure that they turn away from poverty."[89] In spite of the opposition of Francis, as the Franciscan movement spread rapidly throughout Europe it became evident that the need for organization and more precise legislation also necessitated a mitigation of the primitive strict poverty.

Many interesting questions arise in respect to the ideal of St. Francis: Is it possible to follow a literal interpretation of the Gospel teaching on poverty? Did Francis originally envisage groups of mendicant preachers without stability and without affiliation to an organized society rather than a religious order? Did Francis err in emphasizing poverty to such an extent that some friars made it a goal rather than a means? One may speculate on these and other related questions, but the facts of history are that Pope Innocent III and Cardinal Ugolino, protector of the New Order, were also of the opinion that Francis' rules on poverty were much too severe. It seems that the authorities of the Church were almost reluctant to give full approval to the manner of life envisaged by St. Francis.

The principal events of the life of St. Francis and the growth of the Friars Minor can be summarized briefly.[90] In 1212, at Assisi, St. Francis and St. Clare founded the cloistered Franciscan nuns, known as Poor Clares, and Francis composed a rule of life for them. Ever desirous, like St. Dominic, of going to the Far East as a missionary, Francis made two unsuccessful attempts. It is said that in 1213 he got as far as Santiago de Compostela in Spain. He did succeed in going to Morocco and Tunisia in 1219 in order to preach to the Moors, and it is said that he also made a pilgrimage to the Holy Land. In 1221 he established what is known today as the Third Order of St. Francis, composed of priests or laity desirous of living according to the spirit of St. Francis. By this time, twelve years after its beginning, the Franciscan Order numbered more than three thousand friars.

St. Francis resigned as head of the Order in 1220 and Brother Peter became Minister General, but he died within the year and was followed by Brother Elias. The General Chapter of 1220 approved and promulgated a new version of the Rule, but it seems that Cardinal Ugolino advised Francis to modify the text before submitting it for the approval of the Holy See. St. Francis complied and the General Chapter approved the "second" Rule in 1223; Pope Honorius officially approved it in November of the same year. The principal themes of the final Rule were poverty, manual labor, preaching, missions among the infidels, and the balance between action and contemplation.[91]

St. Francis then dedicated himself almost exclusively to preaching, penance and prayer. On September 17, 1224, he received the grace of the stigmata in the hermitage of Mount Alverno. This is the first recorded instance in the history of Christian spirituality in which an individual has been visibly marked with the signs of the passion of Christ; it has been repeated numerous times in subsequent history, and even in modern times.[92]

In April of 1226 St. Francis composed his *Testament*, in which he made his final appeal for the strict observance of poverty and fidelity to the Rule. This *Testament* became the occasion for another crisis in the Order; some wanted it to have the force of law and others, while respecting the authority of their founder, were unwilling to consider it anything more than a paternal exhortation. The case was finally settled by Pope Gregory IX, who stated in his bull

Quo elongati (1230) that the *Testament* did not bind as law but he appointed a *nuntius apostolicus* who would handle all financial matters for the Franciscans and thus enable them to preserve the strict observance of poverty.

Meanwhile, weak and exhausted, almost blind, and frequently vomiting blood, Francis composed his beautiful *Canticle to Brother Sun*. As he realized that his death was approaching, he commanded his friars to lay him naked on the ground, but then accepted a rough woollen garment from one of the friars. On the evening of October 3, 1226, he intoned Psalm 141 and the friars chanted it with him. Then, one of the friars, at Francis' request, read aloud Chapter 13 of St. John's Gospel, and during the reading Francis passed into eternal life. Two years after his death he was canonized by Pope Gregory IX.

St. Francis died amid a severe crisis in his Order. The Friars Minor had begun to lessen the severity of their poverty even during his lifetime, but after his death the Order was fragmented into "observants", "conventuals", and "spirituals". In spite of the efforts of St. Bonaventure as Minister General from 1257 to 1274, it was impossible to bring all the friars to a consensus on the life style proper to Franciscans. As recently as 1909 Pope Pius X, in his apostolic letter *Septimo iam pleno*, declared that the three branches of the First Order of Franciscans are established *in perpetuum* as Friars Minor of the Leonine Union (O.F.M.), Friars Minor Conventual (O.F.M. Conv.) and Friars Minor Capuchin (O.F.M. Cap.) and that all three Ministers General are successors of St. Francis because all three Orders are branches of the same tree.

Several other factors played a part in the modification of the original ideal of St. Francis: the ordination of friars to the priesthood, the apostolate of preaching and teaching, and the need to defend the mendicant orders against its detractors. From the very beginning, following the example of Francis himself, the early friars were dedicated to itinerant preaching, and although some basic education was required, the Franciscans were unwilling to inaugurate courses of study because of St. Francis' attitude toward learning. When, finally, they entered the universities, they, with the Dominicans, became victims of the violent opposition of the diocesan clergy.[93]

Both of these mendicant orders had established houses near the University of Paris and as early as 1229 a Dominican held a chair of theology there, to be followed by a Franciscan in 1231. Unfortunately, in 1252 the secular clergy, under the leadership of William of

Saint-Amour, began to attack the friars. William wrote a strongly worded tract in 1255 in which he tried to have all friars excluded from professorships. Gerhard of Abbeville and Nicholas of Lisieux continued the attack from 1269 to 1272. Thanks to St. Thomas Aquinas and St. Bonaventure,[94] the position of the friars was vindicated and Pope Alexander IV took them under the protection of the Holy See.[95]

ST. BONAVENTURE

The three principal names in Franciscan learning are St. Bonaventure, St. Anthony of Padua and John Duns Scotus. Numerous others of course, must be added to the total list: John of Rochelle, Alexander of Hales, John Peckham, Roger Bacon, Peter Auriol, Francis de Meyronnes, Nicholas of Lyre, William of Ockham and John of Ripa. We shall restrict our study to St. Bonaventure, whom Pope Leo XIII called "the Prince of Mystics" and whom many hail as the second founder of the Franciscan Order.[96] We can surely assert with safety that he is the greatest theologian of the spiritual life among the Franciscans. Cayré says of him: "He carried on the tradition of Alexander of Hales and prepared the way for Duns Scotus, who gave the final form to Franciscan Augustinism."[97]

St. Bonaventure (1221–1274) was a contemporary of St. Thomas Aquinas at the University of Paris and although they differed radically in their ideas, they were very close personal friends, as were Francis and Dominic before them. They differed not only in their approach to theology – Bonaventure was voluntaristic and mystical while Thomas was intellectual and analytic – but also in their definitions of theology, as Congar explains:

> For St. Bonaventure, theology is a production of grace. It is to be considered a consequence of the communications which God gave us of himself. Theology therefore is situated for St. Bonaventure ... "between faith and appearance." ...
>
> The first light received from God is reason. But when Bonaventure considers reason's concrete possibilities, he severely limits them, since he claims that man in his present state cannot come to know superior truths simply by reason. ... However this does not mean that philosophy is not the first step toward wisdom. ...
>
> In the order of grace and Christian wisdom, progress toward the perfect possession of wisdom ... is marked by three stages or grades. First, the grade of virtues, in which faith opens our eyes to help us find God in everything, next, the grade of gifts and, third, the grade of beatitudes. Now the acts of virtues, gifts, and beatitudes are respectively

defined as: *credere* (believing); *intelligere credita* (understanding the things believed); *videre intellecta* (seeing the things understood). ...

Hence, this knowledge of mysteries, which is the object of theology, is for Bonaventure an intermediary stage between the simple assent to faith and the vision. ...

Theology, for St. Bonaventure, is a gift of God. ... Hence it is not a purely intellectual gift. It presupposes not a dead faith, but a living faith of prayer, the exercise of the virtues and the yearning for a union of charity with God.

Here we arrive at an essential point, where the theology of Bonaventure and Thomas Aquinas are clearly distinguished. For the latter, theology is the growth of the convictions of faith and the construction of these convictions into a body of knowledge consonant with human reason. Like all things, it develops under God's providence and is rooted in supernatural faith, but it is strictly a rational construction. The wisdom of theology is distinguished from the infused gift of wisdom, which develops as an experimental and affective body of knowledge. On the other hand, theology is an intellectual wisdom, acquired by personal effort, which tries intellectually to comprehend and reconstruct the order of the works and the mysteries of God by tying them up with the mystery of God himself.[98]

St. Bonaventure's theological masterpiece is his commentary on the *Book of Sentences* by Peter Lombard and almost everything else that he wrote is in some way based on this work.[99] The fundamental characteristic of his doctrine is that it is traditional, following the teaching of St. Augustine through Alexander of Hales. His principal writings on the spiritual life are *Breviloquium, `De triplici via, Itinerarium mentis ad Deum, Soliloquium de quatuor mentalibus exercitiis,* and *Lignum vitae,* and it is in the field of spiritual theology that Bonaventure excels.[100] Smeets says that the works of St. Bonaventure manifest not only his orthodoxy but his sanctity and virtues: "They show that the holy doctor was permeated with the Franciscan spirit and that he had no other guide than his seraphic father, St. Francis."[101] This is particularly evident in Bonaventure's conciseness of style, humble submission to authority, veneration of theologians, respect for the opinions of others, and his calm and peaceful temperament.

De Wulf says of Bonaventure that "his mysticism is the incarnation of the best of thirteenth-century mysticism."[102] This is another way of saying that the spiritual doctrine of St. Bonaventure is the traditional doctrine taught by St. Augustine, pseudo-Dionysius, St. Bernard and the School of St. Victor. His spiritual doctrine is eminently Christocentric and while he agrees with Thomas Aquinas that the purpose of the incarnation was the redemption, he sees Christ as the center of the entire created universe. The fundamental virtue of Christian spirituality is humility; grace is a likeness to God which is received both by the soul and its faculties; the essence of Christian perfection is charity, which is perfected as wisdom, to which the mystical graces are related; contemplation is the perfection of charity and wisdom and it is much more a savory experience of God than it is the vision; it is entirely passive and infused and usually accompanied by some form of ecstasy which Bonaventure calls *excessus*.

St. Bonaventure canonized the classification of the spiritual life into the three ways and uses the same terminology as pseudo-Dionysius: purgative, illuminative and unitive or perfect. He does not see them as progressive and separate stages, however, although at a given time one or another will predominate. The ultimate goal for all Christians is holiness and as they pass through the various stages of spiritual growth, each one bestows its own gift. Thus, the *purgative way* leads to peace of soul and is characterized by meditation, examination of conscience and consideration of the passion of Christ; the *illuminative way* leads to truth, and its predominant exercises are consideration of the benefits received from God and frequent meditation on the passion and death of Christ; the *unitive way* terminates in charity, union with God through love and an awareness of the divine beauty through contemplation of the Trinity.[103]

MULTIPLICATION OF RELIGIOUS ORDERS

In spite of the prohibition of the Fourth Lateran Council, there was a remarkable increase in religious institutes during the last half of the thirteenth century.[104] Some of them were not really new, however, but were a modernization and adaptation of ancient orders, such as the Carmelites and Augustinians. Others were inspired by the mendicant friars – Dominicans and Franciscans – who had such a prodigious expansion and were so favored by the Holy See. Many of the institutes had only a local character and ceased to exist after a time. In fact, the Council of Lyons (1274) abolished twenty-two religious institutes that had not been approved by the Holy See. But what should be noted, both in the newly founded institutes and the outgrowths of the ancient orders, is the increasing emphasis on the apostolate and a noticeable decline in the number of religious dedicated to the purely contemplative life. As time passed this placed contemplative institutes somewhat on the defensive, but for the time being even the institutes dedicated to an apostolate or ministry were constrained to follow a monastic or conventual type of life. One of the problems was that so many institutes were identical in life and mission.

Among the canons regular we note first of all that the Canons of St. Augustine were already in existence and they consisted of cathedral chapters or communities following the Rule of St. Augustine. But in the twelfth and thirteenth centuries several religious institutes were founded under the title of the Cross. The Crosier Canons, founded by Theodore de Celles, a canon of Liège in 1210, were formally approved in 1248. The rule of the Crosiers is based on the Dominican *Constitutions* and the early members were dedicated to preaching the Crusades and the care of pilgrims. After its approbation, however, the Crosier Order followed the "mixed life" and began to engage in missionary work. It flourished especially in the Low Lands.[105]

The Hermits of St. Augustine, who were much less given to contemplation than their name indicates, were formed out of groups of hermits in Italy who adopted the Rule of St. Augustine. They were approved by Pope Alexander IV in 1256 and classified among the mendicant friars with the Dominicans and Franciscans. Eventually the name "Hermits of St. Augustine" fell into disuse, since they dedicated themselves to all types of apostolate and priestly ministry.[106]

Another group that began with an eremitical spirit was the Servants of Mary, popularly known as Servites. Founded by seven businessmen who desired to live a life of austerity and penance, with special devotion to the Blessed Virgin, they followed the observances of the mendicant friars. They made their first foundation at Florence, Italy, in 1233 and, like most of these new institutes, they also made provision for a feminine branch.[107]

Two other orders of friars that had a glorious history are the Mercedarians, founded by St. Peter Nolasco and aided by the Dominican St. Raymond of Peñafort, and the Trinitarians. Both of these orders were founded for the redemption of captives and consequently their field of labor was at first among the Moors and later in Latin America. In modern times, however, their membership has greatly decreased.[108]

Finally, the Order of Our Lady of Mount Carmel also came into prominence in the thirteenth century, although its origins go back to Mount Carmel in Palestine. Early in the thirteenth century some

Latin hermits lived on Mount Carmel and in due time, for a variety of reasons, the Carmelites spread to Europe. St. Simon Stock (+1265), gradually adapted the Carmelite rule and life to a semi-apostolic religious institute and in 1245 the Carmelites were classified among the mendicant orders. The Carmelite hermits ceased to exist in Palestine in 1291 when the remaining members were murdered by the Muslims, but by that time the Carmelites in Europe had committed themselves to a predominantly active life.[109]

The characteristics of the thirteenth century were basically the same as those we listed for the twelfth century, with the addition of the remarkable influence of the newly-founded religious institutes dedicated to the apostolate and the publication of numerous books and manuals on the basic dogmas and moral instruction. As a result, there was a flourishing of lay groups desirous of living an exemplary Christian life. Most notable among them were the Beghards and the Béguines. They did not feel called to religious life nor did they want to be anchorites; normally they grouped themselves around a religious order.

The Beghards and the Béguines originated in northern France, the Low Lands and the Rhineland. Although they lived a community life, they took no vows, and they lived a celibate life and were obedient as long as they remained in the *béguinage*. They occupied themselves with sewing and embroidery, visiting the sick, caring for the elderly, and sometimes the education of children. They assisted at the liturgy in a group at a neighboring church, and after six years of formation they could obtain permission to live as a recluse.

In time the simplicity of their life caused the Beghards and the Béguines to be the object of criticism and suspicion. Later they were openly attacked for their use of the vernacular for Bible-reading and for their interpretation of Scripture. In 1311 they were officially condemned by the Council of Vienne. The doctrinal basis for the condemnation was quietism and a latent pantheism.

Marie d'Oignies (+1213), one of the leaders of the movement, had an intense love for Christ and desired especially to imitate his poverty. The poor Christ or Christ as a beggar was the predominant object of her veneration and imitation. Juliana of Cornillon (+1258) also belonged to a community of Béguines and was one of the promoters of the feast of Corpus Christi, first approved for the diocese of Liège in 1246 and for the universal Church by Pope Urban IV in 1264. But the most famous of the Béguines was Hadewijch of Antwerp (+1282 or 1297), because of her written accounts of her visions, and her letters and poetry. Her dominant theme was that the soul can attain union with God only through ecstatic love, and this union takes on the symbolism of the mystical marriage. This constitutes the *Brautmystik* and seems to have been a favorite concept with the mystics of the Low Lands and the Rhineland. There is also in the writings of Hadewijch a suggestion of the *Wesenmystik* that will be further developed by Meister Eckhart. Hadewijch is thus a forerunner of the Rhineland mystics.[110]

CHAPTER 7

DIONYSIAN SPIRITUALITY
AND
DEVOTIO MODERNA

Following Cayré,[1] we have decided to designate this chapter as "Dionysian spirituality" but the title requires explanation. First of all, it refers to a revival of neo-Platonic, Augustinian spirituality by the German Dominicans, who then influenced the Christian life in the Netherlands. Secondly, while dependent on the Dominican intellectual tradition, it swings away from that tradition toward the mystical and contemplative spirituality of pseudo-Dionysius, who lived around the year 500. Thirdly, it resulted in the expansion of spiritual influence from the Latin countries to the Germanic and Anglo-saxon countries, introducing at the same time a classification of schools of spirituality according to national cultures and temperaments.

The leader of this new school was Meister Eckhart, a German Dominican who was later accused of pantheistic tendencies. His disciples included John Tauler and Henry Suso, both German Dominicans, and John Ruysbroeck of the Netherlands. In England a more moderate form of Dionysian spirituality was taught by Richard Rolle, Walter Hilton and the author of *The Cloud of Unknowing*.[2] Mention should also be made of the Carthusian, Denis Rijkel, who is in the same school of spirituality and brings the Middle Ages to a close as far as spiritual theology is concerned.

Before noting the contributions of each of the outstanding figures in Dionysian spirituality, we should investigate the circumstances that led to the emergence and success of this spiritual movement. Although theologians of the stature of St. Thomas Aquinas and St. Bonaventure had written about mystical contemplation, it was not until the fourteenth century that this subject became the object of intense and specialized study. One of the principal situations that favoured this theological development was the increasing number of fervent and educated women who were claiming various types of mystical experience and seeking spiritual direction as a result of it.

Early in the fourteenth century there was an amazing number of religious women who composed spiritual treatises in which they described their mystical experiences, many of them being accounts of the mystical espousal or mystical marriage. Eventually this *Brautmystik* (mysticism of spiritual marriage) became one of the chief characteristics of Eckhart's "mysticism of the essence".[3] That this movement had its excesses, there is no doubt, for Sitwell observes that "in the fourteenth century the whole of the Rhine valley was seething with religious enthusiasts, Béguines and Beghards, and Brethren of the Free Spirit, some of them controlled and respectable, some of them not."[4]

As early as 1292 the Council of Aschaffenburg initiated a repression of the Beghards and the Béguines; in 1306 the Council of Cologne accused them of infamy and heresy and blamed them for instigating attacks on the Franciscans and Dominicans. Finally, the Council of Vienne (1311) condemned eight of their doctrinal propositions and denounced their pseudomysticism. Yet, not all the Beghards and Béguines were deserving of condemnation. Mechtild of Magdeburg is an outstanding example of a Béguine who rose to the heights of the mystical life and, together with St. Gertrude and St. Mechtild of Hackeborn, is a jewel in the crown of the Cistercian monastery at Helfta.[5]

THE MYSTICS OF HELFTA

The ruins of the Cistercian monastery of Helfta still stand in Saxony, near Eisleben. Founded by Gertrude of Hackeborn (+ 1291), it produced three saintly women whose writings had a tremendous influence on Christian life in Germany during the late Middle Ages. The first of these, Mechtild of Magdeburg (+ 1282 or 1297), belonged to a community of Béguines who were closely associated with the Cistercian nuns and was already in the mystical state before she entered the monastery of Helfta in 1270. In the monastery she wrote the last chapter of a work she had been composing under the direction of her Dominican director: *The Flowing Light of the Divinity (Das Fliessende Licht der Gottheit)*. Written in Low German, it was later revised in High German and translated into Latin by Henry of Nordlingen (+ 1345).

The book describes the mystical experience and ecstatic union in the form of a dialogue between Christ and the soul. The fundamental point in the teaching of Mechtild is that the soul must empty itself of everything that comes to it through the senses, the memory and the imagination, and even of its own virtues, in order to attain union with God. There, in the very essence of the soul, in its purest state, the transforming union occurs. Following in the tradition of St. Bernard, Mechtild's teaching is eminently Christocentric, but it also contributes to the "mysticism of essence" that will be popularized later by Meister Eckhart.[6]

St. Mechtild of Hackeborn (+ 1299) was a sister of the foundress of Helfta and she became the mistress of novices. Under her guidance many saintly nuns were formed, and among them was St. Gertrude the Great. St. Mechtild of Hackeborn is renowned as a confidant of the Sacred Heart of Jesus and a leader in the propagation of this devotion.

St. Mechtild never wanted to write about the numerous graces she had received from God, but Gertrude the Great made a transcription of these things and gave it to Mechtild for her approval. In this way St. Mechtild's work, *The Book of Special Grace*, came into being. It is a book filled with joy and thanksgiving, without any mention of pain or suffering. The work was widely circulated because it served as a guide for Christian living. It treated of the Christian virtues, devotion to the Heart of Jesus and Mechtild's numerous revelations. It also provided instructions for the reception of Communion, the practice of prayer, and participation in the liturgy.[7]

St. Gertrude the Great (+ 1302) was received into the monastery school at Helfta at the age of five by the foundress, Gertrude of Hackeborn. She was a brilliant student and became so absorbed in literary pursuits that she neglected her spiritual development. As the result of a vision of Christ in 1281, at the age of twenty-six, Gertrude henceforth dedicated herself in earnest to prayer and the reading of the Scripture and the Fathers of the Church, especially St. Augustine, St. Gregory the Great, St. Bernard and Hugh of St. Victor.

Gertrude's spiritual life was centred on the liturgy and most of her mystical ecstasies occurred during Mass, usually as the result of certain words or phrases that captivated her full attention. Like St. Bernard, her spirituality was predominantly Christocentric; she had a great devotion to the Eucharist, to the passion of Christ and to the wound in the side of Christ.[8] In 1284 Gertrude received the stigmata in an invisible form and also experienced the transverberation of her heart.

Between 1261 and 1302 St. Gertrude wrote *The Herald of Divine Love* (which some critics do not consider to be entirely her own) and her greatest work, *Spiritual Exercises*. The doctrinal basis of these works indicates a strong Dominican influence, but the overall tone is that of St. Bernard's Christology. St. Gertrude was an ardent devotee of the Sacred Heart but she sees it as radiant with glory, a treasury of riches, a lamp suspended between heaven and earth, and her dwelling-place. There is nothing of suffering or reparation in her devotion to the Heart of Jesus.[9]

Two other saintly women deserving of mention in this connection are St. Lutgard and St. Brigid of Sweden. A Cistercian nun, St. Lutgard (+1246) was also a promoter of devotion to the Sacred Heart and she focused the entire theology of this devotion on love.[10]

St. Brigid's spirituality was completely Cistercian, concentrating on the passion of Christ and devotion to Mary. After a pilgrimage to Santiago de Compostela, Brigid's husband entered a Cistercian monastery in Sweden and died there a few years later. From that time on, St. Brigid was more and more directed by God towards a prophetic vocation, similar to that of St. Catherine of Siena. By God's command, she advised great rulers and ecclesiastical dignitaries. During a six-month stay in the Holy Land, Brigid received numerous revelations concerning the passion and death of Christ, which were published for the first time in Lübeck in 1492. Brigid was also the foundress of an order of contemplative nuns dedicated to the praise of God and reparation for sinners. Her book of revelations received the approbation of Pope Benedict XIV as private revelations and acceptable on human faith in accordance with prudence.[11]

ECKHART, TAULER, SUSO

During the fourteenth century the Dominicans and Franciscans were especially noteworthy for their spiritual ministrations to the cloistered nuns. At one point, in fact, a Provincial Chapter of the German Dominicans had attempted to withdraw from this ministry, since so many friars were occupied solely with the spiritual care of nuns, but the Holy See insisted that this apostolate should continue. Then, in 1325, the Chapter of Dominicans denounced those friars who were preaching the subtleties of the mystical life to persons who could easily misinterpret the doctrine.

On the intellectual level a group of German Dominicans, without any particular hostility to St. Thomas Aquinas, preferred the teaching of St. Albert the Great and the neo-Platonism of William of Moerbeke. Included among them are Hugh of Strasburg, Ulric of Strasburg and Thierry of Freiburg. In the fourteenth century, when Catholic spirituality inclined very strongly to the mystical element in Christian life and perfection, the neo-Platonic approach seemed to offer a much more suitable vehicle of expression and description than did the speculative and closely-reasoned Aristotelian approach of St. Thomas.

Medieval spirituality was explicitly directed toward contemplation and mystical experience; to attain this goal, certain ascetical means were proposed: total renunciation of self, complete submission to the divine will, and rejection of all sense images (even the humanity of Christ). This, they believed, would lead to a union with God which was so intimate that nothing would intervene between the soul and God as the bond of the union; it would consist in a divinization that for all practical purposes leaves the soul indistinguishable from God.[12]

As could be expected, a doctrine of this type was especially susceptible to a pantheistic interpretation and there seems to be no doubt that some of the authors did make rash and excessive statements concerning the nature of the mystical union with God.[13] On the other hand, one could hardly expect any writer to describe with clarity and precision the nature of the transforming union.

Having surveyed the setting of the spirituality of the fourteenth century, we can turn our attention to the figures that emerged out of this scene and became the promoters of Dionysian spirituality. The leader, beyond any doubt, was the German Dominican, Meister Eckhart (1260–1327). A renowned theologian and preacher, he also held numerous administrative posts of great importance in the Dominican Order.

As a young friar, Eckhart had studied at the Dominican priory in Cologne, where St. Albert the Great died in 1280. Later he became prior at Erfurt and vicar general of Thuringia. On two separate occasions he was a professor at the University of Paris but left there to be prior and professor at the Dominican priory in Strasbourg, ultimately returning to Cologne. It was there that Eckhart, now a famous preacher, became embroiled in controversy and was accused of unorthodox teaching. A forthright and intransigent man, he was also the victim of persecution at the hands of some of his own Dominican brethren.

In 1326 the Franciscan Archbishop of Cologne, Henry of Virneburg, appointed two inquisitors to investigate the teaching of Eckhart, and from his writings and sermons they drew up a list of 108 propositions which they considered suspect. Eckhart defended himself vigorously but to no avail. He admitted that some of his statements, taken literally, could be interpreted in a heterodox sense, but it was never his intention to preach a doctrine that was contrary to orthodox theology. In 1327, in the church of the Dominicans, he publicly revoked all such ill-sounding doctrine. In that same year Eckhart appealed to the Holy See, stating in advance his willingness to comply with any decision. He even defended himself at the papal court in Avignon but died on his return to Cologne. In March, 1329, Pope John XXII condemned 28 propositions from the teachings of Eckhart; the first fifteen and the last two were condemned as erroneous and heretical and the others were condemned as ill-sounding and rash.[14]

As a theologian, Eckhart was a faithful follower of the teaching of St. Thomas Aquinas concerning the supremacy of the intellect over the will, but he also seems to have gone to excess in its application, thanks to the influence of Maimonides of the Averroistic school and of pseudo-Dionysius. It is also likely that the sermons of St. Bernard exerted a strong influence on Eckhart in questions touching the nature of the mystical experience, though Eckhart carried the doctrine to dangerous extremes. Nor should we overlook the fact that Eckhart was very likely acquainted with and perhaps influenced by the spirituality of persons like Margaret Poret, Hadewijch, and Mechtild of Magdeburg, all of whom emphasized very strongly the nothingness of the soul and the necessity of detachment and nudity of spirit. The result of all these influences was a theology of the spiritual life based on two different but complementary themes: the highly speculative "mysticism of essence" and the spirituality of the mystical marriage or *Brautmystik*. Let us now see how Eckhart attempted to combine these two themes in his spiritual teaching.

In God, says Eckhart, *esse* and *intelligere* are identical; moreover, outside of God there is no true existence or being (*"esse est Deus"*). Consequently, all creation, including man, considered in itself, is nothing; whatever it has of being or existence comes from God, in whose divine intellect it has existed from all eternity. Consequently, man is impelled by the necessity of his own nothingness, so to speak, to return to God in whom he has his source. The point of contact or the radical capacity for union between man and God is found in the essence of the intellect, which is designated variously as a power, a spark or the *"Grund der Seele."* As Eckhart says: "There is something in the soul that is uncreated and uncreatable, namely, the intelligence; and if that were the whole soul, that too would be uncreated and uncreatable."[15]

The spark or *Grund* constitutes the seed of the divine life and of the properly contemplative life, which can be attained by means of a

Platonic type of development. Eckhart constantly reverts to the two basic themes of the transcendency of God and the total detachment required for man's return to the unity and image of God by participation. Consequently, although at times his manner of speaking was excessive and could be interpreted in a pantheistic sense, Eckhart preserved the concept of a transcendent God and placed limitations on the degree of union between the soul and God. This is evident from his response to the judges at the time of the investigation at Cologne.[16]

In his explanation of the precise nature of the union between God and the soul, Eckhart states that the mystical experience flows from grace as a supernatural principle and involves immediately an intellectual or contemplative activity on the part of man, though not excluding the activity of the will under the imperation of charity. Thus, through vision and love, the soul that attains the height of mystical union with God is, as it were, identified with the divine essence; it experiences complete beatitude in and through God.

This does not mean, as Eckhart explained in his response to the judges at Cologne, that we are transformed and changed into God, but just as the numerous hosts on various altars are transformed into the one and the same body of Christ, so also, "by the grace of adoption we are united to the true Son of God and made members of the one Head of the Church, who is Christ."[17]

Eckhart not only came very close to pantheistic doctrine in his manner of expression; he also savored somewhat of the Quietism of the Beghards, which he actually condemned with all his strength. The heterodox Beghards taught that man in the present life is able to reach such a high degree of perfection that he is absolutely impeccable and can attain to no further increase of grace; he is no longer obliged to obey the Church or any moral laws because he is above them; whatever acts he may perform are fully in accord with the divine will. Several of Eckhart's statements, condemned by the Church, do admit of a Quietist interpretation.[18]

There is a wide divergence of views concerning the teaching of Eckhart. According to Denifle, Hurter and Mondonnet, Eckhart was a Scholastic of little originality and he was not a mystic; rather, he was a man of mediocre intelligence and unrestrained in his expressions. According to De Wulf, Delacroix, Weber and Otto, he was orthodox in his intention but he voiced the heretical teaching of Erigena and Almaric, and in that respect is a forerunner of Luther. Finally, Gilson, Dempf and Graef maintain that Eckhart was Catholic in his teaching but not properly understood. He is seen by some as the precursor of Kant, Schopenhauer, Spinoza, Hegel, Heidegger and Jasper. It is difficult to understand how a man credited with such influence on later thinkers could be branded a mediocre thinker. Rather, it would seem more accurate to take Eckhart at his word and say that although he may have expressed himself in exaggerated terms, he never intended to veer from orthodox teaching. The fact is that his doctrine exerted a profound influence on the spiritual teaching and practice of later ages.[19]

John Tauler (1300–1361) considered Eckhart his master and teacher, but he did not fall into the excesses of Eckhart. Tauler was a preacher and spiritual director, not a writer; with Henry Suso, he was the founder of the Friends of God (*Gottesfreunde*). The *Institutiones divinae*, attributed to Tauler, was composed by the Carthusian, Laurence Surius, from the sermons of Tauler.[20]

Like Eckhart, Tauler discussed abstract themes and favoured neo-Platonic expressions, although he had a capacity for illustrating his doctrine by simple, picturesque examples. Like Eckhart also, he emphasizes the need for total renunciation of all externals to attain nudity of spirit and an interior recollection or withdrawal into the "*Grund*" of the soul, where one attains mystical contemplation.

God, says Tauler, is nothing, in the sense that he is nothing we can name, comprehend or experience as long as we have not attained that "nudity of spirit" which is essential for contemplation. Meanwhile, we can know what God is not, rather than what he is; consequently our knowledge of God is by way of eminence and not by way of analogy with created beings. Therefore, until the intelligence of man is completely emptied of all sensible and intellectual images, it cannot contemplate God, because God is not knowable in that way. Only through nudity of spirit can the intelligence become sufficiently passive and receptive so that it can experience intimate union with God.

Man, on the other hand, lives on three levels: the sensible, the rational and the superior level called *Gemüt*. By means of mortification and renunciation, a man rises above the intelligibility of ideas and images so that he can enter into the *Grund* of the soul. This involves a detachment from the lower appetites by active asceticism and of the will by total submission to the divine will. It is just as impossible to give a name to the *Grund* of the soul as it is to give a name to God, but the *Grund* or center of the soul is distinct from the faculties, though it gives them their power of operation.

The *Gemüt*, on the other hand, is something more powerful than the faculties of the soul and can be constantly operative even when the intellect and will are dormant. The *Grund* of the soul is the area of mystical experience, and since the intellect and will cannot touch the *Grund* or center of the soul, the contemplative experience is something beyond the natural faculties of the soul.

Now, we exist in God from all eternity, as an idea in the divine intellect, which is identical with the divine existence. Hence, from all eternity we are united with God and our task on earth is to return to unity with the divine. This is achieved when the individual returns to the *Grund* or center of the soul where the Trinity dwells. But since the intellect and will cannot enter the *Grund* to make contact with the Trinity, it is the function of two gifts of the Holy Spirit – understanding and wisdom – to lead the soul to its center, beyond every form of human life or knowledge, to that abyss where God gives himself as he is and is known as he is in himself. This constitutes the mystical union and contemplation in which no created thing intervenes between God and the soul; the divine essence is immediately united to the soul in its center.[21]

Tauler's doctrine was not free from attack, but it was defended by Blosius, St. Peter Canisius and the Carthusian, Laurence Surius. During the sixteenth century the sermons of Tauler were condemned or forbidden in France, Spain and Belgium, and in the seventeenth century his teaching was perverted by the Quietists. Indeed, until the nineteenth century (and then thanks to scholars like Denifle, who restored Tauler to his rightful place in orthodox theology), the doctrine of Tauler was generally seen under the cloud of Quietism. Nevertheless, Crisógono de Jesús maintained that Tauler, with Ruysbroeck, was the greatest mystic prior to St. Teresa of Avila and St. John of the Cross.[22]

Henry Suso (1295–1366), whom Strauch calls "the singer of German mysticism, a spiritual troubador, the last poet of *Mittelhochdeutsch*,"[23] was very likely at some time or other a fellow-student with Tauler under Meister Eckhart.[24] His life was filled with mystical phenomena and intense suffering. His written works comprise the following: *Little Book of Eternal Wisdom*; *Little Book of Truth*; *Little Book of Letters*; and an autobiography which is of dubious authorship.[25]

> The *Little Book of Truth* gives us the road map of Suso's high flights into philosophical and theological speculations; the *Little Book of Eternal Wisdom* depicts him as a prudent ascetic and practical mystic. In his *Sermons* and *Letters* we learn to know him as a trenchant preacher and enlightened spiritual guide, endowed with rare charisms. The *Life* unfolds the successive developments of his ascent to holiness.[26]

Suso wrote from personal experience and while he lacks the force-fulness of Eckhart and the clarity of Tauler, he possesses a sweetness almost to the point of naïveté. He is more of a poet and mystic than a systematic theologian. In *Eternal Wisdom* he begins by advocating meditation of the mysteries, and especially the sufferings, of Jesus and Mary, which should lead the soul to an awareness of the malice of sin, the rigor of divine judgment, and the need for reparation. After offering practical counsel on how to live and how to die, he returns again to meditations on the passion and death of Christ and the sorrows of Mary.

In the *Little Book of Truth* he speaks of the grades of prayer and ecstasies and raptures, but warns against the illusion of extra-ordinary mystical phenomena and the dangers of the excessive passivity of Quietism, taught by the Beghards and the Brethren of the Free Spirit.[27] For Suso, union with God requires that man be reborn, and this calls for renunciation to such a degree that the soul loses awareness of self as distinct from God and experiences a transformation in Christ. The contemplative experience is inde-scribable, but it consists in a union with God, "the One and the Nothing," without any intermediary. The faculties are absorbed in God, so to speak, and the soul is submerged in God; yet, the soul knows and loves God in this experience without understanding what it knows and loves. Even if the soul reaches this sublime union with the divine, there is always the need for humility, because there is always the possibility of sin.

Henry Suso wrote from personal experience of the mystical life, and with such ardor and effusiveness that one would think his entire life was one uninterrupted rapture. Yet, when one considers the asceticism and penitential practices of Henry Suso and the false accusations brought against him, what stands out above everything else is his heroic fortitude. Even within his own Dominican Order he was persecuted and deprived of his teaching position and his academic degree as a lector in theology. He taught the Pauline doctrine of conformity to Christ and in his sufferings he gave witness to the passion and death of Christ. Henry Suso was beatified by Pope Gregory XVI in 1831.[28]

A great number of the other disciples of Eckhart are as yet unknown and their works are only partially preserved. One of the works, *Theologia Germanica* (*Die deutsche Theologie*) probably written at Frankfurt around 1350, by a disciple of Eckhart, is a jewel of spirituality that was so highly esteemed by Martin Luther that he published an incomplete version of it in 1518.[29] The work is a manual for ordinary Christians and treats of the interior life in a manner more traditional than that of Eckhart, Tauler or Suso. It follows the division of the purgative, illuminative and unitive ways and emphasizes the central role of Christ in the journey to perfection. Man in himself is nothing; only God, the perfect being, is the All. In becoming more and more aware of his nothingness, man becomes increasingly humble. Hence, humility is the door to the renunciation and self-abandonment which enable a man to empty himself of self and be filled with God. When that happens, God's "allness" replaces man's nothingness so that man is, so to speak, divinized.

<h2 style="text-align:center">RUYSBROECK</h2>

The first country outside Germany to receive the influence of the Rhineland mystics was the Netherlands,[30] although it is likely that the origins of the Flemish mystics go back to the thirteenth century. The most influential mystical writer was John Ruysbroeck (1293–1381), who spent a good part of his life as a hermit and died as a Canon of St. Augustine in the abbey which he founded at Groenendael. In 1908 Rome approved the cult given him as a blessed. Although he is in the direct line of the Rhineland mystics, some authors hail Ruysbroeck as the leader of a distinct school of spirituality – the Flemish School – and the founder of *devotio moderna*. He is at least a transition point between the Rhineland mystics and Gerard Groote.[31]

Besides the German writers, Ruysbroeck is also indebted to other sources: St. Augustine, pseudo-Dionysius, St. Bernard and the Victorines. Like the Rhineland mystics, the intent of his writings was to explain how and to what degree a man can achieve union with God, yet always avoiding any taint of Pantheism. Indeed, he states specifically in *The Book of the Highest Truth*: "No creature can be or become holy to the point of losing its created nature and becoming God." He had a great reverence for tradition and asserted that mysticism without a historical sense is a source of pride and error.

Ruysbroeck's spiritual doctrine involves three elements: exemplarism, introversion and union. The basis of *exemplarism* is the Trinity. The intimate life of the Trinity is an ebb and flow, a going out and a return, originating in the unity of the Godhead, from which proceed the three divine Persons, who as Trinity return to the unity of infinite perfection. Man can share somehow in this divine life and movement because of the exemplary ideas existing in the divine intellect: the human soul comes forth from God the Creator and possesses the three spiritual faculties of intellect, memory and will.

But the human soul must regain its unity and it does this by means of *introversion*, returning to its interior by three stages: the active life, the interior life and the contemplative life. The active life is the life of the virtues; the interior life is the life of grace and imitation of Christ; the contemplative life is the tasting and experiencing of God.

To make progress in the spiritual life, one must despoil himself of all egoism and attachment to created things. Then he can receive the life of the Father as communicated by the Son and the Holy Spirit. This constitutes the life of *union* with God, which is so intimate that it transcends all purely human experience, and yet the soul always recognizes this life as something distinct from its own.

Of the written works of Ruysbroeck, twelve treatises are extant, but we shall discuss only the most important.[32] The treatise entitled *The Kingdom of the Lovers of God* contains Ruysbroeck's doctrine on the gifts of the Holy Spirit, but because of certain obscurities, he followed it with *The Book of the Highest Truth*. His intention in the latter work is to explain the three phases of contemplative union with God: through an intermediary; without an intermediary; without difference or distinction. "Union through an intermediary" is effected through the grace of God and the works of virtue, presupposing death to sin and to every disordered appetite of man's lower nature. "Union without intermediary" occurs when the soul is united with God through the total capacity of its love and experiences this love in the depth of its being. The symbol used is that of iron in the fiery furnace, which becomes so inflamed that it is indistinguishable from the flames. "Union without difference or distinction" is the most intimate union that is possible between the soul and God, but always respecting the principle that no created being can become one in essence with God. This is the union for which Christ prayed when he asked the Father that his disciples should be one in him as he is one with the Father in the Spirit.

Ruysbroeck's masterpiece, *The Adornment of the Spiritual Marriage* (known in English as *The Spiritual Espousals*), was written against the Brethren of the Free Spirit who followed the heretical teachings of Bloemardinne.[33] What is of interest in this work is Ruysbroeck's descriptions of the active life, the interior life and the contemplative life.

The primary functions of the active life are death to sin and growth in virtue, presupposing, of course, the infusion of grace and conversion to God. The spiritual powers that are most important at this stage of the spiritual life are the moral virtues, particularly the virtue of humility. The goal sought is union with God through faith, hope and charity, stimulated by a desire to see and know Christ as he is in himself.

The interior life is one in which the soul, illumined by grace and purified by Christ in its lower faculties, rids itself of all images and distracting occupations. The superior powers of intellect, memory and will have been so purified and intensified that the soul experiences the divine touch at its very center and recognizes the call to even more intimate union and the promise of mystical experience. The call is realized and the promise is fulfilled in the contemplative life, where the soul experiences "superessential contemplation" of the divine essence in full divine light and in a divine mode. The soul enjoys an encounter with the divine in the center of the soul.

The doctrine of Ruysbroeck, especially as expounded in the third book of *Spiritual Marriage*, was attacked by Gerson as pantheistic but was defended by John of Schoonhoven, Henry Herp and Denis the Carthusian. Some have not hesitated to give him the title, "the St. Thomas Aquinas of mystical theology," and to place him above St. Bernard and St. John of the Cross![34]

THE ENGLISH MYSTICS

Running parallel to the spiritual movements in Germany and the Low Lands was the production of mystical treatises in Catholic England. And the first thing to be noted about the English mystics is that they were not, as in Germany and the Low Lands, inspired or directed by members of religious orders. They were for the most part independent writers and for the most part enamored of the eremitical life. Although their remote source seems to have been the pseudo-Dionysian doctrine, more immediately their preference was for the Victorines. They tended, however, to be eminently practical and were gifted with a realistic and sometimes humorous view of human frailty.[35]

The earliest spiritual treatise, *The Ancren Riwle*, was composed for the spiritual direction of lay anchorites.[36] The first outstanding writer among the English Catholics was Richard Rolle (+ 1349). He became a hermit at an early age and it is possible that he studied theology at the Sorbonne and then returned to England. His most important works are *Incendium Amoris* (translated into English as *Fire of Love*) and *Emendatio Vitae* (translated under the titles, *The*

Mending of Life and *The Form of Perfect Living*).[37] His works, says Sitwell, "are not important for the contribution they make to spiritual literature, but they tell us a good deal about himself, and his life is of great interest as illustrating the spontaneous desire for contemplation which seems to have been a feature of his times."[38]

Although dedicated to the eremitical life (so much so that he seems to have looked upon the cenobitic life with disdain) and although he actually experienced mystical graces rather early, he was greatly preoccupied with rather harsh criticism of the clergy. He likewise exhibits a certain degree of harshness when speaking of theologians trained in the schools, for while the humble contemplative is taught by wisdom from above, "those taught by wisdom acquired, not inshed, and those swollen with folded arguments, will disdain him saying, 'Where did he learn? Under what doctor did he sit?' They do not admit that the lovers of eternity are taught by a doctor from within to speak more eloquently than they themselves, who have learned from men, and studied all the time for empty honors."[39]

Contemplation for Rolle is an operation of the intellect which leads the soul to union with God in love. The object of contemplation is the Trinity, which is unknowable; hence, contemplation is obscure and its primary characteristics are love and joy.

Devotion to Christ, especially in his passion, and to Mary is particularly prominent in the writings of Rolle. The activity of the Holy Spirit, working through his gifts, pertains to the very essence of contemplation. Speaking of Christian sanctity in general, Rolle stresses the primacy of charity; but when treating of charity as love of God and love of neighbor, he accentuates love of God to such an extent that he seems to place it in opposition to love of neighbor. This is perhaps a logical consequence of his preoccupation with contemplation and mystical experience.

However, it does not seem that he merits the judgment against him, to the effect that he believed sensible mystical phenomena to be of the essence of the mystical experience.[40] On the contrary, he states explicitly in *Emendatio vitae* (chap. 11): "In this degree or state of love is love chaste, holy, willing; loving the Beloved for himself alone and not for his gifts." Finally, Rolle gives little or no importance at all to the role of a spiritual director, for he maintains that the true director of the soul should be the virtue of prudence, which is perfected by the gift of wisdom.

Hailed as the most beautiful spiritual treatise of the fourteenth century, *The Cloud of Unknowing*, by an unidentified author, is an

158 DIONYSIAN SPIRITUALITY AND DEVOTIO MODERNA

excellent example of "apophatic" mystical theology because it treats of God by way of negation. Since God is ineffable, we cannot know what he is; we can know only what he is not. The treatise is fully within the tradition that stems from pseudo-Dionysius through Richard of St. Victor and the Rhineland mystics; it will later cross into Spain and be brought to its perfection in St. John of the Cross. It seems excessive, however, to brand *The Cloud of Unknowing* as a depersonalization of God through extreme idealism and apophasis.[41]

The Cloud of Unknowing is the most celebrated but not the only work of the unknown author. A more profound work, entitled *The Book of Privy Counsel,* refers to *The Cloud* and the *Epistle of Prayer* as being the works of the same author. A fourth work is the *Epistle of Discretion of Stirrings.* Three other works are translations and adaptations: *The Denis Hid Divinity* (a free translation of the *Theologia mystica* of pseudo-Dionysius); *A Treatise of the Study of Wisdom that Men Call Benjamin* (from the *Benjamin minor* of Richard of St. Victor); and *A Treatise of Discretion of Spirits* (based on several sermons of St. Bernard).[42]

The basic thesis of all these works is that contemplative prayer is simply an intensification of the ordinary grace offered to every Christian; it is attained through love and not through knowledge. At the very start, the author states the pseudo-Dionysian teaching that "the most godly knowing of God is that which is known by unknowing." He does not deny that God can somehow be known through analogical knowledge, but the mind must be emptied of all concepts and images so that faith can serve as the basis for the "blind stirring of love."

The mystical knowledge of contemplation is grounded on faith, stirred by love and perfected in wisdom. This is exemplified in Mary Magdalen, who was so enraptured by the divinity of Christ that she no longer retained any image or concept of his physical body as she knelt before him. So also, the contemplative sees God in a "dark knowledge" while love reaches out to touch and embrace divinity.

Contemplative knowledge is "supraconceptual" and that accounts for its darkness as well as for the fact that concepts and images would be distractions that hinder contemplation. Therefore, in contemplation there is a shift from conceptual knowledge to intuitive, experiential, imageless knowledge, which calls into play the operations of love. The perfection of this loving knowledge results in wisdom which, says the author, is like a burning candle that throws light both on itself and on everything around it. Thus, the wisdom of contemplation reveals to the Christian his own nothingness and wretchedness and the ineffable glory of God.

The wisdom that is the perfection of contemplative love is a gift from above, although it is received as a logical consequence of the perfection of grace and charity. Yet, it is received only at the cost of purification and the total abandonment of all self-centered desires; and this is a dark night of suffering for the Christian who endures purgation in silent love. To those who endure the dark night successfully, the dawn of a new day breaks with a wondrous vision of God as he is in himself. The Christian then sees himself as a part of the whole and not as he is in himself; he then becomes through grace what God is by nature. Stripped of self, he is transformed in Christ and united to.the Father in the most intimate union possible in this life.

According to the author of *The Cloud of Unknowing*, every Christian, by reason of his baptismal grace, is called to the most perfect possible union with God, but it is only the contemplative who actually experiences this union. Although the contemplative or mystical experience is within the potentialities of "ordinary" grace, since contemplation is simply the perfection of faith, charity and wisdom, nevertheless it is still a gift and is therefore not attained by all Christians.

In distinguishing between those called to salvation and those called to perfection, the author states that those who are called to perfection are also called to contemplation. Man may be saved without contemplation, but he cannot be perfect without it; that is why the Church proclaims the contemplative life as the most excellent. Unlike Richard Rolle, the author of *The Cloud* insists on the necessity of spiritual direction and the discernment of spirits, if only because of the great danger of self-illusion. But the spiritual director must himself be a man who has experienced the spiritual life.

Walter Hilton (d. 1396) was an Augustinian canon and the author of a major work in English spirituality: *The Scale of Perfection*.[43] The work was written for the direction of an anchoress and therefore postulates contemplation as a goal of Christian perfection. Yet Hilton had a more comprehensive view of Christian spirituality than Rolle or the author of *The Cloud*. For example, whereas Rolle manifested almost a disdain for the active life and the author of *The Cloud* restricted Christian perfection to the attainment of contemplative prayer, Hilton taught that union with God can be achieved in both the active and the contemplative life. His intention in *The Scale of Perfection,* however, is to teach a contemplative how to reach the perfection of the contemplative life, and this should be kept in mind during the study of the treatise.

There are, according to Hilton, three types or degrees of contemplation: first, the knowledge of God and of spiritual things as acquired through the teaching of others and the reading of Scripture; secondly, affective contemplation, which is the result of grace and the work of Christ (all can attain it; it is normal for holy people; it terminates in uninterrupted prayer that is peaceful and consoling); thirdly, perfect contemplation, which is the action of the Holy Spirit and frequently accompanied by ecstasy, rapture and detachment.

The third and highest degree of contemplation is a kind of spiritual marriage in which the soul is transformed, so to speak, into the image of the Trinity. It is a special gift, not given to all, but only to those who devote themselves to the solitude of the contemplative life. It is preceded by a period of intense and painful purification.

Hilton's theological development of the theology of contemplation can be summarized as follows: Before the Fall, man was the image of God and he was directed to God by the higher faculties of intellect, memory and will; but after the Fall, he lost this orientation and fell into "forgetfulness and ignorance of God, and into a monstrous love of himself."[44]

The Christian effort consists in restoring or re-forming the image of God in man as it once was. This is made possible to man through the merits of Jesus Christ. If a Christian is in the state of grace, the image of God is re-formed in him in a lower degree; but if he is in the state of grace and also experiences the Holy Spirit working in him, he has the restored image to a much higher degree, which is proper to the contemplative life. Hence, contemplation is an awareness of the life of grace; "the soul understands something of what it knew before only by faith,"[45] thanks to the presence of uncreated Love, the Holy Spirit, in the soul.

The first thing required of the Christian in the contemplative way is a desire for God or "the naked intent of the will unto God." The first response to this desire may prove a disappointment, however, for when the soul turns inward in search of God, it does not find the image of God, but the image of sin. This is in reality a good sign, because the awareness of our own weakness and sinfulness inspires us to eradicate the evil in us so that we can give ourselves completely to God. The death to self and to sin is described as a "pilgrimage to Jerusalem" and a "passage through the night." It involves darkness, suffering, trials, but eventually the soul will come to rest because "Jesus, who is both love and light, is in the darkness whether it is distressing or peaceful."

Julian of Norwich (d. 1442) is of considerable importance in the history of spirituality and precisely because she gives testimony to the workings and manifestations of grace in the mystical life. As Sitwell says of her:

> The recipient of unusual favors and experiences, she is obviously balanced, humble, wise and charitable; marked off by all the gifts of character and grace necessary to prove the genuineness of her claims. In her only book, *The Revelations of Divine Love*, she comes forward not as a teacher and master providing a map and general information for those setting out to explore a country for themselves, or anxious only to learn about it, but as a traveller returned with a first-hand description of what she has seen there."[46]

What she gives by way of doctrine constantly alternates between two poles: the realization and acknowledgment of God's goodness to man and the awareness of one's sinfulness. But her recurrent theme is the reality of love and the confidence that "all will be well."

Julian was an anchoress in the church of St. Julian in Norwich, a city that was a "little Rome" as far as the number of monasteries was concerned. Her book of revelations (or "showings") consists of an account of fifteen revelations received one day and another sixteen received the following night. There are two redactions of *The Revelations of Divine Love*, and the second one, done many years later, is considerably longer.[47]

In spite of her emphasis on divine love and her insistence that souls should have confidence in the divine mercy, Julian herself was preoccupied with the salvation of the souls of her contemporaries. The response given her by the Lord became for her a constant refrain: "All will be well; all will be well." As a result, even sinners can trust in the divine mercy and know that God loves them; in fact, Julian maintains that those who do penance for their sins will find therein a motive for joy. While individuals may be concerned about the future – whether they or others will reach heaven – Julian says that no one can know for certain, but "all will be well." Finally, it is of interest to note that Julian is one of the relatively few spiritual writers in any age who speaks of the maternity of God. All of her revelations occurred when she seemed to be at death's door and had fixed her gaze on a crucifix.

Richard Rolle and Julian of Norwich ... are in marked contrast to the continental mystics, especially Eckhart and Ruysbroeck. Fundamentally they were teaching the same doctrine, but the latter were speculative, interested in trying to analyze and define the nature of the soul's union with God. They were practical too, but the English writers were wholly so. Whether this was to be attributed to their national temperament, which for the most part is not given to abstract speculation, is an open question, but the fact remains and is very striking. There is no doubt that the movement was less widespread in England than it was on the Continent. We hear nothing in this country of sects such as the Beghards and the Brethren of the Free Spirit, who succumbed wholesale to the dangers inherent in an unwise pursuit of contemplation. Nevertheless the movement must have been sufficiently widespread in England to make the authorities aware of the dangers. This is undoubtedly the reason for the suspicions aroused by Margery Kempe,[48] and the trials to which she was subjected.[49]

DEVOTIO MODERNA

Although the influence of Ruysbroeck was perpetuated by writers like the Franciscan, Henry Herp (d. 1478) and was introduced into France and Spain, something more similar to English spirituality was developing in the Low Lands. The new movement was given the name *"devotio moderna"* by John Busch[50] and it gained momentum largely because of the annoyance and boredom of many sincere Christians with the speculative intricacies of the German and Flemish writers. The new trend offered instead an affective type of spirituality which answered the practical needs of earnest Christians, without excessive theorizing about union with God in the higher states of the mystical life. The following excerpts from the *Imitation of Christ* are expressive of the weariness of many persons as regards the speculative approach to the Christian life:

What does it avail you to discourse profoundly of the Trinity if you lack humility and, consequently, are displeasing to the Trinity? In truth, lofty words do not make a man holy and just, but a virtuous life makes him dear to God. I would rather experience compunction than know how to define it. . . .

Leave off that excessive desire to know, because it is the cause of much distraction and deceit. Men of learning are very glad to appear and be called wise. There are many things of which the knowledge is of little or no value to the soul. And he is most foolish who concerns himself with things that do not contribute to his salvation. . . .

If men would only use as much diligence in rooting out vices and planting virtues as they do in proposing questions, there would not be such great evils committed, nor scandals among the people, nor such relaxation in monasteries.[51]

A second reason for the reaction against the German and Flemish writers was the errors and scandals that arose as a result of their doctrine. There can be no doubt that men like Ruysbroeck were often misquoted and unjustly blamed for the illusions and heresies of false mystics, but men like Gerard Groote and John Gerson felt obliged to stem the tide of pseudo-mysticism at any cost. Besides, they could always point to the list of condemned propositions from the preaching of Eckhart.

Thirdly, throughout the entire Church there was manifest need for reform: there was schism in the papacy, moral laxity among the clergy and religious, and false mysticism among the laity. What was needed was a renewal of the Church and a complete overhaul of ecclesiastical structure. The externals of Christian life were deeply entrenched, but lifeless; basic theological principles were being contested; traditional ideals were taught but not practiced.[52] The Church was marching toward the Renaissance, the Protestant Revolt and the Council of Trent.

The leader of the reform movement in the Netherlands was Gerard Groote (1340–1384), a deacon who dedicated his efforts to preaching. Two years after his death his followers formed a community of Brethren of the Common Life at Windesheim.[53] Like all the members of his group, Groote was familiar with the teaching of Ruysbroeck and the Rhineland mystics but his predominant concern was for the reformation of the Church. He protested so strongly against the laxity of the clergy that he aroused the hostility of the hierarchy and the bishop of Utrecht revoked his faculties for preaching. Some authors have seen in Groote the forerunner of the Protestant Reformation,[54] but neither he nor the movement he led was ever disobedient to the Church.

Opposed as he was to the esoteric theories of speculative mysticism, Groote preferred to cultivate a popular, pragmatic teaching that was divorced from intellectualism. He was more interested in the Christian life of the ordinary Christian and had little or no use for the interminable discussions concerning the active and contemplative lives, which he considered to be equivalent.[55]

His teaching on contemplation can be reduced to the simple formula: contemplation is the perfection of charity. What he insists upon, as did the Rhineland mystics, is spiritual poverty, self-detachment and the practice of the virtues. And if the Christian seeks any pattern or model, he will find it in the imitation of Christ in his sacred humanity. Through Christ's humanity, we are led to the contemplation of his divinity, and this involves a certain progression from sensible images to a certain spiritual harmony. Touching mystical phenomena, Groote insists that the basic rule for distinguishing the true from the false is by the fruits they produce, namely, illumination of the intellect and an increase in charity.[56]

Like other members of the Windesheim Congregation, Groote dedicated himself to preaching and spiritual conferences. His style is aphoristic and consists for the most part in brief practical instructions or counsels without detailed explanation or proof. Many religious communities were reformed and renewed as a result of the efforts of Groote and his foremost disciple, Florentius Radewijns (1350–1400), the actual founder and director of the Brethren of the Common Life. Another disciple, Gerard Zerbolt (1367–1398) formulated a method of meditation which was later perfected by Henry de Calcar (d. 1408), prior of the Carthusians at Munnikhuizen, and the Franciscan, Henry Herp. Later, the method of meditation would be still more systematized by John Mombaer (d. 1501) for the benefit of religious.[57]

However, the most celebrated author of the *devotio moderna* is unquestionably Thomas Hemerken à Kempis (1379–1471), for many years the master of novices at Mount Saint Agnes, monastery of the Canons Regular of St. Augustine in Zwolle. It is generally accepted that he was the author of the *Imitation of Christ*, but this is only one of his numerous treatises.[58] All of his works were written for the instruction or edification of persons devoted to Christian living within the framework of the religious life. They are either ascetical, such as the *Imitation of Christ* and *Soliloquy of the Soul,* or historical, such as the biographies of Gerard Groote and St. Lydwina of Schiedam.

The *Imitation of Christ* has periodically been praised or criticized throughout the centuries, but it has perhaps been the most widely circulated book in Catholic history, second only to the Bible. Against its critics we could point out that the *Imitation* came out of the reactionary movement against speculative spirituality; it was written for men living a monastic life; it was composed in an age that clamored for reform and renewal of the Church. This accounts for its apparent anti-intellectualism, its insistence on separation from the world, and its constant emphasis on repentance and conversion. The treatise faithfully follows the basic doctrine of the *devotio moderna*: the true spiritual life is the imitation of Christ, and by meditating on his sacred humanity the Christian arrives at contemplation of his divinity and a union with God which liberates the soul. This goal is possible for all sincere Christians and if in the attainment of contemplation there is a vision of God, it will be one which differs from the beatific vision, both in duration and in nature. Contemplation is essentially the operation of the virtue of charity.

To reconstruct the doctrine of the *Imitation* and present it in an orderly fashion, it is necessary first of all to recognize that the spiritual life is an interior life and, secondly, that the most difficult battles must be waged within the confines of one's own soul. This being understood, the *Imitation* states as a first condition for the spiritual life a knowledge of oneself: "This is the highest and most profitable lesson: truly to know and despise oneself.... The humble knowledge of yourself is a surer way to God than the deepest search after science."[59]

Self-knowledge is acquired, however, only at the cost of turning away from self and from creatures; when the Christian does that he is confronted by his own sinfulness and misery, which prompts him to turn to God in humility and repentance.[60] In this way he quiets his troubled conscience and enjoys peace of conscience. But at this point the soul needs stability, for there is always the danger of falling back, for "the man who is remiss and abandons his re-solution is tempted in many ways."[61] Stability or constancy can be safeguarded only by control of the passions, which are so prompt to respond to stimulation. Then, the task is to die to self-love:

> He that keeps himself in subjection, so that his sensuality is always controlled by reason, and reason is in all things subject to [God], is indeed a conqueror of himself and lord of the world. If you desire to mount this high, you must begin manfully and set the axe to the root, that you may eradicate and destroy your secret inordinate inclination to self and to all selfish and earthly goods. This vice by which a man inordinately loves himself is at the bottom of everything that must be rooted out and overcome.... He who desires to walk freely with [God] must mortify all his wicked and irregular affections, and must not cling carnally with selfish love to any created thing.[62]

The *Imitation* uses a special word to designate death to self: *resignation*, meaning renunciation of self and total abandonment to God.

Actually, there are only two ultimates – God and self; therefore, death to self necessarily implies submission to God. But this can be accomplished only with the help of God's grace, although a powerful incentive is derived from meditation on the "last things."

The second phase of the spiritual life consists in "carefully observing in ourselves the divers movements of nature and grace."[63] As the individual becomes more recollected, grows in self-knowledge, and endeavors to remain completely resigned to God, he experiences the tension between nature and grace. Plotinus had described it in his *Enneads* as a black horse and a white horse attached to a wagon and pulling in opposite directions. St. Paul spoke of man's internal struggle in terms of the law of the spirit versus the law of the flesh (Rom. 7:14–25). Thomas à Kempis describes it in great detail, in a style that is reminiscent of St. Paul's teaching on charity (I Cor. 13:1–13):

> Nature is crafty and draws away many, . . . but grace walks with simplicity, turns away from all appearance of evil, is not deceitful, and does all things purely for God. . . .
>
> Nature is unwilling to be mortified or to be restrained, . . . but grace studies the mortification of self, resists sensuality, seeks to be subject, desires to be overcome, does not aim at following her own liberty, loves to be kept under discipline and desires not to have command over anyone, but ever to live, stand and be under God. . . .
>
> Nature labors for her own interests. . . . but grace does not consider what may be advantageous or profitable to herself, but rather what may be profitable to many.
>
> Nature willingly receives honor and respect, but grace faithfully attributes all honor and glory to God.
>
> Nature is afraid of being put to shame and despised, but grace is glad to suffer reproach for the name of Jesus.
>
> Nature loves idleness and bodily rest, but grace cannot be idle, and willingly embraces labor.
>
> Nature seeks to have things that are curious and fine, . . . but grace is pleased with that which is plain and humble. . . .
>
> Nature highly regards temporal things, rejoices at earthly gain, is troubled at losses and is provoked at every slight, injurious word, but

grace attends to things eternal and does not cling to those that pass with time, neither is she disturbed at the loss of things or exasperated with harsh words. . . .

Nature is covetous, and more willing to take than to give, . . . but grace is bountiful and open-hearted, avoids selfishness, is content with little, and judges it more happy to give than to receive.

Nature inclines to creatures, to her own flesh, . . . but grace draws to God and to virtues, renounces creatures, flees the world, hates the desires of the flesh, restricts wandering about and is loath to appear in public.

Nature willingly seeks external comfort, in which she finds sensible delight, but grace seeks to be comforted in God alone. . . .

Nature does all for her own gain and interest, . . . but grace seeks nothing temporal nor any other recompense but God alone for her reward, nor desires any more of the necessities of this life than are useful for attaining a happy eternity.

Nature rejoices in a multitude of friends and relations, . . . but grace loves even her enemies and is not puffed up with having a great many friends nor sets any value on family or birth; she rather favors the poor than the rich; she has more compassion for the innocent than the powerful. . . .

Nature readily complains of want and trouble, but grace bears poverty with constancy.

Nature turns all things to herself, . . . but grace refers all things to God. . . .

Nature is anxious to know secrets and to hear news . . . and to have experience of many things by the senses, desires to be taken notice of and to do things that win praise and admiration, but grace cares not for hearing news and curious things. . . . She teaches us, rather, to restrain the senses, to avoid vain complacency and ostentation, humbly to hide those things which are worthy of praise and admiration, and from everything and from every kind of knowledge to seek the fruit of spiritual profit, and the praise and honor of God.[64]

In the third stage of spiritual development the Christian achieves a profound awareness of the power of God, his care for all men through divine providence, and the divine goodness which is manifested in man's redemption through Christ. Considering God's knowledge and watchfulness, the Christian reacts with a holy fear, but first place must always be given to charity, which should grow in proportion to one's knowledge of God's goodness to man. The second place goes to humility, which is the constant refrain in *The Imitation of Christ* as it was in the monastic spirituality. And what greater manifestation of God's goodness can be found than in Christ, the Savior? It is in and through Christ, therefore, that the Christian is united with the Father.

The doctrine of the *Imitation* terminates in a Christ-centered spirituality which rests on the biblical statement that Christ is the way, the truth and the life (John 14:6). Perfect resignation to God is preserved by frequent meditation on the passion and death of the Lord; the following of Christ is "the royal way of the cross"; union with Christ is experienced with joy in reception of the Eucharist. Yet, Thomas à Kempis does not let his reader forget that union with Christ also means union with the Father and, indeed, with the Trinity:

> I bless you, O heavenly Father, Father of my Lord Jesus Christ, because you have vouchsafed to be mindful of so poor a wretch as I am. O Father of mercies and God of all comfort, I give thanks to you, who sometimes are pleased to cherish with your consolations me who am unworthy of any comfort. I bless you and glorify you for evermore, together with your only begotten Son and the Holy Spirit the Comforter, to all eternity. O Lord God, my holy Lover, when you shall come into my heart, all that is within me will be filled with joy. You are my glory and the joy of my heart.[65]

JOHN GERSON

While Gerard Groote and Thomas à Kempis waged a "peaceful war" against speculative mysticism by teaching a practical doctrine that was devoid of theorizing, John Gerson, Chancellor of the University of Paris, fought his battles against excessive and false mysticism in the area of doctrine. His predecessor at the University, Peter d'Ailly (1350–1420) was the first to react against the pseudo-mystics, who had turned to astrology and divining in order to prophesy. Unfortunately, d'Ailly hurt his own cause by reason of his vehemence and even more so by reason of his adoption of the moral principles taught by William of Ockham. Briefly, his position was that nothing is right or wrong in itself; all morality depends on the divine will; consequently something is sinful only if God has forbidden it and not because it violates the eternal law in God himself. All morality is relative, therefore, because God could have decreed otherwise than he did.[66]

John Gerson (1363–1429) was much more effective in clarifying the orthodox theology of the spiritual life, partly because he was an expert theologian and partly because of his well-balanced temperament. His doctrinal sources were pseudo-Dionysius, St. Augustine, St. Bernard, the Victorines, St. Albert the Great, St. Thomas Aquinas, St. Bonaventure and the Carthusian, Hugh of Balma. His principal works are: *De theologia mystica speculativa et practica*; *De monte contemplationis*; and *De elucidatione mysticae theologiae*.[67]

Gerson admits, with pseudo-Dionysius, that God is known by negation, but his objection to Ruysbroeck and the Rhineland mystics is that they push this statement to extremes. For Gerson, speculative theology is the result of the reasoning powers, whose object is truth; mystical theology is the fruit of the affective powers, whose object is the good; but in both cases God can be known to some degree in a positive manner, at least as goodness and truth. Moreover, God and his attributes can surely be known by faith in divine revelation. Nor is the object of contemplation exclusively God in himself, for sometimes contemplatives must meditate on Christ, the Christian virtues or the last end.

Regarding the active and contemplative lives, Gerson maintained that not all Christians are called to the contemplative life; therefore it is a dangerous error to try to lead all souls to contemplation. Many Christians, by reason of temperament or the duties of their state in life, are suited only for the active life. Indeed, it could be sinful for those dedicated to the duties of the active life (e.g., pastors, prelates, parents, etc.) were they to neglect their obligations and pursue the contemplative life. Such persons should have some kind of contemplative activity in their lives, but it should normally consist in periods of recollection. Those who are called to the contemplative life should not try to anticipate contemplation before they are prepared for it; moreover, they should occasionally engage in some form of manual work or other occupations, because no one can be continually contemplative in this life.

Since the way of the contemplative is especially beset with dangers, those who feel drawn to the contemplative life should place themselves under the guidance of a spiritual director. The director himself should be a person who not only has knowledge but lives the doctrine himself. Because mystics are usually held in esteem, they are more prone to fall into erroneous or absurd doctrine than less devout Christians. Some, like the Beghards, reached the absurd position of believing that those who attain to mystical union are no longer under obligation to the divine laws; hence the scandalous immoralities which they committed in the name of mystical experience. Others, confusing the natural and the supernatural orders, interpreted the uncontrolled movements of passion and sensuality as operations of grace and an experience of the supernatural, so that they, too, quickly succumbed to the promptings of the flesh. Still others, more inclined to intellectual speculation, constructed a theology that led them inevitably to excessive idealism or to Pantheism, and in their pride and arrogance many of them became insubordinate to the Church and fell into explicit heresy. Finally, some misguided mystics fell into the error of Quietism, which teaches that one should be indifferent to salvation, neglect prayer and good works, and leave himself totally in the hands of God.[68]

To offset the preceding dangers, Gerson drew up a list of rules for the discernment of spirits and the evaluation of mystical teachings. All Christians must accept the doctrines taught by Councils of the Church, popes, bishops and learned theologians, and those who have the gift of discernment of spirits. The teaching of any individual mystic must be in accord with Scripture and tradition. Any teaching that incites the passions or undermines the virtues should be rejected.

The discernment of spirits is a gift from God, although it is possible to acquire a certain degree of facility through study and experience with souls.

The first thing to consider is the mental and physical health of the mystic, because persons with uncontrolled emotions or vivid imaginations may easily be misled. Special care is also needed when dealing with beginners in the spiritual life or with women.

Secondly, it is necessary to go into great detail in the investigation of a revelation or vision, but the director must be most reserved and even skeptical, lest he be prejudiced in favor of the claims of the mystic. Gerson even suggests that the director should act with severity in order to test the humility of the mystic.

Thirdly, the director should discover the motive which prompts the mystic to discuss the revelation or vision, because authentic mystics are usually somewhat loath to discuss these matters even with a director.

Fourthly, but not less in importance, the director must take into account the life of the mystic; for example, how well the individual fulfills the duties of state in life and what virtues are manifested in the life of the mystic, for genuine mystical phenomena should contribute to the perfection of the individual and not become occasions of pride.

The last step – that of the actual discernment of spirits – is the most difficult because it is a question of trying to determine whether the cause is truly supernatural or whether there may be a natural or diabolical explanation. The true coin of a divine cause is distinguished from the false coin of illusion or diabolical intervention by its weight, which is humility; by its flexibility, which is prudence; by its solidity, which is patience; by its shape, which is truth; and by its color, which is the golden hue of charity.[69]

As regards his positive theological teaching, Gerson prefers mystical theology to speculative theology because it facilitates union with God; it produces patience and humility, while speculative theology causes pride. What he understands by mystical theology is the experiential knowledge of God, although he treats of it both speculatively and practically. In fact, Gerson admits that it may happen that a speculative theologian may be able better to explain mystical theology than one who actually experiences it; for that reason, practical mystical theology should be guided by speculative mystical theology.

In his speculative treatment of mystical theology Gerson teaches that reflection leads to meditation and the latter leads to contemplation; but contemplation is essentially an affective operation; it is an ecstatic love. Thus, it calls into play the higher appetite of the soul called *synteresis*, leaving behind the operations of the passions (sense appetite) and the will. The love proper to contemplation or mystical experience is one that carries the soul to union with God and fills it with joy and happiness.

Gerson, therefore, identifies ecstatic union with contemplation but he then proceeds to clarify precisely what he means by this type of union. The lower powers, including the imagination and reason, cease to act; they are suspended when the soul is caught up in contemplation. The mind has become fixed on God and the affective powers have been alienated from sensible things; the whole operation is called "simplification of the heart."[70] The soul is transformed into God, but Gerson chooses his words with great care when attempting to describe this transformation. In no case can the soul lose its identity or its own being; consequently, the transformation of the soul in God can never be understood as its return to the eternal exemplar in the mind of God; nor can the love by which this transformation is effected be identified with the Holy Spirit (Peter Lombard); nor can it be equated with the change of a drop of water into wine when dropped into a cask of wine, the change of food into the body of the one who eats it, or the change of the bread and wine into the body and blood of Christ in the Mass. All these comparisons are rejected by Gerson, though he admits that not all of them need to be condemned.

The ecstatic union of contemplation that results in the soul's transformation is the work of love; it unites the soul to God by effecting a conformity of wills between the soul and God. But however intimate the union, the mystic always preserves his identity and personality. In asking to what extent the will of the mystic submits to the will of God, Gerson maintains that it is a dangerous (though perhaps permissible) teaching to seek to identify man's will with God's "permissive" will, whereby sin is "permitted" by God or souls are damned, to such an extent that a mystic could "will" his own past sins or his own damnation. Here Gerson is apparently referring to those mystics who stated that since God in some way wills the sins one commits, the mystics themselves would not desire not to have committed them (Eckhart).[71]

It should also be noted that although Gerson holds for the primacy of love in contemplation and ecstatic union, he does not exclude knowledge. He recognizes that it is impossible for the soul to reach God and enjoy intimate union with him without some previous knowledge. Gerson recognizes the necessity of both knowledge and love in the mystical union of contemplation, but he concludes that since most of the effects of contemplation are the effects of charity, contemplation itself, as "perfect prayer," is the perfection of charity.

Turning to the practical question of conditions and means for the attainment of mystical union or contemplation, Gerson states that the most important means is the faithful practice of meditation. By meditation he means the consideration of divine truths for the purpose of fostering one's growth in love and devotion. He offers no fixed rules or method for meditation; he respects the liberty of the individual to adjust his mental prayer to his needs and the duties of his state in life.

From the foregoing it is evident that Gerson played an important role in adapting the *devotio moderna* to the French *milieu*. An intellectual and at the same time a man of action, Gerson was both polemic and constructive. He combated the pseudo-mysticism of the Low Lands and pointed out the dangers inherent in the teachings of Ruysbroeck so far as they were cast in the same mold as the doctrine of Eckhart. Constructively, he set the course of spirituality for the new age that was dawning and, for the time at least, he produced a harmonious synthesis between affective and speculative spiritual theology. He ended his days at the monastery of the Celestines in Lyons, where he devoted himself to contemplation, literary pursuits and the religious instruction of children.

ST. CATHERINE OF SIENA

While there was a ferment of mysticism throughout the Rhineland and the Low Lands, the papal schism stimulated a sense of Christian realism in Italy. In the literary world the *Divine Comedy* of Dante Alighieri (1265–1321) reflected the concerns of the age and stands as one of the most beautiful witnesses to medieval spirituality. Like Petrarch (1304–1374), who fought for the unity of the Church and the return to orthodoxy, Dante also called for reform. However, the figure that dominated this troubled period and ultimately succeeded in putting an end to the papal sojourn in Avignon was St. Catherine of Siena (1347–1380).

Catherine Benincasa was born into a family of twenty-five children and from the age of six she dedicated herself to God. Later she joined the *Mantellate*, a group of laywomen who were members of the Third Order of St. Dominic. All her life she remained a lay person, first living a life of recollection in the family home, and later serving the needy, the prisoners and the sick.

At the age of twenty-four she began an extensive apostolate as a peacemaker and a promoter of the Crusades, travelling from one city to another to establish concord among the principalities of Italy and to promote the good of the Church. After countless setbacks that would have discouraged even the most determined soul, Catherine prevailed, and Pope Gregory XI returned to Rome on January 17, 1377. Unfortunately, the victory was short-lived, for the election of Pope Urban VI led to another schism which, for all her prayers and pleadings, Catherine was unable to avert.

In the last year of her life, Catherine went daily to the Vatican to pray for the end of the schism and the unity of the Church. Finally, drained of strength, she passed from this life on April 29, 1380. She was canonized by Pope Pius II in 1461 and declared Doctor of the Church by Pope Paul VI in 1970.[72]

Favored with the stigmata – invisible until after her death – and with the ring of mystical espousal, St. Catherine of Siena is a kindred spirit to the energetic and dauntless St. Teresa of Avila. Her principal work is the *Dialogue*, known also as *The Book of Divine Providence*.[73] She also left more than 400 letters and various prayers.

During her lifetime she acted as spiritual director to countless souls – popes, bishops, priests, religious and laity. Since Catherine could neither read nor write, all her doctrine was dictated to secretaries.

In the *Dialogue*, which is a colloquy between the eternal Father and Catherine, Catherine makes four petitions to God; 1) for her own sanctification; 2) for the salvation of mankind and peace in the Church; 3) for the reform of the clergy; 4) that divine providence will direct all things for the salvation of souls.

The spiritual doctrine of St. Catherine, as seen in the *Dialogue* and her letters, is based on a knowledge of God and knowledge of self. The latter is the foundation of humility, which destroys self-love. Aware of our own nothingness, since we have received our very being from God, we realize that God is all. Thus, one day the Lord said to her: "Catherine. I am who am; you are she who is not."

Since the essence of Christian perfection is charity, St. Catherine describes three stages of love in the soul's progress to sanctity: servile love (a love accompanied by fear of punishment for one's sins); mercenary love (a love accompanied by hope of eternal reward); and filial love (the love of God for his own sake, which is the perfection of charity). In the state of perfect love the individual is completely despoiled of his own will and totally abandoned to the divine will.

St. Catherine describes mystical union with great clarity and precision: it is the experience or awareness of the presence of God in the soul and is quite different from the simple union with God through sanctifying grace. In the state of perfection the soul never loses its awareness of God's presence; there is such an intimate and continual union between the soul and God that every time and place is a place for prayer, for communing with God.

St. Catherine of Siena was in every way a faithful and loving daughter of St. Dominic. Consequently, we are not surprised to find that her spiritual teaching is profoundly doctrinal, and indeed Scholastic. At the same time she had an ardor, a sensitivity and a passion that rivalled that of her countryman, St. Francis of Assisi. Her devotion to Christ focuses especially on his Precious Blood, shed for the redemption of mankind but Catherine is at the same time an adorer of the Trinity. Moreover, like her spiritual Father St. Dominic, she is an apostolic contemplative. Finally, because of her childlike love for the Vicar of Christ and her fierce loyalty to the Church, Catherine is both a mother and a daughter of the Church.

DENIS THE CARTHUSIAN

This historical survey of medieval spirituality comes to a close with Denis the Carthusian, whom Krogh-Tonning calls the last of the Scholastics.[74] Perhaps with greater success than most religious, the Carthusians had assimilated the *devotio moderna*, but then, the Carthusians have always preferred a simplified form of spirituality that was eminently practical and affective. Indeed, the Carthusian Order did not produce any writer of note until the end of the thirteenth century.[75] At that time Ludolph produced his *Vita Christi*, an original approach to meditation on the mysteries of Christ. Similar to the life of Christ which was formerly attributed to St. Bonaventure, it was a forerunner of *The Imitation of Christ* and one of the most widely read books of its day.[76]

Much more important in the field of spiritual theology is Denis of Rijkel (1402–1471), who serves as a bridge between the traditional teaching and the new movement in spirituality. His vast literary production and erudition (44 volumes) are amazing when one considers that he spent most of his life as a contemplative monk at the charterhouse in Roermond, near Liège.[77] He studied Scripture assiduously and his theology is in the tradition of pseudo-Dionysius, the Victorines, St. Bonaventure and Gerson.

The great contribution of Denis the Carthusian was to synthesize all previous doctrine on the spiritual life and then to make an evaluation of the various conclusions. His writings are addressed to all Christians and he composed treatises for particular groups as well, such as bishops, parish priests, married persons, widows, soldiers, merchants, and so forth. He was thoroughly convinced of his obligation to be of service to the people of God by his writings. He stated that although the purely contemplative life has a greater dignity and stability than the purely active life, highest of all is the life which includes both contemplation and action, provided the activities are such that they flow from the plenitude of contemplation.

Denis follows St. Bonaventure in dividing the spiritual life into three stages. In the purgative stage the Christian is occupied with overcoming sin and growing in virtue; in the illuminative stage his mind is occupied with the contemplation of divine things; in the unitive stage he experiences a vehement love from his contemplation of the divine, so that his soul is "altogether on fire . . . as though enkindled by the immense fire of the divinity."

Contemplation itself admits of two kinds: the "affirmative speculative," which is an acquired contemplation that is attainable by reason alone, even without grace and charity; and the "mystical and loving contemplation,"" which is infused, but requires the operation of charity and is ultimately perfected by the gift of wisdom. Only when love intervenes in contemplation does it become authentic prayer; and only when it is prayer can contemplation become mystical. It is then an intense experience of one's love of God, accompanied by a kind of "divine touch" which is the contact of the soul with God.

Hence, the secret of contemplation is to love much, although Denis follows St. Thomas Aquinas in giving supremacy to the intellect. The function of love in the contemplative act is to make the knowledge intuitive and immediate. Moreover, he admits with the Rhineland mystics and with pseudo-Dionysius that contemplative knowledge is a dark knowledge of negation because God is in himself other than we can say of him. The language of the mystic who tries to describe the mystical experience must necessarily be the language of negation. It is only in the lower type of contemplation – the "affirmative speculative" – that the individual can know something positive of God, by analogy with created things. Like Gerson, Denis stresses the need for the faithful practice of meditation, which normally leads to contemplation. Yet, one does not strictly prepare himself for contemplation, for it is a gift, and it may be granted by God to the simple and uneducated who approach him with deep faith and ardent love.

Denis the Carthusian brings the "ascetic and mystical Middle Ages to a conclusion."[78] It was not a peaceful conclusion, however, for already in the fourteenth century the seeds of humanistic Christianity and a new paganism had been sown and the rumblings of the Protestant Revolt were faintly audible. At its best, the Renaissance was a correction of the sombre austerity of medieval spirituality and its excessive intellectualism, and as such it received the encouragement of the Church. Unfortunately, it ended up as a pagan humanism which exalted fallen human nature and the natural order, causing man to turn in upon himself to the exclusion of the supernatural order and the life hereafter. There can be no doubt that the Protestant Reformation was in great part a reaction against the pagan humanism of the Renaissance.[79]

Perhaps the most effective weapon against the humanizing of Christianity was the introduction of "spiritual exercises" and methods of mental prayer. In Italy the Benedictine, Louis Barbo (d. 1443), wrote a treatise on meditation and through Garcí de Cisneros the movement was carried to Spain, where a book of "spiritual exercises" was published at Montserrat in 1500. A quarter of a century later, Ignatius Loyola would produce a classical formula for spiritual exercises. Henry Herp, the Franciscan (d. 1477), also exerted a great influence by his efforts to supplant the speculative teachings of Ruysbroeck and the Rhineland mystics with a practical spirituality. Mombaer (d. 1502) and Louis de Blois (Blosius) (1506–1566) likewise contributed greatly to the promulgation of sound doctrine on the practice of prayer and the best methods to practice it.

Despite their efforts, the Church was on the march to a revolt and a schism. Other factors in addition to the Renaissance contributed to the ultimate break: the Black Plague, the schism in the papacy, the scandalous lives of the clergy, the indifference of the ordinary Christians or their downright pessimism. The liturgy was decadent; there was a wave of superstition and diabolism, Christianity was strictly an individual matter of performing good works. Piety had become sentimentality, against which the Protestants would react with a puritanical rigorism. Northern Europe was in turmoil; the papacy had lost its prestige; the revival of Christian spirituality would occur south of the Pyrenees, in Spain.[80]

POST-TRIDENTINE SPIRITUALITY

The period covered by the title of this chapter corresponds to the third volume of Pourrat's *Christian Spirituality*,[1] that is, from the middle of the fifteenth to the middle of the seventeenth century. Several things should be noted about this particular period. First, the schools of spirituality are for the most part classified according to nations and not religious orders, as was true of the previous periods. As Pourrat points out:

> The principle of nationality asserted itself in a very remarkable way, especially from the time of the Renaissance. This tendency of each nation to converge upon the lines of its own genius and language and religion reacted upon every manifestation of its life, and therefore upon its spirituality. Hence we actually find in recent times a Spanish spirituality, an Italian spirituality, and a French spirituality, a spirituality which is fundamentally one and the same so far as it is Catholic, but differs in the way in which it is conceived and presented.[2]

There were, of course, certain individuals and certain religious orders which exerted such a tremendous influence during this period that they could be classified as leaders of distinct schools of spirituality, but even in these cases the national temperament and spirit could be discerned as a distinctive trait. Moreover, it was especially through the religious orders that a continuity with the past was preserved. Abrupt changes in ideas and attitudes are rare in history, and this is especially true of the history of spirituality.

Secondly, the prodigious output of spiritual writings during this period makes it impossible to discuss more than a few outstanding authors. Merely to list the writings and their authors would comprise a large volume. Consequently, we shall concentrate on initiators of new trends or schools which reflect the currents of spirituality between the Council of Trent and the mid-seventeenth century.

SPIRITUAL EXERCISES

The state of the Church at the end of the Middle Ages was one of schism, lack of respect for authority and scandalous moral degradation at all levels of society. The Renaissance introduced a humanism that was at once Christian and pagan, but the self-indulgence of the latter reached such universal proportions that Rabelais stated that the rule of life for many people was simply: "Do as you please";[3] and Erasmus observed in 1501 that even among the pagans none were ever more corrupt than the average Christian.[4]

Faced with such conditions, fervent Christians had to resort to a spirituality that was one of withdrawal from the world, fortified by well-regulated spiritual exercises and definite methods of prayer. This itself was not an innovation in the Christian life, for Christ had taught the necessity of self-discipline, a certain detachment from the world and the practice of prayer. St. Paul had repeated the same doctrine, and the early Christians had lived it to such an extent that the word "ascetics" is applied to those who followed a program of spiritual exercises involving fasting, austerities and continence. The same teaching was incorporated in the monastic tradition, with the insistence that external discipline is ordained to the interior practice of prayer.

Ultimately, through various treatises on prayer composed toward the end of the medieval period,[5] methodical or systematized meditation was introduced in the Low Countries, France, Italy and Spain.[6] It is important to note that methodical meditation was introduced and promulgated primarily as a reform measure; it seemed to be a sure way to lead the clergy and religious back to a truly Christian life.

Spiritual exercises, or methodical mental prayer seem to have appeared for the first time in the Low Countries among the Canons of Windesheim and the Brethren of the Common Life.[7] It is probable that John Wessel Gransfort (+1489), a friend of Thomas à Kempis, constructed the first method of meditation. It comprised three stages; preparation for meditation by ridding oneself of distractions and selecting the material for meditation; the actual meditation by the application of mind, judgment and will; and the summation of the meditation, directing to God the desires that have been stimulated.[8] The effectiveness of meditation as a means of spiritual reform was soon evident, for it is difficult to imagine, as St. Teresa of Avila would later remark, the possibility of remaining in sin and at the same time practising daily meditation.

The practice of meditation soon spread to France, through the

influence of John Mombaer (+ 1502), abbot of a Benedictine monastery near Paris. His principal treatise, *Rosetum*, is based on the
practices of Windesheim and is methodical to the point of weariness. Basically, his method is the same as the one drawn up by
Gransfort, although he also advocated meditation on the mysteries
of the rosary.[9]

We have stated that methodical meditation was utilized primarily
as a means of reforming religious life, and that was nowhere more
true than in the Benedictine monasteries of Italy and Spain. According to Watrigant,[10] the introduction of methodical mental prayer in
Italy was the result of a direct influence of the Flemish *devotio
moderna*. However, other authors such as Tassi and Petrocchi either
reject this theory outright or say it is too early to make such a
judgment.[11] A safer conjecture would be that there was a parallel
development in southern Europe rather than an import from the
Low Lands.[12]

In Italy the two great reformers of the clergy and religious were
St. Laurence Justinian (+ 1455) and Louis Barbo (+ 1443). For both
of them the instrument of reform was the practice of methodical
mental prayer or meditation. St. Laurence Justinian was a Canon
Regular of St. George and later became Patriarch of Venice. He
composed numerous treatises – on compunction, on humility, on
disdain for the world, on the degrees of perfection, on divine love –
but in all of them he strove to inculcate the practice of meditation.[13]

Louis Barbo was also a Canon Regular of St. George, but he
transferred to the Benedictine monastery at Padua, where he
became abbot. Later, he was named bishop of Treviso. His reforming influence was felt at Montecassino and, through García de
Cisneros, at Valladolid and Montserrat in Spain.

Barbo's treatise on prayer is entitled *Forma orationis et meditationis*
or *Modus meditandi*, and was first published in Venice in 1523. It
describes three types of prayer: *vocal prayer*, which is best suited for
beginners; *meditation*, which is a higher type of prayer suited for
those who are more advanced; and *contemplation*, the highest type of
prayer, to which one may rise through meditation. At the request of
Pope Eugene IV, Barbo wrote to the Benedictines at Valladolid,
Spain, to acquaint them with methodical meditation, and it
was from this abbey in 1492 that García de Cisneros went, with
twelve monks, to reform the famous abbey of Montserrat, near
Barcelona.

Although he did not attain the fame of St. Ignatius, even in Spain,
García de Cisneros must be recognized as one of the most influential

figures in the Tridentine reform of the Church and in early Spanish spirituality.[14] He left two works which were printed in Spanish at the printing press of Montserrat in 1500: *Ejercitatorio de la vida espiritual* and *Directorio de las horas canónicas*, and it is the first of the two that became a standard directory for spiritual exercises (in Spanish, *ejercicios*).

Normally, three weeks were assigned for the spiritual exercises; the fourth part of the directory is intended specifically for contemplatives. The method of making the exercises is spelled out in some detail, as are the themes for the meditations. At the appointed time the monk goes to chapel, kneels, blesses himself, and recites the prayer "Come, Holy Spirit," after which he recites three times: "O Lord, come to my aid; O Lord, make haste to help me." Then, recollecting himself in the presence of God, he meditates on the three points given for that particular day, concludes with a prayer of petition, and then, striking his breast, repeats three times: "O God, be merciful to me, a sinner." He then stands to recite a psalm and a prayer and leaves the chapel in a state of recollection. The topics assigned for the purgative week are meant to arouse holy fear and contrition: sin, death, hell, judgment, the Passion of Christ, the Blessed Virgin, heaven.

In the illuminative week more freedom is given as regards method, and if devotion or love move the individual, he may abandon the method entirely. On the other hand, if necessary, the monk may spend as long as a month on the purgative meditations. In the illuminative week emphasis is placed on preparation for a worthy confession, sorrow for sin, and the arousal of love of God. The topics considered are creation, the supernatural order, religious vocation, justification, blessings received, divine providence, heaven; or one could meditate on the life of Christ or the saints or on the Lord's prayer.

The unitive way presupposes purification from sin and illumination from God; the individual is totally converted to God, desires to serve God alone, and is detached from the goods of this world. At this stage the soul rises to God more out of love than through use of the intellect. There are six degrees of unitive love, according to Cisneros, terminating in rapture.[15] The topics for the unitive way are God as principle of all things, as the beauty of the universe, as the glory of the world, as infinite charity, as rule of every creature, as governing all things, as supremely generous.

For those who have reached contemplation, Cisneros is much more permissive in regard to subject matter and method. His material is practically a transcription of Gerson's *De monte contemplationis*, but he does propose three ways of contemplating Christ: first, to consider the sacred humanity, as St. Bernard teaches; secondly, to look at Christ as God and man; thirdly, to rise above the sacred humanity and focus on the divinity of Christ. Each person, says Cisneros, should follow his own spiritual attraction, according to the degree of his prayer life.

Like Cisneros, another renowned Benedictine, Louis de Blois, known as Blosius (+ 1566), contributed to the Benedictine reform in the Low Lands through the practice of meditation and spiritual exercises. Blosius stated that external exercises such as the chanting of the Divine Office, recitation of vocal prayers, outward signs of devotion, fasting and vigils are no doubt pleasing to God, but infinitely superior are the spiritual exercises which enable a man to be interiorly and supernaturally united with God.[16] Blosius was an avid reader of the works of Tauler and Suso.

The works of Blosius are as follows: *Institutio spiritualis* (1551); *Consolatio pusillanimum* (1555); *Conclave animae fidelis* (1558); *Speculum spirituale* (1558). These treatises were quickly translated into all the vernacular languages and circulated throughout the monasteries of Europe. In fact, just as some of the Benedictine monks had resisted the efforts of Louis Barbo, so now some monks were fearful that the practice of mental prayer would threaten the devotion of the monks to liturgical prayer, the *opus Dei*.

Eventually the spiritual exercises were practiced by more and more of the laity, as García de Cisneros had intended. Numerous devout laymen would go to the monasteries for the purpose of making the spiritual exercises, as very likely was the case with Ignatius Loyola at Montserrat in 1522. The Dominicans officially adopted the practice of meditation as a community exercise in 1505; the Franciscans followed suit in 1594.

CHRISTIAN HUMANISM

The spiritual exercises were not the only weapon used against the encroachment of the pagan humanism of the Renaissance. A more direct attack was waged by the "Christian humanists." They have sometimes been criticized as the forerunners of the Protestant Revolt under Martin Luther. While it is true that many of their criticisms did provide ammunition for the attacks of the Protestants against the Church, the devout humanists were sincere; they can hardly be accused of deliberately preparing for a schism in the Church. Their basic aims were to preserve Christians from the corruption of pagan humanism, to foster the interior life and the practice of prayer, and to encourage a return to the reading of Scripture, not for theologizing but for inspiration and instruction. Among the outstanding Christian humanists were Nicholas of Cusa, Pico della Mirandola, Lefévre of Etaples, St. Thomas More and Erasmus, but only Erasmus is of interest to us in the history of spirituality.[17]

Born at Rotterdam between 1464 and 1466, Erasmus was educated at the school of the Brothers of the Common Life. Later he entered the Augustinians and, after being dispensed from his religious vows, was ordained a priest in 1492 by the Bishop of Cambrai. Renowned throughout Europe for his vast knowledge, he was highly esteemed by Pope Julius II, Pope Leo X, King Charles V, King Francis I, and King Henry VIII. He was an enemy of the monastic life and of Scholastic theology, as can be seen in his satirical treatise, *Stultitiae laus*. He was intensely dedicated to the formation of a new theology based on Scripture and the Fathers of the Church. His doctrine can be found in *Enchiridion militis christiani* (1504), *Paraclesis* (1516) and *Ratio seu methodus perveniendi ad veram theologiam* (1518).[18] He died at Bâle in 1536, while superintending the edition of his works.

For Erasmus, the Christian life is one of constant warfare against the world, the devil and our own passions. The principal weapons to be used by the Christian are prayer, which strengthens the will, and knowledge, which nourishes the intellect. The practice of prayer requires that the Christian flee from the world and concentrate on Christ, for the goal of the Christian life is the imitation of Christ. Even the external practices of religion, if not rightly used, can become obstacles to the true faith and may lead to a pharisaical observance which Erasmus calls "the religion of the common people."

In the *Enchiridion* (chap. 8) he gives twenty-two directives for the imitation of Christ and victory over sin and temptations. And if the Christian finds it difficult to detach himself from the world, Erasmus reminds him of the vanity of this world, the inevitability of death and the certainty of man's ultimate separation from the goods of this world. The same emphasis on death will be found later in the writings of Montaigne and many of the Spanish spiritual writers of the sixteenth century.

Erasmus is much more emphatic, however, when he discusses the type of knowledge which the Christian must have in order to be successful in combat. First of all, knowledge of self, which is a primary condition for victory. Secondly, knowledge of the truths revealed in Scripture; not the speculative and argumentative theology of the Scholastics, but the practical theology which leads to a holy life and is found in the authentic source which is the Bible. Everyone, says Erasmus, should read the Bible because the doctrine of Christ is for everyone. And in order not to go astray, one should heed the definitions of the Church and follow the teaching of the Fathers and commentators. In questions that have not been decided by the Church, it is the Holy Spirit that instructs the reader, but only if the reader approaches Scripture with faith and devotion. But anyone who reads only the literal sense in Scripture might just as well be reading a fable or a legend; Scripture is sterile unless one perceives the meaning hidden beneath the literal interpretation.

The humanism of Erasmus, Lefèvre and their companions has been severely criticized by many Catholic historians, in spite of the fact that educated Catholics of the sixteenth century found much sound instruction and guidance in the devotional treatises composed by these men and in spite of the fact that the Christian humanists dissociated themselves from Luther and the Protestant movement as soon as it was condemned by Pope Leo X in 1520.[19]

There are, however, several good reasons for the criticism of the Christian humanists. First, in their zeal for a "new theology" which was based exclusively on Scripture and the Fathers of the Church, they rejected all the theological wisdom of the Middle Ages and also weakened, unwittingly perhaps, the authority of the magisterium of the Church. Secondly, through their intensive study of the Greek and Latin classics they formed an erroneous opinion concerning man's inherent goodness, with the result that they underestimated the effects of original sin and man's need for mortification and self-denial. Thirdly, the very fact that Luther spoke approvingly of some of the theses of the humanists was sufficient to discredit them, just as Tauler and Gerson became somewhat suspect among Catholics because Luther quoted from their writings.[20] Thus, by an odd twist of events, the Christian humanism that attempted to reform the Church and renew the Christian life became a victim of its own excesses and helped to set the scene for the division of the Church. True Christian humanism would not appear until early in the seventeenth century, with St. Francis de Sales as its greatest exponent. What this devout humanism is has been described by Bremond as follows:

Devout humanism applies to the needs of the interior life and brings within the reach of all both the principles and the spirit of Christian humanism.... In theology, Christian humanism accepts the theology of the Church purely and simply.... Without neglecting any of the essential truths of Christianity, it prefers to bring into the light those that are the most comforting and cheering, in a word, the most human, which it further regards as the most divine and, if one may say so, as the most in accord with infinite goodness. Thus, it does not look upon original sin as the central doctrine, but on the Redemption.... Thus, too, it does not question the need of grace, but, instead of measuring it out parsimoniously to some of the predestined, it sees it freely offered to all, more anxious to reach us than we can be to receive it....

The humanist does not regard man as contemptible. He is always and with all his heart on the side of our nature. Even if he sees it miserable and impotent, he makes excuses for it; he defends and restores it.[21]

ST. IGNATIUS LOYOLA

The Renaissance, as we have intimated, had much less influence on spirituality than one could have hoped; and as regards the Church as a whole, its effects seem to have been more divisive than reforming. The new trends initiated by Lefèvre and Erasmus never succeeded in causing a complete break with the great currents of medieval spirituality; rather, the personalities that emerged in the spirituality of the sixteenth century manifested a fidelity to the past by further developing the practice of methodical mental prayer, which, as we have seen, had its roots in the monastic tradition. This is especially evident in the case of St. Ignatius Loyola (1491–1556) and the Spanish school of spirituality.

Actually, we are indebted to St. Ignatius for two outstanding contributions: he perfected the spiritual exercises and he gave to the Church a new form of religious life. Born in 1491 in the Basque province of Guipúzcoa, he became a soldier but had to abandon a military career when his right leg was injured in the defense of Pamplona against the French in 1521. During the period of convalescence it seems that the reading of Ludolph of Saxony's *Life of Christ* and James of Voraginé's *Golden Legend* turned his thoughts toward conversion. After some wavering, scruples and doubts, he began his search for the discernment of God's will in his regard.[22]

Ignatius had contact with a variety of religious orders. At the start he gave some thought to becoming a Carthusian. Many of his relatives were Franciscan tertiaries and a cousin was foundress of a monastery of Poor Clares. He spent a long time at the Dominican priory in Manresa, where the prior was his confessor and director.

Later, a group of Dominicans defended and aided the approbation of the Society of Jesus. But perhaps the most fruitful contact was with the Benedictines at Montserrat, where Ignatius very likely came into contact with the *devotio moderna* and the spiritual exercises of García de Cisneros. Ignatius composed the first draft of the *Exercises* under divine guidance; he retouched it at Paris in 1534, and in 1548 the *Exercises* were approved by Pope Paul III.[23]

St. Ignatius assigns a period of four weeks to the *Spiritual Exercises*, although the time may be lengthened or shortened according to the needs of the retreatant and the judgment of the director. Originally, each retreatant was under the guidance of a director, but by 1539 the Jesuits started to give the *Exercises* to groups. Likewise, it was at first required that the retreatant be a Christian of good will, desirous of serving God more fervently, and possessing sufficient spiritual background; later, the *Exercises* were offered to a wider clientele. From the twenty annotations given by St. Ignatius in the introduction to the *Exercises*, we may note the following: a statement of the aim of the *Exercises*, namely, to help the retreatant purify his soul in order to discern his vocation and follow it faithfully; allowance for personal initiative so that the retreatant may abandon *discursus* and practice prayer when so moved; the necessity of adhering as strictly as possible to the schedule and method of the *Exercises*, but adapting them to the age, health, knowledge and state of life of the retreatant; a warning to the director not to intervene too much or try to influence the choices or resolutions of the retreatant.

At the very outset, St. Ignatius advises the retreatant to cultivate a holy indifference toward created things, stating that man is created to praise, reverence and serve God and thereby save his soul; all created things are for the use of man in striving for the end for which he was created; therefore, man is to use created things so far as they help him achieve his eternal goal and rid himself of them so far as they are obstacles to that goal. Very early in the first week he insists that all should be done for the service and praise of God, a thought that would later become the motto of the Jesuits and a characteristic of Ignatian spirituality: *Ad majorem Dei gloriam*.

St. Ignatius then introduces the subject matter for the meditations of the first week, which are sin and hell. He advises the retreatant to bring the three powers to bear on the subject; that is, to recall to one's memory the sin in question, using composition of place as much as possible; then to reflect on it with the intellect; and finally to move the feelings with the will. To meditation is added the particular examen, which St. Ignatius considers as important for spiritual progress as meditation itself. At the end of the material for the first week, he lists ten "additions" which instruct the retreatant on various matters such as comportment and penances.

During the second week the retreatant meditates on the life of Christ, as far as Palm Sunday. The goal of the second week, which may be extended to a period of twelve days, is to make one's election in response to God's call. On the first day the retreatant compares the response of good and loyal subjects to a liberal and kind king with the response Christians should give to Christ the King; he then provides meditations for the first three days. On the fourth day St. Ignatius introduces the symbol of the "two standards," that of Christ and that of Lucifer, and he explains that Christ wants to bring all souls to spiritual – and even actual – poverty, willingness to suffer contempt, and humility. From the fifth to the seventh day the meditations return to the life of Christ, after which St. Ignatius explains the three types of humility: that which is necessary for salvation, that which is more perfect, and that which is most perfect.

At the end of this second week, the retreatant is supposed to make his election, and this must be done in view of the glory of God and the salvation of one's soul. If the election does not concern the choice of one's vocation or some other matter that needs to be decided, it is suggested that one make an election concerning the reform of his own life or some detail that pertains to his state in life. But in every case, the glory of God must be the primary factor in the choice that is made.

The subject matter for the meditations of the third week is the passion and death of Christ, so that the retreatant will find motives for fidelity to Christ and will also be able to petition the graces and strength needed to carry out his election. This particular section of the *Spiritual Exercises* concludes with detailed rules for abstinence in food and drink. St. Ignatius here manifests his great prudence in matters of penance and he advises the retreatant to imagine how Christ acted in the matter of food and drink and then to imitate him.

The fourth and final week consists of meditations on the events of Christ's life from the resurrection to the ascension and the emphasis is not so much on asceticism, as in the third week, but on temperance and moderation. St. Ignatius then offers some outlines for meditations aimed at fostering growth in love and he follows this with directions on three different kinds of mental prayer: to make a reflection and self-examination on the Ten Commandments, the capital sins or the faculties of soul and body; meditation on one word or pausing at a word of a prayer for as long as one gains benefit from it, then moving on to the next one; or, thirdly, making a one-word aspiration each time one draws and exhales a breath or going through the Our Father or Hail Mary in his way.

Last of all, St. Ignatius gives a lengthy list of rules for the discernment of spirits, which are valuable for both the retreatant and the director and are to be studied especially during the first and second weeks of the retreat. Then, some rules for the distribution of alms, the famous and characteristically Jesuit rules for thinking with the Church, and a section on scruples complete the book of the *Exercises* proper.

From the beginning, the *Spiritual Exercises* proved a most effective weapon against the paganism of the Renaissance and the Quietism of Lutheranism. Many of the Catholic clergy and religious were converted to a better life and the *Exercises* received the endorsement of Louis de Blois, St. Charles Borromeo and St. Vincent de Paul. In 1920 Pope Benedict XV proclaimed St. Ignatius the patron of spiritual retreats and in 1948 Pope Pius XII stated that "the *Exercises* of St. Ignatius will always remain one of the most efficacious means for the spiritual regeneration of the world, but on the condition that they continue to be authentically Ignatian."

St. Ignatius never lost sight of the fact that man must exert every effort to cooperate with God's grace; he was equally insistent that growth in grace is more God's doing than man's. He therefore emphasizes the importance of the prayer of petition for obtaining God's assistance, but because of the spiritual climate of his day, he also had to encourage the individual's cooperation with grace. Ignatian spirituality, therefore, will not tolerate passivity; it is a spiritual combat in which the chief weapons are meditation and particular examen. But it is an interior combat, a warfare which one wages against his own sins and predominant faults in order to prepare himself for the action of the Holy Spirit and the works of the apostolate.[24]

Since the sixteenth century the Church has been especially indebted to St. Ignatius for the following contributions to Christian spirituality: the practice of spiritual exercises or retreats; a successful method for the practice of mental prayer; the universal popularity of the general and particular examen; recognition of the need for mortification, but adjusted to the conditions and strength of the individual; the importance of the spiritual director; a theology of the apostolate as an obligation for all Christians; and an adaptation of religious life to the needs of the times.

With regard to the adaptation of religious life, it should be noted that St. Ignatius was as creative a founder as were St. Dominic and St. Francis in their time. They took the monk out of the solitude of the cloister, away from manual labor, and sent him forth to preach the Gospel. St. Ignatius took from the friar his monkish habit, the choral Office, the monastic liturgy and monastic observances and gave the Church a new kind of religious. The Jesuit was to have no distinctive garb other than that worn by the diocesan priest of a given locality; he was to consider the Divine Office as an important exercise of prayer, but recite it privately; the liturgy would be a primary source of spiritual life; and finally, Jesuits would practice daily mental prayer according to a determined method, general and particular examen, and would submit to mandatory spiritual direction. The Church would not witness such a change in the consecrated life until the sudden growth of secular institutes in the twentieth century; and the majority of new religious institutes in the intervening period would implicitly or explicitly follow the pattern of the Society of Jesus.[25]

ST. TERESA OF AVILA

St. Teresa of Avila (1515–1582) has a double title to the preeminent place she holds in the history of spirituality: reformer of Carmel and unsurpassed authority on the theology of prayer. Born at La Moneda, near Avila, in 1515, she was from her earliest years drawn to God and her devout spirit was fostered by the example of her parents. When Teresa was thirteen, her mother died, and the young girl was sent to a boarding school conducted by Augustinian nuns. She left the school a mature young woman and assumed the duties of managing the family household for her father. By 1536 Teresa was convinced that her vocation was to religious life and in spite of her father's initial unwillingness, she entered the Carmelite monastery of the Incarnation at Avila.

Once professed, Teresa determined to strive for perfection, but perhaps with more fervor than prudence, for she soon became so seriously ill that her father had to take her to a neighboring town for treatment. However, the treatment was worse than the illness, and Teresa was brought back to her father's home in Avila, to await death. She did in fact sink into such a coma that for four days she lay as if dead. Her grave was prepared at the Incarnation and the only thing that saved her from being buried was her father's refusal. Gradually she recovered enough to return to the monastery, but she was completely paralyzed for some time. When at last she was completely recovered, she attributed her cure to the intercession of St. Joseph, and thereafter she always had a deep devotion to him.

However, life at the Incarnation was far from the eremitical spirit proper to Carmelites and Teresa herself spent much time at the parlor grille. The admonitions of her Dominican confessor, Father Barrón, were of no avail. What converted her was the impression made on her by a realistic representation of the *Ecce Homo*. From that day on, her interior life improved; she became more recollected and drawn to solitude. Another great help that she received was from a Jesuit confessor. Baltasar Alvarez, only twenty-five years old, but gifted with unusual discernment and the ability to recognize the workings of God in the soul of Teresa. Later she spent almost three years in the home of a very devout widow who was under the spiritual direction of the Jesuits.

At that time the law of enclosure was not observed strictly; indeed, in many respects the monastic life was very lax. In 1560 Teresa and a few companions decided that what was needed was a reform of Carmelite life. Shortly thereafter Teresa received the command from heaven to lead the group. After numerous difficulties and delays, the first monastery of the Reform was opened at Avila in 1562 and placed under the patronage of St. Joseph.

For the rest of her life St. Teresa was engaged in the absorbing task of making numerous foundations throughout Spain; she was almost constantly beleaguered by the attacks and criticisms coming from ecclesiastical prelates, members of the nobility and her own fellow-Carmelites. Yet at the same time God provided good friends and loyal defenders; he also showered her with numerous mystical graces. Teresa passed to her eternal reward on October 4, the feast of St. Francis of Assisi, in 1582 at Alba de Tormes.[26]

As a teacher of the stages of prayer, St. Teresa has never been equalled, much less surpassed. Since her day, practically all spiritual writers have been influenced to some extent by her writings. St. Alphonsus Liguori and St. Francis de Sales are especially noteworthy in this respect. She wrote primarily for the nuns and friars of the Carmelite Order and the success of her writings is all the more remarkable when we consider the heterodox tendencies that prevailed in sixteenth-century Spain: Spanish-Arabian mysticism, the illuminism of the *Alumbrados*, the traces of Lutheran Quietism. Nor should we overlook the severe Spanish Inquisition, personified in the zealous and ruthless Dominican, Melchior Cano.[27]

The teaching of St. Teresa can be found in her three major works, *The Life*, *The Way of Perfection*, and *The Interior Castle*, of which the last-mentioned is her masterpiece.[28] Unlike many of the treatises on prayer before the time of St. Ignatius, the works of St. Teresa are practical rather than theoretical, descriptive rather than expository, with invaluable psychological insights drawn from personal experience and a penetrating observation of the conduct of others. Using *The Interior Castle* as a guide, we shall trace the path of progress in prayer as outlined by St. Teresa.

She pictures the soul as a castle composed of numerous suites or apartments (*moradas*), in the center of which Christ is enthroned as King. As the soul progresses in the practice of prayer, it passes from one apartment to another until eventually, after passing through seven apartments, it reaches the innermost room. Outside the castle there is darkness and in the moat surrounding the castle there are loathsome creatures crawling in the mud. Once the soul resolves to follow the path of prayer and detaches itself from created things, it enters the castle and begins to follow the path of prayer, which leads first through three stages of active or ascetical prayer and then through four stages of passive or mystical prayer. What does St. Teresa understand by prayer?

"In my opinion," she says, "mental prayer is nothing else but friendly conversation, frequently talking alone with him whom we know loves us." It is a loving dialogue between friends, and one's progress in prayer is a sure indication of one's progress in the spiritual life. Although she realizes the importance of knowledge, St. Teresa insists that progress in prayer consists not so much in thinking a great deal but in loving a great deal. Moreover, like St. John of the Cross, she is a great defender of the freedom of the soul to submit to the action of the Holy Spirit. For that reason, she is always alert to protect the soul from the tyranny of a set method. St. Teresa did not equate the entire spiritual life with the practice of prayer; she also treats of a variety of other topics such as self-knowledge, humility, fraternal charity, spiritual direction, spiritual friendships, asceticism and the apostolate.[29]

Coming now to trace the journey of the soul through the stages of prayer, according to *The Interior Castle*, we find that in the first "mansions" or apartment the soul is in the state of a beginner, living in the state of grace but still greatly attached to the things of earth and always in danger of falling away from its good desires. The practice of prayer at this stage is purely vocal prayer.

Upon entering the second "mansions," the soul begins to practice mental prayer in earnest, although there are frequent periods of dryness and difficulty which tempt the soul to give up the effort. The prayer characteristic of this stage is discursive meditation. Although discursive prayer is a reflective type of prayer, it should not consist entirely in reasoning but should terminate in love. For those who have a tendency to "use their intellects a great deal," St. Teresa recommends that they meditate on Christ and converse with him; for those who find difficulty in controlling their faculties in meditation, she suggests that they recite or read some vocal prayer slowly and think about the words.

Moving on to the third "mansions," the soul enters upon the last stage of natural or acquired prayer, which is called the prayer of acquired recollection. It is a consciousness of the presence of God that is so vivid that all the faculties are united in a state of recollection and attention to God. St. Teresa advises that this type of prayer can be fostered if the soul cultivates an awareness of God's presence within it, submits itself totally to the divine will, and strives habitually to live in the presence of God even when engaged in occupations other than the practice of prayer. Since this stage of prayer represents a transition from ascetical to mystical prayer, it may be experienced in various degrees of intensity.[30]

The fourth "mansions" introduces the soul to the first type of mystical prayer, which is a supernatural, infused prayer, called by the generic name of prayer of quiet. It is an infused or passive recollection which consists essentially in an intimate union of the intellect with God, so that the soul enjoys a vivid awareness of God's presence.[31]

However, the perfection of prayer in the fourth "mansions" is the prayer of quiet properly so called. It is a type of prayer in which the will is inundated by divine love and is united to God as its highest good. However, the memory and imagination are still free or "unbound" and they may sometimes threaten to disturb the soul. Therefore St. Teresa advises that one should remain quiet and recollected before God, submitting oneself entirely to the arms of divine love.

The goal of the divine operation on the soul is to captivate all the faculties and fix them on God. Consequently, in the fifth "mansions" the soul is introduced to the prayer of union, which admits of a variety of degrees of intensity. In the prayer of simple union, all the powers of the soul are recollected in God. Then the soul realizes that God is present in such a way "that when it turns in on itself, it cannot doubt that it is in God and God is in it."[32]

As God gains more and more dominion over the soul and floods it with his light and consolations, the soul experiences the prayer of ecstatic union, which is the beginning of the sixth "mansions" and the introduction to the "mystical espousal." As in the highest stages of ascetical prayer, so here at the heights of mystical prayer, the soul undergoes great trials and suffering, the difference being that now they are mystical or passive purgations.[33] It is not infrequent to find that souls at this stage of prayer are favored with extraordinary mystical phenomena such as raptures, flights of the spirit, locutions, visions, and so forth. Then, entering the seventh and last "mansions," the soul realizes the petition of Christ to his heavenly Father: "That they may be one as we also are one; I in them and thou in me" (Jn. 17:22-23). This is the state of mystical marriage or the transforming union and St. Teresa states that there is such a close relationship between the mystical espousal and the mystical marriage that the sixth and seventh "mansions" could well be joined together.[34]

In the transforming union the three divine Persons communicate themselves in an ineffable manner, often by an intellectual vision, and it is not unusual for Christ to reveal himself to the soul in his sacred humanity.[35] The result is that the soul is totally forgetful of self, it thirsts for suffering and rejoices in persecution, and it experiences a great zeal for the salvation of souls. Thus, the summit of mystical contemplative prayer is crowned with apostolic fervor. As St. Teresa says, "Martha and Mary work together."[36]

Although St. Teresa had read spiritual works such as the *Confessions* of St. Augustine, *The Third Spiritual Alphabet* by Francis de Osuna, *The Ascent of Mount Sion* by Bernandine of Laredo and possibly *The Life of Christ* by Ludolph the Carthusian, her doctrine is not from books. In fact, in reading books she usually discovered that they verified her own experience. According to her own testimony, the source of her teaching is God alone.

But it would be an error to think that St. Teresa's doctrine was exclusively mystical. She wrote for contemplative nuns, it is true, but she realized that not all of them were in the mystical state. In fact, she frequently stated that sanctity does not consist in the extraordinary but in doing ordinary things extraordinarily well. The basis of sanctity is complete conformity with the will of God, "so that as soon as we know that he wills a thing, we subject our entire will to it. . . . The power of perfect love is such that it makes us forget to please ourselves in order to please him who loves us.''[37] And the surest and quickest way to reach this perfection of love, says St. Teresa, is obedience, by which we completely renounce our own will and submit it totally to God.[38] As means of growth in holiness she gives special attention to the reception of Communion; the cultivation of humility, obedience and fraternal charity; the observance of poverty; but above all, the love of God.[39]

ST. JOHN OF THE CROSS

One cannot discuss St. Teresa of Avila without thinking of her great collaborator, St. John of the Cross. They are so closely related in their life and work and doctrine that they are the two pillars on which is constructed the Carmelite school of spirituality. St. John of the Cross (1542–1591) is not as widely known and read as he deserves, and there are several reasons for this: he wrote primarily for souls that are already advanced on the path of perfection; his teaching on detachment and purgation is too demanding for some Christians; his language is often too subtle and metaphysical to suit the taste of modern readers. Yet, his writings and those of St. Teresa complement each other so perfectly that one of the best ways to understand either one is to study the works of the other. There is, of course, a noticeable difference between them but it is a difference of approach rather than essentials.

To understand St. John of the Cross and St. Teresa it is necessary to consider the state of the Christian life in Spain in the sixteenth century. Persons who claimed to be favored with revelations, visions, and other extraordinary mystical phenomena were greatly admired and sought after. Some persons earnestly desired to receive these special gifts; others actually simulated the stigmata or visions in order to impress the faithful. Illuminism gained great headway, especially in relaxed religious houses, as a means to eminent holiness without the practice of asceticism or the effort of acquiring virtues. All the structured and institutional aspects of religion were rejected as obstacles or as totally unnecessary for immediate union with God in mystical experience. Pseudo-mysticism was the object of intense investigation by the Spanish Inquisition, which managed to control the situation but at the expense of further development of authentic, orthodox spirituality.[40] Some of the statements in the works of St. Teresa and St. John of the Cross may be open to misinterpretation if the reader does not take into account the Spanish situation in the sixteenth century.

Born Juan de Yepes at Fontiveros, near Avila, St. John of the Cross (1542–1591) was only a few months old when his father died. Reduced to poverty, the family moved to Medina del Campo, where John worked at various trades and attended the Jesuit school from 1559 to 1563. At the age of twenty-one he entered the Carmelite Order and was sent to Salamanca for his theological studies. Returning to Medina del Campo for his first Mass, John met St. Teresa of Avila. He had been thinking seriously about transferring to the Carthusians, but Teresa convinced him that he should join the Carmelite Reform.

The first house of the Carmelite friars of the Reform was founded at Duruelo and John and Anthony of Jesus were the founding Fathers. For the next few years John of the Cross held various offices: master of novices, rector of the college at Alcalá, and confessor for the Carmelite nuns at the Incarnation in Avila. It was in this last assignment that he was kidnapped by the Calced Carmelites (1577) and held prisoner in the monastery in Toledo for nine months.

On escaping from Toledo, John spent most of the remaining years of his life in Andalusia and was elected to various posts of importance. However, in the Provincial Chapter of 1591, held at Madrid, John disagreed publicly with the Vicar General, Nicholas Doria, who immediately deposed John. Humiliated, but happy to be able to return to a life of greater solitude and recollection, St. John of the Cross ended his days at Úbeda, where he died after much suffering. He was canonized by Pope Benedict XIII in 1726 and declared a Doctor of the Church by Pope Pius XI in 1926.[41]

The major works by St. John of the Cross are *The Ascent of Mount Carmel* (1579–1585); *The Dark Night of the Soul* (1582–1585); *The Spiritual Canticle* (first redaction in 1584 and second redaction between 1586 and 1591); *The Living Flame of Love* (first redaction between 1585 and 1587 and second redaction between 1586 and 1591). All of these works are commentaries on poems composed by St. John of the Cross, but the first two treatises were never completed. However, it is commonly agreed that the two treatises *Ascent – Dark Night* cover the entire subject matter contained under the division of the active and passive purgations of the senses and the spiritual faculties.[42]

Having studied at Salamanca, St. John of the Cross was trained in Thomistic theology, but he also read the works of pseudo-Dionysius and St. Gregory the Great. However, the author that most influenced St. John seems to have been Tauler, although it is quite certain that he was familiar with the works of St. Bernard, Ruysbroeck, Cassian, the Victorines, Osuna and, of course, St. Teresa of Avila.[43] Nevertheless, John of the Cross was not a slavish imitator of others; his works have a distinctive character all their own.

The fundamental principle of St. John's theology is that God is All and the creature is nothing. Therefore, in order to arrive at perfect union with God, in which sanctity consists, it is necessary to undergo an intense and profound purification of all the faculties and powers of soul and body. *The Ascent – Dark Night* traces the entire process of purgation, from the active purification of the external senses to the passive purification of the highest faculties; *The Living Flame* and *The Spiritual Canticle* describe the perfection of the spiritual life in the transforming union. The entire path to union is "night" because the soul travels by faith. St. John of the Cross presents his teaching in a systematic manner, with the result that it is spiritual theology in the best sense of the word; not because it is systematic, but because it uses as its sources Sacred Scripture, theology and personal experience.

In speaking of the union of the soul with God, St. John states that he is speaking of supernatural union, and not the general union by which God is present to the soul simply by preserving it in existence. The supernatural union of the mystical life is a "union of likeness" which is produced by grace and charity. But in order that this union of love be as perfect as possible and as intimate as possible, the soul must rid itself of all that is not God and of every obstacle to the love of God so that it can love God with all its heart and soul and mind and strength.

Since any deficiency in the union of love is due to the soul and not to God, St. John concludes that the soul must be completely purified in all of its faculties and powers – those of the sensory order and those that are spiritual – before it can be fully illuminated by the light of divine union. This results in the "dark night," which is so called because the point of departure is a denial and deprivation of one's appetite or desire for created things; the means or the road along which the soul travels to union is the obscurity of faith; and the goal is God, who is also a dark night to man in this life.[44]

The necessity of passing through this dark night is due to the fact that from God's point of view, man's attachments to created things are pure darkness, while God is pure light, and darkness cannot receive light (Jn. 1:5). Stated in philosophical terms, two contraries cannot coexist in the same subject. The darkness which is attachment to creatures and the light which is God are contraries; they cannot both be present in the soul at the same time.

St. John then proceeds to explain how the soul must mortify its appetites or concupiscence and must journey by faith through the active purgation of the senses and spirit. And although the treatment may sound negative and severely ascetical, he never tires of insisting that this purgation or nudity of spirit is not a question of the lack of created things, but the denial and uprooting of one's desire for them or attachment to them.[45] St. John gives a simple method for effecting the purgation: have a habitual desire to imitate Christ; and to do this, study Christ's life and works and then do as Christ did.[46]

In Book 2 of *The Ascent*, St. John discusses the active night of the spirit. He states that the purgation of intellect, memory and will is effected through the operation of the virtues of faith, hope and charity, and then explains why faith is the dark night through which the soul must pass to union with God. Turning then to the practice of prayer, he gives three signs by which the soul may know that it is passing from the practice of meditation to contemplative prayer. First, it is impossible to meditate as one was accustomed to do; secondly, there is no desire to concentrate on anything in particular; thirdly, there is a longing for God and for solitude. What the individual experiences is a "loving awareness of God," and this is a type of contemplative prayer.[47]

The passive purgations are explained in *The Dark Night* and at this stage God brings to completion the efforts of the soul to pure itself on the sensory level and in its spiritual faculties. The soul is gradually led into the dark contemplation that pseudo-Dionysius described as a "ray of darkness" and St. John calls "mystical theology."[48] And although one would expect that mystical contemplation would be delightful, St. John explains that the reason it causes pain is that when the divine light of contemplation strikes a soul that is not yet entirely purified, it causes spiritual darkness, for it not only transcends human understanding, but it deprives the soul of its intellectual operation.

Nevertheless, even during this dark and painful contemplation the soul can see the streaks of light which announce the coming of the dawn. In *The Spiritual Canticle* St. John describes the soul's anxious search for God and the ultimate encounter of love, using the symbol of a bride seeking the bridegroom and finally attaining to the perfect union of mutual love. God draws the soul to himself as a powerful magnet draws the metal particles, and the journey of the soul to God is increasingly more swift until, having left all else behind, it enjoys the most intimate union with God that is possible in this life: the mystical marriage of the transforming union.

Then, in *The Living Flame of Love* St. John describes the sublime perfection of love in the state of transforming union. The union between the soul and God is so intimate that it is singularly close to the beatific vision, so close that "only a thin veil separates it." The soul asks the Holy Spirit to tear now the veil of mortal life so that the soul may enter complete and perfect glory. The soul is so close to God that it is transformed into a flame of love wherein the Father, the Son, and the Holy Spirit are communicated to it. It enjoys a foretaste of eternal life.[49]

> And it should not be held as incredible in a soul now examined, purged, and tried in the fire of tribulations, trials, and many kinds of temptations, and found faithful in love, that the promise of the Son of God be fulfilled, the promise that the Most Blessed Trinity will come and dwell with anyone who loves him (Jn. 14:23). The Blessed Trinity inhabits the soul by divinely illumining its intellect with the wisdom of the Son, delighting its will in the Holy Spirit, and by absorbing it powerfully and mightily in the delightful embrace of the Father's sweetness.[50]

Taken together, St. Teresa of Avila and St. John of the Cross have given the Church a spiritual doctrine that has never been surpassed. So great was their influence and so brilliant their exposition that they have far outshone all the other writers of the golden age of Spanish spirituality.

SPAIN'S GOLDEN AGE

Sixteenth century Spain produced a wealth of spiritual literature and an amazing number of saints. To some extent this was due to the historical situation of the period and the geographical location of Spain. Cut off as it was by the Pyrenees from France, Germany and the Low Countries, Spain was not greatly upset by the effects of the Protestant Reformation as were the countries to the north. By comparison, Spain was enjoying the climate of peace that is necessary for the development of spirituality and the writing of treatises on the Christian life. And although the Inquisition prevented the amount of freedom that one may have desired, it nevertheless allowed for the emergence of some spiritual literature of the highest quality. Unfortunately, in men like Melchior Cano the Inquisition was also the cause of much suspicion, excessive severity, unjust accusation and, at last, a definitely anti-mystical trend that is completely alien to the Spanish temperament.[51] Some of the most illustrious spiritual writers of the period were imprisoned as suspect and many more saw their works listed on the Index.

On the other hand, there was good reason why the Inquisition doggedly pursued the *Alumbrados*. In the early sixteenth century pseudo-mysticism, with all its immorality and false visions, stigmata and ecstasies, had attracted many followers, especially from uneducated religious. From 1524 there was a gradual dissemination of Lutheran doctrine in Spain: a denial of objective morality, the rejection of good works and the claim of individual guidance by the Holy Spirit. Spiritual writers from the Franciscan and Dominican Orders tried to correct the exaggerations of the pseudo-mystics, but by 1551 it became evident that more severe measures were indicated, namely, the Spanish Inquisition.

The Franciscans were the first to provide the spiritual doctrine that was so sorely needed. Alonso of Madrid (+ 1521) published an ascetical treatise under the title *The Art of Serving God*. He first explained the basic theology of the spiritual life and warned against all types of sentimentality and illusion; then he developed three fundamental themes: self-knowledge, growth in virtue and the practice of mental prayer. St. Teresa of Avila recommended this work very highly for her nuns.

In 1527 Francis de Osuna (+ 1540) published his *Third Primer of Spirituality*, a mystical treatise on prayer which had a profound influence on St. Teresa of Avila.[52] In a manner reminiscent of the Rhineland mystics, Osuna insists that recollection in God can be attained only by detachment from the senses and that the perfection of the prayer of recollection consists in thinking of nothing in particular so that the soul can be completely absorbed in God. All this, however, must be done with a joyful spirit, for Osuna declares that those who are sad or downcast make little progress in the life of prayer. The entire treatise is developed from a psychological point of view, which greatly appealed to St. Teresa and characterized her own writings.

Bernardine of Laredo (+ 1540), a physician who became a Franciscan lay brother, published *The Ascent of Mount Sion* in 1535, and then in 1538 he published a new version which reflected considerable change in his doctrine. St. Teresa of Avila states that she found a great deal of enlightenment and consolation in *The Ascent* at a time when she was particularly concerned about her ability to meditate on Christ. It is interesting to note that, whereas the edition of 1535 follows the mystical teaching of Richard of St. Victor, the edition of

1538 reflects the teaching of pseudo-Dionysius, Hugh of Balma, the Carthusian, and Henry Herp.

The Ascent is divided into three parts, of which the first part deals with the process of spiritual self-annihilation, wherein the soul destroys sin and cultivates virtue, with self-knowledge and humility as indispensable elements. Bernardine maintains that contemplative prayer is not reserved for monks and friars but that all Christians can attain it if they cultivate humility and follow Christ. The second part of *The Ascent* provides meditations on the mysteries of the life, death and resurrection of Christ. Then, in the third part of the treatise, the teaching is entirely on contemplative prayer. In the edition of 1535 Bernardine stresses the role of the intellect in contemplation (following Richard of St. Victor); in the edition of 1538 he speaks of mystical contemplation in terms of the will, which surpasses the intellect by aspirations of love.[53]

Lastly, among the Franciscans we should mention St. Peter Alcántara (+ 1562), a reformer of the Franciscan Order in Spain and an advisor of St. Teresa of Avila. There has been a great deal of dispute concerning the authorship of the *Treatise of Prayer and Meditation* which is attributed to St. Peter. St. Teresa herself states that he was "the author of some little books on prayer, written in Spanish and widely used at the present time."[54] The most commonly accepted hypothesis is that St. Peter made an adaptation of the *Book of Prayer and Meditation*, first written by Louis of Granada in 1554. Then Louis of Granada made a new edition of his work in 1555 and a definitive version in 1566. Both of these authors exerted a great influence beyond the Pyrenees, and their doctrine on prayer was used as a source by St. Francis de Sales.

Louis of Granada (+ 1588) was the outstanding spiritual writer among the Spanish Dominicans of the sixteenth century, although he did not escape the vigilance and condemnation of the Spanish Inquisition. Nevertheless, his books had such wide diffusion that they were soon translated into every language, including the languages of some of the mission countries. After several of his works were placed on the *Index*, Louis submitted the same books to the Council of Trent and received formal approbation for his teaching. What seemed to be the ruin of his vocation as a spiritual writer was turned into a victory beyond Granada's expectations, for in 1562 he received the title of Master of Sacred Theology by direct concession of the Master General of the Dominican Order. For thirty-five of the eighty-four years of his life he dedicated his efforts to preaching and writing, and at his death in 1588 the General

Chapter of the Dominicans issued the terse statement: "*Vir doctrina et sanctitate insignis et in toto orbe celebris.*"

After St. Ignatius Loyola, Louis of Granada was the first spiritual writer to formulate a method of prayer for the laity, a method which was adopted by some of the religious orders in Spain. It comprised six steps: preparation (usually the night before); reading of the material for meditation; meditation proper (which consisted of consideration, application, resolution); thanksgiving; offering; and petition. Louis distinguished between imaginative meditation (using scenes from the life of Christ) and intellectual meditation (consideration of a divine attribute or a theological truth). Few writers have excelled Louis of Granada as an expert on discursive meditation.

In addition to his works on prayer, Louis also composed treatises which were aimed at the conversion of Christians to a more devout life. Whether or not his early brush with the Inquisition had made him cautious, Louis of Granada rarely treats of mystical matters, but this is one of the reasons for his universal popularity. Great saints have eulogized his writings, among them: St. Teresa of Avila, St. Charles Borromeo, St. Vincent de Paul, St. Louise de Marillac and St. Francis de Sales.

The basic theme which runs through the works of Louis of Granada is that all Christians are called to perfection, and although it is not obligatory that one be perfect here and now, all are obliged to do the best they can to strive for excellence. Each Christian should seek the goal of perfection in accordance with his temperament, his state in life, and the gifts he has received from God.

All will not follow the same path to holiness and therefore Louis enumerates the various ways: the direct way of prayer, the way of the practice of the virtues, contempt of the world, the painful way of the Cross, the imitation of the saints, the simple way of obedience to the commandments, and the contemplation of God in creation and then of the order of grace and the supernatural.

Whatever the path that is followed, Louis always insists that the Christian should live the life of Christ and be identified with Christ through the grace he merited for us by his passion and death and communicates to us through the Church and the sacraments. But again and again Louis returns to the notion that the most direct and effective way to holiness is the way of the practice of prayer. For him, this is simply a logical consequence of the theological principle that the essence of Christian perfection consists primarily in charity;

hence, prayer is the language of love and therefore an essential element in the Christian life.[55]

Similar to Louis of Granada in his apostolate and in his suffering at the hands of the Spanish Inquisition was the diocesan priest, St. John of Avila (+ 1569), known as the apostle of Andalusia. He was so universally respected that practically every person of recognized holiness had some contact with him. St. Teresa of Avila had correspondence with him on several occasions, and he was responsible for the conversion of St. Francis Borgia and St. John of God. He possessed the gift of discernment of spirits to a remarkable degree, and in his personal life he attained great heights of mystical experience.

Like Louis of Granada, St. John taught a type of meditation that was simple, Christocentric and suited to persons of every walk of life. A man of great caution in dealing with mystical matters, he nevertheless defended mystical experience against those who suspected it. Thus, when St. Teresa sent him a copy of *The Life*, he stated in his letter to her that she should correct certain expressions and give a better explanation of others.

John of Avila was denounced to the Spanish Inquisition in 1531 and spent more than a year in prison before he was exonerated. In 1556 his treatise, *Audi, filia, et vide*, was published without his permission and was placed on the Index in 1559. It was not republished until 1574, after the death of the author. It was greatly modified, however, and for this reason historians of spirituality have lamented the fact that the Inquisition acted as a restraint on great mystics like John of Avila who dared not put into print the lofty theology which they preached in their sermons and conferences.

John of Avila's greatest apostolate was among the priests of his day, and although he himself did not found a religious institute for priests, many who came under his influence entered the Jesuits, which Avila himself had desired to do but never succeeded. The disciples of John of Avila promoted a spirituality that was characterized by filial obedience to their director, the practice of mental prayer, cultivation of a spiritual theology based on the Gospels and St. Paul, and an apostolate of preaching. Anyone who came under his spiritual guidance soon realized that John of Avila was exceptionally gifted with an insight into the meaning of the mystery of Christ. His Christocentric spirituality can be summarized in the following statements: all blessings come to us through Christ; in the measure of our union with Christ we share in the fruits of redemption; our incorporation in Christ begins with faith and baptism and is perfected through the Eucharist; total dedication to Christ produces in us the fruits of hope and joy.[56]

Among the Augustinians the most renowned spiritual writer was Louis of León (1528–1591), professor at the University of Salamanca and literary editor for the first edition of the writings of St. Teresa of Avila. Well versed in Hebrew, he made a translation and a commentary on the Canticle of Canticles, for which he was arrested by the Inquisition and imprisoned for almost five years.

The masterpiece of Louis of León is undoubtedly *The Names of Christ*.[57] The work is based on biblical and patristic sources, although some scholars have detected traces of the spirituality of Germany and the Low Countries as well as similarities with the style of St. John of the Cross. Although the writings of Louis of León have been highly and deservedly praised, he is perhaps regarded more for his literary and esthetic contributions than for his influence on spirituality.[58]

The Jesuits made no contribution to Spanish spiritual literature until the seventeenth century, although individual Jesuits were very much involved with contemporary trends. It is not difficult to find reasons for this lack of Jesuit writers during the golden age of Spanish spirituality. First of all, the Society of Jesus was still young enough to be seeking its definitive form and was at the same time struggling for survival in the face of the opposition of some of the bishops and older religious orders. Secondly, St. Ignatius had firmly established the *Spiritual Exercises* as the framework of Jesuit spirituality, and there was little incentive for the Jesuits to seek elsewhere for methods of prayer or a theology of the spiritual life. Thirdly, the Spanish Inquisition was a constant menace, and a newly founded religious institute was not likely to risk incurring its animosity. Lastly, the Jesuits themselves were faced with an internal crisis concerning the correct balance between contemplation and action within the Society.[59]

When St. Ignatius died in 1556 almost two-thirds of the members of his Society were Spaniards. Orientated as they were to a life of action and living in a period in which most spiritual writing emphasized the practice of prayer with a view to mystical contemplation, the Jesuits had to make a decision concerning the practice of obligatory formal prayer. When no agreement could be reached in the Second General Congregation of 1565, the delegates left the matter in the hands of the newly elected Superior General, Francis Borgia. A month later he prescribed a full hour of formal prayer each day for all the members of the Society.

Gradually more prayers were added until the Third General Congregation of 1573 again took up the question of formal prayer, hoping to return to the original practice instituted by St. Ignatius. But Mercurian, the Superior General, refused to make any changes, although in March of 1575 he forbade the reading of certain authors as not in keeping with the spirit of the Society: Tauler, Ruysbroeck, Mombaer, Herp, Llull, St. Gertrude, St. Mechtild, and others.[60]

In the course of the dispute concerning the place of formal prayer in the life of the Society a good number of Jesuits transferred to the Carthusians, but the argument continued and it eventually was formulated as follows: discursive meditation is the type of formal prayer that is proper to the Society of Jesus; affective prayer and contemplative prayer are foreign to the Jesuit spirit. A few Jesuits continued to defend and teach the practice of affective prayer, notably Cordeses, who was condemned by Mercurian in 1574, and Báltasar Alvarez, who was silenced by the same Superior General in 1577.[61]

Alvarez had been ordained to the priesthood in 1558 and his first assignment was to Avila, where he had the distinction of being named the spiritual director of St. Teresa of Avila. He was only twenty-five years old at the time, and St. Teresa was going through a very difficult period, as she says in her autobiography. Later, when he was transferred to Medina del Campo, he himself experienced mystical prayer, and on the order of his provincial he composed a little treatise to explain the prayer of quiet. It is one of the best refutations of the false mysticism of the *Alumbrados*.[62]

Although there was a real opposition between the Jesuits who fostered affective and contemplative prayer and those who held for what they believed to be the authentic teaching of St. Ignatius on discursive prayer, the division must not be exaggerated. Those of the contemplative persuasion were totally dedicated to the apostolic ends of the Society and those who defended discursive prayer were convinced of the need for an interior life and formal prayer. The crisis was definitively resolved by the fifth Superior General, Aquaviva, who seems to have desired above all else to preserve the unity of the Society of Jesus. He decided in favor of discursive prayer and asceticism, but he also pointed out that it would be an error to evaluate prayer exclusively in terms of the apostolate. Prayer is a value in itself and its essential function is to lead us to a knowledge and love of God – even to contemplation. Prayer is in itself a very noble goal, but in the Society it may never be dissociated from the active vocation of the Jesuits. Aquaviva preferred not to set any specific limit to formal prayer, but to leave it to the needs and the circumstances of the individual, which is much more in accordance with the teaching of St. Ignatius.[63] After the generalate of Aquaviva the Jesuits began to produce a literature of the spiritual life.

The first name on the list of Jesuit writers of the seventeenth century is that of St. Alphonsus Rodríguez (+ 1617), a humble coadjutor brother who seems to go directly contrary to the spirituality endorsed by Aquaviva for the Society of Jesus. Having been refused admittance to the Society on two occasions, he was finally accepted by Cordeses, the provincial of Aragon. Alphonsus entered as a widower and spent his entire religious life as porter at the Jesuit college in Palma de Mallorca. At the request of his superiors he left an autobiography of his spiritual life, which was one of many trials, severe temptations, and the highest degrees of mystical prayer.[64] Most of his writings were not published until the nineteenth century and for that reason Alphonsus did not enjoy the popularity that he deserves. He was a mystic who reached the heights of contemplative prayer by the path of humility, total resignation to God and literal obedience.

Totally different from St. Alphonsus and much better known is Alphonsus Rodríguez (+ 1616), Jesuit novice master in Andalucia, whose lengthy work was published under the title *Ejercicio de la perfección y las virtudes cristianas*.[65] Rodríguez was over seventy years of age when the book was compiled from the spiritual conferences he had given to Jesuit novices. They are almost exclusively ascetical and moral in tone, but since the material concerns the formation of novices, it seems unfair to accuse Rodríguez of being anti-mystical simply because he did not spend much time on mystical topics. Yet Rodríguez seems to make too wide a distinction between ascetical or discursive prayer and mystical prayer, to the point that he seems to see mystical contemplation as something extraordinary, and he does not make allowance for any kind of transitional prayer between discursive and mystical prayer. His *Practice of Christian Perfection* was widely distributed and, once it was translated into French, it was adopted by many religious institutes as obligatory spiritual reading, although in modern times it has fallen into disuse because of its legalistic morality and extreme asceticism.

Louis de la Puente (+ 1624) began his career as a writer when he was over fifty years of age, beginning with a two-volume study entitled *Meditations on the Mysteries of our Holy Faith*.[66] From the days of his tertianship in the Society he was greatly influenced by Báltasar Alvarez, and toward the end of his life he wrote a biography of Alvarez. Although his teaching is almost entirely restricted to ascetical grades of prayer, he helped to break down the prejudice against mystical prayer and the mystical state.

Logically, Louis advocates the use of the *Spiritual Exercises* and he admits that although mystical prayer is a special gift from God, it is usually given to those who have been faithful to the practice of meditation and recollection on the divine mysteries. He gives a variety of names to contemplative prayer: prayer of the presence of God, prayer of repose, prayer of silence, prayer of interior recollection. But in describing contemplation, de la Puente is in the orthodox tradition of the great teachers: "contemplation ... by a simple gaze regards the sovereign truth, admires its greatness and delights in it."[67]

Of all the Jesuit authors of this period, however, Alvarez de Paz (+ 1620) was the first to make a complete synthesis of ascetical and mystical theology. Other writers had composed treatises that touched upon both the ascetical and mystical phases of the spiritual life, but they were books of spiritual direction rather than books of spiritual theology. Alvarez de Paz labored in Peru, where he wrote his books in Latin and then had them published in France (likely through fear of the Spanish Inquisition). The titles of his three published volumes indicate the vastness of the theological project that he had envisioned: *De vita spirituali ejusque perfectione* (1608); *De exterminatione mali et promotione boni* (1613); and *De inquisitione pacis sive studio orationis* (1617). He had also intended to write a volume on the active life of the apostolate but he never finished it.

The author defines the spiritual life as the life of sanctifying grace, which admits of various degrees, and then he explains how the individual soul, in either the active or the contemplative life, can strive for the perfection of the spiritual life by an ever increasing charity. He treats at some length of the avoidance of sin, the importance of cultivating humility, chastity, poverty and obedience, and the practice of mortification.

Alvarez de Paz divides mental prayer into four basic types: discursive meditation, affective prayer, inchoate contemplation and perfect contemplation. He provides something that others before him had failed to do, namely, a form of prayer that would serve as a transition between ascetical prayer and mystical prayer. He can also be credited with introducing a classification that is original – affective prayer – and the name has been preserved by succeeding writers. He is careful to insist, however, that just as discursive prayer cannot be exclusively the work of the intellect (which would turn prayer into study), so affective prayer is not exclusively an activity of the affections. It is simply a question of what predominates in the particular type of prayer, but man must use both intellect and the affections in all forms of prayer. The aim of prayer is to increase charity, and therefore affective prayer is a more pure form of prayer than discursive prayer. It may be practiced in three ways: by repeated acts of love made under the impulse of grace, by a simple, pure act of love in the presence of God, and by a special operation of God on the soul (inchoate contemplation).

Perfect contemplation, on the other hand, is of two kinds: first, the extraordinary gifts which are sometimes given to the soul by God as mystical phenomena (raptures, visions, and so forth) and, secondly, "a simple knowledge of God ... effected by the gift of wisdom, which elevates the soul, suspends the operations of its faculties, and places it in a state of admiration, joy and ardent love."[68] Souls may desire contemplation and even humbly request it of God because "it is the most efficacious way of attaining perfection."

With this, we conclude our survey of Spanish spirituality and although we have discussed only a few of the spiritual writers who are the glory of Spain's golden age, we must note that no other Catholic nation has contributed so much to spiritual theology. The Spain that gave the Church St. Teresa of Avila, St. John of the Cross and St. Ignatius Loyola also produced founders of apostolic orders, countless missionaries to Latin America and the Orient and, in recent times, one of the most flourishing institutes of consecrated life: Opus Dei.

ITALIAN SPIRITUALITY

While Spanish spirituality was from the outset psychological in its approach and, after the golden age, tended to become academic and speculative,[69] Italian spirituality in the sixteenth and seventeenth centuries was practical and tended towards the cultivation of a reforming spirit. Even great mystics like the Carmelite St. Magdalen of Pazzi and the Dominican St. Catherine de Ricci were preoccupied to a great extent with the reform of the Church. The reason for this was the alarming inroads made by the pagan customs of the Renaissance throughout the whole of Italy, and spiritual writers, in the tradition of Savanarola, were soon demanding that steps be taken to restore both the clergy and the laity to an authentic Christian life. The effort was further complicated by the fact that fear of the Protestant Revolt led to the establishment of the Inquisition, so that even the advocates of reform had to exercise great caution. The Italians were more afraid of heresy than they were of worldliness and sensuality.

One of the prime movers in the Italian reaction against the pagan influence of the Renaissance was the Dominican John Baptist da Crema, a renowned preacher, director of souls and spiritual writer. After his death in 1552 his works were placed on the Index by the Italian Inquisition and it was not until 1900 that they were removed.[70] His spirituality was one which placed great emphasis on personal effort, cooperation with grace and the eradication of vice. Because of his insistence on voluntary effort and his inadequate treatment of the doctrine of pure love, some critics claimed to find the taint of semi-pelagianism in his doctrine. Nevertheless, the movement which he began was to bear fruit in several areas: the emergence of the clerics regular as a new form of religious life and the publication of *The Spiritual Combat*, attributed to Laurence Scupoli.

John Baptist da Crema had been the spiritual director of some very holy people, among them, St. Cajetan, the founder of the Theatines (1542) and St. Anthony Zaccaria, the founder of the Barnabites (1530). Like St. Ignatius, who had come to Rome in 1537, these men were convinced that the only way to reform the clergy was by way of example and by personal influence on small groups. As a result, the clerics regular were founded precisely as a vehicle for the reformation of the clergy.

The clerics regular did not live a monastic style of life nor did they observe poverty in the manner proper to the mendicants; rather, they emphasized interior poverty and detachment from the goods of this world. Their practice of prayer was free and simple, unlike the methodical prayer of the Ignatian *Exercises*, although they did follow the system of self-combat advocated by St. Ignatius.

In this period of reform, Italy produced numerous saints and a large number of new religious institutes, dedicated either to the reform of the Church or the apostolate of the works of mercy. Thus, we may mention St. Robert Bellarmine, St. Philip Neri (founder of the Oratorians), St. Charles Borromeo (founder of the Oblates), St. Cajetan (founder of the Theatines), St. Angela Merici (founder of the Ursulines), St. Anthony Zaccaria (founder of the Barnabites), St. Camillus (founder of the Fathers of a Good Death), and so forth. In spite of the reforming spirit of Italian spirituality, it never became harsh or severe; it was always a spirituality of interior mortification, cultivation of divine love, tenderness and joy, as was manifested in the lives of the saints that it produced.

The most influential spiritual literature of the period was *The Spiritual Combat*, the work of the Theatine, Laurence Scupoli (+ 1610).[71] Reflecting as it does a period of Church reform and renewal, *The Spiritual Combat* aims primarily at conversion from sin and the cultivation of an interior life. It states as a fundamental principle that the spiritual life does not consist essentially in external practices but in the knowledge and love of God.

Christian perfection is primarily interior and therefore it demands death to self and complete submission to God through love and obedience. Again and again it stresses the pure love of God and a desire for his glory as the proper motives for Christian living, although fear of hell and a desire for heaven may be good motives for beginners. Considering man's sinful state, perfection can be achieved only by constant warfare against self. The chief weapons in this spiritual combat are distrust of self (of ourselves we can do nothing); trust in God (in him we can do all things); proper use of our faculties of body and soul; and the practice of prayer.

The Spiritual Combat, as the name indicates, is concerned primarily with the proper use of our faculties and powers, and to this end it treats in particular of the various faculties, offers advice on how to control them, and urges constant custody. Nevertheless, there is no attempt to smother the senses or to imply that they are necessary sources of evil and sin. Rather, it is a question of learning how to reach God through the proper use of the senses, much as was explained by St. Ignatius in his *Exercises*.

As regards the practice of prayer, we find none of the detailed explanations that characterize Spanish spirituality. Three styles of prayer are recommended, and all of them are ascetical: meditation, especially on the passion and death of Christ; communion with God by frequently recollecting oneself in his presence and making use of ejaculations or short vocal prayers; and examination of conscience, which is not prayer in the strict sense of the word, although it may lead to prayer. There is, finally, the suggestion to receive Communion as frequently as possible and, when that is not possible, to practice "Communion of desire" or spiritual Communion.

Two renowned mystics of the period also exercised a social and reforming mission, very similar to that of St. Catherine of Siena. The first, a Carmelite named St. Magdalen of Pazzi (+ 1607), was an ecstatic who was gifted with phenomenal mystical gifts. Her written works were all dictated while in ecstasy and she used the services of six secretaries who were hard pressed to copy down the torrent of words that she expressed. Her works can be divided under five headings: contemplations on the mysteries of faith and the life of Christ; the religious life and the virtues; commentaries on Sacred Scripture; contemplations on the divine perfections; and exclamations similar to those composed by St. Teresa of Avila.[72]

Like St. Magdalen, St. Catherine de Ricci (+ 1590), Dominican, was a mystic totally dedicated to the reform of the Church, but unlike St. Magdalen, she carried on her apostolate by means of letters addressed to the persons concerned.[73] In spite of her zeal for the reform of the Church and her intense suffering on receiving the stigmata of the Lord's passion, her biographer, Serafino Razzi, relates that God flooded Catherine's soul with indescribable joy. Other mystics of the time manifested the same concern for the reform of the Church and received similar mystical phenomena, for example, the Dominican tertiary Blessed Osanna of Mantua and the Poor Clare Blessed Battista Varani.

The happiness of the Italian mystics is especially noteworthy in St. Philip Neri (+ 1595),[74] who has been called "the loving saint *par excellence.*" He is in many ways a forerunner of the spirit of St. Francis de Sales, for he maintained that "the spirit of joy wins Christian perfection more easily than does the spirit of sadness." Nevertheless, he also insisted on the importance of interior mortification and, with St. Charles Borromeo, on the practice of prayer. Indeed, he maintained that mortification is one of the best preparations for the practice of prayer. In periods of dryness his advice was the same as that of St. Teresa of Avila: under no circumstances should one abandon the practice of prayer. If a book were used, St. Philip advocated that one should read until devotion is aroused and then close the book and begin to pray. "Prayer," said St. Philip, "is in the supernatural order what speech is in the natural order."[75]

St. Philip Neri dedicated himself as often as possible to the care of the sick. He even maintained that nursing the sick is a short path to perfection. His biographer, Cardinal Capecelatro, says of him: "[He] made himself the master of a mild, sweet, tender, compassionate asceticism. Throughout his life hardly two or three instances of moderate severity are to be met with; and, on the contrary, an infinite sweetness of charity towards one's neighbor is seen at every step."[76]

One characteristic of Italian spirituality at this period is the theme of divine love. Historically, it can be traced back to St. Catherine of Genoa (+ 1510), the foundress of Italian hospitals.[77] One of her disciples, Ettore Vernazza, founded a religious group under the title, *Oratorio del divino Amore*, and it very quickly spread throughout Italy.

The writings of St. Catherine of Genoa were edited by Ettore Vernazza and Cattaneo Marabotto, St. Catherine's confessor, in 1530; then, in 1548, Battista Vernazza composed the *Dialogues*, which were added to St. Catherine's *Life* and *Treatise on Purgatory* in the edition of 1551. Although not the work of St. Catherine herself, the *Dialogues* do faithfully reflect her teaching on divine love. The importance of the *Dialogues* is that they correspond with the mystical experiences of several saints of the time; they propose a high degree of love of God which is free from self-interest; and they place as a condition for the attainment of this perfect love the expression of love of neighbor. The devotion of divine love led to a proliferation of "companies," a title that was used by numerous new institutes dedicated the apostolate of the corporal works of mercy in various cities of Italy.

ST. FRANCIS DE SALES

"St. Francis de Sales forms a school of spirituality by himself alone. He is its beginning, its development, its sum-total."[78] Philip Hughes states that it is in Francis de Sales that "the French Renaissance is baptized and humanism becomes devout."[79] He is also a bridge between the Renaissance and the modern period and has been one of the strongest single influences on spirituality from the seventeenth century to the present day.

Born at Savoy in 1567, Francis de Sales studied under the Jesuits at Paris and then went on to Padua, where he received his doctorate in civil and canon law. Ordained to the priesthood in December of 1593, he was named Provost of the Chapter of Geneva, an office second only to that of the bishop. Immediately he dedicated himself with great vigor to the evangelization of the Calvinists and he succeeded so well that he was named coadjutor to the Bishop of Geneva; then, on December 8, 1602, he was consecrated Bishop of Geneva. Until his death in 1622, he dedicated himself to preaching, spiritual writing and the direction of souls as well as the administration of his diocese. Together with St. Jane Frances de Chantal he founded the religious institute of the Visitation of the Blessed Virgin, a semi-cloistered community for young women and widows. In 1887 Pope Pius IX declared St. Francis de Sales a Doctor of the Church, the first time this honor was bestowed on a French-man.[80]

From his earliest years St. Francis de Sales was strongly attracted to the things of God and various incidents in his life give every indication that his call to the clerical life was an immediate divine vocation. Michael de la Bedoyere says that Francis de Sales is "the greatest of the saints – at least for modern times. And I base this conviction on the sense I had all the time that here was the human being of our period of Western history who, naturally, instinc-tively, as well as supernaturally, reflected most directly the charac-ter and way of Christ our Lord."[81]

The doctrine taught by St. Francis de Sales was not new, but he did present spiritual teaching in an original manner and he deserves credit for removing Christian spirituality from the monastic framework in which it had been confined for many centuries. Trained as he was by the Jesuits, St. Francis was clearly Ignatian in his spiritual practices, but in his theology he is an Augustinian with the realism and optimism of a Thomist. Very likely he was familiar with the writings of the Flemish school, St. Catherine of Siena (for whom he had a great love), St. Catherine of Genoa, St. Philip Neri, and numerous writers of the Spanish school, especially St. Teresa of Avila, St. John of the Cross, Louis of Granada, John of Avila and García de Cisneros. *The Spiritual Combat* was a favorite meditation book since his days at Padua. In Paris he had contacts with the Capuchin, Richard Beaucousin, Bérulle, the Carmelite nuns and Mme. Acarie.

The critical edition of the works of St. Francis de Sales comprises twenty-seven volumes, of which twelve volumes contain his letters. The rest of the edition contains *The Defense of the Standard of the Holy Cross, Introduction to the Devout Life, Treatise on the Love of God, Spiritual Interviews*, his controversies and four volumes of sermons. For our purposes it will suffice to summarize the doctrine contained in *Introduction to the Devout Life*.

The *Introduction to the Devout Life* first appeared in 1609 and a final edition, made by St. Francis himself, was published in 1619. The book was written precisely for the laity and perhaps St. Francis de Sales is the first spiritual writer to compose a treatise of lay spiritual-ity. As he states in his preface, those who have written previously on the spiritual life have done so for the instruction of persons who have given up association with the world or they have taught a spirituality that would lead persons to do so. The intention of St. Francis, however, is to give spiritual instruction to those who remain in the world, in their professions and in their families, and falsely believe that it is impossible for them to strive for the devout life.

What does St. Francis understand by the devout life or true devotion? First of all, it does not consist in any kind of extraordinary grace or favor, and St. Francis states this quite emphatically:

> There are certain things which many people esteem as virtue and they are not that at all.... I refer to the ecstasies, raptures, insensibilities, impassibilities, deific unions, elevations, transformations and other similar perfections discussed in certain books which promise to raise the soul to a purely intellectual contemplation, to the essential application of the spirit and a supereminent life ... These perfections are not virtues; rather, they are rewards that God gives for virtues or small samples of the delights of the future life.... Nevertheless, one should not aspire to such graces, because they are in no way necessary for loving and serving God well, which should be our only aim.[82]

Secondly, true devotion does not consist in any particular spiritual exercise:

> I hear nothing but perfections, and yet I see very few people who practice them.... Some place their virtue in austerity; others in abstemiousness in eating; some in almsgiving, others in frequenting the sacraments of penance and the Eucharist; another group in prayer, either vocal or mental; still others in a certain sort of passive and supereminent contemplation; others in those gratuitously given, extraordinary graces. And all of them are mistaken, taking the effects for the causes, the brook for the spring, the branches for the root, the accessory for the principal, and often the shadow for the substance. For me, I neither know nor have experienced any other Christian perfection than that of loving God with all our heart and our neighbor as ourselves. Every other perfection without this one is a false perfection.[83]

True devotion, which for St. Francis de Sales is the same as Christian perfection, is the fulfillment of the twofold precept of charity enunciated by Christ (Mt. 22:34–40). In the *Introduction to the Devout Life* he gives a detailed exposition which is similar to the definition of devotion according to Louis of Granada:[84]

> True and living devotion, Philothea, presupposes the love of God; indeed, it is nothing else but the true love of God, but it is not just any kind of love. Insofar as divine love beautifies our souls, it is called grace and makes us pleasing to the divine Majesty; insofar as it gives us the

power to do good it is called charity; but when it reaches a degree of perfection in which it not only makes us do good, but makes us do it carefully, frequently and promptly, then it is called devotion.[85]

Although he mentions the good works that flow from true devotion, St. Francis is insistent that the devout life is essentially an interior life. Moreover, the devout life will be lived differently by persons in different vocations or professions; all, therefore, should seek the perfection of the devout life, but each one in accordance with his personal strength and the duties of his state in life.

Immediately after stressing the universal call of all Christians to perfection, St. Francis de Sales insists on the need for a spiritual director. He admits that a good director is hard to find and he states that he must be a man of charity, learning and prudence. He also warns that spiritual direction must never impede the working of the Holy Spirit or be an obstacle to the freedom of the soul, for all persons are not called by the same road to perfection. This, of course, is the same advice that was offered by St. Teresa of Avila and St. John of the Cross.

The first task facing the soul is purgation from sin, and here St. Francis follows the teaching of St. Ignatius Loyola, proposing meditation on the last ends and a general confession. Then, there must be a complete renunciation of all attachment to sin, without which there can be no lasting conversion and no progress in perfection. To achieve this second and more profound purgation it is necessary to avoid all occasions of sin and to be involved in worldly affairs only when necessity requires and not out of love for created things. And although the soul must sometimes learn to live with its own imperfections and weaknesses, it should never willingly accept the faults that proceed from temperament or habit. To grow in virtue, says St. Francis, we must overcome even our indeliberate faults.

In the second part of the *Introduction* St. Francis proposes a daily schedule of spiritual exercises in which the practice of mental prayer holds a central position. Basically, they are the same spiritual exercises as listed in *The Spiritual Combat* and followed by the clerics regular: daily mental prayer, morning and evening prayers, examination of conscience, weekly confession and frequent Communion, spiritual reading, and the practice of interior recollection.

The Salesian method of mental prayer is simple, clear and brief. In many respects it resembles the forms of prayer taught by Louis of Granada, St. Ignatius Loyola and *The Spiritual Combat*. At the very outset, following the teaching of St. Bernard, St. Teresa of Avila and St. John of the Cross, Francis de Sales emphasizes the importance of meditation on the life of Christ.

The body of the meditation proper consists in the application of the intellect and the will to the subject matter. Calmly and without haste, the mind should meditate on the various aspects of the mystery proposed for consideration, and as soon as it finds inspiration and delight in any point, it should pause and dwell on that point. Then the meditation will produce good movements in the will such as the love of God and neighbor, zeal for the salvation of souls, imitation of Christ, confidence in the goodness and mercy of God.

The result of these movements of the affections should be twofold: conversation with God and practical resolutions for the future. Since the purpose of meditation is growth in virtue and the love of God, St. Francis insists that the soul should not be satisfied with arousing affections and conversing with God, but should make particular resolutions to put into practice during the day.

"To all this," says St. Francis, "I have added that one should gather a little bouquet of devotion, and this is what I mean: .... when our mind considers some mystery through meditation, we should select one or two or three points which we have found to be most suitable to our taste and most helpful for our advancement, in order to recall them during the rest of the day...."[86]

St. Francis also offers counsels concerning the behavior of the individual after meditation is completed: seek an occasion for putting into practice one's resolutions; remain in silence for a time and then calmly take up the duties of the day. Then, returning to the practice of meditation, St. Francis states that although he has provided a method of procedure, the soul must always yield at once to any holy inspirations and affections aroused in prayer. Holy affections are never to be restrained, but all resolutions should be made only at the end of the meditation.

In the third part of the *Introduction* St. Francis considers the practice of virtue, selecting those which are particularly necessary for the Christian layman. Of all the virtues treated we could say that, after charity, the predominantly Salesian virtue is meekness. Thus, St. Francis writes in one of his letters: "Remember the principal lesson, the one which [our Lord] has left us in three words, so that we would never forget it and which we should repeat a hundred times a day: 'Learn of me for I am meek and humble of heart.' That is all. Just keep your heart meek in regard to your neighbor and humble in regard to God."[87]

Finally, in the last two parts of the *Introduction* St. Francis treats of temptations, sadness, consolations and aridity and concludes the work with a series of self-examinations and considerations whereby the soul can judge its progress in true devotion. Thus, in its totality the *Introduction to the Devout Life* provides a complete program for the spiritual advancement of the laity.

Whereas the *Introduction* was composed for all Christians of good will, the *Treatise on the Love of God* was addressed to a select group. According to Dom Mackey, it also reveals the soul and heart of Francis de Sales at the height of his holiness.[88] The doctrine contained in the *Treatise* was not always esteemed as highly as it should have been, due to the fact that the Jansenists, the Quietists and Fénelon attempted to use the teaching of Francis de Sales in defense of their errors. According to Dom Mackey, even Bossuet did harm to the teaching of St. Francis when he tried to refute the errors of Fénelon.[89] The result was that St. Francis did not enjoy the influence on the French school that he might otherwise have had.

The purpose of the *Treatise* is to trace the progress of the soul from its fallen state to the heights of divine love, which constitutes Christian perfection and holiness. St. Francis provides the psychological explanations which are necessary for understanding the theology of love. He then develops the theme of the divine origin of love, showing that man's love for God is a participation in the eternal charity of God himself. And since it is the nature of love to increase or to fall away, St. Francis treats of growth in charity, which can be effected by even the most insignificant actions; the obstacles to charity; and the various ways in which a soul may abandon divine love for the love of creatures. He emphasizes the distinction between love of complacency and love of benevolence, stating that the former is proper to glory, where love is experienced in contemplation and repose, while the latter is proper to the soul in this life.

In speaking of mystical prayer and the ecstatic experiences that may accompany it, St. Francis, who constantly expressed a fear of illusion and a repugnance for mystical phenomena,[90] seems to be writing of something that he himself had experienced. But the life of charity does not consist exclusively in the delight of mystical prayer; it is also a question of obedience and suffering. Therefore St. Francis discusses the "love of conformity," by which the soul obeys the commandments, the counsels and particular inspirations, and the "union of our will with the divine will of good pleasure," by which the soul accepts suffering.

The *Treatise* ends with a summary of the theology of charity. St. Francis discusses the precepts of love of God and neighbor; charity as the bond and impulse of all the virtues; the gifts and fruits of the Holy Spirit; and precise suggestions for performing one's actions as perfectly as possible.

From a doctrinal point of view, one of the most significant contributions of St. Francis de Sales to spiritual theology was to unify all Christian morality and holiness under the bond of charity. This doctrine, to be sure, had been taught explicitly by St. Thomas Aquinas[91] and other medieval theologians, but by the time of St. Francis de Sales it was necessary to insist again that Christian perfection does not consist in any particular exercise or practice but in the love of God and neighbor. Few authors have treated of charity and the other virtues with greater unction and power of persuasion. Another contribution was the insistence that the perfection of charity is the vocation of all Christians, regardless of their vocation or state in life. Lastly, he explained in detail two exercises that are fundamental to the Christian life: the practice of mental prayer and the cultivation of the virtues proper to one's state in life. St. Francis de Sales may rightly be called the father of modern spirituality, although changing events prevented his influence from being as effective as one would have hoped.

CHAPTER 9

MODERN SPIRITUALITY

The period covered under the heading "modern spirituality" extends from the seventeenth to the nineteenth century and the focal point is France. While it is true that modern spirituality retains something of the affective flavor of the teaching of St. Francis de Sales, except for Italy, the Salesian influence has not been predominant. Rather, the spirituality fashioned by the French school was eminently Christocentric, firmly rooted in the Christology of St. Paul and the theology of St. Augustine.

"We would have expected that period to produce some masterpieces in theology," says Florand, "but when we list Chardon's *Cross of Jesus*, the *Sermons* of Bossuet, the *Meditations* of Malebranche, we have practically named them all. The *Pensées* of Pascal are but 'a woodpile in disorder'."[1] Nevertheless, the Christocentric spirituality of the French school was diffused so widely that for all practical purposes Catholic spirituality in modern times could be characterized as French spirituality. This is especially evident when we consider the vast influence of French culture and religion on countries throughout the world, particularly during the eighteenth and nineteenth centuries.

In order to evaluate the strength and the weakness, the orthodoxy and the distortions of the French school of spirituality, it will be necessary to retrace our steps somewhat in order to investigate its origins and trace its development.

SOURCES OF FRENCH SPIRITUALITY

France in the sixteenth century was the scene of intense religious activity, directed principally against the Protestants. But life within the Church was anything but fervent. The regulations of the Council of Trent were in large part a dead letter; the king was absolute sovereign of all religious holdings; bishops were worldly, priests were ignorant and immoral, and religious life was at a low ebb. Reaction against the Protestants was practically the only restraint and the only unifying factor.

The first move toward actual reform of the life of the Church must be credited to the Capuchins (who came to France in 1573), the Carmelite nuns (who introduced Spanish spiritual teaching through Anna of Jesus), the Jesuits (established in France in 1553), the professors at the Sorbonne, and the Carthusians.

The Capuchin, Benedict Canfeld (1562–1610; born William Fitch in Essex, England, and a convert from Puritanism), is of special importance as a forerunner of the French school of spirituality. His treatise, *Règle de perfection*, went through twenty-five editions and was translated into all the European languages and into Latin as well. The theme of the work is the necessity of death to self and total abandonment to God. The sources of his doctrine are impressive: pseudo-Dionysius, Herp, St. Bonaventure, Hugh of Balma, Alphonus of Madrid, the *Institutions* of pseudo-Tauler, Ruysbroeck, *Theologia Germanica*, Blosius, St. Catherine of Genoa, *The Cloud of Unknowing*, and Walter Hilton.

Another Capuchin, Joseph Tremblay (1577–1638), wrote *Introduction à la vie spirituelle par une facile méthode d'oraison*, which is an adaptation of the Ignation *Exercises* to the Franciscan spirit and usage. Tremblay was known as "the gray Eminence" when he became attached to the household of Cardinal Richelieu in 1613.

However, the French school of spirituality starts with Bérulle, although he was influenced to some extent by what is called the "abstract" school of Benedict Canfeld, Dom Beaucousin the Carthusian, and a few Capuchins of mystical tendencies.[2] Only relatively recently has it been possible to study Peter de Bérulle with any degree of objectivity and calmness. During his lifetime (1575–1629) he aroused the hostility of the Carmelites, the Jesuits and Cardinal Richelieu. Through the centuries since his death, authors have tended either to exaggerate his originality (Bremond) or to classify him as a poor transmitter of Ignatian spirituality (Pottier).[3]

From his earliest years Bérulle was drawn to God and divine things. He took his early studies under the Jesuits, made the *Exercises* to determine his vocation, and then studied at the Sorbonne and was eventually ordained a diocesan priest. He knew St. Francis de Sales (who spoke highly of Bérulle) and was instrumental in bringing the Carmelite nuns from Spain to France; he also became their spiritual director. As regards his spiritual doctrine, he had read the works of St. Francis de Sales, St. Ignatius, and St. Teresa of Avila (on his knees), but he was especially devoted to the study of St. Augustine and the Fathers of the Church. He was also influenced at first by Herp and Ruysbroeck, but in systematic theology he followed the teaching of St. Thomas Aquinas. Some authors find traces of the teaching of St. Gertrude and Ludolph the Carthusian in Bérulle's doctrine so far as it is Christocentric.[4]

The first work published by Bérulle was *Brief discours de l'abnéga-tion intérieure* (Paris, 1597) and it reveals that at this early period Bérulle was thinking along the lines of the abstract school. Possibly it was a French adaptation of an Italian treatise composed by Isabella Bellinzaga, assisted by the Jesuit, Achille Gagliardi: *Breve compendio de la perfezzione*. As the title indicates, Bérulle treats of the abnega-tion necessary for total adherence to God.

> The first, a very low estimate of all created things and of oneself above all, acquired by the frequent thought of their baseness and by the daily experience of one's nothingness and infirmity.... The second is a very high idea of God, not by a deep insight into the attributes of the divinity, which is not necessary and which few have, but by the total submission of self to God in order to adore him and give him all power over us and what is ours, without reserving any personal interest.[5]

Several events in the life of Bérulle weaned him from the abstract school and emphasis on self-abnegation; he turned to a spiritual doctrine based on the positive commitment or adherence to Christ. First of all, in 1602 the Carthusian Beaucousin translated into French the *Perla evangelica* (by an unknown Dutch author). Since Beaucousin was Bérulle's spiritual director at the time, it is certain that Bérulle was familiar with this treatise; in fact, in his *Trois discours de controverse* (1609), Bérulle uses the same words, style and doctrine as found in the *Perla evangelica*.[6] The doctrine, of course, is eminently Christocentric.

Secondly, in 1602 Bérulle made the Ignatian *Exercises* under the direction of Father Maggio and was powerfully impressed with the self-humiliation of Christ.

> In thinking of the Incarnation of Jesus Christ, I weighed deeply and at length in the depth of my soul this sovereign goodness of the eternal Word who, as very God, is so exalted above all created things, and has indeed deigned to humiliate and abase himself so low as to place on his throne so vile and abject a nature, and has indeed willed to be associated and united therewith so closely that no greater or more intimate union can be found. As the Incarnation is the foundation of our salvation, I have weighed most deeply how great ought to be the abjection of self by which he who is resolved to labor for the salvation of his soul must begin, since the Son of God deigned to begin it in this mystery by the humiliation and abasement of his divine and eternal person.[7]

Thirdly, through his close association with the Carmelite nuns, whom he introduced into France and then served as spiritual director, and through his reading of the works of St. Teresa of Avila, he became convinced of the central position of Christ in the spiritual life. It was also at this time that Bérulle discovered the works of St. John of Avila and Louis of León, both Christocentric writers.

Finally, Bérulle's disputes with the Protestants, which caused him to write *Trois discours de controverse*, forced him to go back to patristic sources, where he absorbed Christological doctrine, and then to go back to St. Paul and St. John. In this way the spiritual doctrine of Bérulle was gradually elaborated, to be completed by the founding of the Oratory of Jesus (1611), under the patronage of Christ, the Sovereign Priest.

Between 1611 and 1613 Bérulle composed a series of prayers for the use of the members of the Oratory and for the Carmelite nuns under his direction. At this time he extended his spiritual doctrine on Christ to include Mary, and from that time on he never separated the Son from his Mother. Yet in the entire scheme of his doctrine his spirituality did not terminate either in Jesus or Mary; rather Bérulle's concept of the journey to perfection was "to Christ through Mary and through Christ to the Trinity."

Unfortunately, the one thing that was original in Bérulle's teaching aroused the animosity of the Carmelites, Duval and Gallemant, and ended Bérulle's friendship with Mme. Acarie (1566–1618), who had entered Carmel as a lay sister, taking the name of Marie of the Incarnation. It also caused his *Elevations* to be censured by the University of Louvain and the University of Douai.[8]

The point at issue was Bérulle's "vow of slavery to Jesus and Mary." Whether it was due to an excessively pessimistic interpretation of St. Paul and St. Augustine or a reaction to the unwarranted exaltation of human nature and freedom at the hands of the humanists, Bérulle looked upon man as "the most vile and useless creature of all; indeed, as dust, mud and a mass of corruption."[9] Man must therefore wage relentless war against his own misery and sinfulness and at the same time have a deep conviction of his need for God's grace. He must strive to reach the point of total adherence to God, but this can be done only at the cost of heroic self-renunciation. This, in turn, involves various elements: voluntary renunciation of all sensible and spiritual consolations in order to give the soul a "capacity for grace"; a fervent desire to love God with all one's heart, accompanied by humble prayer of petition to this effect; an opening of one's soul to the operations of the incarnate Word, at the same time willing whatever Christ wills; and finally, to maintain the disposition of total self-annihilation before Christ by making the vow of holy slavery to Jesus and Mary. In this way there is nothing left of self, but everything is surrendered to the action of Christ.[10]

Bérulle had intended his vow of slavery only for those persons of the Oratory and Carmel who were advanced in Christian holiness. But as it became more widely known it was subjected to attack by the theologians who could see in Bérulle's doctrine at least the seeds of Jansenism, Quietism, Lutheranism or the abstract spirituality of the Low Countries and pseudo-Dionysius, which by this time was completely out of favor. At the urging of his friends, Bérulle defended and explained his doctrine in his masterly work, *Grandeurs de Jésus*.[11]

The vow of slavery to Jesus and Mary was no longer presented as an action restricted to those in the higher stages of the spiritual life, as formerly, but as a logical consequence of the baptismal vows taken by all Christians. To justify his doctrine, Bérulle shifted his emphasis from man's self-renunciation to the "servitude of Christ's humanity in the hypostatic union." The human nature of Christ, considered apart from the divinity of his person, is "essentially in a state of servitude and remains in this state permanently and perpetually, with regard to the divinity, by reason of its very nature and condition."[12] If, therefore, we place ourselves in a similar state of slavery in relation to Christ, we shall be able to belong to him completely, and thus share in his very life and grace. Hence the vow of servitude to Christ composed by Bérulle:

> With this desire I make to thee, O Jesus my Lord, and to thy deified humanity, a humanity truly thine in its deification and truly mine in its humiliation, sorrows and sufferings; to thee and to it I make an oblation and entire gift, absolute and irrevocable, of all that I am through thee in being, by nature and in the order of grace. . . . I leave myself then wholly to thee, O Jesus, and to thy sacred humanity, in the most humble and binding condition that I know: the condition and relation of servitude, which I acknowledge to be due to thy humanity as much on account of the greatness of the state to which it is raised through the hypostatic union, as also on account of the excess of voluntary abasement to which it became reduced and humbled for my salvation and glory, in its life, its cross, and in its death. . . . To this end and this homage I set and place my soul, my state and my life, both now and forever, in a state of subjection and in relations of dependence and servitude in regard to thee and to thy humanity thus deified and thus humiliated together. (*Oeuvres complètes*, p. 490.)

Because of her exalted dignity as Mother of God, Mary is likewise honored by a vow of holy slavery which Bérulle expresses as follows:

> I vow and dedicate myself to Jesus Christ, my Lord and Savior, in the state of perpetual slavery to his most holy Mother, the Blessed Virgin Mary. In perpetual honor of the Mother and the Son, I desire to be in a state and condition of slavery as regards her office as the Mother of my God, in order to honor more humbly and more holily so high and divine an office, and I give myself to her as a slave in honor of the gift which the eternal Word has made of himself as her Son through the mystery of the Incarnation that he deigned to bring about in and through her. (*Oeuvres complètes*, p. 527.)

After defending the vow of slavery to Jesus and Mary, Bérulle then probed more deeply into the theology of the Trinity and the mystery of the Incarnation.[13] Bérulle's concept of God is pseudo-Dionysian and Platonic, as transmitted by St. Augustine and the Rhineland mystics. He loved to contemplate God in his essence, separated from the world and transcendent, although not as the God of the philosophers but as the God of divine revelation. He also had the same preference as St. Augustine for considering the divine unity, which was for him the principal attribute of God.

He saw the trinity and unity of God as "contrary dialectic moments which are complimentary and ontologically simultaneous."[14] The Father is the principle of the life of the Trinity as source of divinity but he is at the same time alpha and omega. In relation to the incarnate Word, the Father is both father and mother. Bérulle seldom refers to the Word except in terms of the Incarnation, but when he does, he uses the Thomistic terminology: intellectual generation and image of the Father. The Holy Spirit is "produced" as the substantial love which is the result of the mutual knowledge of the Father and the Son.

The Incarnation, according to Bérulle, is God's chief creative act and therefore it would seem that it would have occurred even if it had not been necessary for man's redemption. It is a universal and cosmic event which establishes a new order of grace, of which Christ is the principle and source. We are born of Christ through grace as he is born of the Father by nature. Christ's fatherhood through grace is a recapitulation of all things in God (terminology of St. Irenaeus, based on the doctrine of St. Paul); Christ is a microcosmos (St. Gregory's expression); Christ is the archetype of the entire universe (Platonic expression).

When, however, Bérulle attempted to delve more deeply into the mystery of the hypostatic union, he was attacked by the Carmelites and by the ex-Oratorian, Hersent, for maintaining that in the Incarnation the human nature of Christ is united to the divine essence. Here is his argumentation:

> If the Person of the Word is united to this humanity, the essence and subsistence of the Word are united. And this humanity of Jesus Christ our Lord bears and receives in itself not only the personal being but also the essential being of God; for the Word is God, God is man, and man is God, according to the most familiar and most common notions of the faith. And the Word is God by this divine essence, and God is man by this humanity. And man is God by the divinity which the humanity receives in the subsistence of the eternal Word, and it is not possible to understand how this personal being of God can be communicated in the essential being of God.[15]

Bérulle also referred to the Incarnation as a kind of "second Trinity," because whereas the first is a Trinity "of subsistence in unity of essence," the second is a trinity "of essence in the unity of subsistence," namely, the soul, the body and the divinity of Jesus. The first Trinity is divine and uncreated in its persons and its essence; the second trinity is divine in the Person but human in its two essences. Bérulle defended himself against his accusers by saying that his doctrine on the hypostatic union was based on the teaching of St. Thomas Aquinas.

The remaining years of Bérulle's life were far from peaceful. First of all, he entered into theological conflict with the Jesuits, whom he accused of neo-paganism. In his view they granted entirely too much liberty and responsibility to man in the work of justification and salvation and he wished them to follow more closely the teachings of St. Augustine and St. Thomas Aquinas. Secondly, Bérulle was himself attacked by Cardinal Richelieu, who ridiculed Bérulle's spiritual teaching with great animosity.[16]

Nevertheless, in spite of these troubled years, Bérulle wrote a directory for the superiors of the Oratory, a panegyric in honor of St. Mary Magdalen (said to be one of the most beautiful ever written) and a life of Christ. He died at the altar on October 2, 1629, while celebrating a votive Mass of the Incarnation.[17]

Within fifteen years after his death, Bérulle was almost forgotten, but his spiritual teaching was perpetuated by his disciples, and especially by Bourgoing, who dedicated his entire life to the propagation of Bérulle's Christocentric teaching. A number of reasons can be given for the brevity of Bérulle's posthumous influence, but perhaps the principal one is that he was eclipsed by Condren, Olier and Bossuet, the most illustrious of all. Other factors are: the destructive criticism by Cardinal Richelieu, the enmity of the Jesuits, the indifference of many Oratorians, and the archaic, ponderous style of his writing. Nevertheless, one author stated: "As it is impossible to read the treatises of St. Augustine ... without becoming humble, or those of St. Teresa without loving prayer, so also we cannot read those of Cardinal de Bérulle without becoming filled with reverence for God and the mysteries of his Son."[18]

The foregoing tribute adequately sums up Bérulle's spirituality, which rests on the foundation of the virtue of religion[19] and is directed to participation in the mystery of Christ. Starting with the Augustinian view of man's sin and misery, Bérulle stresses man's need for God. But man also has within himself the imprint of the divine image and a natural desire for God. Only grace through Christ can solve the problem of the tension between man's misery and his desire for God. Thus, two operations are involved in the sanctification of the soul: the work of God in the soul and that of the soul toward God. The first is called grace and the second is virtue. But grace is intimately linked with the mystery of Christ, because Christ is not only the mediator of grace but the very source of grace. Just as the humanity of Christ cannot even exist apart from the divinity of the Person of the Word, so also in the spiritual life we cannot live the life of Christ until we are completely despoiled of self and have put on Christ. Through grace, therefore, a new order is realized in man and its manifestation is "adherence" to God through the virtue of religion.

For Bérulle, participation in the mystery of Christ is not simply "imitation of Christ", which would be something purely external; it is a union with Christ's own life and actions, and especially Christ's prayer, sentiments and adoration of his Father. The most important Christlike activity for the Christian is adoration. Only Christ can give the virtue of religion its plenitude as adoration of the Father; hence, in adhering to Christ, we embrace a spirituality of adoration, an adoration rooted in love because the God we adore is also our last end in which we find happiness and peace.

In explaining how the Christian soul can participate in the mystery of Christ, Bérulle speaks of the mysteries or events in the life of Christ as "states".[20] Each mystery or event is at the same time an historical, transitory action which is finished and will not be repeated, and also the eternal manifestation of "the dispositions and inward feelings of our Lord."[21] The latter is what Bérulle means by "state" and it is eternal; it does not change, because it pertains to the Incarnation, which is an eternal and unchanging mystery. Bérulle says:

> The mysteries of Jesus Christ are in some circumstances past, and in another way they remain and are present and perpetual. They are past as regards their performance but they are present as regards their virtue, and their virtue never passes, nor will the love with which they have been accomplished ever pass.... The spirit of God, by whom this mystery was wrought, the internal state of the external mystery ... is always alive, actual, and present to Jesus. ... This obliges us to treat the things and mysteries of Jesus, not as things past and abolished, but as things present, living, and even eternal, from which also we have to gather a present and eternal fruit.[22]

The liturgy is a marvelous means of participating in the mysteries of Christ because the liturgy is at once a representation of the historical events or mysteries in the life of Christ, and a sacramental means of entering into the interior and eternal states of Christ, as explained above. Indeed, Christ is the great Sacrament of Christian piety and the primary Sacrament of the Christian religion.[23]

Finally to adhere to Christ, the soul needs a capacity for this participation, and this is provided by the intervention of the Holy Spirit. Therefore the soul must be docile to the Spirit and totally detached from self.

Three names are of special importance in the development and refinement of Bérullian spirituality: Condren, Olier and St. John Eudes. Bremond states that the concept of adherence to Christ was expressed in different ways by the leaders of the French school: "Bérulle by a more general 'adherence,' in some way, to the Person of the Word Incarnate; Condren by a somewhat more particularized adherence to Christ, dead and risen again; finally, Olier by an adherence to the most deep, most religious, most persevering and, consequently, most 'really' active and efficacious annihilation of the same Word in the Eucharist."[24] St. John Eudes summarized everything in devotion to the Sacred Heart of Jesus and was the most outstanding promoter of this doctrine in the seventeenth century.

Charles Condren (1588–1641) holds an eminent place among the Oratorians.[25] His personal sanctity was admired by all, but as Superior General of the Oratorians he was dilatory in making decisions. Very likely he would have been an unusually successful spiritual writer, but he preferred to dedicate himself to spiritual direction, conferences and letters. He is much more Augustinian than Bérulle in regard to man's sinful and wretched state; therefore he is much more pessimistic. His main theme in spiritual doctrine is that of sacrifice, which should lead the individual to self-annihilation and complete abandonment to God. Yet sacrifice of self as a victim to God cannot bridge the gap between God's greatness and man's nothingness. This is possible only through the Incarnation; therefore, the humanity of Christ was necessary to offer a fitting sacrifice to God. Three divine perfections especially make a man conscious of his own nothingness and his need for Christ as priest and victim: God's sanctity, his sovereignty, and his plenitude.[26]

Jean-Jacques Olier (1608–1657), founder of the seminary of St. Sulpice, has not yet been studied as he deserves, and his written works have not yet been edited completely.[27] He was a person of difficult temperament and according to some authors he gave signs of mental unbalance, although he is commonly considered an authentic mystic. His best writings were published toward the end of his life and they became standard works on priestly spirituality.[28] Earlier, however, his teaching manifested the pessimism and exaggerations characteristic of the French school of spirituality. Like Bérulle and Condren, his spiritual teaching rests on the two themes of self-abnegation and adherence to Christ.

Taking his cue from the teaching of St. Paul on the opposition between the flesh and the spirit, Olier maintains that man must annihilate himself so that the Holy Spirit may work in him. Even after baptism, which "restores" the soul, the flesh remains corrupt. If, therefore, a man follows the inclinations of his body, he can only sin; for that reason he must hate his flesh and never yield in any way to it. Rather, he must love pain, suffering and persecution; even the necessary functions such as eating and drinking must be kept to the minimum imposed by necessity. This severe self-abnegation is man's way of expressing the reverence, adoration and love that comprise the virtue of religion, which has its perfect manifestation in Jesus Christ.

Thus, Olier comes to adherence to Christ, the principal theme in the French school, but with an emphasis that is particularly his own. He states: "Our Lord has made me see that, desirous of renewing the primitive spirit of the Church in these days, he raised up two persons in order to begin this design; Monsignor de Bérulle to honor him in his Incarnation and Fr. Condren to honor him in the whole of his life, his death and, above all, in his resurrction. But there remains to do him honor after his resurrection and his ascension, as he is in the most august sacrament of the Eucharist.... He was willed to bestow upon myself, as successor to Fr. de Condren, the grace and spirit of this adorable mystery."[29]

According to Olier, the sacred humanity of Christ is annihilated in the Incarnation by being deprived of its own personality; it is clothed with divinity and totally consecrated to the Father. In like manner, we should become annihilated in regard to our own interests and self-love so that we can be clothed with Jesus Christ and, in keeping with the mystery of the Incarnation, be completely consecrated to the service of God. Olier drew up specific practices for preserving one's conformity with Christ, but he designates the Eucharist as the most effective means of union with Christ, and he notes its importance for the renewal of the clergy. Christ in the Eucharist is the model for all priests and the source of all priestly holiness.[30]

St. John Eudes (1601–1680), founder of the Congregation of Jesus and Mary and of the Congregation of Our Lady of Charity (Good Shepherd), was the first to observe the feast of the Sacred Heart of Jesus.[31] Although he was one of the chief proponents of Bérullian spirituality, he avoided the abstract or metaphysical elements in Bérulle's writings, preferring to compose a practical manual for the spiritual life of ordinary Christians.[32] Renowned as a preacher and confessor, his special contribution to the Church in France was the renewal of the parish clergy and the foundation of a seminary for the proper formation of candidates for the priesthood. In the Church at large, however, he is most highly regarded as the apostle of devotion to the Sacred Hearts of Jesus and Mary.[33]

JANSENISM

Time and again in the history of the Church the excesses that emerged in Christian spirituality were rooted in the fundamental problem of the relationship between grace and human nature. In France the traditional doctrine, which states that grace perfects nature, elevates it to a higher level through a participation in the divine life while leaving it intact as human nature, was obscured by a doctrine that either destroyed nature and replaced it with grace, or exalted nature to the point that grace was unnecessary. Jansenism and Quietism, the two excesses that marked the spirituality of the French school, were related to each other in the sense that they both exaggerated the role of grace at the expense of human nature and human effort; in other respects, however, they were poles apart. The upheaval in French spirituality lasted for an entire century – from 1650 to 1750 – and the ill effects were felt in the Church until the twentieth century.

Since theologians and historians have studied these two heretical movements in great depth, it is not necessary to do more than give a cursory survey of the rise and influence of each one.[34] Bérulle and his followers, as we have seen, reacted strongly against humanism by stressing the Augustinian teaching on the baseness and sinfulness of man and his utter dependence on God in the order of grace. Although the Bérullians were unyielding in their opposition to the Jansenists, they may have unwittingly provided some doctrinal leverage for the heretical thrust. Saint-Cyran was a great admirer of Bérulle, and when the latter died and no Oratorian dared to preach the funeral eulogy without risking the wrath of Cardinal Richelieu, Saint-Cyran circulated an open letter in which he paid tribute to Bérulle.[35]

Another factor that contributed to the rise of Jansenism in particular was the effort to combat the errors of Luther and Calvin. To get right to the heart of the difficulty, the humanists decided to soften the Augustinian and Thomistic emphasis on predestination and the gratuity of grace in order to emphasize man's freedom and the necessity of his cooperation with grace. The reaction was not slow in coming. At Louvain, Michael Baius (+1589) asserted that the humanists had gone too far; actually, man is no longer free after original sin; all he can do is sin, until he receives the grace of justification, for which he can do nothing by way of preparation.[36]

Leonard Lessius, a Jesuit professor at Louvain, answered Baius by stating that God from all eternity has determined that grace sufficient for justification be given to each one through the merits of Christ and at the moment that God himself chooses. Sufficient grace becomes efficacious as a result of man's voluntary acceptance and then, since God foresees man's future merits as a result of grace, he predestines man to further graces and to salvation.[37]

In Spain, meanwhile, Dominic Bañez, Dominican professor of Salamanca from 1577 until his death in 1604, rallied to the defense of Augustinian and Thomistic doctrine. According to Bañez, prior to any consideration of man's merits, God decrees the acts of man and the free manner in which man performs those acts.[38] Man, therefore, remains free, but always within the providence of God, for it would be impossible for a man to be so autonomous that he becomes the total cause of his own actions. This would make God dependent on man, at least as regards the knowledge of man's free actions.

In 1588 Louis Molina, S.J., published his famous *Concordia liberi arbitrii cum gratiae donis* at Lisbon. He proposed an original explanation by which man's freedom could be respected without detracting from the infallibility and universality of God's knowledge and causality. Since the exercise of man's free will is conditioned by a variety of circumstances, God does not know them by his *scientia simplicis intelligentiae* (which knows things that could but never will exist) nor by his *scientia visionis* (which knows those things which God has decreed will definitely exist). The conditioned future acts of man's free will are known by a third type of divine knowledge which Molina calls *scientia media*: from all eternity God foresees how a man will act in given circumstances, and in view of that knowledge, God offers to man such and such a grace as he sees that man will react to it.

The Dominicans strongly attacked the Molinist teaching but the Roman congregation *De auxiliis gratiae* (1597) failed to resolve the question, and Molinism enjoyed great popularity until the beginning of the seventeenth century, when once again the Augustinian teaching came into favor. This, as we have seen, was aided to a great extent by Bérulle and his followers.[39] Jansenism, however, is an exaggeration of St. Augustine's teaching and the Bérullian French school was vehemently opposed to the excesses of Jansenism.

The originators of Jansenist teaching were John Duvergier Hauranne (1581–1643), more commonly known as Saint-Cyran because he became abbot there in 1620, and Cornelius Jansen (1585–1638), a doctor at Louvain and later bishop of Ypres. Saint-Cyran and Jansen both felt that humanism and Molinism gave so much freedom to man that for all practical purposes they nullified the necessity of redemption by Christ. So many concessions were made to human nature, especially with the introduction of probabilism and casuistry to moral theology, that Christian moral teaching had become scandalously lax and pagan. Even St. Francis de Sales did not escape their disapproval:

> There are in the saints, in the greatest saints, dangerous qualities which are good only for themselves and which can sometimes be harmful to others who wish to imitate them without having their spirit, grace, and the same blessing of God.... Such are the "mildnesses" of the holy Bishop of Geneva, which made him increase in grace, but which to others could be harmful, either through their own fault or through

ignorance and the bad handling of those in charge of them.... My Lord of Geneva was a holy man, but he was not one of the apostles; and it is their general rules that we have to follow.[40]

Jansen and Saint-Cyran proposed as the "authentic primitive teaching" the following points: because of original sin, human nature is fundamentally corrupt; man is totally incapable of choosing between good and evil; grace alone suffices to necessitate man's actions and choices; only the elect will be saved and only the elect can benefit from the Redemption; sacramental absolution is not to be given until the penance has been performed; perfect contrition is required for absolution from sin; pure love of God is demanded as a requisite for worthy Communion; the primary practice of the Christian life is the performance of penitential acts.[41]

Saint-Cyran accordingly proposed "to abolish the present state of the Church"; he declared that God intended to bring down the existing Church in ruin, and to put a renewed Church in its place.... Jansen took upon himself the reform of doctrine, while Anthony Arnauld was to re-establish the practices to the past. Both worked under the inspiration of Saint-Cyran. It is generally recognized by historians that Jansen and Saint-Cyran together initiated the movement of religious reform, and that the latter, "himself already 'Calvinized,' infected with his heretical poison" the future author of the *Augustinus*.[42]

Under the pretext of making Christians more worthy of God's love and mercy, the Jansenists alienated them from God by inculcating a fear that bordered on despair and a penitential spirit that violated the fundamental laws of charity and piety.[43] Preoccupied as they were with man's need for grace and his inability to do anything to dispose himself for it, they distorted Christianity into a religion of pessimism and scrupulosity. At the same time, their preoccupation with self soon evolved into a consummate pride and egotism, especially evident in Saint-Cyran and Mother Angélique.[44] The result of all this was a spirituality of dour moralism which haughtily cut itself off from the mainstream of Catholic life. As Knox puts it: "Overlooked in its cradle by the mournful faces of Saint-Cyran and Mother Angélique, Jansenism never learned to smile. Its adherents forget, after all, to believe in grace, so hagridden are they by their sense of the need for it."[45]

Although the number of Jansenists was relatively small and centered for the most part in the convent of Port Royal,[46] the spirit of Jansenism lived on long after its death. Various reasons can be given for the stubbornness of the heresy: first, the friends of Port Royal were persons of high position in the Church (Bishops Arnauld, Colbert and Noialles), the royal court (the Duchess de Longueville) and literary circles (Pascal, Racine and Madame de Sévigné); secondly, the tardiness with which Richelieu took action against Saint-Cyran;[47] and thirdly, the clumsy efforts of the French Jesuits to halt the movement.[48]

Ultimately, however, Jansenism ended its tragic course. It had started with the desire to restore the purity of primitive Christian doctrine and practice; almost immediately it became involved in the argument over grace and human freedom; then it manifested itself as a self-conscious asceticism that became increasingly puritanical; and finally it enclosed itself in total separation from the world and from the rest of Christianity by a futile attempt to restore the eremitical life, as if to set up a little church within the Church. The death blow was dealt by Pope Clement XI, who issued the bull *Unigenitus* in condemnation of more than 100 propositions excerpted from the work, *Réflexions morales*, by the ex-Oratorian Quesnel. Many of the French clergy refused to accept the decree of the Pope and in 1718 another bull, *Pastoralis officii*, excommunicated all who refused to yield.[49]

QUIETISM

Although Jansenism was introduced into the Netherlands when Arnauld, Nicole and Quesnel fled there from France, it is essentially a "French disease." Quietism, on the other hand, was a more general infection which ultimately was localized in France. And although one would be led to think that Quietism is a natural outgrowth of Jansenism, the Jansenists and the Quietists were bitter enemies. Knox sums up the situation as follows:

> We are told that, as the result of a "split cell," a twin birth may take the form, not of two similar, but of two complementary and therefore opposite products; what one lacks is emphasized in the other. So it was with Jansenism and Quietism; like Jacob and Esau they were enemies from birth. Jansenism is Lutheranism, with the Fathers substituted for the Bible; and the Jansenists reacted to Madame Guyon exactly as Luther reacted to the prophets from Zwickau – no one is so embittered against mysticism as the mystic *manqué*. Engrossed in the theology of predestination, the Jansenists were disgusted by the appearance of a rival sect which asked whether, after all, one's own salvation mattered so very much. Prone to identify "grace" with sensible devotion, they felt little in common with a system which regarded sensible devotion as a kind of

imperfection, a sign of spiritual inferiority. And, above all, they distrusted Quietism because it seemed to be presenting the world with a soft option, to be underestimating the *difficulty* of being a Christian. . . . Jansenist and Quietist, both have affinities with the Protestantism of the Reformation, but not the same affinities – in fact, just the opposite. Jansenism, as you see it in Pascal, has its doctrine of assurance but will not hear a word about human perfectibility. Quietism believes in perfection but denies even to the most perfect the conviction that he is saved.[50]

An erroneous doctrine does not spring forth, full grown, without any previous preparation of the minds that will receive it. Usually it begins with an emphasis on some particular point of Christian teaching or some aspect of the Christian life and then gradually reaches a point at which the doctrine is exaggerated beyond due proportion. Even the most holy and dedicated persons can be the unconscious promulgators of heterodox teaching. In their zeal they fail to see that they are guilty of exaggeration or they are blind to the logical conclusions that follow from their initial statements. Moreover, heretical doctrines and movements are frequently generated as a reaction to some teaching or practice that is judged to be excessive. Over-reaction and unrestrained zeal can easily lead to a distortion of the faith and its ultimate loss.

In order to understand the impact of the Quietist doctrine and the movement that grew out of it, it is necessary to take a backward glance at those writers whom Pourrat classifies as "pre-Quietists".[51] Some of them were authors whose works were partially or entirely condemned by the Church; others were writers whose teaching was basically orthodox but perhaps badly expressed. As an attitude which concentrates on the pure love of God, perfect abandonment to the divine will and the passivity necessary for genuine contemplative prayer, Quietism has been a phenomenon in Christian spirituality since the early centuries. As Knox says: "Quietism is a morbid growth on the healthy body of mysticism, and mystics of recognized orthodoxy may carry the germs of the disease without developing its symptoms."[52]

The first group to have a marked similarity to Quietism were the *Alumbrados*, who appeared in Seville and Cádiz in 1575 and were condemned by the Inquisition in 1623. Their teaching included the following tenets: vocal prayer is to be discouraged in favor of mental prayer, which is necessary for salvation; the absence of all sensible consolation makes mental prayer more meritorious; the individual must avoid the use of all mental concepts, even the representation of the sacred humanity of Christ; the direct contemplation of God is effected by an illumination which is nearly the *lumen gloriae*; those who have reached perfection do not have to perform virtuous acts and by a special grace they could perform objectively immoral acts without committing sin; the perfect tend to withdraw from all worldly affairs and to disdain marriage and the marriage act.

The Edict of Seville against the *Alumbrados* in 1623 made some Church authorities suspect of even the slightest taint of illuminism, with the result that even orthodox authors sometimes fell under suspicion or outright condemnation. Sometimes, indeed, the inquisitors reached back across the years to condemn authors who were long since dead (e.g., Benedict of Canfeld and John de Bernières, whose works in the Italian translation were condemned in 1689).

The spread of enthusiasm for the "prayer of simple regard" and acquired contemplation contributed in no small measure to the fostering of quietistic tendencies. As Guilloré stated: "The weak and the strong, the mediocre and the good, the most unmortified and ignorant, as well as the most understanding, almost all without distinction crowded into the way of prayer of simple regard."[53] In fact, this type of mental prayer became such a fad that Surin remarked that some deluded persons talked about it endlessly, so that "their spirituality is nothing but words. These people are very far from the simplicity of the spirit of God; their language, their sentiments, their behavior – all are affected."[54]

It will be helpful to identify the individuals whose writings contributed directly to the spread of Quietism and the ultimate controversy between Bossuet and Fénelon. The first name we encounter is that of John Falconi, a Spanish Mercedarian who died at Madrid in 1638 with a reputation for holiness. In 1651 the Mercedarians published his most important work, *Cartilla para saber leer in Cristo*, and in 1662 his complete works were published at Valencia.[55] Even during his lifetime, Falconi was criticized for his emphasis on the passivity of contemplative prayer and the importance of the act of faith, with little or no regard for the other virtues. The goal of Christian perfection, according to Falconi, was to reach the state of "one unbroken act of contemplation." His works were translated into French and Italian and eagerly read by the members of Quietist societies in Italy and France. According to Knox, however, Falconi's works would not have been condemned if it had not been suspected that Molinos was inspired by them.[56]

The second writer, Francis Malaval, was born in 1627 and blinded in an accident at the age of nine months. Nevertheless, he eventually became a doctor of theology and canon law. In 1664 Malaval published at Paris a work that had great success; it was entitled *La pratique de la vraie théologie mystique.* As the title indicates, it treated of contemplative prayer, which for Malaval was "nothing but an unalterable loving gaze upon God present." The purpose of the treatise was to show that God can be found by faith in the depth of one's soul and to explain how the soul should prepare itself for contemplative prayer by withdrawing into self, rejecting all sensible and imaginative images. Like some of his contemporaries, Malaval equated the prayer of simple regard with the prayer of the simple presence of God and he seems to have been unduly anxious to lead people indiscriminately into the ways of mystical contemplation. The French edition of his book was condemned in 1695 and the Italian translation was condemned in 1688. Malaval submitted in all humility and died in 1719 with a reputation for sanctity.

With the third writer, Michael Molinos (1628–1696), we come to the very source of the infection of Quietism. Oddly enough, it is not in his principal work, *Guía espiritual,*[57] that we find any explicit heresy. In fact, when the Jesuits, Bell'huomo and Segneri, wrote against the doctrine they found in the book by Molinos, their own works were promptly placed on the Index.[58] The heresy of Molinos was to be found elsewhere, as Pourrat points out:

> If the *Spiritual Guide*, considered in itself and at its face-value, is little worse than Malaval's *Pratique facile* or Falconi's *Alphabet,* its author's spoken commentary on it is another matter.... Many conpetent men declare that they would be hard put to it to find propositions in the *Spiritual Guide* that could be condemned independently of Molinos' other writings, of his explanations, and of his confession.[59]

Since it is impossible to be sure whether Molinos lived the way he did because of his Quietism or whether he embraced Quietism to defend the way he lived, we must glance briefly both at his life and the doctrine he espoused. He was born in the province of Aragon in Spain in 1627 or 1628; he was educated by the Jesuits and ordained a priest at Valencia in 1652. In 1663 he was sent to Rome to work for the beatification of Francis Simon, a diocesan priest from Valencia. For some unknown reason he was relieved of this assignment but remained in Rome, where he became one of the most sought-after directors in the city of Rome. At the peak of his influence he was under the patronage of Queen Christina of Sweden, who had renounced her throne to become a Catholic.

The first work published by Molinos was a short tract in which he replied in great detail to the Jansenists, who placed severe conditions on the reception of Holy Communion. In the same year (1675) Molinos published his *Guía espiritual*, and in six years it went through twenty editions. The theme of the book is that the soul should abandon itself completely to God through the practice of the prayer of simple regard, rejecting all other devotions and practices and cultivating an absolute indifference to everything that happens to it, whether it be from God, man or the devil. It is not possible to say for certain whether Molinos deliberately set out to start a new spiritual movement or whether he simply took advantage of a quietistic and mystical ferment that was near the surface of Italian spirituality. What is certain is that Molinos became the "darling prophet" of Quietism.[60]

As we have already indicated, there was in the seventeenth century an unusually great interest in the practice of prayer, especially the more passive and affective types of prayer. Acquired contemplation was considered to be within the reach of all, and the means for attaining it were carefully expounded. As a consequence, the Jesuits, who considered formal, methodical meditation to be the normal type of prayer while contemplation was an extraordinary gift reserved for the few, found themselves in the middle of two bitter enemies, and they were attacked from both sides. The Jansenists opposed the Jesuits for being too humanistic and for leaving too much to human effort in the quest for holiness; the Quietists accused the Jesuits of being enemies of the mystical life and incapable of understanding the higher states of prayer. On this latter point the French Carmelites and Oratorians were in complete agreement with the accusations against the Jesuits.[61] In the end, the Jansenists and the Quietists were condemned, but the Jesuits did not win from a theological point of view.

Historians can do no more than surmise the reasons for the condemnation of Molinos. Some historians blame the Jesuits; some blame the doctrine he taught in his conferences and spiritual directions; others attribute it to his moral depravity, related to his teaching on non-resistence to temptation.[62] What we do know is that after two years of investigation, the original 263 statements were reduced to 68, and these were condemned by the Holy Office. In 1687 Molinos submitted and made a public retraction in the Dominican Church of Santa Maria sopra Minerva in Rome. He also confessed his guilt to the charges brought against his personal morality and was condemned to prison for the rest of his life, where he died in 1696.

The scene now shifts to France, where the story of Quietism ends in a violent controversy. The central character in this final scene is Jeanne-Marie Bouvier de la Motte (1648–1717), the widow of Jacques Guyon du Chesnoy and known to us as Madame Guyon. By the time of her husband's death in 1676, Madame Guyon was already living a deep interior life and practising the prayer of simple regard. She was under the direction of a Franciscan priest whose name she does not mention. Another spiritual director who influenced her at the time was Jacques Bertot (+ 1681), confessor to the Benedictine nuns of Montmartre. From 1673 to 1680 she claims to have passed through the "dark night of the soul," and after considering the possibility of entering the Visitandines, she decided to dedicate herself to some form of apostolate.

Leaving her two sons to be cared for by relatives, Madame Guyon went to Geneva with her daughter and busied herself with the instruction of young women who had converted from Calvinism. The Bishop of Geneva appointed the Barnabite, Francis Lacombe as her spiritual director. From 1681 to 1686 Lacombe accompanied Madame Guyon on many journeys to Italy, France and Switzerland; or when Lacombe was transferred or went on business trips, Madame Guyon was not long in joining him. Knox suggests that Lacombe was trying to escape from her, but others think that the relationship was voluntary and immoral.[63] In 1687 Lacombe was arrested in Paris for holding and teaching Quietism, and after being transferred from one prison to another, he died insane at Charenton in 1715.

With all her traveling and numerous activities, Madame Guyon produced thirty-five volumes of writings.[64] Early in her association with Lacombe, he had commanded her to write down the thoughts that came to her, and she did this quite automatically, without reflecting very much on what she was writing. In her autobiography she states that she was overwhelmed by an irresistible urge to write *Les torrents spirituels* and that what surprised her most was that the writing seemed to pour forth from the depth of her soul, without passing through her brain.

Madame Guyon became seriously ill in 1683, at which time she claims to have undergone a mystical transformation. From then on, the Infant Jesus replaced her, so that it was no longer she who acted and willed, but God did all things in and through her. She was no longer personally responsible for anything she did or said. From this time on, she suffered a variety of unusual phenomena which Pourrat brands as hysterical in origin.[65]

Madame Guyon then proceeded to claim an authority that came from God himself and to act with the power of God himself. From this point it was only a short step to the statement attributed to Madame Guyon by Cardinal Le Camus: "It is possible to be so united with God that one could knowingly perform unchaste actions with another person without God being offended thereby." In *Les torrents spirituels* she wrote: "It is the ill will and not the action that constitutes the offense. If one whose will is lost and, as it were, swallowed up and transformed in God were reduced by necessity to doing sinful deeds, he would do them without sinning."[66] Small wonder that she did not go to confession for fifteen years.

At the beginning of 1688 Madame Guyon was confined to the convent of the Visitation in Paris and examined for doctrinal errors, but no evidence was found to indict her. Until 1693 she enjoyed great popularity and extensive influence, especially in high society, but in that same year the bishop of Chartres became alarmed at her doctrine and in 1695 he condemned certain statements taken from *Les torrents spirituels.*

But Madame Guyon had anticipated the condemnation, for as early as 1693, on the advice of Fénelon, she had submitted her writings to Bossuet for examination. In 1694 she requested an examination of her writings and her actions by a board of three judges: Bossuet, Noailles and Tronson. The examiners drew up a list of thirty-four erroneous statements and Madame Guyon signed the documents, promising not to teach those particular points. The matter should have ended there, but it did not. Pourrat states that neither Lacombe nor Madame Guyon would have received so much space in the history of false mysticism had it not been for the controversy about them between Bossuet and Fénelon.[67]

Francis Fénelon was thirty-seven when he first met Madame Guyon in 1688 and his first impression of her was unfavorable.[68] She states in her autobiography that at their first meeting she felt inwardly that he did not approve of her, but after suffering over the matter for eight days, she found herself completely accepted by Fénelon without any reservations. In a short time Fénelon became a willing instrument for the promulgation and defense of her teaching, as he himself testified: "I have full confidence in you on the strength of your uprightness, your simplicity, your experience and knowledge of interior things, and of God's plan for me through you."[69]

Jacques Bossuet was already an old man and he had little sympathy for mystical matters. However, as Pourrat points out, "there was no need to be learned in mystical theology to be able to detect the deplorable practical consequences of Mme. Guyon's teaching – it was inconsistent with the first principles of ascetical theology."[70] Bossuet was determined to stamp out the doctrine and influence of Madame Guyon; Fénelon was equally determined to interpret her doctrine in a favorable light.

The principal points at issue were the theology of "disinterested love" and "passive prayer". When the condemned articles were drawn up in 1695, they had been worded in such a way that both Bossuet and Fénelon were able to hold doctrinal interpretations that were incompatible. When Bossuet sent the manuscript of his *Instruction sur les états d'oraison* to Fénelon in July, 1696, for the latter's approval, Fénelon returned it to him without reading it. He then set to work on his own treatise, *Explication des maximes des saints*, which was published in February of 1697, six months before Bossuet's book appeared.[71]

Fénelon's work found supporters among the Dominicans, Jesuits and Oratorians, but in addition to the grim determination of Bossuet, Fénelon also had to cope with Madame de Maintenon, who was resolved to put an end to his influence.[72] Fénelon appealed to Rome in April and again in August of 1697, and his appeal was supported by Louis XIV. For the next two years the battle was waged on two fronts – Paris and Rome – until the Holy See, on March 12, 1699, condemned twenty-three propositions taken from Fénelon's book. The condemnation was couched in terms as mild as possible, because Pope Innocent XII was sympathetic to Fénelon and the theologians on the investigating commission were themselves divided. Fénelon submitted without reservation and in autumn of the same year he was named a cardinal by Innocent XII.[73]

The errors of Fénelon can be reduced to the following four statements: 1) a soul can reach a state of pure love in which it no longer experiences a desire for eternal salvation; 2) during extreme trials of the interior life a soul may have a conviction that it is rejected by God, and in this state it may make an absolute sacrifice of its own eternal happiness; 3) in the state of pure love a soul is indifferent to its own perfection and the practice of virtue; 4) in certain states contemplative souls lose the clear, sensible and deliberate sight of Jesus Christ.[74] Nevertheless, Fénelon did not explicitly teach Quietism. When he was notified of the condemnation of *Maximes*, he was told that the investigators found difficulty with "certain statements which . . . in their primary sense, the sense that first comes to mind, favor some Quietest errors. It is true that the book contains other statements which exclude the wrong meaning of those just referred to, and which seem to be their correctives. Hence the book cannot be absolutely condemned as containing error."[75]

Both the investigators and the Holy Father felt that there was a danger that persons reading the book could be led into the errors of Quietism, already condemned by the Church. Quietism was thus given the death blow in 1699, but at the same time the fears of Pope Innocent XII were realized: mysticism fell into disrepute and, except for the efforts of a few writers, "the eighteenth century saw almost the complete rout in France of Catholic mysticism."[76]

RETURN TO ORTHODOXY

Since human attitudes and actions usually alternate between action and reaction, it is not surprising that the condemnation of Quietism caused many Christians to conclude that the only safe and sure way in the spiritual life was the "ordinary" way of the virtues and the sacraments. The way of the mystics was considered rare and "extraordinary," and usually suspect. In the first half of the eighteenth century the discredit of mysticism had reached such a point that the standard classical works on the subject were practically unknown.

The revival of Jansenism also contributed to the disaffection for mysticism, since the Jansenists placed emphasis almost exclusively on asceticism, self-denial and the rejection of all human pleasure. Writers such as Caussade, Schram and Emery tried to reinstate mysticism in the face of the reaction against Quietism,[77] and other authors such as Avrillon, Judde and Croiset tried to offset the severity of Jansenism.[78] They represent a group of spiritual writers – many of them French Jesuits – who faithfully followed theologians untainted by any Quietistic or Jansenistic infection.

Many Jesuit writers attained a position of great influence in France after their restoration in 1603.[79] Although the Jesuits themselves did not agree with each other on every point of doctrine, their reputation as Christian humanists was sufficient to make them the enemies of the Quietists and the Jansenists. Louis Richeome (+ 1625) attempted to combat Christian stoicism by emphasizing the shortness of life and the glory of the life to come. He also wrote a treatise on humility, which he divides into six degrees. Stephen Binet (+ 1639), a great admirer of St. Francis de Sales, tried to lead his readers to the love of Christ, but he had little use for mysticism or contemplation. Paul de Barry (+ 1661) was excessively moralistic in his writings, which were criticized for his teaching on good works and for advocating bizarre devotions to Mary. Peter Coton (+ 1626), who enjoyed a close friendship with Bérulle, wrote a book of spirituality for persons living in the world. He wished to supernaturalize every human act and was criticized for blurring the distinction between the natural and the supernatural.

The man who dominated the mystical trend among the French Jesuits was Louis Lallemant (1588–1635), and yet he himself never published anything. His conferences were taken down by two of his disciples, John Rigoleuc and J. J. Surin; later they were edited by Peter Champion and published in 1694 under the title, *La doctrine spirituelle du P. Louis Lallemant.*[80] As a spiritual writer, he was somewhat outside the Jesuit school of his time and he was denounced to the Superior General.[81]

There is no doubt that Lallemant was in disagreement with the common Jesuit teaching on several points, but he was completely faithful to St. Ignatius in Christology. He held, for example, that the mystical state is not the result of extraordinary grace but the normal (though rare) development of sanctifying grace, the virtues and the gifts of the Holy Spirit. Lallemant develops his entire doctrine of mysticism on the Thomistic teaching on the gifts of the Holy Spirit, due perhaps to the influence on him by the German and Flemish mystics. In fact, the Superior General, Vitelleschi, admonished Lallemant to confine his teachings to the sources and methods approved by the Society of Jesus.[82]

For Lallemant the basic theme is always the same: the striving for perfection, which consists ultimately in perfect conformity to the divine will. The active phase of the spiritual life is ascetical and it comprises all those exercises which effect a cleansing of the heart. However, Lallemant does not dedicate a great deal of time to this aspect; he develops the passive phase and consequently treats in detail of the gifts of the Holy Spirit. To explain the passivity that marks the soul under the direction of the Holy Spirit, Lallemant compares the infused supernatural virtues to the oars by which one rows a boat and the gifts of the Holy Spirit to the sail which catches the wind and thus causes the movement of the boat.

Treating of contemplative prayer, Lallemant distinguishes between ordinary and extraordinary contemplation. The first is infused contemplation and it is a normal development of the life of grace, activated by the gifts of the Holy Spirit; extraordinary contemplation is accompanied by extraordinary mystical phenomena. Meditation is the prayer proper to those in the purgative state; affective prayer is typical of those in the illuminative state; and contemplation and the prayer of union are attained in the unitive state. The initial stage of contemplation occurs in the prayer of silence or simple gaze. However, Lallemant is unwilling to separate contemplative prayer from the apostolate; rather, he sees it as a fruitful source of apostolic activity. Indeed, the object of contemplation need not be God alone, but it may be anything seen as related to God.[83]

Among the Carmelites, John Cheron wrote *Examen de théologie mystique* (1657), in which he maintains the distinction between infused contemplation and acquired contemplation (which is available to all through ordinary grace and the practice of discursive prayer). Cheron was particularly concerned with excesses in mystical teaching, the vagueness of theological terminology, and the emphasis on experience rather than theological knowledge. In a similar vein, another Carmelite, Philip of the Trinity insisted that mystical doctrine must always rest on sound theology and he explained the distinction between acquired and infused contemplation as follows:

> Christian contemplation is divided into acquired and infused. The first is natural; the second, supernatural. The distinction is similar to that between acquired moral virtue, which is obtained by efforts of the will and is a natural virtue, and infused moral virtue, which God produces in us without any effort on our part.[84]

The Carthusians also opposed Quietism and their Minister General, Dom Innocent Le Masson (1628–1703), branded it as a pernicious and devilish teaching. In order to give proper guidance to the Carthusians, he wrote *Direction pour se former avec ordre et tranquillité au saint exercice de l'oraison mentale* (1695).

Among the Dominicans the outstanding authors of the period were Chardon, Massoulié, Contenson and Piny. *La croix de Jésus* by Louis Chardon (+ 1651) is one of the few great spiritual works to appear in seventeenth-century France.[85] According to Florand, the passages on the simplicity and unity of infused contemplation rival the most celebrated texts of Origen, St. Gregory of Nyssa, Tauler and St. John of the Cross. "The few writings that we have from Chardon demonstrate a strong antipathy to the doctrine of Descartes, and I do not doubt that the confidence which Bérulle

placed in Descartes explains the indifference of the French Dominicans of that time to the entire spiritual movement of Bérulle.''[86]

Vincent Contenson (+ 1674) is famous for his *Theologia cordis et
mentis*, which consisted of a spiritual commentary on the *Summa
theologiae* of St. Thomas Aquinas, question by question.[87] In 1699,
the year of the condemnation of Fénelon, A. Massoulié published
Traité de la véritable oraison oú les erreurs des quiétistes sont refutées.
According to Massoulié, contemplative prayer may be acquired or
infused; the former is ordinary and can be attained with the help of
grace like any other virtue, but the latter is extraordinary in the
sense that it is infused by God on those whom he pleases. Infused
contemplation is not required for Christian perfection because it is
totally unmerited and because it may be granted to souls that are less
advanced than others in the way of perfection.[88]

Alexander Piny (+ 1674) advocated a type of prayer which consists in a simple concentration on one of the divine attributes,
without images or concepts that might distract the soul. He is also a
proponent of the practice of the pure love of God, stating that to will
to love God is itself an effective love of God.[89]

The Franciscans of this period were generally faithful to the spirit
and tradition of St. Francis of Assisi and the theology of St.
Bonaventure. There were also notable influences from the Rhineland mystics, Henry Herp and Benedict Canfeld, and traces of the
Bérullian spirituality on the question of mortification and self-
annihilation. As regards the practice of prayer, the Franciscans had
accepted methodical prayer, but always with great insistence on the
role of grace in the practice of prayer. Normally they classified the
grades of prayer as discursive prayer, affective prayer, acquired
contemplation, infused contemplation and supereminent contemplation. The soul could pass from one grade to another, but the
highest state of prayer was considered to be entirely gratuitous and
extraordinary. The most important Franciscan writers on prayer
are Francis Le Roux, Paul de Lagny, Maximilian de Bernezay,
Ambrose Lombez and Severin Rubéric.[90]

Three more spiritual writers complete our survey of the authors
who perpetuated the basic teaching of Bérulle in the seventeenth
and into the eighteenth century in France. St. John Baptist de la Salle
(1651–1719), founder of the Brothers of the Christian Schools, gave
great importance to the practice of discursive prayer and composed
an extensive treatise on the method to be followed by the members
of his Congregation.[91] Of the three parts in the discursive prayer
described by La Salle – preparation for prayer through recollection,

application to the subject of prayer and thanksgiving – the first part is original. The other two parts are also found in Salesian and Sulpician prayer; recollection in the presence of God seems to be based on the teachings of Louis of Granada and St. Francis de Sales. La Salle explains that God can be present to us in a variety of ways: in the place where we are (by his omnipresence or because several are gathered together in his name), in ourselves (either by the divine power which keeps us in existence or by the special presence of grace and his Spirit), or in the church (because it is God's house or because of his sacramental presence in the Eucharist). For La Salle it was absolutely essential for mental prayer that the individual first become aware of the presence of God; nothing else was as effective for withdrawing the soul from external things and for cultivating the interior life. Indeed, the practice of the presence of God is to be maintained through all the stages of the spiritual life; by beginners "by vocal prayer and repeated reasonings," for the advanced by "occasional and extended reflections" and for the more perfect by the prayer of simple regard. Some souls may even attain the state in which God's presence and action are practically the only object of the soul's attention.[92]

The Jesuit John Grou (1731–1803), was a disciple of Surin and a follower of Bérulle. He served, in fact, as a perpetuator of Bérullian doctrine in the eighteenth century, which was so sterile in spiritual literature. The theme of Grou's writing was that God is all and the soul is nothing by comparison; therefore, the gift of self to God is the foundation of all spirituality. The gift of self in one word is "devotion," which for Grou meant "close attachment, absolute and willing dependence, affectionate zeal, ... a determination of mind and heart to submit to all the wishes of another, to anticipate what he wants, to make his interests one's own, to give up all for him." It is "the holiest and most irrevocable act of religion."[93]

The soul, says Grou, should desire perfection, but less for its own sake than for the glory of God, and this constitutes disinterested love, which at first glance would seem to militate against the virtue of hope. Actually, however, disinterested love purifies hope of all selfish love. Grou was criticized for denigrating the virtue of hope and while he refined his teaching, he lamented the fact that some persons are so hypercritical that they make it necessary to write of spiritual matters only in the most general and vague terminology. Grou's best writings are those which treat of Christ as our pattern and model. "For a Christian," he says, "knowledge is to know Jesus Christ; happiness is to love him; holiness is to imitate him."[94]

More closely related to Bérulle's doctrine than La Salle or Grou was Louis Grignion de Montfort (1673–1716), who studied at Saint-Sulpice, where he cultivated an ardent devotion to Mary. He did not separate devotion to Mary from devotion to Jesus, but in his hands Bérulle's vow of slavery became a servitude to Jesus and Mary. He developed his doctrine by stating that all our perfection consists in being conformed, united and consecrated to Jesus Christ; therefore, the most perfect of all devotions is devotion to Christ. But Mary was the most perfectly conformed to Christ, and hence the best way for us to be conformed to Christ is through devotion to Mary. "The more a soul is consecrated to Mary, the more it is consecrated to Jesus." Then, speaking explicitly of servitude to Mary, he says:

> The principal mystery we celebrate and honor in this devotion is the mystery of the Incarnation, wherein we can see Jesus only in Mary.... Hence it is more to the point to speak of the slavery of Jesus in Mary and of Jesus residing and reigning in Mary.... Jesus is altogether in Mary and Mary is altogether in Jesus; rather, she exists no more, but Jesus alone is in her.[95]

The formula of consecration to Jesus in Mary, which continues to attract many clients, is a complete surrender to Mary of all one's natural and spiritual goods:

> I deliver and consecrate to thee, as thy slave, my body and soul, my goods, both interior and exterior, and even the value of all my good actions, past, present and future; leaving to thee the entire and full right of disposing of me, and all that belongs to me, without exception, according to thy good pleasure, for the greater glory of God, in time and in eternity.[96]

ST. ALPHONSUS LIGUORI

According to Pourrat, when Quietism was condemned, Italian spirituality became aggressive and was characterized primarily by its opposition to Quietism. Yet, the Italian writers were careful not to discredit authentic mysticism, as is evident in the books of Segneri, one of the most effective opponents of Quietism.[97] As a result, Italy did not suffer the serious infection from heresy that we have just witnessed in France. Three authors are of special importance in the seventeenth and eighteenth centuries: Cardinal Bona, J. B. Scaramelli, St. Alphonsus Liguori.

John Cardinal Bona (1609–1674), a Cistercian, was a highly

respected liturgist and spiritual writer. His spiritual doctrine is completely orthodox and traditional, drawn from a large number of authors ranging from the Fathers of the Church to his contemporaries. He wrote for the laity especially and traces the path of Christian perfection in view of man's ultimate end. He discusses numerous theories of mysticism but his own doctrine is the traditional doctrine of the classical authors. For him, contemplation is a work of the Holy Spirit, operating especially through the gift of wisdom, as was taught by St. Thomas Aquinas. He also holds for the possibility of an intuitive vision of the divine essence, but it would be a rare privilege and only a momentary vision. Cardinal Bona places great importance on the use of succinct, ejaculatory aspirations for persons in every stage of the spiritual life because they provide an opportunity for the Christian to practice constant prayer and retain a spirit of recollection in the presence of God.

Cardinal Bona is best known for his work on the discernment of spirits, *De discretione spirituum*, and seems to be one of the first to attempt to compile an exhaustive treatise on the subject.[98] It is based on the teaching of the Fathers, theologians and the experience of the mystics. Although he admits that discernment of spirits may be a charismatic gift, it is more often the result of study and experience, and therefore it is an art that can be acquired. A soul may be led by any one of three spirits: human, diabolical or divine, and the task of the director is to attempt to discern which spirit is at work in a given instance. Among the rules for discernment listed by Cardinal Bona, we find the following:

> The divine spirit inclines the soul to what is good, holy, perfect; the evil spirit moves her toward vanity, sensuality, aimless longings.

> God's way is to lead the Christian progressively from the imperfect to the perfect, having regard to one's age, state of life and measure of spiritual life. Satan follows no such orderly progress; and he shams untimely fervor, ecstasies and things of that nature.

> God usually gives beginners spiritual consolations to encourage them; Satan tries to make the beginner's way very hard, in order to discourage him from perseverance in perfection.

> When he receives some spiritual gift a little out of the ordinary, a man who is led by the divine spirit is always afraid that he is being tricked by a delusion. The evil spirit inclines him to grasp it at once and be proudly pleased about it.

God moves a man toward kindness to his neighbor; Satan does the opposite.

When the divine spirit is at work there is always an atmosphere of quiet, good order and caution, even when something very difficult is to be done. The evil spirit calls attention to himself by disturbances, making the soul act excitedly and without self-control.

God gives peace to the righteous and inspires the sinner with remorse; Satan makes the sinner complacent and torments the righteous.

The best indications for detecting the origin of such phenomena as ecstasies, visions and revelations are these: When there is nothing objectionable, nothing contrary to the Christian faith or to good morality in the way these phenomena happen, they may be divine; but this is not enough to give certitude. The mystic's true advance, over a long period of time, in the practice of all the virtues to an exceptional degree is the only practically certain sign.[99]

The Jesuit theologian John Baptist Scaramelli (1687–1752) also studied discernment of spirits and published a book entitled *Discernimento degli spiriti* in 1753. This work had great authority, but Scaramelli is more widely known for two other works: *Direttorio ascetico* (1752) and *Direttorio mistico* (1754). The first work treats of the nature of Christian perfection and the virtues that must be acquired in order to attain it; the second work, which became a classic, treats of the mystical states and the degrees of mystical prayer.

Scaramelli held that infused contemplation is an operation of the gift of wisdom, but he considered it to be an extraordinary gift. He defines contemplation as an experimental knowledge of God as present in the soul. In his classification of the grades of mystical prayer he lists twelve, and although some theologians followed his classification, the majority have preferred to accept the division given by St. Teresa of Avila.[100]

The most important effect of Scaramelli's teaching on Christian spirituality was the arguments that ensued as a result of his division of asceticism and mysticism and his proposal of two kinds of Christian perfection. Postulating as he did a gratuitous and extraordinary character for all infused contemplation and mystical acts, and asserting that the attainment of mystical contemplation is not at all common among fervent Christians, but very rare, he logically concluded that the ascetical state does not lead to the mystical state.

Rather, asceticism and mysticism are two distinct paths to Christian perfection and there is, moreover, a distinct type of perfection proper to each state. The majority of Christians are called to ascetical perfection, which is the life of the virtues; a small minority are called to mystical perfection, which is a life in which the gifts of the Holy Spirit operate in the soul.

As a result of this distinction, it would follow that there is no need for directors of souls to be preoccupied with mysticism, since most Christians need only be preserved in the state of grace and encouraged to live the life of the virtues. It also follows that for these same Christians the evangelical counsels have no application, for their life is lived exclusively under the guidance of the Ten Commandments and the precepts of the Church. While this doctrine seems to have resolved the problems raised by the Quietists, it was in reality an innovation in spiritual theology and a departure from the traditional Catholic teaching.

In a Brief dated April 26, 1950, Pope Pius XII named St. Alphonsus Liguori patron of confessors and moral theologians. The reasons given were St. Alphonsus' "well known and outstanding erudition, prudence, perseverence and patience in the confessional", his efforts to improve the preparation of confessors, the clarity and mildness of his moral theology, and his success against the rigorism of the Jansenists. He was above all a pastor of souls and a spiritual director who possessed extraordinary gifts of nature and grace. Even in his later years, when he himself suffered anxieties of conscience, St. Alphonsus retained his remarkable prudence in the direction of souls and his ability to discern spirits.

St. Alphonsus Liguori was born at Naples in 1696 and at the age of sixteen he had obtained the doctorate in both civil and ecclesiastical law. He practiced law with brilliant success for eight years but abandoned it to study for the priesthood. Ordained at the age of thirty, he founded the Congregation of the Holy Redeemer in 1732. In 1762 he was ordained a bishop but thirteen years later he resigned and returned to his Congregation, where he suffered greatly from some of the Redemptorists and from scrupulosity. St. Alphonsus died in 1787.

St. Alphonsus was not primarily a speculative theologian but an expert in what would be called today pastoral theology. Nevertheless, he was not a casuist, in the pejorative sense of that word. He was always aware of man's vocation to sanctity, and in his moral and ascetical works he endeavored to lead souls along the paths of virtue and the practice of prayer. He was, however, opposed to the rigorism of the Jansenists, and for that reason he found it necessary to place great emphasis on the sacrament of penance as the tribunal of mercy and forgiveness. He likewise insisted on the minimum good required of the Christian, the necessity of pursuing Christian perfection according to one's ability at a given time, and the reality of the value of the lesser good. St. Alphonsus also rejected the excesses of those who misinterpreted the theology of the "pure love" of God.

St. Alphonsus was a prodigious writer[101] and a large part of his works pertain to the spiritual life. His spiritual teaching dominated the Christian life in eighteenth-century Italy to such an extent that we can say that he was for Italy in his time what St. Francis de Sales was for France and Louis of Granada was for Spain in their time. St. Alphonsus was a voracious reader and his works give evidence of his knowledge of the Fathers of the Church and the great doctors of theology. He had a particular admiration for St. Teresa of Avila (whose doctrine on prayer he follows literally), Alphonsus Rodríguez and Louis of Granada. His doctrine is always centered on Jesus and Mary and his constant theme is love of God and abandonment to the divine will. The instrument of salvation and Christian perfection is the practice of prayer. It will suffice for our purposes to provide a summary of the spiritual teaching of St. Alphonsus.

God wills all men to be saints and therefore the Christian who does not have a desire to become a saint may be a Christian, but he will not be a good Christian. Each one should strive for perfection according to his state of life – the layman as a layman, the religious as a religious, and the priest as a priest. The question of one's vocation is therefore of great importance, and one should embrace the state of life which God desires. The spiritual director should never decide another person's vocation.

All sanctity consists in the love of God and the minimum requisite for the pursuit of holiness is freedom from serious sin. But to love God, the Christian must attach himself to Jesus Christ because the "devotion of all devotions is love for Jesus Christ, and frequent meditation on the love which this amiable Redeemer has borne and still bears for us."[102] Indeed, says St. Alphonsus, "the whole sanctity and perfection of a soul consists in loving Jesus Christ, our God, our sovereign good, and our Redeemer."[103]

If love is the essence of Christian holiness and if love is friendship, then the love that constitutes perfection will necessarily imply conformity to God's will; this, in turn, requires detachment from all that is an obstacle to union with the divine will. The goal, then, is to will only what God wills and thus attain a state of holy indifference to everything but God. Such comformity bears fruit in obedience to God's laws, which are the expression of his will for us.

St. Alphonsus treats in detail of the means for attaining the love of conformity and total detachment. On the positive side, there must be a desire for perfection and a complete submission to God without reserve; on the negative side there must be contempt of self, mortification of the passions, purification of all affections and the effort to avoid all deliberate venial sin. The auxiliary aids are the reception of the sacraments, the practice of prayer, acts of self-denial, daily Mass, visits to the Blessed Sacrament, spiritual exercises and the particular examen.[104] But of all the means for attaining the perfection of charity, the practice of prayer is the most important. St. Alphonsus reasons as follows:

> The generality of theologians.... teach that prayer is necessary for adults, not only because of the obligation of the precept (as they say), but because it is necessary as a means of salvation. That is to say, in the ordinary course of providence, it is impossible that a Christian should be saved without recommending himself to God and asking for the graces necessary to salvation. St. Thomas teaches the same.[105]

Turning to the question of mental prayer, St. Alphonsus maintains that mental prayer is morally necessary for the faithful in order to obtain from God the graces they need to advance along the way of salvation, to avoid sin and to use the means that lead to Christian perfection. Taking the words directly from St. Teresa of Avila, he adds: "It is impossible for him who perseveres in mental prayer to continue in sin; he will either give up meditation or renounce sin.... Mental prayer and sin cannot exist together." Prayer is thus the language of love and, indeed, a proof of one's love, because "he who loves God, loves prayer." However, mental prayer should not only proceed from love but it should terminate in love. Since mental prayer is morally necessary for all Christians, it should be simple enough for all to practice it.

It has been said that the spiritual doctrine of St. Alphonsus is oriented to the ascetical life, and that is true, but it is an asceticism which serves as an excellent preparation for the mystical state.[106] He places great stress on total renunciation, complete conformity to the divine will, and an intense life of prayer, all of which are favorable predispositions in mysticism. Like no other theologian of his time,

St. Alphonsus made the traditional doctrine on the spiritual life practical and popular, yet he was well within the tradition of the great masters such as St. Augustine, St. Thomas Aquinas, St. Teresa of Avila, St. John of the Cross and St. Francis de Sales.

When treating specifically of contemplative prayer, St. Alphonsus distinguishes between active contemplation, which he calls the prayer of natural recollection, and passive contemplation, which is supernatural and infused. Active or acquired contemplation is the simple gaze on "those truths of which one has hitherto acquired knowledge by means of hard thought and effort."[107] This degree of prayer is within the grasp of all and it constitutes the perfection of the Christian in the life of prayer, barring the possibility that God chooses to lead the soul to a higher, passive type of contemplation. But before doing so, God will first prepare the soul by means of the passive purgations. Then the soul will experience supernatural or passive recollection, "which God brings about in us by means of an extraordinary grace whereby he puts the soul into a passive state. Consequently, there is supernatural recollection (infused, to speak more correctly), when the recollection of the soul's faculties is not caused by the soul's own efforts, but through the gift of light with which God illuminates her and sensibly kindles a divine love."[108]

St. Alphonsus never wrote any systematic manual of spiritual theology nor did he compose a complete treatment of the practical aspects of spirituality. He seems to have presumed in his readers a knowledge of fundamental systematic theology and simply proceeded to give particular instructions and practical applications. Everything he wrote was intended to lead souls to a more perfect Christian life. His works are for the most part in the domain of the ascetical, but with an orientation to the perfection of charity. Among his spiritual sons we find such outstanding souls as St. Gerard Majella (+1757), St. Clement Maria Hofbauer (+1820) and J. Schrijvers.[109]

GERMAN RATIONALISM AND MYSTICISM

Unlike other European countries, Germany in the eighteenth century was a ferment of mysticism and extraordinary phenomena and the result was an unusually large number of works on questions related to those areas. Among the reasons for this concentration on mysticism, we may list the following: the rise of the Protestant Pietist movement under the leadership of Philip James Spener;[110] German rationalism; and the visions and stigmata of Anna Catherine Emmerich. The historian Dru describes the scene:

At first sight the *Reichskirche*, at the end of the eighteenth century, seems to conform to the ecclesiastical fashion of the age and to differ in no essentials from the pattern of the Latin countries. . . . But the externals are in some important respects misleading. The *Reichskirche* was not, and never had been, a State Church in the modern meaning of the term. . . .

By the Peace of Westphalia (1648) its possessions had been drastically reduced, by nearly half; and what remained were broken up and scattered, large portions becoming an archipelago of Catholic islands in a Lutheran and Calvinist sea. While the Gallican Church was being centralized under Richelieu and Louis XIV, and isolated as the Huguenots were driven into exile, the *Reichskirche* underwent the opposite process. It was further decentralized, forced to live in close proximity with other denominations and in cultural surroundings that were sometimes alien to its way of life or beliefs. Catholicism in Germany was exposed to a number of dangers, but these did not include isolation, stagnation or complacency. Neither clergy nor laity could hope to seal themselves off successfully from the trend of the times or become separated from the nation. . . .

The Church in Germany was supremely fortunate in experiencing a bloodless revolution. The *Reichskirche* was not violently overturned, but legally buried; in part because circumstances favoured a peaceful end, but also because it had not been passionately hated. . . .

In France the Revolution was primarily political and it divided the nation. In Germany it was first and foremost a cultural metamorphosis, a sort of second Reformation, which unified the nation even before it achieved economic and political unity. . . . For sixty years the intellectual life of Germany was at or near boiling point, and the national genius flowered as it had done in France in the seventeenth century – only that it was not classical but romantic. . . . It forms a single, unbroken process of regeneration in which Germany became conscious of itself. . . ." The revolution which has occurred in the minds of thinking men in Germany during the last thirty years," Mme. de Staël wrote in 1811, in *De l'Allemagne*, "has brought almost all of them back to the feelings of religion."[111]

The claims of visions and revelations by certain Protestant Pietists and the circulation of *The Mystical City of God* by Mary of Agreda (a Spanish Franciscan nun)[113] occasioned the publication of a treatise against the Pietists by the German Franciscan Melchior Weber in 1714.[113] This work was followed in 1744 by a more extensive but excessively severe book by the Augustinian canon, Eusebius Amort, who attempted to establish the rules of discernment concerning visions and private revelations.[114] He then applied the rules to three mystics: St. Gertrude, St. Elizabeth of Schönau and Mary of Agreda, but perhaps he was prejudiced against them from the start. Later, Dominic Schram, concerned about the lethargy of the Catholic theologians and the continuing interest of the Pietists in mystical questions, composed a complete work on spiritual theology and mystical phenomena.[115]

A much more serious problem for the Christian life in Germany was the rise of romanticism, which placed the religious beliefs and practices of Catholicism on a par with the pagan cults of India and Egypt and then dismissed them all as superstitions. In the age of enlightenment (*Aufklärung*), which involved such great thinkers as Fichte, Schelling, Goethe, Schleiermacher and Kant, anything beyond the scope of the human mind was rejected. More than any other man, John Sailer (1751–1832) restored Catholicism to a reputable state in Germany. His writings run to forty volumes and he was read by both Protestants and Catholics.[116]

Geiselmann states: "It is not to Möhler, or even to Scheeben, but to Johann Michael Sailer that we owe the fact that the theology of the nineteenth century rediscovered the mystical conception of the Church as opposed to the legal conception derived from the controversial theology (of the post-Reformation period)."[117] Sailer broke with the Scholasticism of the eighteenth century, so out of touch with the needs of the age, and studied not only Catholic authors, but also the works of Protestants and unbelievers. He was not primarily a systematic theologian, but was dedicated to a pastoral approach which started with the situation and needs of the people rather than theoretical principles. He was familiar with the works of Eckhart, Tauler, Suso, St. Teresa, St. John of the Cross, Fénelon and Thomas à Kempis and he used these works against the teachings of the rationalists of his day. He was accused of being a follower of Kant and a pseudo-mystic, but perhaps Dru is correct when he states that Sailer was simply a man ahead of his time, the forerunner of the Tübingen school.[118] Sailer can be credited especially for stemming the tide of Rationalism and bringing Protestants and Catholics to a state of peaceful coexistence.

John Joseph Görres (1776–1848) is hailed as "the greatest figure in the annals of German Catholicism."[119] That may be true in the wider context of the religious movement in nineteenth-century Germany; it is certainly not true as regards his place in spirituality and mysticism. A layman who returned to Catholicism after holding rationalist teachings for a time, he gained renown by his lectures on mysticism at the University of Munich. Later, these lectures formed the basis of his four volumes entitled *Christliche Mystik* (1836–1842). Although his lectures and writings sparked a new interest in mystical questions, the doctrine of Görres is dated and of little value today. His purpose was to prove the existence and credibility of the supernatural by demonstrating the existence of the mystical. Mysticism for Görres was of three types: divine, natural and diabolical. Only divine mysticism could bring a soul into union and experience with God, although natural mysticism could make an individual aware of the secret and hidden powers of material nature, while diabolical mysticism referred to some kind of contact and influence of devils. Görres was not critical enough in his selection of materials; his physical and physiological theories have long since been proven inadequate; and his concept of mysticism was theologically inaccurate. Nevertheless, his influence continued long after his death.[120]

Even while Görres was writing his book on mysticism, a controversy was being carried on in Germany concerning the visions and mystical phenomena of Anna Catherine Emmerich, an Augustinian nun who died in 1824. The phenomena began to occur after the convent was suppressed by the government of Jerome Bonaparte in 1811 and Anna Catherine took up residence with a widow at Dülmen. The stigmata appeared in 1812 and it consisted at first of two blood-colored crosses on her breast; the following year she bore the bleeding wounds on her hands and feet and the marks of a crown of thorns on her head. Her visions lasted over a period of years, during which time she revealed facts about the Old and New Testament which have since been verified by Scripture scholars and archaeologists.

Anna Catherine was personally a most fervent and exemplary Christian and there is no evidence of any deliberate intent to deceive. However, her case is complicated by the fact that prior to the mystical phenomena she had suffered a serious illness. This prevented the investigators from stating positively that the phenomena were completely supernatural in origin, although they did confess that they could adduce no natural explanation. Among the throngs that flocked to see her, against her wishes, was Clement Brentano, a poet of the German Romantic school, who became her disciple and remained such until her death.[121]

In 1833 Brentano published *The Dolorous Passion of Our Lord Jesus Christ*; later he started a work entitled *The Life of the Blessed Virgin Mary* and it was completed by his brother and sister-in-law after Brentano's death. These books added to the controversy because numerous knowledgeable people accused Brentano of adding his own ideas and teachings to the revelations of Anna Catherine. The controversy has never been settled to everyone's satisfaction but it did stimulate an interest in mysticism and resulted in a flurry of books and articles.[123]

REVIVAL IN ENGLAND

England was occupied with the work of restoration of the Church after the Catholic Emancipation Act of 1829 and the establishment of a Catholic hierarchy in 1850. Prior to that, however, two outstanding spiritual writers deserve special mention: Augustine Baker and Richard Challoner.

David Augustine Baker (1575–1641), says Pourrat, "revived mystical traditions in England. He is the link between the fourteenth-century mystics and modern times."[123] A convert from practical atheism, he entered the Benedictines at Padua and ultimately was assigned to the English Benedictine Congregation, now Ampleforth. He practiced intense mental prayer all his life and seems to have reached an exalted degree of infused contemplation. He wrote approximately sixty treatises, though all of his published works were edited by others.[124] He was strongly opposed to methodical mental prayer but encouraged the practice of affective prayer, which he saw as a disposition for infused contemplation. His best writing is on the topics of mortification and prayer.

Richard Challoner (1691–1781) typifies the best of English Catholicism and his spirit still survives in England. A convert from the Presbyterian Church, he studied at Douai and remained there as a professor after his ordination and ultimately became vice-president of the college. In 1741 he was consecrated coadjutor to the vicar apostolic of London and followed in that position in 1758. He labored to revitalize the English Catholic spirit, but was careful to preserve the link with tradition at the same time that he adjusted to the needs of the times. He revised the Douai-Rheims version of the Bible for English readers, in the hope that he could bring the faithful to an appreciation of the reading of Scripture, but his most successful effort was a prayer book, *Garden of the Soul.*

The purpose of the book was to provide a manual for devout Catholic laymen, and in keeping with the English temperament, it was characterized by common sense, sobriety and moderation.[125] Challoner also composed two books of meditations, *Think Well On't* (1728) and *Meditations for Every Day in the Year* (1764), because he felt the necessity of promoting the practice of mental prayer

among the English Catholics. He wrote nothing about mystical
prayer, but he translated St. Francis de Sales' *Introduction to the
Devout Life*. Cartmell observes:

> Mystical prayer was somewhat in favour in Challoner's time owing to
> the dangers, partly real and partly imaginary, of Quietism. Directors
> encouraged the devout to keep to meditation; it was safe and salutary; it
> did not encourage illusions, it schooled the soul in virtue, and it was a
> valuable ascetic discipline. Challoner therefore was at one with his age in
> stressing the value of meditation to the apparent exclusion of other
> forms of mental prayer. He was, of course, aware of others, higher
> forms; of the prayer of faith or acquired contemplation from his reading
> of St. Francis de Sales, and of infused contemplation in its several
> degrees from the works of St. Teresa. That he had experience of any of
> these higher forms can only be conjectured.[126]

The religious revival in nineteenth century England, which culmi-
nated in the Oxford Movement, was in a sense a blossoming of the
seeds sown by Baker and Challoner. As Thureau-Dangin says,
Christianity had become a quiet, decent, cold, traditional formality,
necessary to a well-organized society; there seemed to be nothing
supernatural about it, nor was there any devotion or fervor, much
less mysticism.[127] What was needed was a life of prayer, and this is
evidenced from the fact that under Anglican auspices the works of
Fénelon, Grou, Lallemant, St. Francis de Sales, Scupoli, and the
Exercises of St. Ignatius were brought out in English translation.
Three men deserve special attention, Faber, Newman, and Manning, although there were others, such as Wiseman, Ullathorne
and Hedley, who contributed to the religious revival in England.[128]

The spiritual writings of F. W. Faber (1814–1863), an Oratorian,
are well known throughout the English-speaking world. They are
not, however, typically English, because Faber preferred the style of
St. Alphonsus Liguori. Today, however, the works of Faber are
seldom even mentioned, due primarily to the style in which they are
written rather than to the doctrine as such. Renowned as a preacher,
in the florid style of his day, Faber wrote in the same manner, with
the result that his works are diffuse and full of digressions. As
Pourrat puts it, Faber's books "are full of doctrine, but they are full
of words as well. . . . The preacher is never separated from the writer
in Faber. When he writes, he talks, and he talks pleasantly, without
ever seeming pressed for time."[139]

Of the eight books written by Faber, six of them are meditations
on the Christian mysteries, written in the manner of the school of

Bérulle (man's nothingness before God the Creator and the central role of the mysteries of Christ in the soul's sanctification). The remaining two are books of spiritual direction.[130] His best books are *All for Jesus* and *Growth in Holiness*. The theme of his spiritual writing is found in *The Creator and the Creature*, in which he states that his intention is to write a "primer of piety" and then goes on to say: "All our duties to God, and to ourselves no less, are founded on the fact that we are creatures. All religion is based on the sense that we are creatures."[131] Therefore, man's first duty is to give glory to God, and this is done primarily by love. "It is neither the wonderful character of its doctrines, nor the pure simplicity of its precepts, nor the supernatural power of its assistances, which make religion what it is, but the fact of its being the creature's personal love of the Creator."[132]

Faber then proceeds in the rest of his spiritual books to concentrate on the mysteries of Christ as the central point of Christian holiness.

> What would the world be without Jesus? ... An earth without hope or happiness, without love or peace, the past a burden, the present a weariness, the future a shapeless terror – such would the earth be, if by impossibility there were no Jesus.... Besides this, Jesus is bound up with our innermost lives. He is more to us than the blood in our veins. We know that he is indispensable to us; but we do not dream how indispensable he is. There is not a circumstance of life in which we could do without Jesus.... But, if he is thus indispensable in life, how much more will he be indispensable in death? Who would dare to die without him?[133]

Faber made it clear that he was not writing a theology of the spiritual life for select souls; he was, in the spirit of the founder of the Oratory, St. Philip Neri, writing a book of instructions for ordinary Christians. For this, Faber could find no better focal point than the mystery of Jesus Christ. His doctrine was so optimistic that some criticized him for making the Christian life too easy and not mentioning the need for asceticism and self-denial.

In his two works on spiritual direction, *Growth in Holiness* and *Spiritual Conferences*, Faber reveals himself as an uncommonly acute psychologist, well versed in the various ways of the spiritual life. Like most authors, he divides the path to perfection into three stages: that of beginners ("a wonderful time, so wonderful that nobody realizes how wonderful it is till they are out of it, and can look back on it"); secondly, the stage of hardship and asceticism ("a vast extent of wilderness, full of temptation, struggle and fatigue, a place of work and suffering"); and finally the stage reached by chosen souls ("the land of high prayer, of brave self-crucifixions, of mystical trials, and of heights of superhuman detachment and abjection").[134] Faber considered that most devout Christians find themselves at some point in the extensive second stage and they usually die in that stage; consequently, these were the souls for whom he was especially writing.

Henry Edward Manning (1832–1892), founder of the Oblates of St. Charles, was named a cardinal in 1875 and took a leading part in Vatican Council I. Like others in the Oxford Movement, he had a great devotion to the Holy Spirit and he wrote two books on this subject: *The Temporal Mission of the Holy Ghost* (1865) and *The Internal Mission of the Holy Ghost* (1875). As the presence of the Holy Spirit in the Church throughout the ages is the basis of its infallibility, so the presence of the Holy Spirit in the souls of the just is the source of their holiness.

Manning's other principal works are *The Glories of the Sacred Heart* (1876) and *The Eternal Priesthood* (1883). It is the book on the priesthood that had the widest circulation and for which he is chiefly remembered. His theology on the priesthood is traditional and orthodox and does not add anything new to the theology of sacerdotal spirituality. Unfortunately, Manning accused religious of judging that diocesan priests could not attain a high degree of perfection and he made an issue out of the term "secular priest," as if it necessarily connoted a wordly priest. Apart from that, his doctrine is similar to that of Newman, but his literary style is more like that of Faber.

John Henry Newman (1807–1890) was primarily an apologist of the first rank and although he dominated his own times, he can be fully appreciated only with the passage of time. He was not a spiritual writer in the strict sense nor did he deal *ex professo* with ascetical and mystical matters; nevertheless, through his sermons he did provide valuable insights into the theology of the spiritual life. In fact, he had intended to compose a book of devotion but never completed it. The work, *Meditations and Devotions*, was compiled from materials collected after Newman's death and published by the Oratorian W. P. Neville in 1895.

Even before he entered the Catholic Church, and while still a leader in the Oxford Movement, Newman was searching for an interior life and was himself a man of deep prayer. He had a special

predilection for solitude and as early as sixteen years of age, he was
convinced that God had called him to lead a life of celibacy.
Moreover, he was completely convinced that he was being led by an
interior light which would gradually become brighter and reveal
God's plan to him. The inspiring story of his search for truth and his
entrance into the Catholic Church give evidence of a spiritual life
that was interior, totally subjected to God's plan, and guided by a
powerful faith in divine providence. Thus, Newman writes:

> God knows what is my greatest happiness, but I do not. There is no rule
> about what is happy and good; what suits one would not suit another.
> And the ways by which perfection is reached vary very much; the
> medicines necessary for our souls are very different from each other.
> Thus God leads us by strange ways; we know he wills our happiness,
> but we neither know what our happiness is, nor the way.... Let us put
> ourselves into his hands, and not be startled though he leads us by a
> strange way.... Let us be sure he will lead us right, that he will bring us
> to that which is, not indeed what we think best, nor what is best for
> another, but what is best for us.[135]

Even while confessing his utter dependence on God, and even as
God's design for him was revealed, Newman was humbled by the
thought that "there were many men far better than I by nature,
gifted with more pleasing natural gifts, and less stained with sin. Yet
thou, in thy inscrutable love for me, hast chosen me and brought me
into thy fold."[136]

The spiritual life for Newman was not something theoretical or
speculative; it was a pulsating reality and a hidden mystery, as the
following passages indicate:

> A true Christian may almost be defined as one who has a ruling sense of
> God's presence within him. As none but justified persons have that
> privilege, so none but the justified have that practical perception of it....
> In all circumstances, of joy or sorrow, hope or fear, let us aim at having
> God in our inmost heart.... Let us acknowledge him as enthroned
> within us at the very springs of thought and affection. Let us submit
> ourselves to his guidance and sovereign direction.... This is the true life
> of saints.[137]

> The kingdom of God spreads externally over the earth, because it has an
> internal hold upon us, because, in the words of the text, "it is within us,"
> in the hearts of its individual members. Bystanders marvel; strangers try
> to analyze what it is that does the work; they imagine all manner of
> human reasons and natural causes to account for it, because they cannot

see, and do not feel, and will not believe, what is in truth a supernatural influence.[138]

Finally, for Newman as for all theologians, the primacy belongs to charity, but a charity which is a love of complacence in God and tends to contemplative activity. "Love is the gentle, tranquil, satisfied acquiescence and adherence of the soul in the contemplation of God; not only a preference of God before all things, but a delight in him because he is God, and because his commandments are good."[139]

Yet there is room for Martha as well as Mary because "both of them glorify him in their own line, whether of labor or of quiet, in either case providing themselves to be not their own, but bought with a price, set on obeying, and constant in obeying his will. If they labor, it is for his sake; and if they adore, it is still from love of him."[140]

CHAPTER 10

THE TWENTIETH
CENTURY

If Christian spirituality in the twentieth century is indebted to any nation more than others, that nation is France. Indeed it would be safe to say that until Vatican Council II, practically all the aspects of the life of the Church – liturgy, exegesis, theology, philosophy, mission work and spirituality – received their most powerful impetus and orientation from French experts and leaders. Even officials of the Roman Curia were sometimes prodded into renewal and adaptation by French theologians and ecclesiastics.

Yves Congar has aptly stated that "the beacons which the hand of God has set aflame on the threshold of the atomic century are called Thérèse of Lisieux and Charles de Foucauld." There are other lights as well, not only as examples of Christian holiness but as experts in various fields that relate to the spiritual life, but it is worth noting that in an age of intense activism and flourishing technology, the Holy Spirit has raised up those two great witnesses to the power and efficacy of the contemplative life.

ST. THÉRÈSE OF LISIEUX
After St. Teresa of Avila and St. John of the Cross, St. Thérèse of Lisieux is the third great luminary of Carmelite spirituality. Although she lived in the nineteenth century (1873–1897), her impact on the twentieth century is nothing short of remarkable. This is all the more true when we consider that she spent her youth in the closed circle of the Martin family, tenderly protected by a loving father and older sisters, and the remainder of her short life was hidden in the cloister of the Carmel of Lisieux.

Thérèse was the last of the nine children born into the Martin family, of which four children died in their infancy. Four of the girls became Carmelite nuns at Lisieux and the fifth became a Visitandine. From her earliest days, Thérèse felt the call to the cloister, but when she made the formal request for admittance to Carmel, the superiors refused her because of her youth. Thérèse even travelled to Rome with her father and Celine, to seek a dispensation from Pope Leo XIII. Finally, on April 9, 1888, she was admitted to Carmel and made her religious profession on September 8, 1890.

In 1894 the prioress, Mother Agnes, a blood sister of Thérèse, asked her to write the memories of her childhood. This was the beginning of Thérèse's autobiography, known as *Story of a Soul*.[1] In 1895 Sister Thérèse of the Child Jesus and the Holy Face (to give her full title as a Carmelite nun) offered herself to God as a victim soul. The following year she completed the first section of her auto-biography and in the same year she suffered her first hemorrhage. Nevertheless, she began the second section of her autobiography at the urging of another blood sister, Sister Genevieve (Celine). In June of 1897 Thérèse was moved to the infirmary, where she completed the autobiography. She received Communion for the last time on August 19 and died on September 30, 1897.

The following year, on September 30, the autobiography was published under the title, *L'Histoire d'une âme*, and immediately became one of the most widely read books of the time. In 1925 Thérèse was proclaimed a saint by Pope Pius XI; in 1927 she was declared co-patroness of the missions with St. Francis Xavier; in 1944 Pope Pius XII named St. Thérèse co-patroness of France, together with St. Joan of Arc.[2]

In spite of her contemplative vocation, St. Thérèse of Lisieux has rightly been proposed as a model for the countless "little souls" (she called them *petites âmes*) who to all appearances never receive any extraordinary gifts of grace nor experience the lofty heights of mystical union. As a result, St. Thérèse emphasized the need for fidelity to the ordinary duties of one's state of life, the importance of love as a motivating power, and the cultivation of a filial trust in the heavenly Father.[3] Consequently, Pope Pius XI declared that Thérèse's form of spirituality is "an expression of the fundamental teaching of the Gospel." And St. Thérèse said of herself: "I have never given the good God anything but love and it is with love that he will repay."[4]

Judging from her own written testimony, St. Thérèse did not practice extraordinary penances or mortifications, although her mortal illness, coupled with her observance of the Carmelite life, surely constituted a severe form of asceticism. Nor do we find in her life the numerous charisms and extraordinary phenomena com-monly recorded in hagiography, although Thérèse asserts in her autobiography that she was cured of a serious and strange illness in 1882 through the intervention of the Blessed Virgin;[5] moreover, she describes how she experienced the mystical flame of love after entering Carmel:

> I was beginning the Way of the Cross; suddenly, I was seized with such a violent love for God that I can't explain it except by saying it felt as though I were totally plunged into fire. Oh! What fire and what sweetness at one and the same time! I was on fire with love, and I felt that one minute more, one second more, and I wouldn't be able to sustain this ardor without dying. I understood, then, what the saints were saying about these states which they experienced so often. As for me, I experienced it only once and for a single instant, falling back immediately into my habitual state of dryness.[6]

St. Thérèse also stated that at the age of fourteen she had experienced transports of love but it was only after she had made her "oblation to Merciful Love" that she experienced the flame of love. St. John of the Cross had described this experience in *The Living Flame of Love*, stanza 2 of the second redaction.

St. Thérèse of Lisieux is above all an apostle of love and a witness to the theological axiom that it is not works that make us holy, but love. Because of her childlike love and trust in the heavenly Father, she was able to practice perfect abandonment to the divine will and embrace wholeheartedly her vocation as a victim soul. Shunning any and all extraordinary favors and practicing utmost fidelity to the ordinary tasks of her daily life, she offers hope and encouragement to all the "little souls" who seek to follow Christ by performing their ordinary tasks extraordinarily well.

ELIZABETH OF THE TRINITY

Born at Bourges, France, in 1880, Elizabeth Catez entered the Carmel at Dijon in 1901 and died in 1906. The publication of *Souvenirs*, containing the biography of Elizabeth of the Trinity and a number of her writings, met with immediate success in France. Men of great authority were impressed with her doctrine, among them, Cardinal Mercier, John G. Arintero, R. Garrigou-Lagrange and M. M. Philipon. Like St. Thérèse of Lisieux, she was doctrinally nourished by the assiduous study of the works of St. John of the Cross, and to this she added her meditation on the Epistles of St. Paul.

In a letter to the Carmel of Dijon in 1927, John G. Arintero stated: "What I most admire in this servant of God is her profound understanding of the great mysteries of the Christian life: our incorporation in Christ, whose mission we must continue; the indwelling of the Blessed Trinity in our hearts. . . . Through this grasp of the great mysteries, identical with St. Paul's, she became a faithful interpreter of some of the most sublime passages of his profound Epistles."

Reginald Garrigou-Lagrange has made the following observation concerning Elizabeth of the Trinity:

> To be led to the heights of sanctity, it would be enough for a soul to live intensely but one of these truths of our faith. . . . The servant of God, Elizabeth of the Trinity, was one of those enlightened and heroic souls able to cling to one of these great truths, which are both the simplest and the most important, and, beneath the appearance of an ordinary life, to find therein the secret of a very close union with God. This mystery of the indwelling of the Blessed Trinity in the depths of her soul was the great reality of her interior life.[7]

Elizabeth made a private vow of virginity at the age of fourteen, but when her mother refused permission for her entrance into Carmel, Elizabeth took an active part in the social life of her circle and greatly enjoyed the vacation trips during the summer holidays. Amid all this activity, however, Elizabeth yearned for the Carmelite life and her friends were amazed at her ability to be so deeply recollected in prayer when the occasion offered. Her greatest challenge during this period was to control her violent outbursts of temper and to do so she practiced immediate and total obedience to her mother. At the time she was reading St. Teresa's *Way of Perfection* and was able to verify certain divine touches that she had been experiencing. It was at that time also that she met the Dominican, Iréné Vallée, who frequently preached and gave conferences to the Carmelites of Dijon. On asking him about her spiritual experiences, he acquainted her with the doctrine of the indwelling of the Trinity in the soul through grace. Elizabeth at that moment discovered the secret of her own spiritual life and henceforth the indwelling of the Trinity was the foundation of her interior life.

Elizabeth entered Carmel in 1901 but she did not live to enter fully into the community of professed nuns. In 1904 she composed her sublime prayer to the honor of the Blessed Trinity:

> O my God, Trinity whom I adore! Help me to become utterly forgetful of self, that I may bury myself in thee, as changeless and as calm as though my soul were already in eternity. May nothing disturb my peace or draw me out of thee, O my immutable Lord! but may I at every moment penetrate more deeply into the depths of thy mystery!

Give peace to my soul; make it thy heaven, thy cherished dwelling place, thy home of rest. Let me never leave thee there alone, but keep me there, all absorbed in thee, in living faith, adoring thee and wholly yielded up to thy creative action!

O my Christ, whom I love, crucified by love, fain would I be the bride of thy Heart; fain would I cover thee with glory and love thee. . . . until I die of very love. Yet I realize my weakness and beseech thee to clothe me with thyself, to identify my soul with all the movements of thy own. Immerse me in thyself; possess me wholly; substitute myself for thee, that my life may be but a radiance of thy own. Enter my soul as Adorer, as Restorer, as Savior!

O Eternal Word, Utterance of my God! I long to pass my life in listening to thee, to become docile, that I may learn all from thee. Through all darkness, all privations, all helplessness, I crave to keep thee ever with me and to dwell beneath thy lustrous beams. O my beloved Star! so hold me that I cannot wander from thy light!

O consuming Fire! Spirit of Love! descend within me and reproduce in me, as it were, an incarnation of the Word; that I may be to him another humanity wherein he renews his mystery!

And thou, O Father, bend down toward thy poor little creature and overshadow her, beholding in her none other than thy Beloved Son in whom thou hast set all thy pleasure.

O my "Three," my All, my Beatitude, Infinite Solitude, Immensity wherein I love myself! I yield myself to thee as thy prey. Bury thyself in me that I may be buried in thee, until I depart to contemplate in thy light the abyss of thy greatness![8]

In the middle of Lent, 1906, Sister Elizabeth was transferred to the infirmary, although until shortly before her death she kept all the observances of the Carmelite life. Diagnosed as suffering from an incurable disease, Elizabeth obtained permission to make a final retreat in preparation for her passage to eternal life. It was during that time that she composed her *Last Retreat of Laudem Gloriae* (the name she had taken for herself). Two other documents came from her hand: in the summer of 1906 she compiled retreat notes entitled *Heaven on Earth*, and a few weeks before her death she sent a lengthy letter to her lifelong friend, Marguerite, entitled *Last Spiritual Counsels*.[9]

A few days before her death Sister Elizabeth wrote with failing hand to one of the nuns: "It seems to me that in heaven my mission will be to draw souls, by helping them to go out of themselves in order to adhere to God by a very simple, wholly loving movement and to maintain them in that great inner silence which allows God to imprint himself on them and to transform them into himself."

Elizabeth was beatified by Pope John Paul II on November 25, 1984.

CHARLES DE FOUCAULD

Born in Strasbourg in 1858, and orphaned at the age of five, Charles de Foucauld passed a difficult childhood. At the age of twenty-three he enlisted in the army and then later, from 1883 to 1884, he explored Morocco scientifically, for which he received a decoration from the French government. Converted from atheism in 1886, Charles thought of entering the religious life. After a visit to the Holy Land, he entered the Trappists in France but after six months he was transferred to a Trappist monastery in Syria, where he made his religious profession in 1892.

The Trappist life did not satisfy Charles de Foucauld, for he wanted to found his own religious order in which there was no distinction between choir monks and lay brothers, no choral office, and the monks would support themselves completely by manual labor. He left the Trappists and went to Palestine, where he found work as a laborer for the Poor Clares and spent many hours of the day and night in mental prayer. Later he returned to France, where he was ordained to the priesthood in 1901. He then returned to Africa, where he intended to work for the conversion of the Arabs by a hidden life of continual prayer and penance.

Dressed as an Arab, and living in a small hut, Charles passed through the dark night of suffering and abandonment. His spirituality was eminently Trinitarian and he rejoiced that he could surrender everything and simply have the happiness of realizing that God is God. This great "apostle of the Sahara" was murdered by Arabs in 1916.

The hidden life of Charles de Foucauld has produced abundant fruit in the twentieth century. The Little Brothers of Jesus and the Little Sisters of the Sacred Heart of Jesus were established in 1933 and are flourishing throughout the world. In 1939 another congregation inspired by Charles de Foucauld was founded – The Little Sisters of Jesus – and they exercise an apostolate among non-Christians and among the abandoned masses. Finally, there are several fraternities that follow the spirit of Brother Charles. The spirit and mission of the Little Brothers of Jesus was described by Charles de Foucauld:

> The Little Brothers of the Sacred Heart have a special call, first, to imitate our Lord Jesus Christ in his hidden life at Nazareth; secondly, to live in mission countries, there to practice perpetual adoration of the Blessed Sacrament exposed.... By taking the altar and its tabernacle into the midst of unbelieving peoples, they sanctify those peoples without speaking a word, as Jesus silently sanctified the world for thirty years at Nazareth.... It is true that we do not take part in the glorifying of God, the work of our Lord, the saving of souls, by preaching the Gospel; but we do so effectively by taking to people the Eucharistic presence of Jesus, Jesus offered in the holy Sacrifice, and the evangelical virtues, the charity of Christ's heart which we do our best to practice. We have not received a call from God to the ministry of the word; so we bless and preach by silence.[10]

In the *Directory* for the association of prayer which he founded in France, de Foucauld stated that he and his followers would direct their efforts to the conversion of "those who are spiritually the poorest, the most crippled, the blindest, the infidel peoples of missionary countries; those who know not the Good News; who have no tabernacle, nor priest; the most abandoned souls, those who are most sick, the sheep that are indeed lost."[11] Thus, Charles de Foucauld promoted a missionary activity which was simply a vocation of presence among the people he wished to lead to Christ. A new form of contemplative life was introduced, a contemplative life lived in the world, with silence as a means of influence, presence as a method of communication, and poverty as a witness to fraternal love for the poor and needy in whose midst the Little Brothers and the Little Sisters live. Far from being an apostolate of social service, however, it is an apostolate of sharing the same sufferings of the poor and giving witness of the Gospel teaching. Contemporary followers of the ideal of Charles de Foucauld have gone into the "desert" of the slums and the factories to bring the "presence of Christ" through the example of virtue and contemplative prayer.

There were others, too, who contributed to the spirituality of the twentieth century, and although we cannot discuss all of them, we can at least refer to some of the leading figures. To do so, we shall relate them to the specific areas in which they played a significant role: the liturgical movement, the remarkable expansion of the foreign missions, holiness among the laity and developments in systematic spiritual theology.

LITURGICAL REVIVAL

The revival of liturgical spirituality can be credited to the Benedictine, L. P. Guéranger, the restorer of the Benedictine Order of France. The traditional practice of methodical mental prayer had been so well established between the sixteenth and the twentieth centuries that the liturgical revival inaugurated by Guéranger and the monks of Solesmes in 1837 seemed to be in conflict with the individual piety fostered by mental prayer. Guéranger (1805–1875) made his position very clear: "By asserting the immense superiority of liturgical over individual prayer, we do not say that individual methods should be suppressed; we would only wish them to be kept in their proper place."[12] Nevertheless, some of his followers went so far as to deny any place at all to the practice of mental prayer in the monastic tradition. The most famous works of Guéranger are: *L'année liturgique*, in 15 volumes (1841–1901), and the three volumes of *Institutions liturgiques* (1840–1851).

The efforts of Dom Guéranger were seconded and carried to fulfillment in large part by Pope Pius X (1835–1914), who settled the argument on frequent Communion by issuing a decree on frequent and daily Communion for all Christians in the state of grace and having the proper dispositions.[13] The same Pontiff encouraged the active participation of the faithful in the liturgy of the Church. The effort was successful, more in some localities than others, and E. Masure has described the results as follows:

> Like theology, . . . the liturgy never ceased to exist in the Church, but at the beginning of the century it was given new life and was lifted up to heights that would have astonished Dom Guéranger himself. . . . Christian worship has new vitality. Souls are lifted to the invisible by music, chant, drama, texts with their pictures, symbols with their meaning – and the Christian community once more in ceremonies finds its sacramental unity.[14]

The success of the liturgical revival was due to the dedication and zeal of the French Benedictines, and especially to the monks of Solesmes. But, as we have seen, it received its official promulgation from Pope Pius X. However, it was through the efforts of the Belgian Benedictine, Dom Beauduin (1873–1960), that the liturgical movement became more popularized, more pastoral and less monastic. As a result, the Catholic faithful gained a deeper appreciation for the Eucharist as the center of Christian life. Nor should we fail to recognize the great contribution made by the monastery of

Maria-Laach in Germany and the contribution of writers such as Dom Casel (1886–1948) and Pius Parsch (1884–1954). Finally, we note the encyclical, *Mediator Dei*, by Pope Pius XII, which set into motion the liturgical reforms that would be implemented by Vatican Council II.

MISSIONARY EXPANSION AND CATHOLIC ACTION

The name of Pauline Jaricot (1799–1862) will always be held in reverence by missionaries because she was the foundress of what is known as the Society for the Propagation of the Faith. At the age of seventeen she made a private vow of perpetual virginity and founded the Union of Prayer in Reparation to the Sacred Heart, an organization composed of working girls. She founded an association for the missions in 1820 and collected modest donations from the ordinary faithful. In 1826 she established the Loretta house, a home for working girls, and founded the Association of the Living Rosary. When a new group of twelve laymen banded together in Paris for the purpose of soliciting financial aid for the foreign missions, the members decided to join forces with the Association founded by Pauline Jaricot and this was done on May 3, 1822. Such was the beginning of the Society for the Propagation of the Faith, but Pauline Jaricot has always been considered the foundress. She spent the last years of her life in abject poverty and the victim of derision and slander. "May God do what he wills," she said, "without being turned one iota from his holy purpose in my regard by my sufferings, my tears, my prayers or my complainings."[15]

During this same period, France was the scene of the foundation of numerous religious institutes dedicated to the foreign missions; to a lesser extent the same can be said of Italy and Germany. The number of missionary institutes increased with amazing rapidity and the Catholics of Europe and the United States contributed generously to the support of the foreign missions. One of the disastrous effects of the Second World War was the curtailment of missionary activity, and yet this prepared the way for a native hierarchy in those countries which had been evangelized.

Living at the same time as Pauline Jaricot and, like her, dedicated to the works of mercy, was Frederick Ozanam (1813–1853). Descended from a Jewish family, he was educated at Lyons. Eventually he became a professor of foreign literature at the Sorbonne, as a specialist on Dante. While in Paris he was in contact with the outstanding literary and religious thinkers of the day: Lacordaire, Chateaubriand, Montelambert, and others. In 1833 he founded the

"Conference of Charity" and in 1835 the organization took as its formal title the "Society of St. Vincent de Paul." Since that time the Society has flourished throughout the world, especially in the United States, and has become a symbol of charitable work on behalf of the poor and needy.[16]

The works of Pauline Jaricot and Frederick Ozanam provide us with the proper setting in which to describe briefly the historical evolution of Catholic Action. The precursors of the promotion of the lay apostolate were St. Vincent Pallotti, Pope Pius IX, who called for the collaboration of the laity in the work of the Church, and Pope Leo XIII, who promoted the organization of Catholic Action. It was also fostered by Pope Pius X, and historians of Catholic Action usually point to him as the Pope who understood what Catholic Action should be.[17] But the actual creation of Catholic Action as a lay apostolate was the work of Pope Pius XI.

Congar lists three original concepts of Catholic Action that are the contribution of Pope Pius XI: the insistence on its apostolic character; it embraces all classes and categories of the Catholic laity; and it is an apostolate of the layman as a Christian in the world doing God's work in the world.[18] Pope Pius XI defined Catholic Action as "the participation of the laity in the apostolate of the hierarchy." In 1923 Joseph Cardijn founded the J.O.C., or Young Christian Workers (Y.C.W.), and it prospered so greatly that in 1935 there were more than one hundred thousand delegates from fifteen countries in attendance at its Congress. Pope Pius XII finalized the definition and structure of Catholic Action.[19]

SANCTITY AMONG THE LAITY

Since all Christians are called to the perfection of charity, we would expect to find outstanding examples of holiness among the laity of every century. In addition to Pauline Jaricot and Frederick Ozanam, we should mention St. Gemma Galgani and Elizabeth Leseur.

Born near Lucca, Italy, in 1878, Gemma was orphaned at an early age and was taken into the household of Matteo Giannini, where she remained until her death in 1903. She suffered from chronic illness, which prevented her from entering the monastery of the cloistered Passionist nuns at Lucca. Nevertheless, she experienced extraordinary favors from God, such as the stigmata, continual raptures, and visions of Jesus, Mary and the Passionist St. Gabriel, for whom she had great devotion.

St. Gemma did not write any work for publication, but we know her doctrine through her letters, her autobiography and her life, written by the Passionist, Germano of St. Stanislaus. Her outstanding virtue was humility and because of the countless miracles worked through her intercession, she is one of the most venerated saints of modern times. She was canonized in 1940.[20] Together with St. Gabriel, she is an exponent of Passionist spirituality.

Elizabeth Leseur, born in Paris in 1866, is an impressive example of sanctity within the married life and an active social life. From her earliest years she followed a rule of life in which the practice of prayer, the study of religious doctrine and a constant effort to overcome her faults played an important part. At the age of twenty-one she married Felix Leseur, who had lost his faith completely, and although he had promised to respect Elizabeth's practice of her religion, he soon began a relentless attack to make her lose her faith.

After seven years of marriage, Elizabeth abandoned the practice of religion, but on reading Renan's *History of the Origins of Christianity*, she saw through the falsity of his arguments. As a result, she began to read the works of the Fathers of the Church, St. Augustine, St. Thomas Aquinas, St. Teresa of Avila, St. Francis de Sales, but above all, the Bible. The result was her conversion back to the faith of her youth and an intense practice of the Christian life.

During a trip to Rome with her husband in 1903, Elizabeth had a mystical experience of the presence of Christ within her and a complete renewal of her interior life. She abandoned herself to Christ without reserve. One of her greatest consolations and supports thereafter was in the reception of Communion. At the same time, she worked unceasingly for the conversion of her unbelieving husband, not by arguments, but by the witness of her own holy life and by her prayers. She died in 1914, without seeing the conversion of her husband.

However, in 1905 she had written in her diary that eventually her husband would be converted, and this did occur, three years after the death of Elizabeth. She had died of cancer and early in her illness she had offered her life for the conversion of Felix. After her death he entered the Dominican Order and became a priest. He died at the age of sixty-two, blessing the memory of his wife, who had offered her sufferings for his conversion. Elizabeth had written various works in addition to her *Spiritual Journal*, but her best writing was on the subject of Christian endurance of suffering.[21]

Since we have selected St. Gemma and Elizabeth Leseur as examples of Christian holiness among the laity, this is a suitable place to say a word about secular institutes as a form of consecrated life in the twentieth century. The origins and development of the profession of the evangelical counsels by persons living in the world are described in *Provida Mater Ecclesia*, issued by Pope Pius XII in 1947.[22] However, as early as 1889 Pope Leo XIII had promulgated the Decree, *Ecclesia Catholica*, in which he referred to associations of pious Christians living in the world, to which he gave the name "pious sodalities."[23] But it was only with the promulgation of the Apostolic Constitution of Pope Pius XII, *Provida Mater Ecclesia*, the Motu Proprio, *Primo feliciter*, and the Instruction of the Congregation of Religious, *Cum Sanctissimus*, that secular institutes received their own proper legislation.[24]

Throughout the history of the Church there had always been single individuals or groups who had embraced the life of the evangelical counsels – poverty and continence in particular. But in 1948 the Holy See officially recognized and approved this mode of life for persons who are not religious but secular. Now religious and members of secular institutes are both listed under the general title "consecrated life".

According to *Provida Mater Ecclesia*, the secular institutes are a type of society or association, and in this respect they are similar to a pious union or a third order. Since they are *secular* institutes, the members are described as "remaining in the world" and the note of "secular" is emphasized throughout the legislation. This means that the members not only do not necessarily live in community, as religious are required to do, but they dedicate themselves to an apostolate and have contact with society to a degree that is not proper to religious. But the essential distinction would seem to be that the members of a secular institute remain individuals working in their particular professions or trades and on becoming members of the institute they do not enter a different "state of life," as would be the case of a layman who becomes a priest. In recent years the secular institutes have flourished and multiplied but, as so often happens with associations of the laity and diocesan priests, some of them have already begun to take on the appearance of religious institutes and to lose their specifically "secular" character.

SYSTEMATIC SPIRITUAL THEOLOGY

The fact that at its very beginning the twentieth century was the scene of a sudden increase of interest in mystical questions and systematic spiritual theology may be attributed in large part to the writings of Joseph Görres and his German contemporaries.[25]

Moreover, shortly after the First World War, theologians in France, Spain and Italy became involved in a dispute concerning basic principles of ascetico-mystical theology. For several decades books and articles were published in defense of incompatible views concerning such questions as the call to perfection; the relation between mystical experience and Christian perfection; the distinction between acquired contemplation and infused contemplation; and the unity or diversity of the path to perfection.

The "mystical question" has been a source of controversy since the early days of the Church, when the Apostolic Fathers attempted to defend orthodox Christian gnosis against pagan Gnosticism. With the passage of time and the deeper investigations of theologians, the term "mystical theology" gradually became more refined, so that pseudo-Dionysius, writing at the beginning of the sixth century, could apply the term to an experience of the divine, passively received. Until the seventeenth century, theologians of the spiritual life generally accepted the fact that individuals who cooperate fully with the graces received, can attain to a mystical experience of God.

Although he was not the first to do so,[26] it seems that the Jesuit John Baptist Scaramelli (+ 1752) had the greatest influence in propagating the theory that the perfection of the Christian life does not necessarily comprise the mystical experience nor, indeed, are all Christians called to that degree of perfection. In his two works, *Direttorio ascetico* and *Direttorio mistico*, he made a complete separation between the ascetical and mystical aspects of the spiritual life and posited two distinct types of Christian perfection.

The theological reasoning behind this division can be summarized as follows: since all Christians are called to the perfection of charity, and since relatively few souls attain the mystical state of infused contemplation, it would seem that the "ordinary" perfection of the Christian life is realized in the ascetical state. The theological conclusions that follow from this statement are numerous: 1) the ascetical state and ascetical perfection are the normal, ordinary perfection of the Christian life; the mystical state and mystical perfection are extraordinary and therefore in the class of *gratiae gratis datae*; 2) there are two paths to perfection and actually two distinct types of perfection at the end of these paths; 3) since the mystical state is extraordinary, it is unlawful to pray for or desire the mystical state, mystical experience or any of the phenomena that accompany them; 4) there is a distinction between acquired contemplation and infused contemplation and the former does not lead to the latter; 5) the perfection of charity does not necessarily involve for all Christians the operation of the gifts of the Holy Spirit nor infused contemplation nor a mystical experience of God's presence; 6) Christian perfection does not necessarily require the passive purgations.

This theology of the spiritual life was challenged by Saudreau in his book, *Les Degrés de la vie spirituelle* (1896), and later by Poulain in the work, *Des grâces d'oraison* (1901).[27] The controversy broke out in earnest when the Capuchin Ludovic of Besse criticized Poulain's doctrine on the distinction between asceticism and mysticism. Then, in 1908, Poulain attacked the doctrine contained in Saudreau's book, *Faits extraordinaires de la vie spirituelle*.[28] At this point the controversy spread from France to Italy and Spain, and precisely because Poulain defended the distinction between acquired and infused contemplation.

At the very time that the mystical controversy was at its height in France, a Spanish Dominican, John Arintero (1860–1928), abandoned his career as a specialist in the natural sciences and devoted the rest of his life to ascetical and mystical theology. His masterpiece in spiritual theology, *La Evolución mística*, won for him immediate recognition as an unusually gifted theologian.[29] Calling upon the teaching of the Fathers of the Church, the greatest theologians in the Catholic tradition and the experiences of the mystics themselves, he successfully defended the unity of the spiritual life, the place of infused contemplation as a normal development of the life of grace, and mystical experience (necessarily involving the operation of the gifts of the Holy Spirit) as a universal possibility, since all Christians are called to the perfection of charity.

In the short time that he taught at the Angelicum in Rome, Arintero inspired Reginald Garrigou-Lagrange to take up his pen and write for the same cause. Garrigou-Lagrange became known throughout the world as his works in spiritual theology were translated into various languages.[30] Nevertheless, to Arintero belongs the credit for being the champion of the return to traditional teaching in spiritual theology and in this field he must likewise be considered the master of Garrigou-Lagrange.

At the outset, Arintero became involved in controversies with Jesuits, Carmelites and some of his Dominican brethren. But today, except for a few scattered points of doctrine, the position of Arintero has generally been accepted by theologians throughout the world.

Among the Carmelites the outstanding modern author on

spirituality is Gabriel of St. Mary Magdalen (1893–1953), close friend of Garrigou-Lagrange and professor of spiritual theology in Rome from 1931 until his death in 1953. A prolific writer, Gabriel of St. Mary Magdalen based his spiritual theology on St. Thomas Aquinas, St. Teresa of Avila and St. John of the Cross. He was a staunch defender of the one path to perfection and the universality of the call to the greatest possible union with God through love. He likewise pointed to Mary, Queen of saints, as the model of Christian perfection, since she was totally submissive to the action of the Holy Spirit and yet lived an apparently ordinary life.[31]

Joseph de Guibert (1877–1942) was professor of spiritual theology at the Gregorianum in Rome and a highly respected retreat master and spiritual director. He is perhaps the most authoritative Jesuit author of spirituality in the twentieth century. Theologically, and typical of the Jesuit stance, he takes a middle position between the extremes defended by the theologians who were engaged in the arguments previously described. His approach to the treatment of ascetico-mystical theology is eminently practical and pastoral, for which reason he leans heavily on psychological data. Basing much of his teaching on the *Spiritual Exercises* of St. Ignatius Loyola, he concentrates more on the ascetical than the mystical aspect of Christian holiness.[32]

Several Benedictine authors are also deserving of special mention, and first of all Dom Columba Marmion (1858–1923), the saintly abbot of Maredsous. His most famous trilogy comprises *Jesus Christ, Life of the Soul* (1917); *Jesus Christ in His Mysteries* (1919); and *Jesus Christ, Ideal of the Monk* (1922). A posthumous work entitled *Jesus Christ, Ideal of the Priest*, was compiled from the abbot's conferences and letters. The doctrine in these works is that of St. Paul and the constant theme is that we shall be holy in the measure that we are configured to Christ. All spirituality, therefore, must be Christocentric; the entire Christian life and all sanctity can be reduced to becoming through grace what Christ was by nature: Son of God. Pope Benedict XV was a constant reader of *Jesus Christ, Life of the Soul*, which is a work that can serve as a spiritual guide for persons from every walk of life.[33]

Another Benedictine who achieved worldwide fame as a spiritual writer is Dom John-Baptist Chautard (1858–1935), author of *The Soul of the Apostolate*. This is another book that is universal in its application and helpful to persons of every vocation. The basic message contained in the book is that all apostolate and all ministry should flow from an intimate union with God through a deep interior life. Dom Chautard has simply developed the theological principles that charity is the source and the form of all the virtues and that true virtue does not consist in the external acts but in the interior disposition or *habitus*.[34]

We close this survey of the history of spirituality with a layman, a philosopher and theologian of lasting importance and influence throughout the Catholic world. Jacques Maritain was born in Paris in 1882 into a Protestant family. He studied at the Sorbonne and at the end of his studies he became a Catholic and began to write for *Les cahiers de la quinzaines*, edited by Charles Peguy. After studying biology in Germany, and Thomism under Fr. Clérissac in France, Maritain was named professor at the Institute Catholique in Paris. In 1932 he was invited to lecture at the Institute of Medieval Studies in Toronto, after which he taught at Columbia University in New York and at Princeton. From 1945 to 1948 he was ambassador to the Holy See for France and at the death of his wife Raïssa in 1960, he retired to the monastery of the Little Brothers of Jesus in Toulouse, where he died in 1973.

In addition to his numerous works on philosophy, Maritain also wrote several treatises on spirituality in conjunction with his wife, who lived an intensely mystical life. In his eighties, Maritain wrote his last work entitled *The Peasant of the Garonne*, which was his cry of alarm and of warning against those who were misinterpreting the teachings of Vatican Council II.

In the field of spiritual theology Maritain was completely Thomistic and in accord with the doctrine of Arintero and Garrigou-Lagrange. In fact, Maritain made a positive contribution to the development of the theology of the gifts of the Holy Spirit. Rather than maintain that every mystic will necessarily enjoy habitual infused contemplation in the mystical state, he proposed that since the gifts of the Holy Spirit are divided into intellectual and affective operations, it is possible that some mystics will be moved predominantly by the gifts that operate through the affective faculties.[35]

Undoubtedly the ecclesiastical event of greatest significance in the twentieth century was the Second Vatican Council, celebrated during the pontificates of John XXIII and Paul VI. Officially convoked in 1961, the first session began in October of 1962 and the closing session was held in December of 1965. The Council produced sixteen magnificent documents which will serve as guides and orientations for many years to come.

Since the Council had as one of its goals the renewal of the

Christian life, it is logical that great emphasis was placed on the Christian call to holiness and indeed to holiness as a mark of the Church. This theme was stated repeatedly and in various forms in the fundamental document of the Council, *Lumen Gentium*. Some of the key passages serve well as a conclusion to this survey of the origins and development of holiness in the Church.

> The Church, whose mystery is set forth by this sacred Council, is held, as a matter of faith, to be unfailingly holy. This is because Christ, the Son of God, who with the Father and the Spirit is hailed as "alone holy," loved the Church as his Bride, giving himself up for her so as to sanctify her (cf. Eph. 5:25–26); he joined her to himself as his body and endowed her with the gift of the Holy Spirit for the glory of God. Therefore all in the Church, whether they belong to the hierarchy or are cared for by it, are called to holiness, according to the apostle's saying: "For this is the will of God, your sanctification (I Th. 4:3; cf. Eph. 1:4) This holiness of the Church is constantly shown forth in the fruits of grace which the Spirit produces in the faithful and so it must be; it is expressed in many ways by the individuals who, each in his own state of life, tend to the perfection of love, thus sanctifying others; it appears in a certain way of its own in the practice of the counsels which have been usually called "evangelical". . . .
>
> The Lord Jesus, divine teacher and model of all perfection, preached holiness of life (of which he is the author and maker) to each and every one of his disciples without distinction: "You, therefore, must be perfect, as your heavenly Father is perfect" (Mt. 5:48). For he sent the Holy Spirit to all to move them interiorly to love God with their whole heart, with their whole soul, with their whole understanding, and with their whole strength (cf. Mk. 12:30), and to love one another as Christ loved them (cf. Jn. 13:34: 15:12). . . .
>
> It is therefore quite clear that all Christians in any state or walk of life are called to the fullness of Christian life and to the perfection of love, and by this holiness a more human manner of life is fostered also in earthly society. In order to reach this perfection the faithful should use the strength dealt out to them by Christ's gift, so that, following in his footsteps and conformed to his image, doing the will of God in everything, they may wholeheartedly devote themselves to the glory of God and to the service of their neighbor. . . .
>
> The forms and tasks of life are many but holiness is one – that sanctity which is cultivated by all who act under God's Spirit and, obeying the Father's voice and adoring God the Father in spirit and in truth, follow Christ, poor, humble, and cross-bearing, that they may deserve to be partakers of his glory. Each one, however, according to his own gifts and duties must steadfastly advance along the way of a living faith, which arouses hope and works through love.[36]

NOTES

Chapter 1 Sacred Scripture and the Spiritual Life

1. "Dogmatic Constitution on Divine Revelation," nn. 21–24, *passim*. All quotations from Vatican II documents are taken from A. Flannery (ed.), *Vatican Council II: The Conciliar and Post Conciliar Documents*, Costello Publishing Company, Northport, N.Y., 1975.
2. Y. Congar, "Christ in the Economy of Salvation and in our Dogmatic Tracts," in E. Schillebeeckx and B. Willems (ed.), *Who is Jesus of Nazareth?*, Paulist Press, Glen Rock, N.J., 1965, pp. 5–6. By "economic," Congar means the realization of God's plan in human history; by "functional," he means the conditioning of revelation in relation to salvation.
3. Cf. Y. Congar, *art. cit.*, p. 6.
4. P. Grelot, "God's Presence and Man's Communion with Him in the Old Testament," in P. Benoit and R. F. Murphy (ed.), *The Breaking of Bread*, Paulist Press, Glen Rock, N.J., 1969, p. 7.
5. "Dogmatic Constitution on Divine Revelation," n. 2.
6. Y. Congar, *art. cit.*, p. 23.
7. H. U. von Balthasar, "The Gospel as Norm and Test of all Spirituality in the Church," in C. Duquoc (ed.), *Spirituality in Church and World*, Paulist Press, Glen Rock, N.J., 1965, p. 14.
8. Cf. P. Grelot, "Exégèse, théologie et pastorale," in *Nouvelle revue théologique*, Vol. 88, 1966, pp. 3–13; 132–148.
9. Cf. C. Charlier, *The Christian Approach to the Bible*, tr. H. J. Richards and B. Peters, Newman, Westminster, Md., 1963, p. 244.
10. J. P. Jossua, *Yves Congar: Theology in the Service of God's People*, tr. M. Jocelyn, Priory Press, Chicago, Ill., 1968, p. 145.
11. P. Roets, "Scriptural Teaching on Sexuality," in A. Rock (ed.), *Sex, Love and the Life of the Spirit*, Priory Press, Chicago, Ill., 1966, p. 87.
12. P. Grelot, *art. cit.*, p. 7.
13. Cf. J. P. Jossua, *op. cit.*, p. 128.
14. P. Grelot, *art. cit.*, p. 13.
15. According to *The Jerusalem Bible* (p. 1125), the term "Second-Isaiah" signifies that Isaiah 40–55 was probably composed by an anonymous author who was a disciple of Isaiah and a prophet.
16. Cf. A. Lefèvre, "The Revelation of God's Love in the Old Testament," in J. A. Grispino (ed.), *Foundations of Biblical Spirituality*, Alba House, Staten Island, N.Y., 1964, pp. 15–35.

17. Cf. P. Drijvers, *Les Psaumes*, Paris, 1958; J. L. McKenzie, *The Two-Edged Sword*, Bruce, Milwaukee, Wis., 1958.
18. J. P. Jossua, *op. cit.*, pp. 129–130.
19. "Dogmatic Constitution on Divine Revelation," n. 15, *passim*.
20. Y. Congar, *art. cit.*, pp. 24–25.
21. H. Urs von Balthasar, *The Glory of God: A Theological Aesthetics*, Vol. I: *Seeing the Form*, Ignatius Press, San Francisco, Calif., – Crossroads Publications, New York, N.Y., 1982, pp. 224; 227.
22. Cf. J. P. Jossua, *op. cit.*, p. 133.
23. J. G. Arintero, *The Mystical Evolution in the Development and Vitality of the Church*, tr. J. Aumann, TAN Books, Rockford, Ill., 1978. Vol. 2., pp. 349–351, *passim*.
24. C. Marmion, *Christ in His Mysteries*, B. Herder, St. Louis, Mo., 1924, pp. 54–55.
25. Cf. F. Moschner, *The Kingdom of Heaven in Parables*, tr. E. Plettenburg, B. Herder, St. Louis, Mo., 1960.
26. Cf. W. K. Grossouw, *Spirituality of the New Testament*, tr. M. W. Schoenberg, B. Herder, St. Louis, Mo., 1964.
27. J. Bonsirven, *Theology of the New Testament*, tr. S. F. L. Tye, Newman Bookshop. Westminster, Md., 1963, p. 37.
28. Cf. W. K. Grossouw, *op. cit.*, p. 30; P. G. Stevens, *The Life of Grace*, Prentice-Hall, Englewood Cliffs, N.J., 1963, pp. 8–18.
29. Cf. W. K. Grossouw, *op. cit.*, pp. 26–29; E. J. Fortman, *The Theology of Man and Grace*, Bruce, Milwaukee, Wis., 1966, pp. 23–25.
30. W. K. Grossouw, *op. cit.*, p. 45.
31. Cf. *ibid.*, p. 45.
32. Cf. J. P. Jossua, *op. cit.*, p. 137.
33. W. K. Grossouw, *op. cit.*, p. 55.
34. Cf. G. Salet, "Love of God, Love of Neighbor," in J. A. Grispino (ed.), *Foundations of Biblical Spirituality*, Alba House, Staten Island, N.Y., 1964, p. 50.

Chapter 2 Spirituality of the Early Church

1. Cf. P. Carrington, *The Early Christian Church*, 2 vols., London, 1957–1960; F. Mourret, *A History of the Catholic Church*, tr. N. Thompson, B. Herder, St. Louis, Mo., 1931; L. Bouyer, *The Spirituality of the New Testament and the Fathers*, tr. M. P. Ryan, Desclée, New York, N.Y., 1960.
2. In Acts 20:17–28 the words *episkopoi* (bishops) and *presbyteroi* (presbyters) are used interchangeably. In his commentary on St. Paul's Letter to Titus (1:5), St Jerome states that in those early days bishops were sometimes called presbyters. Cf. F. Prat, "Evêques," in *Dictionnaire de Théologie Catholique*, ed. A. Vacant *et al.*, Paris.
3. L. Bouyer, *op. cit.*, p. 167.

4. For further details on the Apostolic Fathers, see F. Mourret, *op. cit.*; B. Altaner, *Patrology*, Herder and Herder, New York, N.Y., 1960; L. Bouyer, *op. cit.*; K. Lake, *The Apostolic Fathers*, 2 vols., Cambridge, 1959; P. Pourrat, *Christian Spirituality*, tr. W. H. Mitchell and S. P. Jacques, Newman, Westminster, Md., Vol. I, 1953; J. Lawson, *A Theological and Historical Introduction to the Apostolic Fathers*, New York, N.Y., 1961.
5. Cf. P. Pourrat, *op. cit.*, Vol. I, p. 56.
6. *Letter to the Magnesians*, 8 and 13.
7. *Letter to the Smyrnaeans*, 1.
8. *Letter to the Philadelphians*, 8.
9. *Letter to the Smyrnaeans*, 8. It seems that St. Ignatius was the first to use the term "catholic" Church. He also defended the real presence of Christ in the Eucharist, the ecclesiastical hierarchy and the primacy of the Bishop of Rome.
10. *Letter to the Magnesians*, 9.
11. *Letter to the Ephesians*, 9.
12. *Letter to the Philadelphians*, 7.
13. The basic notion of Millenarianism was that the second coming of Christ will be preceded by a thousand years during which the kingdom of God will be established on earth. There was no agreement on the starting point of the millenium. Cf. L. Bouyer, *op. cit.*, pp. 171–174.
14. *Didache*, 16.
15. *Letter to the Corinthians*, 49–50.
16. *Letter to the Romans*, 4–5, *passim*.
17. Cf. K. Lake, *The Apostolic Fathers*, Vol. 2, pp. 359–361.
18. L. Bouyer, *op. cit.*, p. 175.
19. *Ibid.*, p. 176.
20. *Didache*, 9. Chapter 10 contains thanskgiving prayers.
21. P. Evdokimov, *The Struggle with God*, Paulist Press, Glen Rock, N.J., 1966, p. 192.
22. For details on liturgy of early Church, cf. L. Duchesne, *Christian Worship: Its Origin and Evolution*, tr. M. L. McClure, 5th edition, London, 1949; G. Dix, *The Shape of the Liturgy*, 2nd edition, London, 1945; D. Attwater, *Introduction to the Liturgy*, Helicon, Baltimore, Md., 1961; A. A. King, *Liturgies of the Past*, Bruce, Milwaukee, Wis., 1959; W. J. O'Shea, *The Worship of the Church*, Newman, Westminster, Md., 1957; O. Rousseau, *The Progress of the Liturgy*, Newman, Westminster, Md., 1951.
23. Cf. L. Bouyer, *op. cit.*, p. 211.
24. Cf. J. Dupont, *Gnosis, la connaissance réligieuse dans les épîtres de saint Paul*, Louvain, 1949.
25. Cf. L. Bouyer, *op. cit.*, pp. 216–236; 245–256. According to heretical Gnosticism there are three classes of persons: 1) the *pneumatics*, an elite class of persons who are predestined to be saved, no matter how

they live; 2) the *psychics*, who live according to the Spirit as best they can, but cannot be saved without God's help; and 3) the *hylics*, who live according to the flesh and are predestined to damnation.

26. *First Apology*, 65–67, *passim*.
27. *Against Heresies*, III, Preface; I, 6, 3; III, 1, 1.
28. This doctrine is found in *Stromata*, 2 and 7.
29. Cf. *Stromata*, 2; 6; 7.
30. Cf. *Stromata*, 5.
31. *Stromata*, 6. The concept of *apatheia* was taken up later by the Cappadocians and Evagrius Ponticus. It is also one of the bases on which some scholars have attempted to attribute a pagan element to early Christian spirituality. Cf. L. Bouyer, *op. cit.*, pp. 273–274.
32. Cf. L. Bouyer, *op. cit.*, p. 282.
33. *Commentary on John*, 32:27.
34. *Contra Celsum*, 3, 28; 32, 27.

Chapter 3 Monasticism in the East

1. Cf. L. Bouyer, *The Spirituality of the New Testament and the Fathers*, tr. M. P. Ryan, Desclée, New York, N.Y., 1960; P. Pourrat, *Christian Spirituality*, tr. W. H. Mitchell and S. P. Jacques, Newman Press, Westminster, Md., 1953, Vol. 1; AA.VV., *Théologie de la vie monastique*, Theologie 49, Paris, 1961.
2. F. Fénelon, "Discours sur les avantages et les dévoirs de la vie réligieuse," in *Oeuvres*, ed. Versailles, Vol. 17, p. 396.
3. Cf. St. Jerome, *Vita S. Malchi monachi*, PL 23, 53.
4. P. Evdokimov, *The Struggle with God*, Paulist Press, Glen Rock, N.J., 1966, p. 94.
5. Cf. I. Clement, 33, 1–2; St. Ignatius, *Letter to Polycarp*, 5, 2.
6. Cf. Tertullian, *De virginibus velandis; De cultu feminarum*; St. Cyprian, *De habitu virginum*.
7. Cf. J. M. Perrin, *Virginity*, tr. K. Gordon, Newman Press, Westminster, Md., 1956; P. T. Camelot, "Virginity," in *New Catholic Encyclopedia*, McGraw-Hill, New York, N.Y., 1967. Vol. 14, pp. 701–704.
8. M. H. Vicaire, *The Apostolic Life*, tr. W. De Naple, Priory Press, Chicago, Ill., 1966, pp. 29–31.
9. Cf. G. Morin, *L'idéal monastique et la vie chrétienne des premiers jours*, Paris, 1921.
10. Cf. P. Evdokimov, *op. cit.*, p. 113.
11. Cf. L. Bouyer, *op. cit.*, p. 144.
12. Cf. J. Quasten, *Patrology*, Newman Press, Westminster, Md., 1950–1960, Vol. 3, pp. 424–482.
13. For details on literary sources of monastic life, see B. Altaner, *Patrology*, Herder and Herder, New York, N.Y., 1960; J. Quasten, *op. cit.*, Vol. 1.

14. Cf. L. Bouyer, *op. cit.*, p. 323.
15. Cf. L. Bouyer, *op. cit.*, p. 330.
16. Cf. J. Gribomont, *Histoire du texte des "Ascétiques" de Saint Basile*, Louvain, 1953, p. 187; P. Pourrat, *op. cit.*, Vol. 1.
17. *Regulae brevius tractatae*, PG 31, 441.
18. Cf. L. Bouyer, *op. cit.*, pp. 336–337, *passim*.
19. *Ibid.*, p. 351.
20. Cf. J. Quasten, *op. cit.*, Vol. 2, pp. 221 ff.
21. *Oratio 7*, PG 35, 785.
22. *Oratio 30*, PG 36, 112.
23. *Oratio 2, 7*, PG 35.
24. See also J. Quasten, *op. cit.*, Vol. 2, pp. 267; 305–310.
25. Cf. J. Tixeront, *History of Dogma*, B. Herder, St. Louis, Mo., 1930, Vol. 2, p. 8. For a rebuttal of this opinion, see J. Daniélou, *Platonisme et théologie mystique: Essai sur la doctrine spirituelle de saint Grégoire de Nysse*, 2 ed., Paris, 1954.
26. Cf. L. Bouyer, *op. cit.*, pp. 351–368.
27. J. Quasten, *op. cit.*, pp. 254–296.
28. *Ibid., loc. cit.*
29. L. Bouyer, *op. cit.*, pp. 352–353.
30. The complete text of *De instituto christiano* can be found in W. Jaeger, *Opera ascetica*, Vol. 8, Leiden, 1952.
31. Quoted by L. Bouyer, *op. cit.*, pp. 360–361.
32. *Ibid.*
33. Cf. *In Canticum Canticorum*, PG 44, 889.
34. Cf. R. F. Harvanek, "St. Gregory of Nyssa," in *New Catholic Encyclopedia*, Vol. 6, p. 795.
35. Cf. L. Bouyer, *op. cit.*, p. 369. Macarius discussed the apparent conflict between work and prayer and he stressed the importance of community life. He also used the expression *"simul justus et peccator"* to designate that even the soul in grace must still be purified before attaining the plenitude of grace. Cf. L. Bouyer, *op. cit.*, pp. 379–380.
36. Cf. L. Bouyer, *op. cit.*, p. 381.
37. H. U. von Balthasar, "Metaphysik und Mystik des Evagrius Ponticus," in *Zeitschrift für Aszese und Mystik*, Vol. 14, pp. 31–34.
38. The only extant versions of this work are the Syriac edition by W. Frankenberg, *Evagrius Ponticus*, Berlin, 1912, pp. 546–553, and the Armenian edition by H. B. V. Sarghissian, *Vie et oeuvres du saint Père Evagre*, Venice, 1907, pp. 12–22.
39. Cf. A. Guillaumont, *Les six centuries des "Kephalaia gnostica" d'Evagre le Pontique*, PO, Vol. 28, Paris, 1958.
40. Cf. H. Gressmann, *Nonnenspiegel und Mönchsspiegel*, Leipzig, 1913, pp. 146–151; 153–165.
41. Cf. PG 79, 1145–1164; 1200–1233.
42. Cf. PG 79, 1165–1200.
43. Evagrius divided Christians into ascetics and mystics. The mystics

are further divided into those who enjoy natural contemplation (*physiké*) and those who attain to the contemplation of God (*theologiké*). Finally, natural contemplation may have as its object either corporeal natures or spiritual natures.

44. Cf. L. Bouyer, *op. cit.*, pp. 420–421.
45. Cf. the excellent article, "Denys l'Areopagite (Le Pseudo-) by R. Roques in *Dictionnaire de Spiritualité*, Vol. 3, col. 244–286.
46. *De ecclesiastica hierarchia*, PG 3, 371.
47. *De divinis nominibus*, 1, 5. PG 3.
48. *De mystica theologia*, PG 3, 997–1000.
49. L. Bouyer, *op. cit.*, pp. 406–410, *passim*.
50. *De divinis nominibus*, PG 3, 648; 681–684.
51. Cf. *De mystica theologia*, PG 3, 997–1000.
52. *Epistola 5*, PG 3, 1073.
53. Cf. P. Evdokimov, *op. cit.*, pp. 105; 113–116.
54. Cf. L. Bouyer, *op. cit.*, pp. 427–433.
55. Cf. L. Bouyer, *op. cit.*, pp. 433–436; P. Sherwood, *St. Maximus the Confessor*, Newman Press, Westminster, Md., 1955.
56. Cf. P. Sherwood, *op. cit.*, pp. 70–99.
57. Cf. L. Bouyer, *op. cit.*, p. 436.

Chapter 4 Monasticism in the West

1. For further details on western monasticism, see L. Bouyer, *The Spirituality of the New Testament and the Fathers*, tr. M. P. Ryan, Desclée, New York, N.Y., 1960; M. Wolter, *The Principles of Monasticism*, tr. B. R. Sause, B. Herder, St. Louis, Mo., 1962; R. Lorenz, "Die Anfänge des abendländischen Mönchtums, im 4 Jahrhundert," in *Zeitschrift für Kirchengeschichte*, 77, 1966.
2. Eusebius, *Historia ecclesiastica*, 6, 43, 16.
3. St. Jerome, *Epistola* 127; cf. J. N. D. Kelly, *Jerome*, Harper & Row, New York, N.Y., 1975.
4. Cf. A. Paredi, *Ambrose: His Life and Times*, University of Notre Dame Press, Notre Dame, Ind., 1964.
5. Cf. J. Lienhard, *Paulinus of Nola and Early Western Monasticism*, Hanstein, Cologne, 1977.
6. Cf. J. Fontaine, *Vie de Saint Martin*, Ed. du Cerf, Paris, 1967–1969; N. Chadwick, *Poetry and Letters in Early Christian Gaul*, Bowes & Bowes, London, 1955.
7. Cf. O. Chadwick, *John Cassian*, Cambridge University Press, Cambridge, 2 ed., 1968.
8. Cassian enumerates eight capital sins, as did Evagrius. St. Gregory the Great substitutes envy for pride and combines sloth with sadness. There are seven capital sins according to common teaching: pride, sloth, covetousness, lust, anger, envy and gluttony.

9. *Conferences*, 3, 6.

10. *Conferences*, 9, 9–15.

11. *Ibid.*, 23, 3.

12. Cf. *Adversus Jovinianum*, 1, 1.

13. In the Latin Church clerical celibacy was not obligatory until the fourth century, when the Council of Elvira (Spain) imposed it on subdeacons, deacons and priests. The custom spread throughout the Church and eventually became a universal law for the Church in the West.

14. Cf. I. Hausherr, "L'erreur fondamentale et la logique du messalianisme," in *Orientalia christiana periodica*, 1, 1935, pp. 356–360.

15. Cf. E. Portalié, *A Guide to the Thought of St. Augustine*, tr. R. J. Bastian, Regnery, Chicago, Ill., 1960.

16. *De natura et gratia*, 70, 84.

17. *De doctrina christiana*, 3, 10, 15–16.

18. *De perfecta justitia hominis*, 3, 8.

19. *Sermo* 170, 8; cf. *Enarratio in Ps. 82*, 10.

20. *De quantitate animae*, 33, 70–76. In his commentary on the beatitudes and on Isa. 11:2, St. Augustine divides the stages according to the gifts of the Holy Spirit, beginning with fear of the Lord and terminating with wisdom.

21. *Enarratio in Ps. 41*.

22. *Tractatus in Joann.*, 124, 5.

23. Cf. *De consensu evangelistarum*.

24. *Sermo 169*.

25. *De civitate Dei*, 19, 19.

26. P. Pourrat, *Christian Spirituality*, tr. W. H. Mitchell and S. P. Jacques, Newman Press, Westminster, Md., 1953, Vol. I, p. 164.

27. Cf. L. Bouyer, *The Spirituality of the New Testament and the Fathers*, tr. M. P. Ryan, Desclee, New York, N.Y., 1963, p. 495.

28. Cf. *ibid.*, pp. 498–499.

29. Cf. L. Verheijen, *La règle de Saint Augustine*, Etudes Augustiniennes, 2 vols., 1967.

30. *In Ps.* 132, 6.

31. C. Peifer, "Pre-Benedictine Monasticism in the Western Church," in *The Rule of St. Benedict*, ed. T. Fry, Liturgical Press, Collegeville, Minn., 1981, p. 63.

32. Cf. C. Peifer, *art. cit.*, p. 64; R. Lorenz, *art. cit.*, footnote 1 *supra*.

33. Cf. F. Cabrol, *Saint Benedict*, Burns & Oates, London, 1934; J. McCann, *Saint Benedict*, Sheed & Ward, New York, N.Y., 1937; J. Chapman, *Saint Benedict and the Sixth Century*, Greenwood Press, Westport, Conn., 1972; T. F. Lindsay, *St. Benedict: His Life and Work*, Burns & Oates, London, 1949; I. Schuster, *Saint Benedict and His Times*, B. Herder, St. Louis, Mo., 1951; T. Maynard, *Saint Benedict and His Monks*, P. J. Kenedy, New York, N.Y., 1954.

34. C. Peifer, "The Rule of St. Benedict," in *op. cit.*, p. 73.

35. For discussion of relation between Rule of St. Benedict and *Regula Magistri*, cf. C. Peifer, *art. cit.*, pp. 79–90.
36. All quotations from the *Rule of St. Benedict*, ed. T. Fry, Liturgical Press, Collegeville, Minn., 1981.
37. *The Rule of St. Benedict*, ed. T. Fry, pp. 191–201.
38. *Ibid.*, chapter 73.
39. Cf. J. F. Kenney, *The Sources for the Early History of Ireland*, New York, N.Y., 1929; J. Ryan, *Irish Monasticism: Origins and Early Development*, Talbot Press, Dublin, 1931; L. Gougaud, *Christianity in Celtic Lands*, London, 1932.
40. Cf. J. Wilson, *Life of St. Columban*, Burns & Oates, London, 1952; F. MacManus, *Saint Columban*, Sheed & Ward, New York, N.Y., 1952.
41. Cf. F. Cayré, *Manual of Patrology*, tr. H. Howitt, Desclée, Paris, 1930, Vol. 2, p. 237.
42. Cf. C. Peifer, *art. cit.*, p. 78. However, L. Cilleruelo maintains that the members of St. Gregory's monastery were refugees from Monte Cassino after its destruction by the Lombards. Cf. "Literatura espiritual de la Edad Media," in B. J. Duque and L. S. Balust (ed.), *Historia de la Espiritualidad*, Juan Flors, Barcelona, 1969, Vol. 1, p. 685.
43. Cf. F. H. Dudden, *Gregory the Great: His Place in History and Thought*, Russell and Russell, New York, N.Y., 2 vols., 1967.
44. Cf. J. Leclercq, F. Vandenbroucke, L. Bouyer, *The Spirituality of the Middle Ages*, Burns & Oates, London, 1968.
45. Cf. *Moralia*, 2, 76–77; 31, 87; 35, 15; *In Ezech.*, 1, 4, 8; 1, 7, 7; 2, 4, 4.
46. Cf. G. C. Carluccio, *The Seven Steps to Spiritual Perfection according to St. Gregory the Great*, Ottawa, 1949.
47. *Hom. in Ezech.*, 2, 2, 8.
48. *Ibid., loc. cit.*
49. *Moralia*, 6, 61; *Hom. in Ezech.*, 1, 3, 9.
50. *Moralia*, 29.
51. Cf. *op. cit.*, 6, 56.
52. *Hom. in Ezech.*, 11, 11, 12.
53. *Op. cit.*, 2, 19, 20.
54. Cf. *Moralia*, 31, 104; *Hom. in Ezech.*, 9, 31; 2, 1, 16; 2, 10, 21.
55. Cf. *Hom. in Ezech.*, 2, 77; *Moralia*, 18, 81.
56. Cf. J. Leclercq *et al., op. cit.*, chapter 3.
57. PL 94, 657–658.
58. Cf. J. Leclercq *et al., op. cit.*, pp. 57–60.
59. Cf. *ibid.*, p. 67.

Chapter 5 Benedictine Spirituality

1. Cf. J. Lortz, *Geschichte der Kirche*, Münster, 1950; J. Leclercq, F. Vandenbroucke, L. Bouyer, *The Spirituality of the Middle Ages*, Burns

& Oates, London, 1968; L. Génicot, *La spiritualité médiévale*, Paris, 1958; J. F. Rivera Recio, "Espiritualidad popular medieval," in *Historia de la Espiritualidad*, ed. B. J. Duque-L. S. Balust, Juan Flors, Barcelona, 1969, pp. 609–657.

2. Cf. P. J. Moullins, *The Spiritual Life according to St. Isidore*, Catholic University, Washington, D.C., 1940.
3. Cf. M. T. A. Carroll, *The Venerable Bede: His Spiritual Teaching*, Catholic University, Washington, D.C., 1946.
4. Migne has two volumes (97 and 98) on Charlemagne under the title *Beati Caroli Magni Opera Omnia*. See also A. Fliche–V. Martin, "L'epoque carolingienne," in *Histoire de l'Eglise*, Vol. 7, E. Amann, Paris, 1947.
5. Cf. J. Leclercq *et al.*, *op. cit.*, pp. 75–76.
6. For a detailed study, cf. J. Winandy, *Ambroise Autpert, moine et théologien*, Paris, 1953.
7. Cf. M. Mähler, "Alcuin," in *Dictionnaire de Spiritualité*, Vol. 1, pp. 296–299.
8. L. Cilleruelo, "Literatura espiritual de la edad media," in *Historia de la Espiritualidad*, Vol. 1, p. 702.
9. Cf. PL 103, 701–1380.
10. Cf. J. Semmler, ed., *Corpus consuetudinum monasticarum*, F. Schmitt, Siegburg, 1963, Vol. 1, pp. 423–582.
11. Cf. J. Winandy, "L'oeuvre monastique de saint Benoît d'Aniane," in *Mélanges Bénédictines*, Fontenelle, 1947, pp. 237–258.
12. C. Peifer, "The Rule in History," in *The Rule of St. Benedict*, ed. T. Fry, Liturgical Press, Collegeville, Minn., 1981, pp. 122–123.
13. Cf. J. Leclercq, "Profession according to the Rule of St. Benedict," in *Rule and Life*, ed. M. B. Pennington, Cistercian Publications, Spencer, Mass., 1971, pp. 117–150.
14. Cf. C. Peifer, *art. cit.*, pp. 124–125.
15. Cf. A. Schroll, *Benedictine Monasticism as Reflected in the Warnefrid-Hildemar Commentaries on the Rule*, Columbia University, New York, N.Y., 1941.
16. Cf. P. Salmon, "Obligation de la célebration de l'office," in *L'office divin*, Paris, 1959, pp. 30–31.
17. Cf. J. Leclercq, "Dévotion et théologie mariales dans le monachisme au moyen âge," in *Maria*, Paris, 1952, Vol. 2, p. 552.
18. Cf. C. Peifer, *art. cit.*, p. 126.
19. *Ibid., loc. cit.*
20. In the beginning the *conversi* were not monks but men dedicated to a life of manual labor and accepted as *familiares* or oblates in the monastic community. Cf. J. Dubois, "The Laybrothers' Life in the 12th Century: A Form of Lay Monasticism," in *Cistercian Studies*, Vol. 7, 1972, pp. 161–213.
21. Cf. C. Peifer, *art. cit.*, p. 127; cf. J. Leclercq, "La crise du monachisme au XIe et XIIe siècles," in *Aux Sources de la spiritualité occidentale: Étapes*

et constantes, Ed. du Cerf, Paris, 1964, pp. 175–199; J. Leclercq et al., *op. cit.*, pp. 68–126.

22. Cf. A. Wilmart, "Auteurs spirituels et textes dévots du moyen âge, in *Maria*, Paris, 1952, Vol. 2, p. 552; J. Leclercq–J. Bonnes, *Un maître de la vie spirituelle* au XIIe siècle, Jean de Fécamp, Paris, 1946.
23. Cf. G. Sitwell, *Spiritual Writers of the Middle Ages*, Hawthorn, New York, N.Y., 1961, p. 26.
24. Cf. A. Wilmart, *op. cit.*, p. 127.
25. J. Leclercq–J. P. Bonnes, *op. cit.*, p. 182.
26. Cf. K. Bihlmeyer–H. Tüchle, *Church History*, tr. V. Mills–F. Muller, Newman Press, Westminster, Md., 1959, Vol. 2, pp. 103–166.
27. PL 103, 575–663.
28. Cf. P. Doyere, "Erémitisme," in *Dictionnaire de Spiritualité*, fasc. 28–29, 1960. Several eremitical communities were founded during this period: Vallombrosa in 1038; Grandmont in 1076; Fontévrault in 1101; and a congregation of Scottish monks in Germany in 1075. Fontevrault was a double monastery of men and women under the jurisdiction of an abbess.
29. Cf. J. Leclercq *et al.*, *op. cit.*, pp. 150–156.
30. PL 153, 420–606; cf. A. Wilmart, "La chronique des premiers char- treux," in *Rev. Mabillon*, Vol. 16, 1926, pp. 77–112.
31. J. Leclercq *et al.*, *op. cit.*, p. 153.
32. PL 184, 475 ff.
33. *Ibid.*, *loc. cit.*
34. Cf. L. Lekai, *The White Monks*, Okauchee, Wis., 1953; B. Lackner, *The Eleventh Century Background of Citeaux*, Cistercian Publications, Washington, D.C., 1972.
35. G. Sitwell, *op. cit.*, p. 43.
36. Cf. J. Leclercq *et al.*, *op. cit.*, p. 187; J. M. Mattoso, "Espiritualidad monástica medieval," in *Historia de la Espiritualidad*, Vol. 1, p. 895.
37. Cf. Introduction to J. Dubois, *De l'amitié spirituelle*, Bruges, 1948.
38. Cf. J. Lekai, *op. cit.*; L. Bouyer, *La spiritualité de Citeaux*, Paris, 1955.
39. Cf. PL 182, *praef. gen.*, p. 23.
40. G. Sitwell, *op. cit.*, p. 44.
41. A. H. Bredero, "Etudes sur la *vita prima* de St. Bernard," in *Analecta S. Ord. Cist.*, Vol. 17, 1961, and Vol. 18, 1962.
42. For details on the life and work of St. Bernard, cf. AA.VV., *Bernard of Clairvaux*, Paris, 1963; J. Leclercq, *op. cit.*, pp. 191–204; E. Vascan- dard, "Saint Bernard," in *Dictionnaire de Théologie Catholique*, Vol. 1, pp. 746–785; A. de Bail, "Bernard," in *Dictionnaire de Spiritualité*, Vol. 1, pp. 1454–1499.
43. The works of St. Bernard are found in PL 182–183.
44. W. Yeomans, "St. Bernard of Clairvaux," in *Spirituality through the Centuries*, ed. J. Walsh, P. J. Kenedy, New York, N.Y., 1964, p. 109.
45. I Jn., chap. 4.

46. *De diligendo Deo*, PL 182, 274. The phrase was also used by Severus of Milevum and attributed to St. Augustine.

47. Cf. *De gradibus humilitatis*, PL 182, 941 ff.

48. Cf. W. Yeomans, *art. cit.*, p. 117.

49. Letter 34, PL 182, 440.

50. Letter 91, PL 182, 224.

51. *De diligendo Deo*, PL 182, 974.

52. Cf. *In cantica*, PL 183. Cf. also the authoritative work by E. Gilson, *The Mystical Theology of St. Bernard*, tr. A. Downes, Sheed & Ward, London, 1940. According to D. Ramos, *Obras completas de San Bernardo*, BAC, Madrid, 1953, St. Bernard considered the highest degree of love to be most rare in this life, but something to which all should aspire.

53. *In cantica, loc. cit.* When speaking of the mystical union, St. Bernard always refers to God as the object, as do St. Augustine and the pseudo-Dionysius. The role of the humanity of Christ in mystical experience was discussed by Cassian, the Rhineland mystics, Thomas à Kempis, Gerson and St. Teresa of Avila.

54. Cf. *De diversis*, Sermon 87; *In cantica*, Sermons 1, 68, 83–85.

55. Cf. *In cantica*, Sermons 9, 20, 23, 25, 33, 41, 42, 49, 56, 57, 76, 78.

56. Cf. *In cantica*, Sermon 79.

57. *Ibid.*, Sermon 41.

58. *Op. cit.*, Sermon 23.

59. *In cantica*, Sermon 49.

60. Cf. W. Yeomans, *art. cit.*, p. 116.

61. Cf. J. Leclercq *et al.*, *op. cit.*, p. 254.

62. G. Sitwell, *op. cit.*, p. 57.

63. The works of William of St. Thierry are found in PL 180, 205–726; 184, 365–408. The pioneer in research on William is J. M. Déchanet: *Guillaume de Saint-Thierry. L'homme et son oeuvre*, Bruges–Paris, 1942; and *Aux sources de la spiritualité de Guillaume de Saint-Thierry*, Bruges, 1940. Cf. also O. Brooke, "The Trinitarian Aspect of the Ascent of the Soul to God in the Theology of William of Saint-Thierry," in *Recherches de theologie ancienne et médiévale*, Vol. 26, 1959, pp. 85–127.

64. Cf. J. Déchanet, *Aux sources de la spiritualité de Guillaume de Saint-Thierry*, Bruges, 1940.

65. Cf. G. Sitwell, *op. cit.*, p. 60.

66. Cf. *Epist. ad Fratres de Monte Dei*, PL 184, 315–316. William here follows Cassian's division of prayer. "The different techniques of mental prayer had not yet been worked out, and contemplation was not connected specifically with prayer as it later came to be" (G. Sitwell, *op. cit.*, p. 58).

67. Our source for this material is O. Brooke, *art. cit.*, and "William of St. Thierry," in *Spirituality through the Centuries*, ed. J. Walsh, pp. 121–131.

68. Cf. O. Brooke, "William of St. Thierry," in *Spirituality through the Centuries*, pp. 125–126. William states in *Speculum fidei*: "The Mediator . . . though he is God eternal, became man in time, in order that through him who is eternal and yet subject to time, we may pass through the temporal to the eternal" (PL 180, 382–383).

69. *Aenigma fidei*, PL 180, 426.

70. O. Brooke, *art. cit.*, pp. 126–127.

71. Cf. *ibid.*, p. 127.

72. *Epist. ad Fratres de Monte Dei*, PL 184, 348.

73. Cf. *Speculum fidei*, PL 180, 393; *Aenigma fidei*, PL 180, 399.

74. Cf. *Epist. ad Fratres de Monte Dei*, PL 184, 349.

75. *De contemplando Deo*, PL 184, 376. "The great contribution of William of St. Thierry is to have evolved a theology of the Trinity which is essentially mystical, and a mystical theology which is essentially Trinitarian. He is therefore the initiator of the tradition of Trinitarian mysticism, which is to be found especially in the writings of Ruysbroeck, Eckhart, Tauler and Suso" (O. Brooke, *art. cit.*, p. 130).

76. Aelred's works can be found in PL 195, 210–796 and PL 184, 849–870.

77. *Speculum caritatis*, PL 195, 566.

78. Cf. J. Leclercq *et al.*, *op. cit.*, p. 208. For further details cf. W. Daniel, *The Life of Aelred of Rievaulx*, London, 1950.

79. Cf. E. Power, *Medieval Women*, Cambridge University Press, Cambridge, 1976; R. Bridenthal–C. Koonz, *Becoming Visible: Women in European History*, Houghton Mifflin, Boston, Mass., 1977.

80. Cf. Appendix 1, *The Rule of St. Benedict*, ed. T. Fry, Liturgical Press, Collegeville, Minn., 1981.

81. Cf. J. Leclercq, *op. cit.*, p. 129.

82. Cf. M. Bernards, *Speculum virginum*, Cologne, 1955.

83. The works of St. Hildegarde are in PL 197. Cf. also *Vies des saints et bienheureux*, published by the Benedictines of Paris, 1950, Vol. 9, pp. 336–371.

84. Cf. F. W. Roth, *Das Gebetbuch der Hl. Elisabeth von Schönau*, Augsburg, 1886; D. Besse, *Les mystiques bénédictins*, Paris, 1922; pp. 202–215; *Vies des saints et bienheureux*, Paris, 1950.

85. J. D. Mansi, *Sacrorum Conciliorum nova et amplissima collectio*, Austria, 1961, Vol. 13, p. 660.

86. Apostolic Constitution *Ne in agro,* Corp. Iur. Can., Vol. 2, 1086.

87. Apostolic Constitution *Regularis disciplinae restitutione*, Bull. Rom., Vol. 10, 773.

88. An excellent study on lay brothers has been done by D. K. Hallinger, "Woher kommen die Laienbrüder?", in *Analecta S. Ord. Cist.*, Vol. 13, 1957, pp. 1–104; cf. also M. Wolter, *The Principles of Monasticism*, tr. and ed. B. Sause, B. Herder, St. Louis, Mo., 1962, pp. 459–461;

481–486; P. Mulhern, *The Early Dominican Lay Brother*, Washington, D.C., 1944.
89. Cf. J. Leclercq *et al.*, *op. cit.*, p. 183.

Chapter 6 *Spirituality of the Middle Ages*

1. Cf. J. Leclercq, F. Vandenbroucke, L. Bouyer, *The Spirituality of the Middle Ages*, Burns & Oates, London, 1968, pp. 142–144; L. Génicot, *La Spiritualité Médiévale*, Paris, 1958, pp. 43–44.
2. Cf. J. D. Mansi, *Conciliorum Nova et Amplissima Collectio*, Austria, 1961, Vol. 23, pp. 197 and 329; J. F. Rivera Recio, "Espiritualidad Popular Medieval," in *Historia de la Espiritualidad*, ed. B. J. Duque–L. S. Balust, Juan Flors, Barcelona, 1969, Vol. 1, p. 633.
3. Cf. K. Richstätter, *Christusfrömmigkeit in ihrer historischen Entfaltung*, Cologne, 1949.
4. The standard reference is E. Mâle, *L'art réligieux du XIIᵉ siècle en France*, Paris, 1922; cf. also E. de Bruyne, *L'esthétique au moyen âge*, Louvain, 1947.
5. P. de Blois, *Liber de confessione sacramentali*, PL 207, 1088–1089.
6. The hymn has been erroneously attributed to St. Bernard. Cf. A. Wilmart, "Le 'jubilus' sur le nom de Jésus, dit de saint Bernard," in *Ephem. liturg.*, Vol. 57, 1943, p. 285.
7. Gerboh of Reichersberg (1169), *De aedificio Dei*, PL 194, 1302.
8. The First Lateran Council (1123) and the Second Lateran Council (1139) made strict laws to enforce celibacy on priests and monks. At this time celibacy was made obligatory for all clerics in major orders in the Latin Church.
9. J. Leclercq *et al.*, *op. cit.*, pp. 260–261. For a description of extreme practitioners of poverty, cf. pp. 261–268.
10. Some say that the elevation of the Host began in Paris in 1210; others maintain that it was already the practice early in the twelfth century. Cf. J. Jungmann, *The Mass of the Roman Rite*, tr. F. A. Brunner, 2 vols., New York, N.Y., 1951–1952.
11. Denz. 437.
12. Cf. E. W. Kemp, *Canonization and Authority in the Western Church*, London, 1948.
13. St. Bernard, *De laude novae militiae*; cf. J. Leclercq, C. H. Talbot, H. Rochais, *S. Bernardi Opera*, Rome, 1959, Vol. 3, pp. 213–239; R. Grousset, *Histoire des croisades et du Royaume franc de Jérusalem*, Paris, 1934–1939, 5 vols.
14. Cf. D. Rops, *L'Eglise de la catédrale et de la croissade*, Paris, 1952; A. Fliche–V. Martin, *L'Histoire de l'Eglise*, Paris, 1940, Vol. 7, pp. 483–487; Vol. 8, pp. 462–478.
15. Letter of January 28, 1092 (PL 151, 338); cf. C. Dereine, "Chanoines," in *Dictionnaire d'hist. et de géog. ecclés.*, Vol. 12, 1963, cols. 385–386; J. Leclercq *et al.*, *op. cit.*, pp. 137–145.

16. M. H. Vicaire, *The Apostolic Life*, tr. K. Pond, Priory Press, Chicago, Ill., 1966, p. 53.

17. Cf. G. Bardy, "Chanoines," in *Catholici me*, Paris, 1949, Vol. 2, pp. 900–902; A. Schmitz, "Chanoines Reguliers," in *Dictionnaire de Spiritualite*, Vol. 2, p. 469; M. H. Vicaire, *op. cit.*, pp. 55–56.

18. Cf. M. H. Vicaire, *op. cit.*, pp. 66–77. Hildebrand strongly criticized the canonical rule of Aix-la-Chapelle for not imposing poverty on the diocesan priest canons.

19. Cf. J. Leclercq, *et al.*, *op. cit.*, pp. 127–130.

20. *Contra clericos regulares proprietarios* in PL 145, 486.

21. For the disputes concerning the *vita apostolica*, cf. M. H. Vicaire, *op. cit.*, pp. 84–87.

22. Cf. *op. cit.*, pp. 82–83.

23. PL 213, 814–850.

24. Other communities of canons are: Canons Regular of the Lateran (Rome); Canons of St. Rufus (Avignon); Canons Regular of the Holy Sepulchre (Jerusalem); Canons of Holy Cross, known as Crosiers (Low Lands).

25. Hugo, the successor of St. Norbert as head of the Premonstratensians, described their life as eremitical according to the canonical profession; cf. *Annales Ord. Praemonstr.*, Nancy, 1734, Vol. 1, chap. 42.

26. Cf. F. Petit, *La spiritualité des Prémontrés aux XIIe et XIIIe siècles*, Paris, 1947; P. Lefèvre, *Les statuts de Prémontré*, Louvain, 1946; H. M. Calvin, "The White Canons in England," in *Rév. d'hist. ecclés.*, Vol. 46, 1951, pp. 1–25.

27. Cf. J. Bulloch, *Adam of Dryburgh*, London, 1958.

28. St. Norbert also made provisions for a feminine branch of the Order and for lay brothers, although the Norbertines are a clerical institute.

29. Cf. J. Leclercq *et al.*, *op. cit.*, pp. 149–150.

30. Cf. M. D. Chenu, *La théologie au XIIe siècle*, Paris, 1957; J. Leclercq *et al.*, *op. cit.*, pp. 239–242,

31. R. G. Villoslada, *Historia de la Iglesia*, BAC, Madrid, Vol. 2, p. 897.

32. K. Bihlmeyer–H. Tüchle, *Church History*, Newman Press, Westminster, Md., 1958, p. 247.

33. M. Grabmann, *Die Geschichte der scholastischen Methode*, Freiburg. 1909–1911, Vol. 2, p. 259.

34. Hugh of St. Victor's works are found in PL 175 to 177.

35. *In Eccles.*, sermon 1, PL 175, 117–118.

36. Cf. *In Eccles.*, loc. cit.; *De modo dicendi et med.*, PL 176, 877; R. Baron, *Science et sagesse chez Hugo de S.-Victor*, Paris, 1957; D. Lasic, *Hugonis a S. Victore theologia perfectionis*, Rome, 1956.

37. F. Cayré, *Manual of Patrology*, tr. H. Howitt, Desclée, Paris, 1930, Vol. 2, p. 453.

38. *De Trinitate*, PL 196, 887–992; cf. also A. M. Ethier, *Le "De Trinitate" de Richard de S.-Victor*, Paris–Ottawa, 1939.

39. *Benjamin minor*, PL 196, 1–63; *Benjamin major*, PL 196, 64 FF.; cf. also J. M. Déchanet, "Contemplation au XIIe siècle," in *Dictionnaire de Spiritualité*, Vol. 2, pp. 1961–1966; P. Pourrat, *Christian Spirituality*, tr. W. H. Mitchell and S. P. Jacques, Newman Press, Westminster, Md., 1953, Vol. 2, pp. 120–129.

40. Richard of St. Victor, *The Mystical Ark (Benjamin Major)*, tr. G. A. Zinn, Paulist Press, New York, N.Y., 1979, p. 157.

41. *Ibid.* St. Thomas Aquinas refers to this definition in *Summa theol.*, IIa IIae, q. 180, a. 3, ad 1, but in speaking of the "movements" of contemplation, he follows the pseudo-Dionysius.

42. *Benjamin major*, PL 196, 64.

43. Cf. *op. cit.*, PL 196, 65.

44. Cf. *op. cit.*, PL 196, 66.

45. Cf. E. Kulesza, *La doctrine mystique de Richard de S.-Victor*, Saint-Maximin, 1924; P. Pourrat, *op. cit.*, Vol. 2, p. 225.

46. Cf. M. D. Chenu, *op. cit.*; Y. Congar, *A History of Theology*, Doubleday, New York, N.Y., 1968.

47. R. W. Southern, *The Making of the Middle Ages*, London, 1953; H. Roshdall–F. M. Powicke, *The Universities of Europe in the Middle Ages*, 3 vols., Oxford, 1942.

48. Cf. J. De Ghellinck, *La mouvement théologique du XIIe siècle*, Paris, 1914, pp. 41–56; 311–338.

49. Cf. Y. Congar, *op. cit.*, pp. 63–65, *passim*.

50. Cf. *Prosologion*, PL 158, 223; 225.

51. *Ibid.*, PL 158, 227.

52. *De Fide Trinit., et de Incarn.*, PL 158, 263.

53. As quoted in Y. Congar, *op. cit.*, p. 68.

54. Cf. PL 191 and 192; "Pierre Lombard," in *Dictionnaire de Théologie Catholique*, Vol. 12, cols. 1941–2019.

55. J. Leclercq *et al.*, *op. cit.*, p. 242.

56. Cf. Laurent, *Monumenta historica S. Dominici*, Paris, 1933, Vol. 15, p. 60.

57. Jordan of Saxony, *Libellus de principiis ordinis praedicatorum*, ed. H. C. Scheeben in *Monumenta O.P. Historica*, Rome, 1935, pp. 1–88.

58. The Fourth Lateran Council forbade the foundation of new religious institutes unless they were extensions of an existing institute or adopted an approved Rule.

59. W. Hinnebusch, *The History of the Dominican Order*, New York, N.Y., 1965, Vol. 1, p. 44. The Rule of St. Augustine was also adopted by numerous other religious institutes founded in the twelfth and thirteenth centuries.

60. Cf. W. Hinnebusch, *op. cit.*, p. 49. On February 17, 1217, a third papal bull, *Jus petentium*, specified that a Dominican friar could not transfer to any but a stricter religious institute and approved the stability pledged to the Dominican Order rather than to a particular church or monastery.

61. *I Constitutiones S.O.P.*, prologue; cf. P. Mandonnet–M. H. Vicaire, *S. Dominique: l'idee, l'homme et l'oeuvre*, 2 vols., Paris, 1938.
62. Cf. W. Hinnebusch, *op. cit.*, p. 84.
63. *Contra impugnantes Dei cultum et religionem.*
64. *I Const. S.O.P.*, prologue; cf. W. Hinnebusch, *op. cit.*, p. 84.
65. *I Const. S.O.P.*, n. 4; cf. W. Hinnebusch, *op. cit.*, p. 351.
66. Cf. M. S. Gillet, *Encyclical Letter on Dominican Spirituality*, Santa Sabina, Rome, 1945; Mandonnet–Vicaire, *op. cit.*; V. Walgrave, *Dominican Self-Appraisal in the Light of the Council*, Priory Press, Chicago, Ill., 1968; S. Tugwell, *The Way of the Preacher*, Templegate, Springfield, Ill., 1979; H. Clérissac, *The Spirit of St. Dominic*, London, 1939.
67. V. Walgrave, *op. cit.*, pp. 39–42.
68. Cf. M. D. Chenu, *Introduction a l'étude de Saint Thomas d'Aquin*, Montreal–Paris, 1950; Y. Congar, *History of Theology*; V. Walgrave, *op. cit.*, pp. 285–318.
69. A. D. Sertillanges, *Saint Thomas Aquinas and His Work*, tr. G. Anstruther, London, 1957, pp. 5–9.
70. "Augustinians" here refers to all who followed the theological system of St. Augustine.
71. Y. Congar, *A History of Theology*, pp. 103–114.
72. St. Thomas treats of Christian perfection and the spiritual life in *Summa theol.*, IIa IIae, qq. 179–183; *De perfectione vitae spiritualis*; *III Sent.*, dist. 35.
73. This Thomistic doctrine is found in *Summa theol.*, Ia IIae, qq. 61–68; 109–113; IIa IIae, qq. 23–27; 179–183. Cf. also R. Garrigou–Lagrange, *The Three Ages of the Interior Life*, tr. T. Doyle, 2 vols., B. Herder, St. Louis, Mo., 1948–1949; J. G. Arintero, *The Mystical Evolution*, tr. J. Aumann, B. Herder, St. Louis, Mo., 2 vols., 1950–1951; J. Aumann, *Spiritual Theology*, Sheed & Ward, London, 1980.
74. Cf. *Summa theol.*, IIa IIae, qq. 179–182.
75. Cf. J. Aumann, *Action and Contemplation*, in the English translation of the *Summa theologica*, McGraw-Hill, New York, N.Y., 1966, pp. 85–89; 114–123.
76. Cf. *Summa theol.*, IIa IIae, q. 180.
77. Cf. *ibid.*, *loc. cit.*
78. *Ibid.*
79. *Summa theol.*, IIa IIae, q. 180, art. 5.
80. Cf. P. Lejeune, "Contemplation," in *Dictionnaire de Theologie Catholique*, vol. 3, cols. 1616–1631; J. Aumann, *Action and Contemplation*, pp. 103–108.
81. Cf. *Summa theol.*, IIa IIae, q. 23, art. 1.
82. Cf. *op. cit.*, q. 24, art. 8.
83. *Summa theol.*, Ia, q. 82, art. 3.
84. *Ibid.*, Ia IIae, q. 3, art. 3–5.

85. Cf. *ibid.*, Ia IIae, q. 3, art. 5.
86. Cf. P. Philippe, "La contemplation au XIII° siecle," in *Dictionnaire de Spiritualité*, Vol. 2, pp. 1987–1988.
87. Thomas of Celano, *Legenda*, 33.
88. Cf. Thomas of Celano, *Vita I*, 51.
89. Cf. ibid., *Vita II*, 70.
90. For biography of St. Francis of Assisi, cf. J. Joergensen, *St. Francis of Assisi*, tr. S. O'Connor, London, 1922; R. M. Huber, *Sources of Franciscan History*, Milwaukee, Wis., 1944 I. Gobry, S. *François d'Assise et l'ésprit franciscain*, Paris, 1947.
91. Cf. E. Alençon, "Frères Mineurs," in *Dictionnaire de Théologie Catholique*, Vol. 6, pp. 809–812.
92. More than a hundred Franciscans have received the stigmata; they are outnumbered only by the Dominicans.
93. Cf. K. Bihlmeyer, *op. cit.*, pp. 322–338; J. Leclercq *et al.*, *op. cit.*, pp. 365–377; F. Cayré, *op. cit.*, pp. 470–690.
94. St. Thomas wrote in defense of the mendicant orders: *De perfectione vitae spiritualis; Contra pestiferam doctrinam retrahentium homines a religionis ingressu.* St. Bonaventure wrote: *De paupertate Christi; Quare Fratres minores praedicent et confessiones audiant.*
95. Cf. *Bullarium O.P.*, Vol. 1, Rome, 1729–1740, p. 338.
96. For details on St. Bonaventure, cf. *Opera Omnia*, Quaracchi, 1882–1892; E. Smeets, "S. Bonaventure," in *Dictionnaire de Théologie Catholique*, Vol. 2, pp. 962–986; P. Pourrat, *op. cit.*, vol. 2, pp. 176–184.
97. Cf. F. Cayré, *op. cit.*, p. 498.
98. Cf. Y. Congar, *op. cit.*, pp. 117–120; E. Gilson, *La philosophie de S. Bonaventure*, Paris, 1924.
99. E. Smeets, "Bonaventure," in *Dictionnaire de Théologie Catholique*, Vol. 2, p. 967.
100. For testimonies to St. Bonaventure, cf. *Opera Omnia*, Quaracchi edition.
101. Cf. E. Smeets, *art. cit.*, p. 977.
102. Cf. De Wulf, *Histoire de la philosophie médiévale*, p. 291; E. Longpré, "La théologie mystique de S. Bonaventure," in *Arch. Francis. Hist.*, Vol. 14, 1921.
103. Cf. F. Cayré, *op. cit.*, Vol. 2, pp. 497–526; P. Pourrat, *op. cit.*, Vol. 2, pp. 176–184; J. Leclercq *et al.*, *op. cit.*, pp. 370–377.
104. Cf. Helyot, *Histoire des ordres monastiques*, Paris, 1721; M. Heimbucher, *Die Orden und Kongregationen der Katolischen Kirche*, 3 ed., Paderborn, 1933–1934; J. Leclercq *et al.*, *op. cit.*, pp. 474–480.
105. Cf. M. Vinken, "Croisiers," in *Dict. hist. géogr. eccl.*, Vol. 13, pp. 1042–1062.
106. Cf. D. Gutiérrez, "Ermites de Saint Augustin," in *Dictionnaire de Spiritualité*, Vol. 4, cols. 983–1018.
107. Cf. A. M. Lépicier, *L'Ordre des Servites de Marie*, Paris, 1929.

108. Cf. C. Mazzarini, *L'Ordine Trinitario nella Chiesa e nella Storia*, Turin, 1964; "Mercedarios," in *Enciclopedia Universal Ilustrada Europeo-americana*, Espasa, Madrid, Vol. 34, pp. 816–819.
109. Cf. J. Zimmerman, "Carmes," in *Dictionnaire de Théologie Catholique*, Vol. 2, cols. 1776–1792.
110. Cf. J. Leclercq, *op. cit.*, pp. 344–372; E. W. McDonnell, *The Béguines and Beghards in Medieval Culture*, New Brunswick, N.J., 1954; J. B. Porion, *Hadewijck d'Anvers*, Paris, 1954; Vernet-Mierlo, "Beghards" and "Béguines," in *Dictionnaire de Spiritualité*, Vol. 1, pp. 1329–1352.

Chapter 7 Dionysian Spirituality and Devotio Moderna

1. Cf. F. Cayré, *Manual of Patrology*, tr. H. Howitt, Desclée, Paris, 1930, Vol. 2, p. 702.
2. Cf. W. Johnston, *The Mysticism of the Cloud of Unknowing*, Desclée, New York, N.Y., 1967.
3. For anthologies of the writings of the Rhineland mystics: S. M. Gieraths, *Reichtum des Lebans. Die deutsche Dominikanermystik des 14 Jahrhundert*, Düsseldorf, 1956; H. Kunisch, *Ein Textbuch aus der altdeutschen Mystik*, Hamburg, 1958; F. W. Wentzlaff-Eggbert, *Deutsche Mystik zwischen Mittelalter und Neuzeit*, Tübingen, 1947.
4. G. Sitwell, *Spiritual Writers of the Middle Ages*, Hawthorn, New York, N.Y., 1961, p. 75.
5. Cf. S. Roisin, "L'efflorescence cistercienne et le courant feminin de la spiritualité au XIIIe siécle," in *Rev. Hist. Eccles*, Vol. 39, 1943, pp. 343–378.
6. For further information on Mechtild of Magdeburg, cf. H. Tillman, *Studien zum Dialog bei Mechtild von Magdeburg*, Marburg, 1933; J. Ancelet-Hustache, *Mechtilde de Magdebourg*, Paris, 1926.
7. Cf. S. Roisin, *art. cit.* Dante introduces St. Mechtild in canto 33 of the *Divine Comedy* as a guide and interpreter with a sweet and melodious voice.
8. Devotion to the wound in Christ's side was extremely widespread during this period and it has its origins in the biblical descriptions of the crucifixion as well as some of the commentaries of the Fathers.
9. Cf. H. Graef, *The Story of Mysticism*, Doubleday, New York, N.Y., 1965, pp. 161–164.
10. Cf. J. Leclercq, F. Vandenbroucke, L. Bouyer, *The Spirituality of the Middle Ages*, Burns & Oates, London, 1961, pp. 452–453.
11. Cf. P. Pourrat, *Christian Spirituality*, Newman Press, Westminster, Md., 1953, Vol. II, pp. 92–98.
12. Thus, Mechtild of Magdeburg stated in *Das fliessende Licht der Gottheit* that the soul shares so intimately in the divine nature that nothing intervenes between the soul and God.

13. For a bibliography of texts, cf. F. W. Oediger, *Über die Bildung der Geistlichen in späten Mittelalter*, Leiden, 1953.
14. Cf. Denz. 501–529; M. H. Laurent, "Autour du procès de Maître Eckhart," in *Div. Thom. F.*, Vol. 39, 1936, pp. 331–349; 430–447.
15. Sermon 12; cf. Denz. 527.
16. Cf. J. Ancelet-Hustache, *op. cit.*, p. 136.
17. Cf. A. Daniels, *Beitr. Geschichte Philos. Mittelalters*, Münster, 1923, Vol. 23, p. 15.
18. Cf. Denz. 501–529. For editions of Eckhart's works, cf. E. Benz–J. Koch, *Meister Eckhart. Die deutschen und lateinischen Werke*, 5 vols., Stuttgart, 1936—; J. Quint, *Meister Eckhart. Deutsche Predigten und Traktate*, Munich, 1955; R. B. Blackney, *Meister Eckhart, A Modern Translation*, Harper & Row, New York, N.Y., 1957; M. O'C. Walshe, *Meister Eckhart: German Sermons and Treatises*, 2 vols., Dulverton & Watkins, London, 1979–1981.
19. Cf. R. L. Oechslin, "Eckhart," in *Dictionnaire de Spiritualité*, Vol. 4, cols. 93–116; F. Vernet, "Eckhart," in *Dictionnaire de Théologie Catholique*, Vol. 4, cols. 2057–2081.
20. The first critical edition of Tauler's sermons was edited by F. Vetter (Berlin, 1910). None of Tauler's letters are extant. Cf. F. Vetter, *Die Predigten Taulers*, Berlin, 1910; A. L. Corin, *Sermons de J. Tauler et autres ècrits mystiques*, 2 vols., Paris, 1924–1929; J. Tauler, *Spiritual Conferences*, tr. E. Colledge and Sr. M. Jane, B. Herder, St. Louis, Mo., 1961.
21. Tauler did not teach that the soul is impeccable as a result of its union with God; it must still work out its salvation in holy fear. Neither did he condemn good works; in fact, he strongly opposed the passivity taught by the Quietists.
22. For detailed information on Tauler, cf. *Johannes Tauler, ein deutscher Mystiker*, ed. P. Filthaut, Editorial Driewer, Essen, 1961; J. M. Clark, *The Great German Mystics*, Macmillan, New York, N.Y., 1949.
23. Cf. P. Strauch, *Allgemeine deutsche Bibliographie*, Vol. 38, p. 171.
24. Henry Suso was born Henry von Berg, but he used his mother's maiden name, Seuss or Seuse. Cf. E. Amann, "Suso, Le bienheureux Henri," in *Dictionnaire de Théologie Catholique*, Vol. 14, cols. 2859–2864; S.M.C., *Suso: Saint and Poet*, Oxford, 1947; J. M. Clark, *op. cit.*; J. A. Bizet, *Mystiques allemands*, Paris, 1957.
25. Cf. K. Bihlmeyer, *Henrich Seuse, deutsche Schriften*, Stuttgart, 1907, transcribed in modern German by E. Diederich, Iena, 1911. For an excellent English translation of Suso's works, cf. N. Heller, *The Exemplar*, tr. Sr. Ann Edward, 2 vols., Priory Press, Chicago, Ill., 1962.
26. N. Heller, *op cit.*, Vol. 1, p. xviii.
27. The Brethren of the Free Spirit should not be confused with the *Gottesfreunde*. The latter were members of an orthodox spiritual movement under the leadership of John Tauler, Henry Suso and Henry von Nördlingen.

28. Cf. J. M. Clark, *op. cit.*; C. Gröber, *Der Mystiker Heinrich Seuse*, Freiburg, 1941.

29. There is a dispute concerning the original text: whether it is the one published by Luther in 1516 and 1518 or the one re-edited by Pfeiffer in 1851. Cf. G. Baring, *"Neues von der 'Theologia Deutsch' und ihrer Weltweider Bedeutung,"* *Archiv. f. Reformationsgeschichte*, Vol. 48, 1957.

30. Cf. M. A. Lücker, *Meister Eckhart und die Devotio Moderna*, Leiden, 1950; G. I. Lieftinck, *Die middelnederlansche Taulerhandschriften*, Groningen, 1936.

31. *See* St. Axters, *La spiritualité des Pays-Bas*, Louvain-Paris, 1948; J. Huijben, "Y a-t-il une spiritualité flamande?" in *Vie Spirituelle. Suppl.*, Vol. 50, 1937, pp. 129–147; L. Brigué, "Ruysbroeck," in *Dictionnaire de Théologie Catholique*, Vol. 14, cols. 408–420.

32. The works of Ruysbroeck were known in France, Italy and Spain through the translation of Surius, *D. Joannis Rusbrochii opera omnia*, Cologne, 1552, 1555, 1609, 1692; for English versions cf. *The Spiritual Espousals*, tr. E. Colledge, New York, N.Y., 1963; *The Seven Steps of the Ladder of Spiritual Love*, tr. F. S. Taylor, London, 1944.

33. "What little we are told of Bloemardinne by Pomerius, the early fifteenth-century biographer of Ruysbroeck, shows plainly enough that she had preached . . . . a Manichaean dualism which taught that those who in this life attain to a region of grace can no longer sin, that they are 'free in spirit' from the flesh, which may be left to do as it pleases, and from the law, which binds only the imperfect" (E. Colledge, "John Ruysbroeck," in *Spirituality through the Centuries*, ed. J. Walsh, New York, N.Y., p. 201).

34. Cf. E. O'Brien, *Varieties of Mystic Experience*, Holt, Rinehart & Winston, New York, N.Y., 1964, p. 186. For other evaluations of the work and influence of Ruysbroeck, cf. D'Aygalliers–A. Wautier, *Ruysbroeck the Admirable*, Dutton, 1925; A. Ampe, "La théologie mystique de l'ascension de l'âme selon le Bx. Jean de Ruusbroec," in *Revue d'ascétique et de mystique*, Vol. 36, 1960, pp. 188–201; 273–302.

35. Cf. W. A. Pantin, *The English Church in the Fourteenth Century*, Cambridge, 1955; H. Graef, *The Story of Mysticism*, Doubleday, New York, N.Y., 1965, pp. 205–212.

36. Editions of the *Ancrene Riwle* have been made by M. Day, London, 1952, and A. C. Baugh, London, 1956. Cf. J. Leclercq, F. Vandenbroucke, L. Bouyer, *op. cit.*, pp. 275–277.

37. For additional information cf. E. Allen, *Writings Ascribed to Richard Rolle and Materials for his Biography*, London, 1927; *The Fire of Love and Mending of Life*, tr. R. Misynand and ed. F. M. Cowper, London, 1920; *English Writings of Richard Rolle*, ed. H. E. Allen, Oxford, 1931; *Richard Rolle of Hampole, an English Father of the Church, and his Followers*, ed. C. Horstman, 2 vols., London, 1927; E. Arnould, *The*

Melis Amoris of Richard Rolle, Oxford, 1957; E. McKinnon, *Studies in Fourteenth Century English Mysticism*, Urbana, Ill., 1934.

38. G. Sitwell, *op. cit.*, pp. 88–89.
39. *Incendium amoris*, II, chap. 3.
40. Cf. D. Knowles, *English Mystics*, London, 1927, pp. 78–80.
41. Cf. G. Hart, *Sense and Thought: A Study in Mysticism*, London, 1936. For editions of *The Cloud*, cf. *The Cloud of Unknowing*, edited by P. Hodgson, London, 1958; translation in modern English by J. McCann in the Orchard Series, 6 rev. ed., London, 1952; see also detailed study by W. Johnston, *The Mysticism of the Cloud of Unknowing*, New York, N.Y., 1967.
42. Cf. W. Johnston, *op. cit.*, pp. 1–2.
43. *The Scale of Perfection*, ed. E. Underhill, London, 1923; also translated into modern English by G. Sitwell, London, 1953. Cf. H. Gardner, "The Text of the *Scale of Perfection*," in *Medium Alvum*, Vol. 5, 1936, pp. 11–30, and "Walter Hilton and the Mystical Tradition in England," in *Essays and Studies*, Vol. 22, pp. 103–127.
44. *The Scale of Perfection*, tr. G. Sitwell, London, 1953, p. 64.
45. Cf. G. Sitwell, *op. cit.*, p. 246.
46. Cf. G. Sitwell, *Spiritual Writers of the Middle Ages*, p. 100; A. M. Reynolds, *A Showing of God's Love*, London, 1958; P. Molinari, *Julian of Norwich*, New York–London, 1958; *Julian of Norwich: Showings*, tr. E. Colledge-J. Walsh, Paulist Press, New York, N.Y., 1978.
47. Cf. R. Hudleston (ed.), *Julian of Norwich*, Newman, Westminster, Md., 1952.
48. *The Book of Margery Kempe*, a modern version by W. Butler-Bowden, London, 1936.
49. Cf. G. Sitwell, *op. cit.*, p. 104.
50. J. Busch, *Chronicon. can. reg. Windesemensis*, Antwerp, 1621, Vol. 2, p. xvii; P. Desbognie, "Devotion moderne," in *Dictionnaire de Spiritualité*, Vol. 3, cols. 727–747.
51. *Imitation of Christ*, I, chaps. 1–3, *passim*.
52. "For example, Wyclif in the late fourteenth century was calling in question the justification of the whole religious life in its technical sense, the life of the three vows, and when Gerson wrote a treatise on clerical celibacy in 1413, he was able to quote many opinions demanding its suppression" (G. Sitwell, *op. cit.*, p. 108).
53. Cf. P. Pourrat, *Christian Spirituality*, Newman, Westminster, Md., 1953, Vol. 2, p. 254; A. Hyma; *The Brethren of the Common Life*, Grand Rapids, Mich., 1950; G. Axters, *La spiritualité des Pays-Bas*, Louvain, 1948; J. Tousaert, *Le sentiment réligieux en Flandre à la fin du moyen-âge*, Paris, 1963; T. P. Zijl, *Gerard Groote, Ascetic and Reformer*, Washington, D.C., 1963.
54. Cf. C. Ullmann, *Reformatoren vor der Reformation*, Gotha, 1866; G. Bonet-Maury, *Gerard de Grote, un précurseur de la Reforme au XIVᵉ siècle*, Paris, 1878.

55. Cf. J. Leclercq, F. Vandenbroucke, L. Bouyer, *The Spirituality of the Middle Ages*, pp. 428–431.

56. Cf. *De quatuor generibus meditationum seu contemplationun*, ed. A. Hyma, in *Geschiedenis Aartsbisdom Utrecht*, Vol. 49, 1924, pp. 304–325.

57. Mombaer's *Rosetum exercitiorum* inspired García de Cisneros and he, in turn, influenced St. Ignatius Loyola; cf. P. Debognie, *Jean Mombaer de Bruxelles*, Louvain, 1928.

58. Cf. L. M. J. Delaissé, "Le manuscrit autographe de Th. à K. et l'Imitation du Jésus-Christ," in *Examen archéologique et édition diplomatique du Bruxellensis*, Antwerp, 1956, Vol. 2, pp. 5855–5861; J. Huijben-F. Debognie, *L'auteur ou les auteurs de l'Imitation*, Louvain, 1957; *Opera omnia Thomae Hemerken à Kempis*, ed. Pohl, Freiburg-im-Breisgau, 1910–1922, 7 vols.

59. *Imitation of Christ*, I, chaps. 1 and 2.

60. *Imitation of Christ*, I, chap. 22; III, chap. 52.

61. *Ibid.*, I, chap. 13.

62. Cf. *op. cit.*, III, chap. 53.

63. *Ibid.*, III, chap. 54.

64. Cf. *loc. cit.*; for a hymn of praise to charity, see III, chap. 5.

65. Cf. *ibid.*, III, chap. 5.

66. Peter d'Ailly's teaching is found in the works of Gerson: *Opera omnia*, Antwerp, 1706, *De falsis prophetis*, Vol. 1. pp. 499–603. See also E. Vansteenberghe, "Ailly (Pierre d')," in *Dictionnaire de Spiritualité*, Vol. 1, cols. 256–260, and in *Dictionnaire de Théologie Catholique*, Vol. 1, cols. 642–654. Gerson based his moral teaching on the principle: "God does not will certain actions because they are good, but they are good because he wills them; conversely, certain actions are evil because he forbids them" (*Opera omnia*, Vol. 3, p. 13).

67. The *Opera omnia* of Gerson was published by E. du Pin at Antwerp in 1706; a new critical edition of Gerson's works by L. Mourin was scheduled to start publication in 1946. For further studies on Gerson, cf. J. Connolly, *John Gerson, Reformer and Mystic*, Louvain, 1928; M. J. Pinet, *Le vie ardente de Gerson*, Paris, 1929; P. Glorieux, "La vie et les oeuvres de Jean Gerson," in *Arch. Hist. M.A.*, Vol. 18, 1950, pp. 149–192.

68. Cf. *Opera omnia*, Vol. 1, pp. 80–82, 174; Vol. 3, pp. 369, 470, 571–572; Vol. 4, p. 3.

69. Cf. *ibid.*, Vol. 1, pp. 43–45.

70. *Opera omnia*, Vol. 3, pp. 390–393; 457–467.

71. Cf. *op. cit.*, Vol. 3, pp. 390–393; 457–467.

72. Cf. M. de la Bedoyére, *The Greatest Catherine*, Bruce, Milwaukee, Wis., 1947; J. Jorgensen, *Saint Catherine of Siena*, tr. I. Lund, Longmans Green, London, 1939; I. Giordani, *Saint Catherine of Siena, Doctor of the Church*, tr. T. J. Tobin, St. Paul Editions, Boston, Mass., 1975; *St. Catherine of Siena* (*Legenda major*, or her life by

Raymond of Capua), tr. C. Kearns, M. Glazier, Wilmington, Del., 1981.

73. Catherine of Siena, *The Dialogue*, tr. S. Noffke, Paulist Press, New York, N.Y., 1980; *Selected Letters of Catherine Benincasa*, tr. V. D. Scudder, E. P. Dutton, New York, N.Y., 1927.

74. Cf. K. Krogh-Tonning, *Der letzte Scholastiker*, 1904.

75. Cf. Y. Gourdel, "Cartusians," in *Dictionnaire de Spiritualité*, Vol. 2, cols. 705–776.

76. Cf. M. I. Bodenstedt, *The Vita Christi of Ludolphus the Carthusian*, Washington, D.C., 1944.

77. The *Opera omnia* of Denis the Carthusian was published by Montreuil in Tournai between 1896 and 1935. Cf. A. Stoelen, "Denys the Carthusian," in *Spirituality through the Centuries*, ed. J. Walsh, P. J. Kenedy, New York, N.Y., 1964.

78. P. Pourrat, *op. cit.*, Vol. 2, p. 316.

79. Cf. J. Guiraud, *L'Eglise et les origines de la Renaissance* Paris, 1902; A. Baudrillart, *L'Eglise catholique, la Renaissance, le Protestantisme*, Paris, 1904.

80. Cf. J. Nohl, *The Black Death*, London, 1926; H. Pirenne, A. Renaudet, E. Perroy, M. Handelsman, L. Halphen, *La fin du moyen age*, Paris, 1945; J. M. Clark, *The Dance of Death in the Middle Ages and the Renaissance*, Glasgow, 1950.

Chapter 8 Post-Tridentine Spirituality

1. Cf. P. Pourrat, *Christian Spirituality*, tr. W. H. Mitchell, 3 vols., Newman Press, Westminster, Md., 1953.

2. P. Pourrat, *op. cit.*, Vol. 3, p. v.

3. Cf. *Gargantua*, 5, 47.

4. Cf. Erasmus, *Enchiridion militis christiani*, 5, 40, 8.

5. Cf. Guigo I, *Scala claustralium*, PL 184, 476; Aelred, *De Vita eremetica*, PL 32, 1461; David of Augsburg, *De exterioris et interioris hominis compositione*, Quaracchi, 1899.

6. Cf. P. Pourrat, *op. cit.*, Vol. 3, pp. 4–22.

7. Cf. P. Pourrat, *op. cit.*, Vol. 3, p. 13.

8. J. W. Gransfort, *Tractatus de cohibendis cogitationibus et de modo constituendarum meditationum*, in *Opera omnia*, Amsterdam, 1617.

9. *Rosetum exercitiorum spiritualium et sacrarum meditationum*, Paris, 1494. The *Rosetum* was widely circulated and reprinted in many places.

10. Cf. H. Watrigant, *Quelques promoteurs de la méditation méthodique au XVe siècle*, Enghien, 1919.

11. Cf. I. Tassi, *Ludovico Barbo* (1381–1483), Rome, 1952; M. Petrocchi, *Una "devotio moderna" nel Quattrocento italiano? ed. altri studi*, Florence, 1961.

12. Cf. the excellent study by A. Huerga, "*La vida cristiana en los siglos*

XV–XVI," in *Historia de la Espiritualidad*, ed. B. Duque–L. S. Balust,
Juan Flors, Barcelona, 1969, Vol. 1, pp. 34–41.

13. Cf. N. Barbato, *Ascetica dell'orazione in S. Lorenzo Giustiniani*, Venezia, 1960.
14. Cf. E. Allison Peers, *Studies of the Spanish Mystics*, London, 1930, Vol. 2, pp. 3–37.
15. This is in the tradition of St. Bonaventure and Richard of St. Victor. Some authors add two more degrees of unitive love: sense of security and perfect tranquillity.
16. Cf. L. Blosius, *The Book of Spiritual Instruction*, London, 1925, chap. 5.
17. Few of the Christian humanists were concerned explicitly with spiritual theology. Pico della Mirandola, who died at the age of thirty-one (1494), wrote the *manifesto* of Christian humanism, of which thirteen theses were declared heretical. Lefèvre, the greatest French humanist, wrote commentaries on part of the Bible and on pseudo-Dionysius; he also translated and commented on the works of Aristotle. Luther used the works of Lefèvre to defend his doctrine on justification by faith alone. Cf. F. Robert, *L'humanisme essai de définition*, Paris, 1946.
18. Cf. R. G. Villosleda, "*Erasme*," in *Dictionnaire de Spiritualité*, Vol. 4, pp. 925–936; *Opera omnia*, Leyden, 1703, 10 vols.; *Opus epistolarum*, ed. P. S. Allen and H. M. Allen, Oxford, 1906–1947.
19. Cf. P. Pourrat, *op. cit.*, Vol. 3, pp. 59–62.
20. Cf. P. Pourrat, *op. cit.*, Vol. 3, pp. 72–79.
21. M. Bremond, *Histoire littéraire du sentiment réligieux en France*, Paris, 1916, Vol. 1, pp. 10–12, *passim*.
22. Cf. G. de Guibert, *Ignace mystique*, Toulouse, 1950; H. Rahner, *Ignaz von Loyola und das geschichtliche Werden seiner Frommigkeit*, Vienna, 1947; H. Pinard de la Boullaye, *La spiritualité ignatienne*, Paris, 1949.
23. Cf. I. Iparraguirre, *Historia de la Espiritualidad*, Vol. 2, pp. 210–211. For further details on the life and spirituality of St. Ignatius, see P. de Leturia, *Estudios ignacianos*, 2 vols., Rome, 1957. The standard critical edition of the *Exercises* is found in *Obras completas de san Ignacio de Loyola*, ed. I. Iparraguirre, and C. de Dalmeses, Madrid, 3rd corrected ed. 1963. For bibliographies, see I. Iparraguirre, *Orientaciones bibliográficas sobre san Ignacio de Loyola*, Rome, 1957.
24. According to F. Charmot, the teaching of St. Ignatius Loyola is based on two fundamental theological principles: "without me you can do nothing" and the necessity of cooperation with God's grace. The second principle is developed in the *Spiritual Exercises*. Cf. *Ignatius Loyola and Francis de Sales*, B. Herder, St. Louis, Mo., 1966, p. 41.
25. Cf. I. Iparraguirre, *op. cit.*, pp. 207–230.
26. For further details on the life and works of St. Teresa, cf. St. Teresa, *The Life*, tr. E. Allison Peers, Sheed & Ward, New York, N.Y., 1946; Silverio de Santa Teresa, *Saint Teresa of Jesus*, tr. Discalced Carmelite,

Sands, London, 1947; W. T. Walsh, *Saint Teresa of Avila*, Bruce, Milwaukee, Wis., 1954; E. Allison Peers, *Handbook to the Life and Times of St. Teresa and St. John of the Cross*, Newman, Westminster, Md., 1954.

27. Cf. M. Menéndez y Pelayo, *Historia de los Heterodoxos Españoles*, Madrid, 1880, Vol. 2; E. Allison Peers, *Spanish Mysticism, a Preliminary Survey*, London, 1924; A. Huerga, "*La vida* cristiana en los siglos XV–XVI," in *Historia de la Espiritualidad*, pp. 75–103.

28. For information on the autographs and various editions of the works of St. Teresa, cf. *Obras Completas*, ed. E. de la Madre de Dios, Madrid, 1951. For English translations, cf. E. Allison Peers, *The Complete Works of St. Teresa*, 3 vols. Sheed & Ward, New York, N.Y., 1946, and *The Letters of St. Teresa*, 2 vols., London, 1951; K. Kavanaugh-O. Rodríguez, *The Collected Works of St. Teresa of Avila*, 2, vols., ICS, Washington, D.C., 1976–1980.

29. Cf. P. Eugene-Marie, *I Want to See God*, tr. M. Verde Clare, Chicago, Ill., 1953.

30. Cf. *The Way of Perfection*, chap. 28.

31. For a comparative study of St. Teresa's terminology regarding passive recollection and the prayer of quiet, cf. E. W. T. Dicken, *The Crucible of Love*, New York, N.Y., 1963, pp. 196–214. Most authors prefer to speak of passive recollection and the prayer of quiet as specifically distinct: cf. J. G. Arintero, *Stages in Prayer*, tr. K. Pond, St. Louis, Mo., 1957, pp. 24–27; 36–44.

32. Cf. *The Interior Castle*, E. Allison Peers tr. Vol. 2, pp. 253–258; 264–268; *The Life*, E. Allison Peers tr., Vol. 1, pp. 105–110.

33. Cf. *The Interior Castle*, E. Allison Peers tr., Vol. 2, pp. 324–326.

34. Cf. *The Interior Castle*, E. Allison Peers tr., Vol. 2, pp. 287.

35. Cf. *ibid.*, E. Allison Peers tr., Vol. 2, pp. 333–334.

36. Cf. *The Way of Perfection*, E. Allison Peers tr., Vol. 2, p. 129. For studies on the teaching of St. Teresa, E. Allison Peers, *Studies of the Spanish Mystics*, Vol. 1, New York and Toronto, 1927; E. W. T. Dicken, *The Crucible of Love*, New York, N.Y., 1963; J. G. Arintero, *Stages in Prayer*, tr. K. Pond, St. Louis, Mo., 1957; P. Marie-Eugene, *I Want to See God*, tr. M. Verda Clare, Chicago, Ill., 1953, and *I am a Daughter of the Church*, tr. M. Verda Clare, Chicago, Ill., 1955.

37. Cf. *Book of Foundations*, E. Allison Peers tr., Vol. 3, p. 23.

38. Cf. *ibid.*, *loc. cit.*

39. Cf. *The Way of Perfection*, E. Allison Peers tr., Vol. 2, pp. 15–21; 30–37; 57–59.

40. Cf. A. Huerga, "Introduction" to Louis of Granada, *Summa of the Christian Life*, tr. J. Aumann, B. Herder, St. Louis, Mo., 1954, Vol. 1; M. Menéndez y Pelayo, *Historia de los heterodoxos españoles*, ed. BAC, Madrid, 1951, pp. 4–59.

41. For further details on life of St. John of the Cross, cf. M. del Niño Jesús, *Vida y Obras de San Juan de la Cruz*, Madrid, 1950; E. Allison

Peers, *Spirit of Flame*, London, 1943; C. de Jesús Sacramentado, *The Life of St. John of the Cross*, London, 1958; G. of St. Mary Magdalen, *St. John of the Cross*, Mercier, Cork, 1947.

42. Cf. K. Kavanaugh–O. Rodríguez, *The Collected Works of St. John of the Cross*, Doubleday, New York, N.Y., 1964, pp. 54–56.

43. Cf. C. de Jesús, *San Juan de la Cruz: su obra científica y literaria*, Avila, 1929, Vol. 1, p. 51.

44. *The Ascent of Mount Carmel*, Book 1, chapter 2, no. 1.

45. Cf. *ibid.*, Book 1, chap. 3, no. 4.

46. Cf. *ibid.*, Book 1, chap. 13, nos. 3–4.

47. *The Ascent of Mount Carmel*, Book 2, chap. 13, nos. 2–4. Cf. K. Wojtyla (Pope John Paul II), *Faith according to St. John of the Cross*, tr. J. Aumann, Ignatius Press, San Francisco, Calif., 1981.

48. Cf. *ibid.*, Book 2, chap. 5.

49 *The Living Flame of Love*, Stanza 1.

50. *The Collected Works of St. John of the Cross*, tr. K. Kavanaugh–O. Rodríguez, p. 585.

51. Cf. M. Menéndez y Pelayo, *op. cit.*, pp. 4–59.

52. The complete edition of the three *Primers* (*Abecedarios*) was published at Seville in 1554 and the first one written, that of 1527, is placed third in the complete edition. The other two, written in 1528 and 1530, treat of the passion of Christ and ascetical matters. Cf. *Neuva biblioteca de autores españoles*, Madrid, 1911, Vol. 16; F. de Ros, *Un mâitre de sainte Thérèse: le P. François d'Osuna*, Paris, 1936; E. Allison Peers, *Studies of the Spanish Mystics*, Vol. 1, pp. 77–131. For an English version, cf. Francisco de Osuna, *The Third Spiritual Alphabet*, Paulist Press, New York, N.Y., 1983.

53. Cf. F. de Ros, *Un inspirateur de S. Thérèse: Le Frère Bernardin de Laredo*, Paris, 1948; K. Pond, "Bernardino de Laredo," in *Spirituality through the Centuries*, ed. J. Walsh, Kenedy, New York, N.Y., 1964; *The Ascent of Mount Sion*, tr. E. Allison Peers, London, 1952, which contains only the third part on contemplative prayer. See *Vida* 27; E. Allison Peers tr. Vol. 1, 171.

54. *The Life*, E. Allison Peers tr., Vol. 1, p. 194.

55. Cf. A. Huerga, "Introduction" to *Summa of the Christian Life*, tr. J. Aumann, St. Louis, Mo., 1954–1958, 3 vols. This work is now available from TAN Books, Rockford, Ill.

56. Cf. *Obras Completas*, ed. L. S. Balust, 2 vols., Madrid, 1952–1953; A. Huerga, *El Beato Juan de Avila*, Rome, 1963; E. Allison Peers, *Studies of the Spanish Mystics*, Vol. 2.

57. *Los Nombres de Cristo* was published at Salamanca in 1583; for an English version, cf. *The Names of Christ*, tr. E. J. Schuster, B. Herder, St. Louis, Mo., 1955.

58. Cf. E. Allison Peers, *op. cit.*

59. Cf. P. de Leturia, *Estudios ignacianos*, Rome, 1957, Vol. 2.

60. His exact words were: "*Instituti nostri rationi minus videntur congruere.*"

61. Cf. B. Alvarez, *Escritos espirituales*, ed. C. M. Abad and F. Boado, Barcelona, 1961, pp. 134–160. See *Vida* 28, 33; E. Allison Peers tr. Vol. 1, 185–186; 224–225.

62. Cf. L. de la Puente, *Vida del V. F. Báltasar Alvarez*, Madrid, 1615.

63. Cf. P. de Leturia, *op. cit.*, p. 321.

64. Cf. J. Nonell, *Obras espirituales del Beato Alonzo Rodríguez*, 3 vols. Barcelona, 1885; V. Segarra, *Autobiografía. San Alonso Rodríguez*, Barcelona, 1956; *The Autobiography of St. Alphonsus Rodríguez*, tr. W. Yeomans, London, 1964.

65. A Rodríguez, *The Practice of Perfection and Christian Virtues*, tr. J. Rickaby, 3 vols., Chicago, Ill., 1929.

66. Cf. *Meditaciones de los misterios de la nuestra santa fe*, Valladolid, 1605.

67. Cf. *Vida del Báltasar Alvarez*, Madrid, 1612, p. 14.

68. Cf. *De inquisitione pacis*, 5.

69. The Carmelite writers, John of Jesus-Mary (+1615), Thomas of Jesus (+1627) and Joseph of the Holy Spirit (+1674), were principally responsible for introducing the argument on the distinction between acquired and infused contemplation. Later, another Carmelite, Joseph of the Holy Spirit (+1730), published a lengthy theological synthesis entitled *Cursus theologiae mystico-scholasticae* in six volumes.

70. Melchior Cano, the ruthless Spanish inquisitor, considered John Baptist da Crema to be as "dangerous" as Tauler and Herp.

71. The work has sometimes been attributed to the Spanish Benedictine, John Castañiza, or the Italian Jesuit, Achille Gagliardi, but there seems to be little doubt that the work comes from the Italian school of the Theatines. The first edition appeared at Venice in 1589. The treatise was enlarged in later editions.

72. The works of St. Magdalen were published by the Carmelite, Laurence Brancaccio, under the title, *Opera di Santa Maria Maddalena de Pazzi carmelita di S. Maria di Firenze*, Florence, 1609. A later edition at Florence (1893) includes her letters.

73. See *Lettere*, ed. C. Guasti, Prato, 1861.

74. Cf. Cardinal Capecelatro, *Vie de saint Philippe de Néri*, tr. H. Bézin, Paris, 1889, Vol. 1, p. 512.

75. A. Bayle, *Vie de saint Philippe de Néri*, Paris, 1859, p. 247.

76. Cf. Cardinal Capecelatro, *op. cit.*, Vol. 1, p. 483.

77. Cf. F. von Hügel, *The Mystical Elements of Religion as Studied in Saint Catherine of Genoa and her Friends*, 2 vols., London, 1908.

78. P. Pourrat, *Christian Spirituality*, Vol. 3, p. 272.

79. P. Hughes, *A Popular History of the Catholic Church*, Garden City, New York, N.Y., 1954, p. 196.

80. For details on the life of St. Francis de Sales, cf. H. Burton, *The Life of St. Francis de Sales*, London, 1925–1929, M. de la Bedoyere, *François de Sales*, New York, N.Y., 1960; M. Henry-Coüannier, *Francis de Sales and His Friends*, tr. V. Morrow, Staten Island, New York, N.Y.,

1964; F. Trochu, *S. François de Sales*, Lyon-Paris, 1941–1942, 2 vols.; M. Trouncer, *The Gentleman Saint: St. François de Sales and His Times*, London, 1963.

81. Cf. M. de la Bedoyere, *op. cit.*, p. 9. *Oeuvres de Saint François de Sales* (Annecy 1892–1964) 27 v., published under the direction of the Visitandines at Annecy, with introductory material by Dom B. Mackey, O.S.B.

82. Cf. *Oeuvres* 3, 131.

83. Quoted from St. Francis de Sales by Bishop Jean-Pierre Camus. Cf. F. Charmot, *Ignatius Loyola and Francis de Sales*, tr. M. Renelle, St. Louis, Mo., 1966, p. 7.

84. Cf. L. Granada, *Libro de la Oración y Meditación*, 2, 1.

85. *Oeuvres*, 3, 14.

86. Cf. *Oeuvres*, 3, 82–83.

87. Cf. *Oeuvres*, 13, 358.

88. Cf. *Oeuvres*, Vol. 4, Introduction.

89. Cf. *Oeuvres*, Vol. 4, p. vii.

90. Cf. *Oeuvres*, 3, 109; 131–132.

91. Cf. *Summa Theologiae*, IIa IIae, q. 23, art. 4–8.

Chapter 9 Modern Spirituality

1. Cf. F. Florand, *Stages of Simplicity*, tr. Sr. M. Carina, B. Herder, St. Louis, Mo., 1967, pp. 9–10; T. Gannon and E. Traub, *The Desert and the City*, Toronto, 1969, pp. 227–228.

2. Cf. J. Huyben, *Aux sources de la spiritualité; française du XVIIe s.*, in *SupplVieSpirit*, decembre 1930-mai 1931.

3. Cf. H. Bremond, *L'Histoire littérnire du sentiment religieux*, vol. 3, Paris, 1921; J. Dagens, *Bérulle et les origines de la restauration catholique (1575–1610)*, Paris, 1952; P. Cochois, *Bérulle et l'Ecole français*, Paris, 1963; J. Orcibal, *Le cardinal de Bérulle: evolution d'une spiritualité*, Paris, 1965.

4. Cf. A. Molien, "Bérulle", *Dictionnaire de Spiritualité*, Vol. 1, pp. 1539–1581.

5. *Oeuvres complètes de Bérulle*, ed. J. P. Migne, Paris, 1856, p. 879. The abstract school soon waned because it became too Dionysian and because some of its adherents were accused of Lutheran tendencies. By 1623 the abstract school had practically disappeared in France.

6. Cf. A. Molien, *art. cit.*, *DictSpirAscMyst*, Vol. 1, pp. 1539–1581.

7. *Oeuvres complètes de Bérulle*, pp. 1293–1294.

8. Cf. P. Cochois, "Bérulle et le Pseudo-Denys," in *RevHistRel*, 1961, pp. 175–214; "Bérulle hierarque dionysien," in *RevAscMyst*, n. 147, 1961, pp. 314–353; n. 151, 1962, pp. 354–375.

9. Cf. *Oeuvres complètes*, p. 880.

10. Cf. *ibid.*, pp. 159; 567; 1136; 1195; 1573–1579.
11. His work appeared in 1623 under the title: *Discours de l'état et grandeurs de Jésus, par l'union ineffable de la divinité avec l'humanité et de la dépendance et servitude qui lui est due, et à sa très sainte Mère, ensuite de cet état admirable.* It was reprinted four times between 1623 and 1634.
12. Cf. *Oeuvres complètes*, pp. 181; 182–185.
13. See *Grandeurs de Jésus*, discourses 3 and 4.
14. Cf. P. Henry, "La mystique trinitaire du bienheureux Jean Ruusbroec," in *Mélanges Lebreton*, 1952, Vol. 2, p. 340.
15. Cf. *Grandeurs de Jésus*, 9, 4, 231.
16. Some historians believe that Richelieu's animosity toward Bérulle was due in great part to their political differences and that the Jesuits became Bérulle's enemies because the success of the Oratorians was seen as a threat to themselves.
17. In 1637 the Oratorian Gibieuf edited and published the manuscripts that were found after Bérulle's death, under the title *Grandeurs de Marie.* Another Oratorian, Francis Bourgoing, third Superior General of the Oratorians, edited and published the complete works of Bérulle in 1644, republished in 1657 and 1663: *Les Oeuvres de l'éminentissime et révérendissime P. cardinal de Bérulle*, Paris, 1644.
18. P. Amelote, *La vie due P. Charles de Condren*, Paris, 1643.
19. Bourgoing stated that Bérulle revived in the Church the spirit of religion and the cult of adoration and reverence for God (*Oeuvres*, Preface, pp. 102–103).
20. Cf. *Oeuvres*, p. 350.
21. Cf. *op. cit.*, pp. 1052–1053.
22. *Ibid.*, pp. 998; 1022; 1050; 1362, *passim*.
23. Cf. Molien, "Bérulle" in *DictSpirAscMyst*, Vol. 1, p. 1554.
24. H. Bremond, *op. cit.*, Vol. 3, pp. 490–491.
25. Cf. D. Amelote, *La vie du P. Ch. de Condren*, Paris, 1643, 2 vols.; *Lettres du P. Ch. de Condren*, ed. P. Auvrey, and A. Jouffrey, Paris, 1643.
26. For details on Condren's doctrine, cf. P. Pourrat, *Christian Spirituality*, Vol. 3, pp. 350–352; 371–377. Claude Séguenot (1596–1676) an admirer and follower of Condren, in a treatise on prayer (*Conduite d'oraison pour les âmes*, 1634), was strongly opposed to methods of prayer, since prayer occurs in the core of the soul and not in the faculties; it is more God's doing than man's. He also attacked religious life, saying that the vows add nothing to Christian perfection nor to the baptismal vow. The just man does not live under the law; therefore, he should not bind himself to the law by vows.
27. Cf. *Oeuvres complètes de M. Olier*, ed. Bretonvilliers, Paris, 1856; L Bertrand, *Bibliothéque sulpicienne ou Histoire littéraire de la Compagnie de Saint-Sulpice*, Vol. 1, Paris, 1900; P. Pourrat, *Jean-Jacques Olier*, Paris, 1932.
28. *Journée chrétienne* (1655); *Catéchisme chrétien pour la vie intérieure*

(1656); *Introduction à la vie et aux vertus chrétiennes* (1657); *Traité des saints ordres* (1675).

29. Cf. E. Faillon, *Vie de M. Olier*, Paris, 1873, Vol. 2, p. 209.

30. Olier also promoted devotion to the Sacred Heart; cf. P. Pourrat, *op. cit.*, Vol. 3, pp. 396–398.

31. Devotion to the Sacred Heart dates back to St. Gertrude and St. Mechtild in the thirteenth century, but St. John Eudes is the outstanding promoter of the liturgical celebration of this devotion. The first revelation to St. Margaret Mary Alacoque occurred on December 27, 1673.

32. Cf. *La vie et le royaume de Jésus dans les âmes chrétiennes* (1637). For biographical data, cf. E. Georges, *St. Jean Eudes*, Paris, 1925; D. Sargent, *Their Hearts be Praised: The Life of St. John Eudes*, New York, N.Y., 1949; P. Hérambourg, *St. John Eudes: A Spiritual Portrait*, tr. R. Hauser, Westminster, Md., 1960.

33. *Le Coeur admirable de la très sacrée Mère de Dieu* by St. John Eudes was published posthumously in 1681. For an English version of his works: W. E. Myatt, and P. J. Skinner, *Selected Works*, New York, N.Y., 1946–1948. The *Oeuvres complètes* were published in Paris in six volumes between 1905 and 1909.

34. Cf. P. Pourrat, *Christian Spirituality*, Vol. 4, pp. 1–288; R. A. Knox, *Enthusiasm*, Oxford, 1950; L. Cognet, *Spiritualité moderne*; Paris, 1966.

35. Cf. M. J. Orcibal, *Saint-Cyran et le jansénisme*, Paris, 1961.

36. The doctrine of Baius was condemned by Pope Pius V in 1567 and by Pope Gregory XIII in 1579.

37. Cf. L. Lessius, *Thèses théologiques* (1585); *Leonardi Lessii opuscula*, Antwerp, 1613. St. Francis de Sales accepted the doctrine of Lessius and incorporated it in his *Treatise on the Love of God* (Part 3, chap. 5).

38. Cf. St. Thomas Aquinas, *Summa theologiae*, Ic, q. 23, art. 1–8.

39. For example, Gibieuf, who had been a Molinist before joining the Oratorians, was converted to the Augustinian and Thomistic doctrine by Bérulle and later wrote a book against Molinism. Cf. H. Bremond, *op. cit.*, Vol. 4, p. 28.

40. Cf. P. Pourrat, *op. cit.*, Vol. 4, p. 12.

41. For detailed account of Jansenistic doctrine, cf. P. Pourrat, *op. cit.*, Vol. 4, pp. 1–33; H. Bremond, *op. cit.*, Vol. 4; Abercrombie, *The Origins of Jansenism*; L. Cognet, *op. cit.*, pp. 453–495; M. J. Orcibal, *Les origenes du Jansenisme*; *Sainte-Cyran et le jansenisme*, Paris, 1961.

42. Cf. P. Pourrat, *op. cit.*, Vol. 4, p. 13. Arnauld, the brother of Mère Angélique of Port-Royal, published a work against frequent Communion. Jansen's work, *Augustinus*, appeared at Louvain in 1640. Cf. J. Carreyre, "Jansenisme" in *Dictionnaire de Théologie Catholique*, Vol. 8, cols. 318–529.

43. Saint-Cyran considered it an inspiration from God to stop celebrating daily Mass: "Now that God has led me away from that, I find my

consolation and nourishment in the least word of the Scriptures; and I learn by experience the truth of what our Lord says in the Gospel, that man does not live by bread alone (and this applies even to the holy bread of the Eucharist), but by the word that comes from the mouth of God." Cf. *Rech. RechScRel*, 1913, p. 373.

44. Cf. H. Bremond, *op. cit.*, Vol. 4; R. A. Knox, *op. cit.*, pp. 192–196.

45. R. A. Knox, *op. cit.*, pp. 212–213.

46. Port-Royal, originally a Cistercian convent, was the patrimony of Angélique Arnauld, and with her sister, Agnes, she set out to reform the religious life there. Jansenism was introduced to the convent through her association with Saint-Cyran, who replaced Sebastian Zamet as her director. In 1709 the convent of Port-Royal was razed to the ground. Cf. R. A. Knox, *op. cit.*, pp. 177–182.

47. "If Richelieu had imprisoned Saint-Cyran when controversy arose over the *chapelet secret*, there would have been no Jansenism" (R. A. Knox, *op. cit.*, p. 185). When Richelieu finally acted, Jansenism was well established and the imprisonment of Saint-Cyran made him a martyr in the eyes of his followers.

48. Two facts should be kept in mind regarding the Jesuit opposition to Jansenism: they were not fighting from a position of strength because they had only recently been restored in France; perhaps they were more interested in avenging themselves on the Arnauld family than in overcoming the excesses of Jansenism. Cf. R. A. Knox, *op. cit.*, pp. 183–188.

49. Among the opponents of *Unigenitus* was the deacon, Francis of Paris, who died in 1727 and was buried in the cemetery of Saint-Médard. It was at his tomb that Jansenist "convulsionaries" experienced pseudo-mystical and spiritualistic phenomena. The cemetery was closed by the government in 1732. Cf. A. Grégoire, *Histoire des sectes religieuses*; R. A. Knox, *op. cit.*, pp. 373–388.

50. R. A. Knox, *op. cit.*, p. 234. For a detailed study of Quietism, R. A. Knox, *op. cit.*, pp. 231–355; P. Pourrat, *op. cit.*, Vol.. 4, pp. 101–260; "Quietisme" in *Dictionnaire de Théologie Catholique*; H. Bremond, *Histoire littéraire du sentiment religieux*, Vol. 4.

51. Cf. P. Pourrat, *op. cit.*, Vol. 4, pp. 103–175; R. A. Knox, *op. cit.*, pp. 231–259.

52. R. A. Knox, *op. cit.*, p. 240.

53. Cf. F. Guilloré, *Maximes spirituelles pour la conduite des âmes*, Nantes, 1668.

54. Cf. J. J. Surin, *Dialogues spirituels ou la perfection chrétienne est expliqué pour toutes sortes de personnes*, 2 vols., Avignon, 1829.

55. The Italian translation of *Cartilla* and two of Falconi's letters of spiritual direction were placed on the Index in 1688.

56. Cf. R. A. Knox, *op. cit.*, p. 244.

57. The complete title of this work, published at Rome in 1675, is *Guía espiritual que desembaraza al alma y la conduce por el interior camino para*

alcanzar la perfecta contemplación y el rico tesoro de la interior paz. It was published in Italian in the same year and in English in 1685.

58. Cf. P. Dudon, *Le quiétisme espagnol: Michel Molinos*, Paris, 1921. This is perhaps the most authoritative study on Molinos. Cardinal Petrucci defended Molinos against Segneri, but later the Cardinal's works were put on the Index and he was removed from his diocese by Pope Alexander VIII.

59. P. Pourrat, *op. cit.*, Vol. 4, pp. 164–165. The document of condemnation, *Coelestis Pastor*, does not mention the *Guía espiritual*. The 68 condemned propositions were taken from letters of Molinos or from depositions of witnesses at the trial.

60. R. A. Knox, *op. cit.*, p. 304.

61. Cf. *ibid.*, pp. 304–311.

62. "He has taught, it appears, that if souls in a high state of prayer are tempted to commit the most obscene and blasphemous actions, they must not leave their prayer to resist the temptation; the devil is being allowed to humiliate them, and if the actions are committed, they are not to be confessed as sins. ... Molinos admits having himself omitted all sacramental confession for the last twenty-two years," R. A. Knox, *op. cit.*, pp. 313–314.

63. Cf. R. A. Knox, *op. cit.*, pp. 322–324; P. Pourrat, *op. cit.*, Vol. 4, pp. 179; 192.

64. Her works were published at Lausanne between 1789 and 1791. Her commentaries on the bible fill twenty volumes. Her most famous works are: *L'explication du Cantique des Cantiques*; *Moyen court et très facile de faire oraison*; *Les torrents spirituels*; *Vie de Mme. Guyon.*

65. Pourrat states that in her infancy Mme. Guyon was subject to "continual fits" and in her childhood she suffered from sudden, strange maladies. Cf. P. Pourrat, *op. cit.*, Vol. 4, pp. 185–186; 188–192.

66. Cf. P. Pourrat, *op. cit.*, Vol. 4, p. 200, footnote 18.

67. Cf. P. Pourrat, *op. cit.*, Vol. 4, p. 198. Mme. Guyon was accused of breaking her promise and in December, 1695, she was confined at Vincennes. From October, 1696, to June, 1698, she was placed in a community at Vaugirard. From 1702 until her death in 1717 she lived in retirement at Blois.

68. For details on Fénelon, cf. G. Joppin, *Fénelon et la mystique du pur amour*, Paris, 1938; *Oeuvres de Fénelon*, Versailles, 1820.

69. Cf. M. Masson, *Fénelon et Mme. Guyon*, p. 114.

70. Cf. P. Pourrat, *op. cit.*, Vol. 4, p. 208.

71. Knox gives a different version of this incident, but we have followed the testimony of Pourrat. Cf. R. A. Knox, *op. cit.*, pp. 342–343; P. Pourrat, *op. cit.*, Vol. 4. pp. 216–217.

72. Cf. R. A. Knox, *op. cit.*, pp. 334–336; 343; L. Cognet, *Post-Reformation Spirituality*, New York, N.Y., 1959, pp. 130–133.

73. For further details on the controversy between Bossuet and Fénelon and the ultimate condemnation, cf. R. A. Knox, *op. cit.*, pp. 344–352;

Cognet, *op. cit.*, pp. 132–136; H. Bremond, *History of Religious Thought in France*, London–New York, 1929–1937, 3 vols.

74. For a commentary on these statements, cf. P. Pourrat, *op. cit.*, Vol. 4, pp. 219–227.

75. Quoted by P. Pourrat, *op. cit.*, Vol. 4, p. 226.

76. Cf. L. Cognet, *op. cit.*, p. 136. For the teaching of Fénelon and Bossuet on contemplative prayer and the state of passivity, cf. P. Pourrat, *op. cit.*, Vol. 4, pp. 227–232.

77. The Jesuit, John de Caussade (+1751) is the author of *Instructions spirituelles en forme de dialogues sur les divers états d'oraison suivant la doctrine de Bossuet, Perpignan*, 1741 and *Abandonment to Divine Providence*, tr. H. Ramière, 1867. The Benedictine, Dominic Schram, published *Institutiones theologiae mysticae* (1720) and the diocesan priest, James Emery, published a condensed version of the works of St. Teresa of Avila in 1775.

78. The Minim friar, John Baptist Avrillon (+1729), was a prolific writer on the love of God and the theological virtues. The Jesuit, Claude Judde (+1735), followed the teaching of Louis Lallemant on docility to the Holy Spirit. Another Jesuit, John Croiset (+1738), composed a series of liturgical meditations entitled *Année chrétienne*, anticipating the work of Dom Guéranger. The teaching of all these writers is basically Bérullian.

79. Cf. H. Bremond, *op. cit.*, Vol. 7; F. Dainvelle, *Naissance de l'humanisme moderne*, Paris, 1940.

80. Available in English as *The Spiritual Doctrine of Father Louis Lallemant*, ed. A. C. McDougall, Westminster, Md., 1946. For biographical data on Lallemant, cf. J. Jiménez, *"Précisions biographiques sur le Père Louis Lallemant"* in *Archivum Historicum Societatis Jesu*, Vol. 33, 1964, pp. 269–332; A. Pottier, *Le P. Louis Lallemant et les grands spirituels de son temps*, 3 vols., Paris, 1927–1929.

81. Cf. P. Dudon, "Les leçons d'oraison du P. Lallemant ont-elles blâmées par ses superieurs?" in *RevAscMyst*, Vol. 11, 1930, pp. 396–406.

82. Cf. P. Pourrat, *op. cit.*, Vol. 4, pp. 46–61.

83. Cf. *The Spiritual Doctrine of Father Louis Lallemant*, ed. A. C. McDougall; A Pottier, *Le P. Louis Lallemant et les grands spirituels de son temps*.

84. Philip of the Holy Trinity, *Summa theologiae mysticae*, Paris, 1874, Vol. 2, pp. 45–46.

85. English version, tr. R. Murphy, and J. Thornton, *The Cross of Jesus*, 2 vols., B. Herder, St. Louis, Mo., 1959.

86. F. Florand, *Stages of Simplicity*, tr. M. Carina, B. Herder, St. Louis, Mo., 1967.

87. *Theologiae mentis et cordis, seu speculationes universae doctrinae sacrae*, Lyon, 1668–1669.

88. This is substantially the same doctrine taught by the Spanish

Dominican, Thomas Vallgornera, in *Mystica theologia D. Thomae utriusque theologiae scholasticae et mysticae principis*, Barcelona, 1662. It seems that Vallgornera leaned heavily on the teaching of the Carmelite, Philip of the Trinity (*Summa theologiae mysticae*).

89. A Piny, *L'oraison du coeur ou la manière de faire oraison parmi les distractions les plus crucifiantes de l'esprit*, Paris, 1683; *État du pur amour*, Lyon, 1676; *La clef du pur amour*, 1682; *Le plus parfait*, 1683; *Retraite sur le pur amour*, 1684.

90. For a listing of Franciscan writers, cf. Ubald of Alençon, *Études franciscaines*, 1927.

91. *Explication de la methode d'oraison*, 1739.

92. Cf. G. Lercaro, *Methods of Mental Prayer*, Newman, Westminister, Md., 1957.

93. Cf. *Caractères de la vraie dévotion*, Paris, 1788.

94. Cf. *L'interieur de Jésus et de Marie*, 2 vols., Paris, 1815, p. 13.

95. Cf. *True Devotion to the Blessed Virgin Mary*, tr. F. W. Faber, Bay Shore, New York, N.Y., 1950, pp. 89; 181–182.

96. Cf. *op. cit.*, pp. 228–229.

97. Cf. P. Pourrat, *op. cit.*, Vol. 4, pp. 345–347.

98. Pope Benedict XIV is the author of a similar work which was for many centuries a standard reference: *De servorum Dei beatificatione et beatorum canonizatione* (1734).

99. Cf. P. Pourrat, *op. cit.*, Vol. 4, pp. 351–352.

100. Many of the grades of mystical prayer listed by Scaramelli are described by St. Teresa and others as concomitant phenomena rather than distinct grades of prayer.

101. St. Alphonsus wrote more than a hundred books and opuscula and about two thousand manuscripts. During his lifetime his works went through more than four hundred editions and since his death there have been about four thousand reprintings. His works have been translated into sixty-one foreign languages.

102. Cf. *The Holy Eucharist*, Brooklyn, New York, N.Y., 1934, p. 229.

103. Cf. *op. cit.*, p. 263.

104. Cf. *The Way of Salvation and of Perfection*, Brooklyn, New York, N.Y., 1934, pp. 428 ff.; *The Holy Eucharist*, pp. 392 ff.; 406–407.

105. Cf. *The Great Means of Salvation and Perfection*, p. 26.

106. Cf. P. Pourrat, *op. cit.*, Vol. 4, pp. 383–384.

107. Cf. *Praxis confessarii*, chap. 9.

108. Cf. *loc. cit.* For a description of Liguorian spirituality and further bibliography, cf. G. Cacciatore, "La spiritualità di S. Alfonso de' Liguori," in *Le scuole cattoliche di spiritualità*, Milan, 2nd ed. 1949; R. M. Fernández, *Espiritualidad redentorista*, Madrid, 1959; G. Liéven, "Alphons de Liguori," in *Dictionnaire de Spiritualité*, vol. 1, col. 357–389; R. Telleria, *San Alfonso Maria de Liguorio*, 2 vols., Madrid, 1950.

109. St. Clement Hofbauer introduced the Redemptorists into Poland and

Austria. Joseph Schrijvers was the author of numerous spiritual works of great merit, among them *The Gift of Oneself*, tr. Carmelite nuns of Bettendorf, Iowa, (1934) and *Les principes de la vie spirituelle* (Brussels 1922).

110. Spener (1635–1705) was greatly influenced by his study of John Tauler. Cf. P. Grünberg, *Philipp Jacob Spener*, 3 vols., Göttingen, 1893–1906; J. T. McNeill, *Modern Christian Movements*, Philadelphia, Penn., 1954.

111. A. Dru, *The Contribution of German Catholicism*, New York, N.Y., 1963, pp. 17–24, *passim*.

112. Translated into English by F. Marison, as *The City of God*, 3 vols., Hammond, Ind., 1915.

113. *Secta Pietistarum dissecta gladio verbi dei*, Cologne, 1714.

114. *De revelationibus, visionibus et apparitionibus privatis regulae tutae*, Augsburg, 1744.

115. *Institutiones theologiae mysticae*, Augsburg, 1774.

116. John Sailer entered the Jesuits after completing his secondary studies at Munich, but before he completed his novitiate, the Society was suppressed (1773). Ordained a priest in 1775, he was professor of theology at various schools until he was named bishop of Ratisbon in 1829. He has been called the Francis de Sales and the Fénelon of Germany.

117. R. Geiselmann, *Von lebendiger Religiosität zum Leben der Kirche*, Stuttgart, 1952, p. 248.

118. A. Dru, *op. cit.*, p. 62.

119. A. Dru, *op. cit.*, p. 65.

120. Cf. P. Pourrat, *op. cit.*, Vol. 4, pp. 416–417; A. Dru, *op. cit.*, pp. 65–72.

121. Brentano claimed that Anna Catherine had been selected by God for a special work of revelations to the world and that he had been designated as her secretary. However, the Augustinian, Winifried Hümpfner, who worked on the *Process* for Anna Catherine's beatification, concluded that Brentano had falsified statements made by the visionary and interpolated his own ideas in the text. Cf. T. Wegener, *Emmerich und C. Brentano*, Dülman, 1900; W. Hümpfner, *Klemens Brentano Glaudwürdigkeit in seinem Emmerich-Aufzeichnungen*, Wurzburg, 1923.

122. H. Thurston wrote a series of articles on the Emmerich controversy in *The Month* (1921–1925).

123. P. Pourrat, *op. cit.*, Vol. 4, pp. 436–437.

124. *Sancta Sophia*, ed. S. Cressy, New York, N.Y., 1857; *Holy Wisdom*, ed. G. Sitwell, London, 1964. For details cf. *The Confessions of Venerable Father Augustine Baker*, ed. P. J. McCann, London, 1922; P. Salvin, and S. Cressy, *The Life of Father Augustine Baker*, ed. P. J. McCann, London, 1933; D. Knowles, *The English Mystical Tradition*, New York, N.Y., 1961.

125. Cf. L. Sheppard, *Spiritual Writers in Modern Times*, New York, N.Y., 1967, pp. 27–28.
126. R. Cartmell, "Richard Challoner" in *English Spiritual Writers*, ed. C. Davis, London, 1961, p. 121. For further details cf. M. Trappes-Lomax, *Bishop Challoner*, New York, N.Y., 1936; D. Matthew, *Catholicism in England*, 2nd ed., New York, N.Y., 1950; E. I. Watkin, *Roman Catholicism in England*, New York, N.Y., 1957.
127. Cf. P. Thureau-Dangin, *La renaissance catholique en Angleterre au XIXe siècle*, Paris, 1899, Vol. 1, p. 4.
128. Cardinal Wiseman (1802–1865), first archbishop of Westminster, wrote the famous novel, *Fabiola* (1854). William Bernard Ullathorne (1806–1889), Benedictine, became the first bishop of Birmingham and is the author of *The Endowments of Man* (1880), *The Groundwork of the Christian Virtues* (1882), *Christian Patience* (1886) and an autobiography which was published together with his letters (1891–1892). Cuthbert Hedley (1837–1915), a Benedictine of Ampleforth, wrote treatises on the Eucharist, the priesthood and for use in spiritual retreats.
129. P. Pourrat, *op. cit.*, Vol. 4, pp. 451–452.
130. The books of spirituality are: *All for Jesus* (1853); *The Blessed Sacrament* (1855); *The Creator and the Creature* (1858); *The Foot of the Cross* (1858); *The Precious Blood* (1860); *Bethlehem* (1860). The books of spiritual direction are: *Growth in Holiness* (1854) and *Spiritual Conferences* (1859). Faber also composed *Notes on Doctrinal Subjects* (1866), translated Lallemant's *Spiritual Doctrine* (1853) and published several lesser works.
131. Cf. *The Creator and the Creature*, 15 ed., Baltimore, Md., 1857, Book 1, chap. 1.
132. Cf. *ibid.*, Book 3, chap. 4.
133. *Growth in Holiness*, p. 27; *Spiritual Conferences*, p. 6.
134. *Growth in Holiness*, Newman, Westminster, Md., 1950, p. 27.
135. *Meditations and Devotions*, ed. H. Tristram, London, 1953.
136. Cf. *ibid.*, p. 312.
137. Cf. *Parochial and Plain Sermons*, Vol. 5, p. 225.
138. *Sermons Preached on Various Occasions*, ed. H. Tristram, 1900, n. 4.
139. *Parochial and Plain Sermons*, Vol. 3, p. 321.
140. Cf. *ibid.*, Vol. 5, pp. 10–11. The writings and sermons of Cardinal Newman fill 42 volumes in the standard edition (1868–1913). Studies on Newman are readily available and among the authors, C. Stephen Dessain has special competence.

Chapter 10 The Twentieth Century

1. The most recent English translations of the writings of St. Thérèse are: *Story of a Soul*, tr. J. Clarke, ICS Publications, Washington, D.C.,

1975; *St. Thérèse of Lisieux: Her Last Conversations*, tr. J. Clarke, ICS Publications, Washington, D.C., 1977.

2. For further details on the life of St. Thérèse, cf. *St. Thérèse of Lisieux by Those who Knew her*, ed. and tr. C. O'Mahony, Veritas, Dublin, 1975; J. Beevers, *Storm of Glory*, Image Books, New York, N.Y., 1955; A. Combes, *Spirituality of Saint Thérèse*, Kenedy, New York, N.Y., 1950; I. F. Goerres, *The Hidden Face: The Life of St. Thérèse of Lisieux*, Pantheon, New York, N.Y., 1959; D. Day, *Thérèse*, Templegate, Springfield, Ill., 1979; P. T. Rohrbach, *The Search for St. Thérèse*, Hanover, Garden City, New York, N.Y., 1961; H. U. von Balthasar, *Thérèse of Lisieux*, Sheed & Ward, New York, N.Y., 1954.

3. Cf. J. Clarke (tr.), *Story of a Soul*, ICS, Washington, D.C., 1975, pp. 187–200; 219–229.

4. Cf. J. Clarke (tr.), *op. cit.*, pp. 254–259.

5. J. Clarke (tr.), *Story of a Soul*, pp. 60–67.

6. J. Clarke (tr.), *St. Thérèse of Lisieux: Her Last Conversations*, ICS, Washington, D.C., 1977, p. 77.

7. Cf. M. M. Philipon, *The Spiritual Doctrine of Sister Elizabeth of the Trinity*, Newman Press, Westminster, Md., 1961, pp. xvii–xviii.

8. Cf. M. M. Philipon, *op. cit.*, pp. 53–54.

9. For further details on life and works of Sister Elizabeth, cf. *The Praise of Glory: Reminiscences*, Newman Press, Westminster, Md., 1962; M. M. Philipon (ed.), *Spiritual Writing of Sister Elizabeth of the Trinity*, tr. M. St. Augustine, New York, N.Y., 1962; H. U. von Balthasar, *Elizabeth of Dijon: An Interpretation of Her Spiritual Mission*, tr. A. V. Littledale, New York, N.Y., 1956.

10. For further information on Charles de Foucauld, cf. *Oeuvres spirituelles*, Paris, 1958; R. Bazin, *Charles de Foucauld: Hermit and Explorer*, tr. P. Keelan, London, 1923; A. Freemantle, *Desert Calling*, New York, N.Y., 1949; M. Carrouges, *Soldier of the Spirit: The Life of Charles de Foucauld*, tr. M. C. Hellin, New York, N.Y., 1956; J. F. Six, *Witness in the Desert*, tr. L. Noël, New York, N.Y., 1965; G. Gorrée, *Memories of Charles de Foucauld*, London, 1938.

11. Cf. L. Sheppard, *Spiritual Writers in Modern Times*, New York, N.Y., 1967.

12. Cf. *The Liturgical Year*, tr. L. Sheppard, Newman, Westminster, Md., Vol. 1, p. 7.

13. The decree, *Sacra Tridentina Synodus*, was issued in 1905; in 1910 Pope Pius X extended frequent Communion to children who have reached the age of reason. For details on the dispute over frequent Communion, cf. A. Bride, "La Communion du XVIIIe siècle à nos jours," in *Eucharistia*, Paris, 1947, p. 288.

14. E. Masure, *Some Schools of Catholic Spirituality*, ed. J. Gautier, Desclée, Paris–New York, 1959.

15. For further details, cf. J. Jolinon, *Pauline Jaricot*, Paris, 1956; K. Burton, *Difficult Star: The Life of Pauline Jaricot*, New York, N.Y.,

1947; M. Christiani, *Marie-Pauline Jaricot*, Paris, 1961; J. Servel (ed.), *Un autre visage: Textes inédits de Pauline Jaricot*, Lyons, 1961.

16. For further information, cf. *Oeuvres completes*, 11 vols., Paris, 1859–1865; E. Renner, *The Historical Thought of Frédéric Ozanam*, Washington, D.C., 1959; L. Baunard, *Ozanam d'après sa correspondence*, Paris, 1912.

17. Cf. P. Dabin, *L'apostolat laïque*, Paris, 1931; Y. Congar, *Lay People in the Church*, Newman Press, Westminster, Md., 1957; J. Gaynor, *The Life of St. Vincent Pallotti*, St. Paul Editions, Boston, Mass., 1980.

18. Y. Congar, *Jalons pour une theologie du laicat*, Ed. du Cerf, Paris, 1953, pp. 505 ff.

19. Cf. Pope Pius XII, "Allocution to Italian Catholic Action," AAS, Vol. 32 (1940), p. 362.

20. Cf. *Letters of St. Gemma Galgani*, ed. by Germano of St. Stanislaus and tr. by Dominican nuns of Menlo Park, Calif., 1947; Sr. St. Michael, *Portrait of St. Gemma, a Stigmatic*, New York, N.Y., 1950.

21. Cf. M. L. Herking, *Elizabeth Leseur nous parle*, Paris, 1955.

22. Cf. *AAS*, Vol. 39 (1947), pp. 114 ff.

23. Cf. *ibid.*, Vol. 23 (1931), p. 634.

24. "Provida Mater Ecclesia," AAS, Vol. 39 (1947), pp. 114 ff.; "Primo Feliciter," AAS, Vol. 40 (1948), pp. 283 ff.; "Cum Sanctissimus," AAS, Vol. 40 (1948), pp. 283 ff.

25. The following list gives an indication of the great interest in mystical questions in Germany at the end of the nineteenth century: W. Preger, *Geschichte der deutschen Mystik im Mittelalter* (1874–1893); M. Hausherr, *Die wahre und falsche aszese* (1856); Weibel, *Die Mystik* (1834); J. Haver, *Theologia mystica*; J. Görres, *Christliche Mystik* (1842); Von Bernard, *Theologia mystica* (1847); Hettinger, *De theologiae et mysticae connubio* (1882); Helfferich, *Die Christliche Mystik* (1842).

26. Prior to Scaramelli the "two ways" were defended by the Capuchin, Victor Gelen of Treves (+ 1669) and the Polish Franciscan, Chrysostom Dobrosielski (+ 1676).

27. English versions of these works are: A. Saudreau, *Degrees of the Spiritual Life*, 2 vols., New York, N.Y., 1907; A. Poulain, *The Graces of Interior Prayer*, tr. L. Y. Smith, Celtic Cross Books, Westminster, Vt., 1978.

28. For Poulain's response to Besse, cf. *Etudes*, November, 1903. For the debate between Poulain and Saudreau, cf. *Revue du clergé français*, June, 1908, and *Etudes*, October, 1908, and January, 1909.

29. For the English version, cf. J. G. Arintero, *The Mystical Evolution*, tr. J. Aumann, TAN Books, Rockford, Ill., 1978.

30. In the field of spiritual theology, the following works are available in English: R. Garrigou-Lagrange, *The Three Ages of the Interior Life*, tr. T. Doyle, 2 vols., Herder, St. Louis, Mo., 1947; *Christian Perfection and Contemplation*, tr. T. Doyle, Herder, St. Louis, Mo., 1937.

31. The works of Gabriel of St. Mary Magdalen were published in Italian; however an English translation of his *St. John of the Cross* was published in Ireland by Mercier, Cork, 1946.
32. Most of the works by Joseph de Guibert were written in Latin.
33. Cf. also M. M. Philipon, *The Spiritual Doctrine of Dom Marmion*, tr. M. Dillon, Newman Press, Westminster, Md., 1956.
34. Cf. Dom J.-B. Chautard, *The Soul of the Apostolate*, tr. T. Merton, Image Books, New York, N.Y., 1946.
35. The works of Jacques and Raïssa Maritain are readily available in English translation. *The Peasant of the Garonne* was translated by M. Cuddihy and E. Hughes and published by Holt, Rinehart & Winston, New York, N.Y., in 1968. The American Maritain Association was founded at Niagara University in 1977 "to perpetuate the wisdom, influence and inspiration of Jacques Maritain as a Catholic intellectual, a saintly Christian, and a classical creative exponent of the *philosophia perennis* which has a living Thomism as its main embodiment for today and for the future."
36. "Dogmatic Constitution on the Church (*Lumen Gentium*) in A. Flannery (ed.), *Vatican Council II: The Conciliar and Post-Conciliar Documents*, Costello Publishing Company, Northport, N.Y., 1975, pp. 396–398, *passim*.

INDEX OF NAMES